INTERNATIONAL HANDBOOK
ON CHILD PARTICIPATION IN FAMILY LAW

European Family Law Series

Published by the Organising Committee of the Commission on European Family Law

INTERNATIONAL HANDBOOK ON CHILD PARTICIPATION IN FAMILY LAW

Edited by
Wendy SCHRAMA
Marilyn FREEMAN
Nicola TAYLOR
Mariëlle BRUNING

INTERSENTIA
Cambridge – Antwerp – Chicago

Intersentia Ltd
8 Wellington Mews
Wellington Street | Cambridge
CB1 1HW | United Kingdom
Tel: +44 1223 736 170
Email: mail@intersentia.co.uk
www.intersentia.com | www.intersentia.co.uk

Distribution for the UK and
Rest of the World (incl. Eastern Europe)
NBN International
1 Deltic Avenue, Rooksley
Milton Keynes MK13 8LD
United Kingdom
Tel: +44 1752 202 301 | Fax: +44 1752 202 331
Email: orders@nbninternational.com

Distribution for Europe
Lefebvre Sarrut Belgium NV
Hoogstraat 139/6
1000 Brussels
Belgium
Tel: +32 (0)800 39 067
Email: mail@intersentia.be

Distribution for the USA and Canada
Independent Publishers Group
Order Department
814 North Franklin Street
Chicago, IL 60610
USA
Tel: +1 800 888 4741 (toll free) | Fax: +1 312 337 5985
Email: orders@ipgbook.com

International Handbook on Child Participation in Family Law

ISBN 978-1-83970-056-9
D/2021/7849/62
NUR 822

British Library Cataloguing in Publication Data. A catalogue record for this book is available from the British Library.

ACKNOWLEDGEMENTS

The idea for this Handbook grew out of a collaboration between the four co-editors when we met in London in March 2017, and then in Leiden in October 2017. We agreed to develop an international comparative project based on our shared research interest in child participation in family law contexts. The result of our initiative is this Handbook which includes 17 country chapters, preceded by several chapters on pedagogical and psychological perspectives, human and children's rights standards and private international law in the context of child participation, and which culminates in a comparative analysis chapter. It has become clear that children are now taken more seriously in family law proceedings, but more work is still necessary to fully respect children's right to participate in these contexts.

We would like to express our gratitude in the context of writing this Handbook. First of all, this Handbook was made possible through the support of Intersentia Ltd in response to our project proposal. We would particularly like to thank Ann-Christin Maak-Scherpe, Publisher and General Manager, and Rebecca Moffat, Editor, for their invaluable expertise and collegiality.

We also wish to express our sincere appreciation to all the child and family law experts who contributed to the Handbook. They willingly shared their knowledge and experience of the ways in which children's participation rights are given effect globally or in family law proceedings in their specific jurisdictions.

We are most grateful to Charlotte Mol for her comparative analysis chapter, as it was a complex task to thematise the diverse range of information provided in the 17 national perspectives chapters.

We would also like to thank the Organising Committee of the Commission on European Family Law (CEFL) for accepting this Handbook into the European Family Law Series.

Finally, we would like to thank our universities for their support as we undertook this project: Utrecht University, University of Westminster, University of Otago and Leiden University.

We hope that our Handbook inspires all those who are interested in child participation in the family justice system. In addition, we would like to think that the handbook stimulates further reflection about how best to embed children's right to participation in family law contexts and to initiate more research on this important topic.

CONTENTS

LIST OF CASES

COURT OF JUSTICE OF THE EUROPEAN UNION

EUROPEAN COURT OF HUMAN RIGHTS

AUSTRALIA

BELGIUM

CANADA

DENMARK

ENGLAND AND WALES

GERMANY

ISRAEL

ITALY

THE NETHERLANDS

NORWAY

ROMANIA

SCOTLAND

SOUTH AFRICA

UNITED STATES OF AMERICA

LIST OF CONTRIBUTORS

Nicholas Bala
Professor of Law at the Faculty of Law, Queen's University, Ontario, Canada; Fellow of the Royal Society of Canada.

Felicity Bell
Research Fellow at the Law Society of New South Wales' Future of Law and Innovation in the Profession (FLIP) research stream, University of New South Wales, Sydney, Australia.

Rachel Birnbaum
Professor of Social Work and Cross-Appointed to Childhood Studies (Interdisciplinary Programs) at King's University College at Western University, London, Ontario, Canada.

Ingrid Boone
Associate Professor and Campus Dean of the Faculty of Law, and Director of the Institute for Family Law and Juvenile Law, KU Leuven, Belgium.

Mariëlle Bruning
Professor of Child Law at Leiden Law School, Leiden University, the Netherlands.

Judy Cashmore AO
Professor of Social Legal Research and Policy at Sydney Law School and Professorial Research Fellow in the Research Centre for Children and Families, University of Sydney, Australia.

Charlotte Declerck
Associate Professor of Family and Family Property Law at the Faculty of Law, Hasselt University, Belgium; Member of the Brussels Bar.

Nina Dethloff
Director of the Institute for German, European and International Family Law and Center for Advanced Study 'Law as Culture', University of Bonn, Germany.

Ester di Napoli
Adjunct Professor of European Private International Law at LUMSA University, Rome, Italy; Legal Consultant at the Department for Family Policies, Italian Presidency of the Council of Ministers.

Linda D. Elrod
Richard S. Righter Distinguished Professor of Law and Director of the Children and Family Law Center, Washburn University, Kansas, USA.

Simona Florescu
Doctoral Researcher at Leiden Law School, Leiden University, the Netherlands; Attorney with the Bucharest Bar Association.

Marilyn Freeman
Co-Director of the International Centre for Family Law, Policy and Practice (ICFLPP) and Principal Research Fellow at Westminster Law School, University of Westminster, London, England, UK.

Joe Harman
Judge at the Federal Circuit Court of Australia; Lecturer in Family Law at the University of Sydney, Australia.

Christina G. Jeppesen de Boer
Assistant Professor and Researcher in Comparative Family Law at the Utrecht Centre for European Research into Family Law (UCERF), Utrecht University, the Netherlands.

Annette Kronborg
Associate Professor of Family Law at the Faculty of Law, Southern University of Denmark.

Thalia Kruger
Professor of Private International Law at the University of Antwerp, Belgium; Honorary Research Associate at the University of Cape Town, South Africa.

Nigel Lowe QC (Hon)
Emeritus Professor of Law, Cardiff University, Wales, UK; Senior Bencher of the Inner Temple; Member of the UK International Family Law Committee.

Nataša Lucić
Assistant Professor at the Faculty of Law, Josip Juraj Strossmayer University, Osijek, Croatia.

Francesca Maoli
Contract Research Fellow in European Union Law, University of Genoa, Italy.

Charlotte Mol
PhD Candidate at the Utrecht Centre for European Research into Family Law (UCERF), Utrecht University, the Netherlands.

Tamar Morag
Academic Director of the Child Advocacy Law Clinic, The Hebrew University of Jerusalem, Israel; formerly Vice-Chair of the Israeli CRC Legislation Committee.

Anna Nylund
Full Professor of Law at the University of Tromsø – The Arctic University of Norway.

Stephanie Rap
Assistant Professor in Children's Rights at Leiden Law School, Leiden University, the Netherlands.

Branka Rešetar
Full Professor of Family Law at the Faculty of Law, University Josip Juraj Strossmayer, Osijek, Croatia; formerly President of the Law Commission concerning the reform of Croatian family law.

Wendy Schrama
Professor of Family Law and Comparative Law and Director of the Utrecht Centre for European Research into Family Law (UCERF), Utrecht University, the Netherlands.

Daniela Schröder
Research Assistant and PhD Candidate at the Institute for German, European and International Family Law, University of Bonn, Germany.

Rhona Schuz
Professor of Law and Director of the Centre for the Rights of the Child and the Family, Academic College for Law and Science, and Adjunct Professor at Bar Ilan University, Israel.

Julia Sloth-Nielsen
Professor in the Department of Public Law and Jurisprudence, University of the Western Cape, South Africa; Professor of Children's Rights in the Developing World at Leiden Law School, Leiden University, the Netherlands.

Daisy J.H. Smeets
Assistant Professor of Forensic Family Studies at the Institute of Child Education Studies, Leiden University, the Netherlands.

Nicola Taylor
Professor at the Faculty of Law and Director of the Children's Issues Centre, University of Otago, New Zealand; Holder of the Alexander McMillan Leading Thinker Chair in Childhood Studies.

E. Kay M. Tisdall
Professor of Childhood Policy and Member of the Childhood and Youth Studies Research Group, MHSES University of Edinburgh, Scotland, UK.

Eva Vertommen
Research Assistant at the Institute for Family Law, KU Leuven, Belgium.

Ningning Zhao
Partner of V & T Law Firm Shanghai Office, China; Director of the China International Private Law Society.

INTRODUCTION TO THE INTERNATIONAL HANDBOOK

Nicola TAYLOR, Marilyn FREEMAN, Mariëlle BRUNING
and Wendy SCHRAMA

1. INTRODUCTION

Children's participation is now widely accepted as an important aspect of contemporary family law decision-making processes. Research findings emphasising children's desire for opportunities to be heard in legal proceedings affecting them, with appropriate weight to be attached to their views, coupled with children's Article 12 rights in the United Nations Convention on the Rights of the Child (UNCRC) 1989, have prompted many jurisdictions to enact, or strengthen, statutory provisions and to implement mechanisms to enable children to express their views in the family justice system. These laws and mechanisms vary significantly across the world and so this International Handbook aims to bring together the diverse range of approaches and practices in the field to identify their similarities and differences. The Handbook also highlights current trends and will help to point the way forward globally.

The idea for such a Handbook grew out of a collaboration between the four co-editors when we met in London in March 2017, and then in Leiden in October 2017, and agreed to develop an international project based on our shared research interest in child participation in family law contexts.

Two of us are based in common law jurisdictions (New Zealand, England and Wales), while the other two are from a civil law jurisdiction (The Netherlands). We recognised the exciting opportunity offered by combining our common law and civil law expertise, and by inviting contributions from leading child and family law researchers in our respective networks, to produce a book that would provide a state-of-the-art update on child participation internationally. This seemed especially important given that so many jurisdictions, having embraced child participation, currently grapple with how best to implement this within their dispute resolution processes. The Handbook enables the modes of child participation in these national contexts to be considered within the growing body of research on children's right to be heard in family law proceedings from legal and social science perspectives and from theoretical and international perspectives.

Child and family law proceedings span both private law and public law issues. This International Handbook focuses on private law disputes when separated parents are seeking to resolve their children's future care arrangements (variously called residence, custody, contact, access, etc.). Many divorces involve children and, while the number of children affected by the separation of parents in de facto relationships is generally less ascertainable, the separation rate for de facto relationships is thought to be higher than the divorce rate. Thus, globally, many children are affected by their parents' separation or divorce which, despite the changes in community attitudes, still represents a major life stressor for the family members involved. Most children fare well, but the development and wellbeing of those experiencing violence, abuse or high interparental conflict will be detrimentally affected, particularly when those risk factors are sustained over time. Paying close attention to how children can best participate in the decision-making processes following parental separation and divorce is therefore important as it can help to tip the balance between their good or poor adjustment to this family transition.

The Handbook not only addresses how decisions are made about children's post-separation care arrangements, but also considers (i) relocation disputes when one parent wants to move away to a new domestic or international location with the children; and (ii) international child abduction, as this can be closely associated with the actual, or feared, arrangements for the future care of the children. Only passing mention is made in some chapters of child participation in public law contexts when the state has stepped in to address children's safety, care and protection. The latter context is clearly important, and significant progress has been achieved to enable children at risk of harm, or living in out-of-home care, to express their views and contribute to the decisions being made about them. However, to keep the word length manageable, and to include as many country chapters as possible, we have focused the Handbook on private law proceedings concerning children's post-separation care arrangements.

2. UNITED NATIONS CONVENTION ON THE RIGHTS OF THE CHILD

The UNCRC is one of the core international conventions and covenants aimed at promoting and protecting human rights. In many jurisdictions, its principles have significantly influenced legislative and policy initiatives and professionals' roles regarding child participation in the family justice system. The UNCRC – and Article 12 in particular – thus plays a crucial role in underpinning the analyses presented in this Handbook.

The UNCRC's significance lies in the fact it is the first international instrument bringing together states parties' obligations with respect to the protection, provision and participation rights of children under the age of 18. It is the inclusion of this latter category of rights – particularly Article 12 regarding the child's right to express their views, and have due weight attached to these in accordance with the age and maturity of the child, and Article 13 regarding the child's right to freedom of expression and to seek, receive and impart information – that has added such a significant new dimension to the children's rights agenda internationally. Participation has been identified as one of the four General Principles for interpreting all other provisions within the Convention; the others being the right to non-discrimination, the right to life and development, and the primary consideration of a child's best interests. This has been done to highlight that participation is not only a right in itself, but should also be considered in the interpretation and implementation of all other rights.[1]

The UNCRC's principles are generally regarded as a great strength of modern family law. In many jurisdictions, they have significantly influenced subsequent legislative and policy initiatives and professionals' roles regarding children in the family justice system. The UNCRC – and Article 12 in particular – features in most chapters of this Handbook.

While the phrase 'right to participate' does not actually appear in Article 12, the UN Committee on the Rights of the Child makes direct reference to it in its General Comment on Article 12.[2] This recognises the obligation to implement the right of participation in the context of divorce proceedings:

> all legislation on separation and divorce has to include the right of the child to be heard by decision makers and in mediation processes.[3]

Further, Article 9(2), which relates to children separated from their parents, provides that 'all interested parties shall be given an opportunity to participate

---

1 United Nations Committee on the Rights of the Child, *General Comment No. 12: The Right of the Child to be Heard*, CRC/C/GC/12, 20 July 2009.

2 Ibid.

3 Ibid., para. 52.

in the proceedings and make their views known'. This is considered to include children themselves when family disputes are occurring over their post-separation care.

3. STRUCTURE OF THE HANDBOOK

Part I sets out an evaluative framework for child participation with chapters on the international and regional human rights instruments pertinent to child participation and pedagogical insights on why and how to involve children. In Part II, child participation in the private international law context is addressed through the relevant Hague Conventions and EU instruments. Part III comprises 17 chapters reporting on the ways in which children are currently able to participate in family law proceedings in their particular country. The Handbook concludes in Part IV with a comparative chapter analysing the similarities and differences between the different modes of child participation in the 17 jurisdictions represented by the country chapters. Finally, there is a conclusion written by the four co-editors.

4. PART I: CHILD PARTICIPATION – AN EVALUATIVE FRAMEWORK

4.1. INTERNATIONAL AND REGIONAL HUMAN RIGHTS INSTRUMENTS

Mariëlle Bruning and Charlotte Mol discuss child participation in the context of six international and regional human rights instruments. They note at the outset that Article 12 of the UNCRC is the foundation for the child's right to participate and, together with the UNCRC generally, has acted as a catalyst for the development of five further international and regional instruments that have significance for children's participation in family law proceedings:

- the African Charter on the Rights and Welfare of the Child (ACRWC) 1990;
- the European Convention on the Exercise of Children's Rights (ECECR) 2000;
- the European Convention on Human Rights (ECHR) 1950;
- the Council of Europe (CoE) Guidelines on Child-Friendly Justice 2010; and
- the International Association of Youth and Family Judges and Magistrates (IAYFJM) Guidelines on Children in Contact with the Justice System 2017.

The authors then set out how each of the six international and regional instruments address the different types of family law proceedings in which children are provided with the right to participate. These include the same topics considered in each country chapter of this Handbook – i.e. custody/residence, contact/access, relocation, international child abduction and adoption in the context of both court proceedings and alternative dispute mechanisms like mediation and arbitration. The ECECR is specifically limited to the family law field, but the scope of the other five international and regional instruments extends well beyond this.

Bruning and Mol next consider how these different human rights instruments construe children's participation rights. Multiple participation forms are provided for children, but the two primary ones involve the child being heard (i) directly, or (ii) indirectly via a representative such as a parent, lawyer or other professional like a social worker or psychologist. The right to be heard directly is provided by all the instruments, as are indirect forms, although there is a scale of different options for representation in this regard.

The authors found that participation in family law proceedings is not an absolute right for all children. Rather, the six instruments each set out various conditions that apply in exercising this right – these include, for example, that the child must be capable of forming or communicating their own views; or that due weight should be given to the child's views. While the phrasing and presentation of the respective conditions varies across the instruments, one core requirement, regarding the child's maturity, is shared by them all. However, the child's maturity is also variously expressed through reference to such other factors as age, capacity, sufficient understanding or discernment.

Bruning and Mol review how the international and regional instruments attend to various practical issues, including the location of the child's participation, the methods of communication and the child's right to information and feedback.

They conclude by noting that the binding instruments (the UNCRC, ACRWC and ECECR) all required broad political approval and could not therefore be as specific as the 'soft law' instruments (the CoE Guidelines on Child-Friendly Justice and the IAYFJM Guidelines on Children in Contact with the Justice System). The instruments that came after the UNCRC also had the benefit of being able to build upon its general principles and to explicate them further. All six international and regional human rights instruments are very clear that children have the right to participate in family law proceedings that concern them, but they do not provide a blueprint for how children's procedural inclusion is best achieved in practice. The practical implementation of how children can and should participate is where work needs to occur. In this regard, it is intended that this Handbook will help to fill that void.

4.2. PEDAGOGICAL INSIGHTS

The social and financial consequences of parental separation can detrimentally impact children's developmental outcomes, wellbeing, and parent-child attachments, particularly when interparental conflict and loyalty binds are evident. As part of the Handbook's evaluative framework, Daisy J.H. Smeets and Stephanie Rap consider the pedagogical conditions that enable children to participate effectively in judicial decision-making processes within the context of divorce proceedings. Interaction between law and social science is considered essential to enhance both the quality of family law decision-making and children's developmental trajectories.

The authors provide a brief historical perspective on childhood and child participation. The definition of children, childhood and children's rights has varied greatly across time and place, depending, among other things, on social, economic and cultural circumstances. The Western conceptualisation of childhood has changed markedly over past centuries with children now regarded as worthy of being listened to and as capable of providing their views and opinions in important decisions affecting their lives. However, protecting children's interests is also an important pillar of the UNCRC and, particularly in family law cases involving parental separation and divorce, a tension can arise between protecting children and involving them. Smeets and Rap therefore discuss the dominant theoretical underpinnings of child participation to reach a more nuanced understanding of how children can be involved in a meaningful way, while at the same time having their rights and interests protected.

Definitions of participation vary widely and incorporate both individual and collective elements. Participation can be considered as a process or an outcome, or as an end in itself, as well as a means of achieving other goals, such as the possibility of having an impact on the nature of the decision being made. Roger Hart, Harry Shier and Laura Lundy have each developed models to better conceptualise child participation and to evaluate practice on the basis of children's different levels, or types, of participation. This has helped to highlight the challenges embedded in implementation in practice, including in the settings and contexts for child participation. A persistent criticism is the tokenistic nature of many forms of involvement by children.

The authors consider several empirical, mainly socio-legal, research studies on child participation in family law proceedings. These primarily consist of interviews with children, parents and (legal) professionals about their experiences with child participatory procedures and/or involve observations of court hearings. Children's desire to be included in decision-making processes seems to outweigh their concerns. However, Smeets and Rap discuss the research findings showing how children's right to participate is not always fully satisfied. Children do not always feel heard and may not be adequately informed. Major barriers thwarting child participation include professionals' lack of skills and time, children's loyalty conflicts and related fears, and adults' concerns about children's cognitive capacities.

The conditions for effective child participation need to be based on pedagogical and psychological knowledge on how to involve and talk with children.

Three important conditions are reviewed: (i) access to legal procedures and informing children; (ii) stimulating a safe environment; and (iii) communication skills. Guidance is provided on how child participation can best be facilitated in family law proceedings, given the particular challenges posed in relation to hearing children's views in post-separation parenting contexts.

5. PART II: PRIVATE INTERNATIONAL LAW

While private international law instruments do not usually impose direct duties to hear the child, and leave the modalities for doing so to national law, Thalia Kruger and Francesca Maoli set out how the influence of human rights law is being clearly felt in the private international law contexts governing child protection, international child abduction, parental responsibility and maintenance.

Kruger and Maoli highlight and discuss the careful nudges by supranational legislators to better respect children's right to participation, paying particular attention to the 1980 Hague Convention on the Civil Aspects of International Child Abduction, which they concede, in itself, does not greatly enhance child participation. However, they conclude that the obligation to hear the child in return proceedings under the 1980 Convention has become even more stringent in light of the different understanding of such proceedings by the European Court of Human Rights (ECtHR) and that a coherent interpretation of the 1980 Convention with the UNCRC, and, where applicable, the European Convention on Human Rights and the EU Charter of Fundamental Rights, guarantees children's participation rights. They are clear that the 1980 Hague Convention can be applied in a way that is respectful of children's participation rights.

The 1996 Hague Child Protection Convention includes just one mention – in its chapter on recognition and enforcement – of a child's right to be heard. While this provides a useful reminder to judges to grant children the opportunity to be heard to avoid the decision not being recognised or enforced, the authors note that the Convention does not introduce, or refer to, an international standard for child participation.

Kruger and Maoli acknowledge the value of small steps as they examine the development of the EU Regulations on parental responsibility, Brussels II*bis* and *ter*, the latter of which will come into force in August 2022, and which uses the language of the UNCRC in relation to giving children capable of forming their own views the opportunity to express those views, and for due weight to be given to these in accordance with their age and maturity. This opportunity must be genuine and effective, thus further enhancing child participation, and giving important nudges to national judges.

Their assessment that private international law instruments can create incentives to cautiously move national procedures in the right direction provides welcome encouragement for the child participation field.

6. PART III: NATIONAL PERSPECTIVES

Leading researchers were also invited to contribute to the International Handbook and we are delighted to have 17 country chapters detailing the approach to child participation in family law proceedings in Australia, Belgium, Canada, China, Croatia, Denmark, England and Wales, Germany, Israel, Italy, the Netherlands, New Zealand, Norway, Romania, Scotland, South Africa, and the USA. Each country author was asked to follow a standardised template developed by the co-editors to ensure that each of these chapters addressed similar issues. These included:

- a general introduction to the jurisdiction, its demographic profile, and an overview of the key decision-making processes and roles of key actors;
- the statutory provisions relevant to child participation in family law proceedings and whether these have any age/maturity/capability/capacity requirements;
- the modes of child participation: (i) direct forms of participation (e.g. judicial meetings with children); (ii) representation forms of participation (e.g. by children's legal representatives); and (iii) whether or not a child can litigate on their own behalf by commencing litigation or by appealing a decision;
- the types of proceedings and leading case law on child participation issues in legal/court proceedings for custody/residence, contact/access, relocation, international child abduction; and, where relevant, parentage and adoption (note that children's participation in proceedings relating to child protection, family and domestic violence were not included);
- out-of-court family dispute resolution processes (e.g. mediation)
- research on child participation in the jurisdiction, if available;
- significant policy or practice developments or initiatives (e.g. recent, or forthcoming, legislation or new policies/practices); and
- consideration as to whether the requirements of Article 12 of the UNCRC are being met in the jurisdiction, and how/how not.

We acknowledge the many gaps in the global coverage of countries included in this Handbook. Notwithstanding this, the 17 jurisdictions that are represented provide valuable insight into how child participation is undertaken within each family justice system. This reveals the range of legislative provisions, modes of participation, and roles and types of professionals involved in engaging with children.

7. PART IV: COMPARATIVE ANALYSIS

The Handbook includes a comparative analysis chapter, authored by Charlotte Mol, which identifies the similarities and differences between the different modes of child participation in the 17 jurisdictions represented by the country chapters.

This chapter begins by addressing the types of family law proceedings in which children are allowed to participate and those in which their participation rights may be more limited. Globally, there are many specific types of proceedings for divorce, custody/residence, contact/access and parentage issues. The delineation between these types of family law proceedings differs between jurisdictions and child participation opportunities can be fragmented between different types of proceedings even within a single jurisdiction. In most jurisdictions, the modes of participation available to the child depend on the type of proceedings. Sometimes these modes are available in most proceedings but, other times, they may only be available for a very specific type of proceeding. It is therefore difficult to compare the modes of participation available by the type of proceedings so the comparative analysis focuses on four modes of participation independent of the type of proceedings:

- *Direct modes:* The hearing of a child by the court, or a judicial meeting, was found to be available in all 17 jurisdictions.
- *Representation modes:* Many different modes of representation were identified in the jurisdictions. These representatives are mostly lawyers, but non-legal representatives such as laypersons, relatives, recommended citizens, psychologists and pedagogical experts are also evident. The purpose of the representation also varies between representing the child's views/wishes and/or the child's best interests/welfare.
- *Indirect modes:* In nine jurisdictions children's views can be expressed by means of an expert/specialist report.
- *Party status and litigation by children:* Children generally have no party status in family law proceedings and, in the small number of jurisdictions where this is possible, it is limited and used in a minority of cases. The potential for children to initiate litigation on their own behalf is also either non-existent or limited to specific types of cases or through requirements of understanding/maturity.

The comparative analysis then addresses child participation in (i) international child abduction proceedings, where most jurisdictions offer similar participation opportunities for children in these proceedings as they do in domestic family law proceedings; and (ii) alternative dispute resolution (ADR) processes like mediation, which parents are required to, or voluntarily, use to try to reach agreement prior to any commencement of family law proceedings. Children's right to participate in ADR is regulated by law in a few jurisdictions, but most lack any specific laws regarding how children should be able to express their views in ADR processes. This can mean little involvement by children in ADR, although several jurisdictions report child participation is increasing over time. Child-inclusive models have, however, been developed in other jurisdictions through soft-law or service-based protocols.

The chapter then discusses two overarching issues regarding the requirements for child participation and children's right to receive information about their opportunities to participate in the proceedings and to receive feedback on the decisions made. Age and maturity requirements are popular criteria, albeit often phrased in different ways across the jurisdictions – the child has to, for example, have 'sufficient age and maturity', the 'capacity to express views', the 'capacity to instruct' a representative, be 'capable of understanding the meaning and legal consequences' of litigation, or have 'sufficient understanding'. In some jurisdictions these norms are complemented by a presumption that children of a certain age can be automatically granted the opportunity to express their views, while younger children will have to fulfil maturity requirements. These age limits vary from six years to 15 years, with some jurisdictions (such as Germany) hearing even younger children (aged three) in practice.

8. CONCLUSION

As long-term researchers in the field of child participation within various family law contexts, we recognised at the outset the wide range of approaches to child participation which exists globally in family law decision-making. Our aim as editors was to mine this information with the help of international children's rights specialists to identify current and best practice around the world, and bring together the results of that collaboration for your consideration. This Handbook details the undoubted progress that has been made towards the dual ambitions of honouring the right of children to be heard and involved in decisions affecting their lives, and protecting their interests. However, it is clear that there remains more to do to ensure that children and young people feel that they have been adequately informed and properly heard when they wish to participate.

We hope you will enjoy delving into the rich array of child participation material provided in this Handbook in both national and international contexts, and that it may act as a springboard for further comparative research as we, the international family law community, look together to ways in which child participation may continue to flourish around the world.

PART I

CHILD PARTICIPATION: AN EVALUATIVE FRAMEWORK

CHILD PARTICIPATION IN INTERNATIONAL AND REGIONAL HUMAN RIGHTS INSTRUMENTS

Mariëlle BRUNING and Charlotte MOL

1. INTRODUCTION

The child's right to be heard in all matters affecting the child, including the views of the child being given due weight in accordance with their age and maturity, is not only one of the core elements of the UN Convention on the Rights of the Child (UNCRC), but can also be distilled from other sources of international and regional human rights. This right includes the opportunity to be heard in any judicial and administrative proceedings affecting the child, for example in family law proceedings. The child's right to be heard is a fundamental aspect of children's participation and has led to extensive research and policy on 'child participation', although the term itself does not appear in international and regional human rights documents.

The child's right to participate in legal proceedings encompasses the right to be heard directly or indirectly, a right to representation, and procedural rights such as the right to commence proceedings, access to all relevant files, or to appeal, as an independent party to the proceedings with legal status or indirectly via legal or other forms of representation.[1] The UNCRC and other international and regional instruments cover elements of the child's right to participate in legal proceedings. The relevant sources are covered in this chapter, both binding and non-binding, international and regional.[2] This chapter provides a foundation for the other chapters in this Handbook. It discusses the core themes related to child participation in legal proceedings which will also be dealt with in each corresponding country chapter: the types of proceedings in which children may participate, the forms of participation available to children, conditions for participation, the location in which participation ought to take place and the method of communication, and the role of information and feedback in the participation process. For each theme, the rights or guidelines provided by the international and regional instruments are described.

From a human rights perspective, Article 12 of the UNCRC is regarded as the foundation for the child's right to participate. The UNCRC, both generally and Article 12 specifically, was the catalyst for further international and regional developments on the topic of child participation. The African Charter on the Rights and Welfare of the Child (ACRWC) was a regional response to the UNCRC, which was adopted in 1990, coming into force in 1999.[3] Another regional response emerged from the Council of Europe (CoE) through the European Convention on the Exercise of Children's Rights of 1996 (ECECR), which entered into force in 2000.[4] More recently, two sets of guidelines have

---

1 The right to access to justice for children will not be addressed in this contribution; this right is grounded in the right of the child to seek remedies in the event of (alleged) rights violations, hence the right to legal action against rights violations (see e.g. UN High Commissioner for Human Rights, *Access to justice for children. Report of the United Nations High Commissioner for Human Rights*, UN Doc. A/HRC/25/35, 2013; this report stresses that children should preferably be heard directly in court and legal proceedings should be child-sensitive to safeguard effective access to justice, see also T. Liefaard, 'Access to Justice for Children: Towards a Specific Research and Implementation Agenda', *The International Journal of Children's Rights*, Vol. 27, No. 2, 2019, pp. 195–227). This chapter focuses on the right to participation of children in (family law) proceedings.

2 The Charter of Fundamental Rights of the European Union will not be addressed in this contribution as its scope of application is limited to the functioning of the EU institutions and the implementation of EU law and thus is of little relevance for the domestic laws on child participation. Additionally, the Brussels II*bis* or Brussels II*ter* Regulations, as well as the 1980 Hague Convention on the Civil Aspects of International Child Abduction, are discussed in the contribution by T. Kruger and F. Maoli in this Handbook, which deals with private international law and the relevant EU instruments in relation to international child abduction.

3 African Charter on the Rights and Welfare of the Child, adopted July 1990 (entered into force 29 November 1999) OAU Doc. CAB/LEG/24.9/49 (1990).

4 European Convention on the Exercise of Children's Rights 1996, ETS No. 160.

been adopted: the Guidelines on Child-friendly Justice (CoE Guidelines) were adopted by the Council of Ministers of the Council of Europe on 17 November 2010;[5] and the International Association of Youth and Family Judges and Magistrates (IAYFJM) adopted and ratified the Guidelines on Children in Contact with the Justice System (IAYFJM Guidelines) in 2017.[6] Although the latter guidelines are not 'soft law' as the CoE Guidelines are, they do provide relevant best practice and are a form of international professional standards. Finally, a general regional source of human rights law is also of relevance for this topic, i.e. the European Convention on Human Rights 1950 (ECHR). Contrary to the UNCRC, the ECHR does not contain a separate article on the child's right to participate. Nevertheless, it is an important source for this right thanks to the unique position of the European Court of Human Rights (ECtHR) and its case law, as is explained below. We commence with a brief introduction of the status and relevance of these six sources.

2. THE SIX INTERNATIONAL AND REGIONAL INSTRUMENTS

2.1. UN CONVENTION ON THE RIGHTS OF THE CHILD 1989

Central to the UNCRC is the idea that children are no longer regarded as mere objects of rights, but rather as rights holders who have agency to realise their rights enshrined in the UNCRC. Article 12 adds to that, providing that every child who is capable of forming their own views has the right to express those views freely in all matters affecting the child, the views of the child being given due weight in accordance with the age and maturity of the child (Article 12(1)). The child shall in particular be provided the opportunity to be heard in any judicial and administrative proceedings affecting the child, either directly or through a representative or an appropriate body, in a manner consistent with the procedural rules of national law (Article 12(2)). It is important to underscore that the child has the right not to exercise their right to be heard: expressing views is a choice for the child, not an obligation.[7] Article 12 provides that states parties 'shall assure' the right of the child to express their views and thus imposes a clear obligation on states parties to introduce opportunities for the child to do so.

---

5 *Guidelines of the Committee of Ministers of the Council of Europe on child-friendly justice*, 17 November 2010.

6 International Association of Youth and Family Judges and Magistrates, *Guidelines on Children in Contact with the Justice System*, 2017 (aimjf.org).

7 UN Committee on the Rights of the Child, *General Comment No. 12: The Right of the Child to be Heard*, CRC/C/GC/12, 20 July 2009, para. 16; CoE Guidelines, above n. 5, IV(D), para. 46.

The UNCRC Committee has pronounced this provision as one of the four general principles of the UNCRC.[8] This implies that the right to be heard is an overarching right that is particularly necessary for the fulfilment of all other rights. Article 12 is closely connected to both Article 5 UNCRC in which 'the evolving capacities of the child' are mentioned as a guiding tool to provide appropriate direction and guidance in the exercise by the child of the UNCRC rights, and Article 3 that is also considered as one of the four fundamental principles of the UNCRC ('in all action concerning children … the best interests of the child shall be a primary consideration'). In addition, Article 9 UNCRC can be seen as a specification of Article 12 for children who face or experience separation from their parents against their will. The UNCRC has almost universal ratification (by all countries in the world except the United States) and is therefore in this respect the most successful human rights document in history. The UNCRC Committee has launched a General Comment on 'The right of the child to be heard' in 2009 (General Comment No. 12) that can be seen as an interpretative tool. The aim of this General Comment was to provide a better understanding of what Article 12 entails and how to fully implement it for every child, taking into consideration the many impediments to fully realising this right.[9] The UNCRC is a binding convention to Member States and has had an enormous influence in recent history.[10] Although the UNCRC has recently celebrated its 30th anniversary, still many challenges lie ahead regarding the further implementation of its rights.

2.2. AFRICAN CHARTER ON THE RIGHTS AND WELFARE OF THE CHILD 1990

The ACRWC echoes Article 12 UNCRC through Article 4(2): the right to be given an opportunity for the child's views to be heard either directly or through

8 UN Committee on the Rights of the Child, *General Comment No. 5: General Measures of implementation of the Convention on the Rights of the Child*, CRC/GC/2003/5, 27 November 2003, para. 12; this highlights the fact that Art. 12 UNCRC not only establishes a right in itself, but should also be considered in the interpretation of all other rights. The other three general principles are the principle of non-discrimination (Art. 2), the best interests of the child principle (Art. 3(1)), and the right to life, survival and development (Art. 6).

9 General Comment No. 12, above n. 7, para. 4.

10 See e.g. K. Arts, 'Twenty-Five Years of the United Nations Convention on the Rights of the Child: Achievements and Challenges', *Netherlands International Law Review*, Vol. 61, No. 3, 2014, pp. 267–303. It is relevant to note that internally states adopt different attitudes as to the enforceability of the UNCRC; this depends in part on whether a state has a 'monist' or 'dualist' system. In monist systems, ratified conventions can be enforced directly in national courts, whereas in dualist systems treaties cannot be enforced until they have been incorporated into national law via national legislation.

an impartial representative in all judicial or administrative proceedings affecting them and that those views must be taken into consideration. More generally, Article 7 provides children with the right to communicate views and express opinions freely. The ACRWC is a binding regional convention to which the African Member States of the African Union can be parties. At present, 49 out of 55 states have ratified the ACRWC.[11]

2.3. EUROPEAN CONVENTION ON THE EXERCISE OF CHILDREN'S RIGHTS 2000

The ECECR was intended to be a general European response to the UNCRC. However, it ended up focusing on procedural, rather than substantive, children's rights to complement the UNCRC in providing children with options to exercise their rights.[12] These rights include, amongst others, the right to express views and to be appointed a representative. The Convention has been ratified by 20 of the 47 CoE Member States. While not considered a 'key' convention, it is binding and has regular ratifications.[13]

2.4. EUROPEAN CONVENTION ON HUMAN RIGHTS 1950

The ECHR, as the general European human rights convention, does not explicitly recognise the child's right to participate. However, together with the ECtHR, it occupies a unique position within the human rights framework. This has led to the introduction of a child's right to participate through interpretations of Article 6 and Article 8 ECHR in the ECtHR's judgments.[14] By ratifying the ECHR, states accepted the establishment and jurisdiction of the ECtHR and the possibility of individual applications to this Court.[15] The monitoring system of the ECtHR combined with the 'golden rule' of evolutive interpretation is an important means

---

11 See https://au.int/en/treaties/1168 for the current status list.

12 K. Herbots, 'Het nieuwe Europees Verdrag inzake de uitoefening van de rechten van het kind en de situatie in België', *Tijdschrift voor Privaatrecht*, 1997, pp. 1763–1823, p. 1767.

13 See the Report by the Secretary General on the Review of Council of Europe Conventions, SG/Inf(2012)12. In 2015 both Malta and Spain ratified the Convention. In total 20 states have ratified the Convention: Albania, Austria, Croatia, Cyprus, Czech Republic Finland, France, Germany, Greece, Italy, Latvia, Malta, Montenegro, Poland, Portugal, Slovenia, Spain, the former Yugoslav Republic of Macedonia, Turkey and Ukraine. A further eight states have signed the Convention: Hungary, Iceland, Ireland, Luxembourg, the Russian Federation and Sweden.

14 See M.R. Bruning et al., *Kind in proces: van communicatie naar effectieve participatie*, Wolf Publishers, Nijmegen 2020, pp. 80–122.

15 Arts. 19, 32 and 34 ECHR.

of achieving children's rights in Europe.[16] Individuals (including children) can bring cases to the Court themselves and thus raise alleged (children's) rights violations.[17] In recent decades, the ECtHR has increasingly focused on children's rights and made use of children's rights in the UNCRC and other international documents as an aid to interpretation. In the Court's case law there is the explicit recognition of the child's right to sufficient involvement in the decision-making process under Article 8 ECHR. This was introduced in the *M and M* judgment, where the ECtHR concluded that the parent's right to sufficient involvement applies *mutatis mutandis* to children, meaning children ought to be provided the opportunity to be heard and express their views.[18] Additionally, the ECtHR has repeatedly held that 'as children become mature and able to formulate their own opinion ... the courts should give due weight to their views and feelings and to their right to respect for their private life'.[19]

2.5. COUNCIL OF EUROPE GUIDELINES ON CHILD-FRIENDLY JUSTICE 2010

In addition to the ECERC and the ECHR, the CoE introduced its own guidelines in Europe. The CoE Guidelines focus on the broader right to participate and make very specific recommendations for child-friendly procedures. The Guidelines provide detailed guidance to the Council of Europe Member States; they are not binding but do provide impetus, amongst others, to the ECtHR's interpretation of children's rights. During the drafting process it was decided

---

16 U. Kilkelly, 'The Best of Both Worlds for Children's Rights? Interpreting the European Convention on Human Rights in the Light of the UN Convention on the Rights of the Child', *Human Rights Quarterly*, Vol. 23, 2001, pp. 308–326, p. 311; and M. Burbergs, 'How the right to respect for private and family life, home and correspondence became the nursery in which new rights are born' in E. Brems and J. Gerards (eds.), *Shaping Rights in the ECHR: The Role of the European Court of Human Rights in Determining the Scope of Human Rights*, Cambridge University Press, Cambridge 2013, pp. 315–329.

17 Art. 34 ECHR. See also L. Graziani, 'Access to Justice: A Fundamental Right for All Children' in T. Liefaard and J. Sloth-Nielsen (eds.), *The United Nations Convention on the Rights of the Child: Taking Stock after 25 Years and Looking Ahead*, Brill/Nijhoff, Leiden 2017, pp. 125–141, p. 130.

18 ECtHR *M and M v Croatia* (Appl. No. 10161/13), 3 September 2015, para. 181. This principle has been reaffirmed in three subsequent judgments: ECtHR *NTs and others v Georgia* (Appl. No. 71776/12), 2 February 2016, para. 78; ECtHR *ES v Romania and Bulgaria* (Appl. No. 60281/11), 19 July 2016, para. 59; and ECtHR *C v Croatia* (Appl. No. 80117/17), 8 October 2020, para. 73.

19 ECtHR *Płaza v Poland* (Appl. No. 18830/07), 25 January 2011, para. 71; ECtHR *Gobec v Slovenia* (Appl. No. 7233/04), 3 October 2013, para. 133; and ECtHR *Khusnutdinov and X v Russia* (Appl. No. 76598/12), 18 December 2018, para. 86.

that the guidelines should not extend beyond the standards already set out in international law (e.g. Article 12 UNCRC; case law of the ECtHR).[20]

2.6. INTERNATIONAL ASSOCIATION OF YOUTH AND FAMILY JUDGES AND MAGISTRATES GUIDELINES 2017

On a different note, in 2017, the IAYFJM adopted and ratified the Guidelines on Children in Contact with the Justice System (IAYFJM Guidelines).[21] These guidelines mirror many of the principles contained in the Guidelines on Child-Friendly Justice and reflect many aspects of the child's right to participation in court proceedings, more specifically in the context of family and child law proceedings. The guidelines are not binding, but can be seen as a reflection of youth and family judges' perceptions of the child's right to participate in family law proceedings and therefore as an international professional standard.

3. TYPES OF PROCEEDINGS

The first theme addressed is the type of proceedings in which children are provided the right to participate in each of the instruments. More specifically, the different types of family law proceedings are considered.

Children must be able to express their views 'in all matters affecting' them, according to Article 12(1) UNCRC. The UNCRC Committee supports a broad definition of 'matters' since a wide interpretation of matters affecting the child helps to include children in the social processes of their community and society.[22] Opportunities to be heard have to be provided, in particular, in 'any judicial and administrative proceedings affecting the child' (Article 12(2) UNCRC). The UNCRC Committee mentions in this regard proceedings of separation of parents, custody, care and adoption and explains that judicial and administrative proceedings may involve alternative dispute mechanisms such as mediation and arbitration.[23] The Committee also notes that the right to be heard applies both to proceedings which are initiated by the child as well as to those initiated by others which affect the child, such as parental separation or adoption.[24]

---

20 T. Liefaard and U. Kilkelly, 'Child-Friendly Justice – past, present and future' in B. Goldson (ed.), *Juvenile Justice in Europe. Past, Present and Future*, Routledge, London/New York 2018, pp. 57–73; the Guidelines are seen as rather weak at certain points, including the relatively weak status, and not really adding anything new, p. 64.

21 IAYFJM Guidelines, above n. 6.

22 General Comment No. 12, above n. 7, para. 27.

23 General Comment No. 12, above n. 7, para. 32.

24 General Comment No. 12, above n. 7, para. 33.

According to Article 9 UNCRC, states parties shall ensure that a child shall not be separated from their parents against their will, except when this is in accordance with the law and necessary for the best interests of the child, such as 'where the parents are living separately and a decision must be made as to the child's place of residence' (Article 9(1) UNCRC). In any such proceedings all interested parties shall be given the opportunity to participate in the proceedings and make their views known.[25]

Turning to the regional sources, the right of the child to communicate views in Article 4(2) of the African Charter is provided for 'in all judicial or administrative proceedings affecting a child'. This phrasing mirrors the text of Article 12(2) UNCRC. The phrase can therefore be understood to include family law proceedings of all types which affect the child.[26]

The material scope of the ECECR is, in principle, limited to family proceedings according to Article 1(3) ECECR and, in particular, proceedings on the exercise of parental responsibilities. The Explanatory Report does suggest that states can opt to apply the Convention to any other proceedings; however, the focus is on family proceedings.[27] In the ratification process of the ECECR, states must specify a minimum of three categories of family proceedings to which the Convention is to apply.[28] The selection of types of proceedings has both benefits and drawbacks. It may make the ratification and implementation of the ECECR more accessible for states;[29] however, it may also lead to fragmentation of rights and a lack of uniformity between different proceedings.[30]

Contrary to the other regional sources, the case law of the ECtHR, by its nature, does not provide a specific scope of application for the child's right to participate. As the ECtHR deals with any complaints brought before it, the case law on child participation rights has not been limited to any type of proceeding.

---

25 Some authors interpret this as another specification of Art. 12(1) UNCRC: the child's right to be heard should be respected in all cases when the separation of the child from their parents is under consideration, e.g. L. Krappmann, 'The weight of the child's view (Article 12 of the Convention on the Rights of the Child)', *The International Journal of Children's Rights*, Vol. 18, 2010, pp. 501–513, p. 504. However, Sandberg states that this provision was not meant to include children to be heard. See K. Sandberg, 'Alternative Care and Children's Rights' in U. Kilkelly and T. Liefaard (eds.), *International Human Rights of Children*, Springer, Singapore 2018, pp. 187–213, p. 200.

26 D. Kassan, 'The Voice of the Child in Family Law Proceedings', *De Jure*, Vol. 36, No. 2, 2003, pp. 164–179, p. 166.

27 Explanatory Report to the European Convention on the Exercise of Children's Rights, Strasbourg, 25 January 1996, para. 15.

28 Art. 1(4) ECECR.

29 I. Jansen, 'Europees Verdrag inzake de uitoefening van rechten van kinderen', *FJR*, No. 6, 1996, pp. 132–138, p. 134.

30 K. Herbots, above n. 12, p. 1774; and N. Lowe, 'The impact of the Council of Europe on European family law' in J.M. Scherpe (ed.), *European Family Law Volume I: The Impact of Institutions and Organisations on European Family Law*, Edward Elgar, Cheltenham 2016, pp. 95–123, p. 104.

There are well-known cases on a variety of family law proceedings. For example, *Sahin v Germany* and *Sommerfeld v Germany* concerned access rights; *M and M v Croatia* concerned custody rights; *Havelka and others v Czech Republic* concerned care proceedings; and *Rouiller v Switzerland* concerned international child abduction proceedings.[31]

The CoE Guidelines on Child-Friendly Justice deal with the issue of children's rights and needs in judicial proceedings and in alternatives to such procedures. These Guidelines apply to all ways in which children are (likely to be) brought into contact with criminal, civil or administrative law. The IAYFJM Guidelines are focused on rights for children who come into contact with the law in any setting, including separation of parents, custody, protection and adoption.[32] They apply to all matters where children are in contact with the justice system. The non-binding nature of the CoE and IAYFJM Guidelines may explain the broad scope of their recommendations, as they concern not only family law proceedings, but also any other criminal, civil and administrative proceedings.[33]

To summarise, all the above-mentioned human and regional human rights sources provide for children's right to participate in family law proceedings. They therefore address all the proceedings central to this Handbook, such as the separation of parents, custody, care, adoption and international child abduction. Some of the instruments also cover alternative dispute mechanisms (e.g. mediation and arbitration). In fact, the scope of most Conventions and Guidelines reach beyond the field of family law – only the ECECR is limited to family law specifically.

4. FORMS OF PARTICIPATION

Participation in legal proceedings is broader than only the right to be heard; it also covers other forms of procedural inclusion in the proceedings discussed above. We now turn to discuss how the different human rights instruments construe children's participation rights.

Children have the right to be heard either directly or through a representative or an appropriate body according to Article 12(2) UNCRC. However, the UNCRC Committee recommends that, wherever possible, the child must be given the opportunity to be directly heard in any proceedings.[34] The representative can

31 ECtHR *Sahin v Germany* [GC] (Appl. No. 30943/96), 8 July 2003; ECtHR *Sommerfeld v Germany* [GC] (Appl. No. 31871/96), 8 July 2003; ECtHR *Havelka and others v Czech Republic* (Appl. No. 23499/06), 21 June 2007; ECtHR *Rouiller v Switzerland* (Appl. No. 3592/08), 22 July 2014; ECtHR *M and M v Croatia* (Appl. No. 10161/13), 3 September 2015.

32 IAYFJM Guidelines, above n. 6, pp. 7–8.

33 CoE Guidelines, above n. 5, I(2).

34 General Comment No. 12, above n. 7, para. 35.

be the parent(s), a lawyer or another person, e.g. a social worker. The UNCRC Committee emphasises that indirect hearing via a family representative (often parent(s)) risks a conflict of interests and it is therefore of utmost importance that the child's views are transmitted correctly to the decision-maker by the representative.[35] The representative must exclusively represent the interests of the child. The UNCRC Committee recommends that codes of conduct should be developed for representatives who are appointed to ascertain and represent the child's views.[36]

It is not clear whether states have the discretion to determine how the child's views should be heard[37] or have to provide for a representative as an option to children in proceedings.[38] According to Mol, it appears that states cannot simply decide to provide children with only one manner in which to be heard; children should – according to General Comment No. 12 – be provided with a choice between forms of participation.[39] Once a child has opted to be heard in a proceeding, they should be provided with the opportunity to decide how to be heard.[40] Still, neither Article 12 UNCRC nor the UNCRC Committee address the question regarding how children should be provided with representation in legal proceedings pursuant to Article 12 UNCRC, nor do they explicitly require representation forms to be available to children.[41] It remains unclear from these sources what the most suitable option is to hear children in family law proceedings.[42] Parkes forewarns that best-interests representation by a guardian ad litem as a means of indirectly hearing the child's voice should be accompanied with the guarantee of presenting the child's own views to the court; this could be realised by a 'tandem model' of both a guardian ad litem and a special lawyer representing the child.[43]

---

35 General Comment No. 12, above n. 7, para. 36.

36 General Comment No. 12, above n. 7, para. 37.

37 R. Hodgkin and P. Newell, *Implementation Handbook for the Convention on the Rights of the Child*, UNICEF, New York 2007, p. 157.

38 A. Parkes, *Children and International Human Rights Law: The Right of the Child to be Heard*, Routledge, London 2013, p. 98.

39 C.R. Mol, 'Children's Representation in Family Law Proceedings', *The International Journal of Children's Rights*, Vol. 27, No. 1, 2019, pp. 66–98, p. 70.

40 General Comment No. 12, above n. 7, para. 35. See also G. Lansdown, *Every Child's Right to be Heard: A Resource Guide on the UN Committee on the Rights of the Child General Comment No. 12*, Save the Children Fund, London 2011; E.E. Sutherland, 'Listening to the Voice of the Child: The Evolution of Participation Rights', *New Zealand Law Review*, Vol. 26, No. 3, 2013, p. 345; and C.R. Mol, above n. 39.

41 C.R. Mol, above n. 39, pp. 74 and 94.

42 A. Parkes, above n. 38, p. 120.

43 A. Parkes, above n. 38, p. 255. With regard to international child abduction cases, Schuz prefers the child to be heard directly by the court; indirectly 'translating' the child's voice should be insufficient to guarantee effective participation of the child; R. Schuz, *The Hague Child Abduction Convention: a critical analysis*, Hart Publishing, Oxford 2013, p. 381.

General Comment No. 14 also addresses the way in which children should participate in court proceedings:

> In civil cases, the child may be defending his or her interests directly or through a representative, in the case of paternity, child abuse or neglect, family reunification, accommodation, etc.[44]

Consistent with the discussion about how an indirect hearing of the child should be shaped, General Comment No. 14 addresses representation of the child by others than the parent(s) or primary carer(s) to realise separate participation in legal proceedings. In paragraph 90 it is stated that in situations where the child's views are in conflict with those of their representative, a procedure should be established to allow the child to approach an authority to establish separate representation for the child (e.g. a guardian ad litem), if necessary. In cases where a child is referred to an administrative or judicial procedure involving the determination of their best interests, they should, according to the UNCRC Committee in General Comment No. 14, be provided with a legal representative, in addition to a guardian or representative of their views, when there is a potential conflict between the parties in the decision.[45] It appears that the UNCRC Committee is more explicit in General Comment No. 14 compared to General Comment No. 12 regarding the child's right to legal representation in situations of (possible) conflict of interests between the child and the (parent) representative.[46] In family law proceedings, the risk of a conflict of interests between parents and child is particularly apparent.

The UNCRC and General Comment No. 12 remain silent about the child's right to commence proceedings, file a request to access relevant files or appeal. However, when the right of the child to be heard in legal proceedings is breached, the UNCRC Committee notes that the child must have access to appeals and complaint procedures.[47] The UNCRC Committee also notes that the giving of feedback to the child by the decision-maker may prompt the child to file an appeal or a complaint.[48] States parties should review or amend their legislation to introduce mechanisms providing children with access to appropriate information, adequate support if necessary, feedback on the weight given to their views, and procedures for complaints, remedies or redress.[49] Thus the UNCRC

[44] UN Committee on the Rights of the Child, *General Comment No. 14: The right of the child to have his or her best interests taken as a primary consideration*, CRC/C/GC/14, 29 May 2013, para. 29.

[45] General Comment No. 14, above n. 44, para. 96.

[46] M.R. Bruning et al., above n. 14, p. 90.

[47] General Comment No. 12, above n. 7, para. 47.

[48] General Comment No. 12, above n. 7, para. 45.

[49] General Comment No. 12, above n. 7, para. 48.

Committee does not explicitly address the possibility of the child independently commencing proceedings or filing an appeal, but appealing against a decision in which the child is heard should be an option for children and they should receive appropriate information and support.

The text of Article 4(2) ACRWC refers to two forms of participation: the child may be heard directly or 'through an impartial representative as a party to the proceedings'. The direct form of participation is similar to that in Article 12 UNCRC, while the indirect form differs in wording. Article 4(2) calls for an 'impartial representative', adding an additional element of neutrality. The option of an indirect hearing through an 'appropriate body' has not been replicated in the ACRWC.[50] The wording of Article 4(2) does add to the direct hearing and the representative the phrase 'as a party to the proceedings'. Chirwa considers that this implies that 'a child has to be a party to given proceedings for him/her to be heard'.[51] It can be understood in this way as providing the opportunity for a child to be included as a party to proceedings, including in family proceedings.[52] However, it can also be understood to refer solely to the position of the impartial representative for the child.[53]

The ECECR provides a range of procedural rights, of which two are mandatory for states to provide, while the others are optional. States are obliged to provide the child with the right to express their views in proceedings, as provided by Article 3 (and mirrored in Article 6) ECECR. Additionally, when the holder(s) of parental responsibility cannot represent the child in the proceedings due to a conflict of interests, Articles 4 and 9 provide for the right to the appointment of a special representative. Article 5 lists a number of procedural rights that states could opt to provide for children. These rights are: the right to apply to be assisted by an appropriate person of their choice when expressing their views, the right to apply for the appointment of a separate representative, the right to appoint their own representative and, finally, the right to exercise some or all of the rights of parties to such proceedings.

The mandatory and optional procedural rights in the ECECR consist of various forms of participation. The first form is the expressing of views by being 'consulted' as provided in Article 3(b) ECECR; this refers to the hearing of the child, either directly by the judicial authority or indirectly through other persons or bodies.[54] Subsequently the ECECR provides for representation.

50 See M. Gose, *The African Charter on the Rights and Welfare of the Child*, Community Law Centre, Bellville 2003, p. 128.

51 D.M. Chirwa, 'The merits and demerits of the African Charter on the Rights and Welfare of the Child', *The International Journal of Children's Rights*, Vol. 10, 2002, pp. 157–177, p. 161.

52 D. Kassan, above n. 26, p. 166.

53 K.-A. Cleophas and U.M. Assim, 'Child Participation in Family Law Matters Affecting Children in South Africa', *European Journal of Law Reform*, Vol. 17, No. 2, 2015, pp. 294–304, pp. 296–297.

54 See Art. 6(b) ECECR and ECECR Explanatory Report, above n. 27, para. 45.

A representative is defined as 'a person, such as a lawyer, or a body appointed to act before a judicial authority on behalf of the child' in Article 2(c) ECECR. Representation is mentioned in four ways: the special representative,[55] the separate representative,[56] the 'own' representative,[57] and the holder(s) of parental responsibilities.[58] The difference between these representatives and their tasks or functions remains, to a certain extent, unclear within the ECECR and its Explanatory Report. The final form included in the ECECR is contained in Article 5(d): the option of the child as a party to the proceedings.

The forms of participation recognised and recommended by the ECtHR are found throughout its case law on the topic. Three forms of participation can be deduced from this case law: direct participation in the form of a direct hearing, indirect participation through representation, and indirect participation through expert reports.

The ECtHR has expressed general principles on children's right to participate in these ways. In *Sahin v Germany*, the Grand Chamber found that 'it would be going too far to say that domestic courts are always required to hear a child in court on the issue of access to a parent not having custody, but this issue depends on the specific circumstances of each case, having due regard to the age and maturity of the child concerned.'[59] This principle has also been slightly amended to apply to other forms of participation. In *Sommerfeld v Germany* the ECtHR used the same formula with regard to the involvement of a psychological expert[60] and in *Wildgruber v Germany* the ECtHR applied the principle equally to the appointment of a curator ad litem.[61]

With regard to the option of representation, the judgment in *NTs and others v Georgia* is relevant as the ECtHR extensively discussed the role of the representative and the children's 'effective representation'. In this judgment, the ECtHR questioned whether the children's interests could be effectively represented if the representative that had been appointed to them in the proceedings had no 'formal procedural role' provided for by the Code of Civil

55 Arts. 4 and 9(1) ECECR.

56 Arts. 5(b) and 9(2) ECECR.

57 Art. 5(c) ECECR.

58 Art. 10(2) ECECR.

59 ECtHR *Sahin v Germany* [GC] (Appl. No. 30943/96), 8 July 2003, para. 73. This principle was reiterated in ECtHR *Iglesias Casarrubios and Cantalapiedra Iglesias v Spain* (Appl. No. 23298/12), 11 October 2016, para. 36; and ECtHR *Getliffe and Grant v France* (dec.) (Appl. No. 23547/06), 24 October 2006.

60 ECtHR *Sommerfeld v Germany* [GC] (Appl. No. 31871/96), 8 July 2003, para. 71. This principle was reiterated in ECtHR *Moog v Germany* (Appl. Nos. 23280/08 and 2334/10), 6 October 2016, para. 78; ECtHR *Wildgruber v Germany* (dec.) (Appl. No. 32817/02), 16 October 2006; and ECtHR *Wildgruber v Germany* (dec.) (Appl. Nos. 42402/05 and 42423/05), 29 January 2008.

61 ECtHR *Wildgruber v Germany* (dec.) (Appl. No. 32817/02), 16 October 2006.

Procedure and no rights or official position in those proceedings.[62] The Court was critical of the fact that the type of representation, the functions, and the powers of the representative were ambiguous. In practice, this meant that during the duration of the domestic proceedings (two years) the representative appointed to the children were various persons of the Social Services Agency, who met the children only a few times, and who solely drafted reports on the situation of the children.[63] Referring to the international standards of the ECECR and the CoE Guidelines, the ECtHR concluded that the representation in practice could not be considered 'adequate and meaningful representation'.[64] More recently, in *C v Croatia* the ECtHR has emphasised that representation, for example by a 'special guardian ad litem', may be specifically relevant for children in a post-divorce custody battle.[65] A representative could then protect the interests of the child, explain to them the court proceedings, decisions and consequences thereof and 'liaise between the competent judge and the child'.[66] In this judgment the Court also emphasises the need for direct participation, particularly when there are 'flaws in the quality' of representation, i.e. when there was no independent representative appointed for the child in a conflict of interests with his parent.[67]

According to the CoE Guidelines, children should be consulted on the manner in which they wish to be heard.[68] These Guidelines also indicate that children should have the right to their own legal counsel and representation, in their own name, in proceedings where there is, or could be, a conflict of interests between the child and the parents or other involved parties;[69] they should have access to free legal aid;[70] and they should be considered as fully fledged clients.[71] The CoE Guidelines explicitly emphasise that in cases where there are conflicting interests between parents and children, the competent authority should appoint either a guardian ad litem or another independent representative for the child.[72] It is unclear whether best interests representation (e.g. via a guardian ad litem) is sufficient according to the Guidelines, since no mention is made of how to choose between a guardian ad litem or another representative.

Moreover, the CoE Guidelines assure access to court and to the judicial process (under D1) and indicate that the possibility of access to court for children who have sufficient understanding of their rights, as well as of the use of remedies to

---

62 ECtHR *NTs and others v Georgia* (Appl. No. 71776/12), 2 February 2016, para. 74.
63 ECtHR *NTs and others v Georgia* (Appl. No. 71776/12), 2 February 2016, para. 75.
64 ECtHR *NTs and others v Georgia* (Appl. No. 71776/12), 2 February 2016, para. 76.
65 ECtHR *C v Croatia* (Appl. No. 80117/17), 8 October 2020, para. 77.
66 ECtHR *C v Croatia* (Appl. No. 80117/17), 8 October 2020, para. 77.
67 ECtHR *C v Croatia* (Appl. No. 80117/17), 8 October 2020, para. 80.
68 CoE Guidelines, above n. 5, IV(D), para. 44.
69 CoE Guidelines, above n. 5, para. 37.
70 CoE Guidelines, above n. 5, para. 38.
71 CoE Guidelines, above n. 5, para. 39.
72 CoE Guidelines, above n. 5, para. 42.

protect these rights, should be facilitated.[73] This provision gives considerable discretion regarding the implementation of access to court for children and the criteria for determining 'sufficient understanding'. Any obstacles to court, such as the cost of the proceedings or the lack of legal counsel, should be removed.[74] The CoE Guidelines require that children should be guaranteed equivalent levels of safeguards in both judicial and out-of-court proceedings.[75]

The IAYFJM Guidelines also aim at guaranteeing the child's right to participate either directly, or through a representative or an appropriate body, in a manner consistent with the procedural rules of national law and thus follow closely the definition of Article 12 UNCRC. Furthermore, the IAYFJM Guidelines provide for extra support tools to enable children to participate in proceedings, such as a psychologist or other expert.[76] This expert support seemingly has two aims, namely both to explain the child's views and to support the child before, during and after the hearing. According to the IAYFJM Guidelines, children must be provided with access to legal assistance and representation in their contacts with justice whenever their interests are at stake. In cases where there is, or could be, a conflict of interest between children and their parents or any other party, children must have their own counsel and representation, in their own name.[77] The IAYFJM Guidelines explicitly indicate that the role of the child's representative is similar to an adult client representative's role, but this role should be executed in a manner that is consistent with the level of understanding and communication of the child.[78] Beyond the legal role, representatives should be aware of the needs of children for general and psychological support throughout the proceedings. Children should be provided with free legal aid and representatives should not be chosen and paid for by the parents, but rather supported by the state.[79] In the IAYFJM Guidelines specific consideration is given to conflicts of interests that frequently arise when children and parents interact within justice systems; for example, separated or divorced parents may be influenced by their personal interests when litigating over the legal custody of their children.[80]

The IAYFJM Guidelines also consider children's access to court or other bodies (section 4.4), comparable to the CoE Guidelines. All children must have access to remedies, and obstacles, such as the cost of proceedings or the lack of legal assistance and representation, should be removed.[81] No further explanation is provided on this aspect of children's participation in court proceedings.

73 CoE Guidelines, above n. 5, para. 34.
74 CoE Guidelines, above n. 5, para. 35.
75 CoE Guidelines, above n. 5, para. 26.
76 IAYFJM Guidelines, above n. 6, para. 2.3.1.
77 IAYFJM Guidelines, above n. 6, para. 3.3.1.
78 IAYFJM Guidelines, above n. 6, para. 3.3.2.
79 IAYFJM Guidelines, above n. 6, para. 3.3.5.
80 IAYFJM Guidelines, above n. 6, section 3.3, pp. 32–33.
81 IAYFJM Guidelines, above n. 6, paras. 4.4.1 and 4.4.2.

Furthermore, the child's right to appeal is enshrined in paragraph 4.7: children must have the right to appeal decisions in which they have an interest. Their appeal must not be lesser than that which adults would have in similar circumstances. Hence, these Guidelines take children's legal rights very seriously and grant children the right to appeal.

Taking all of the human rights sources together, it is evident that there are multiple participation forms provided for children. The right to be heard directly is provided by all instruments. Indirect forms of participation, provided through representatives or other bodies, are also included in all sources, although there is a scale of different options for representation in this regard. The child's right to legal representation and professional support is recognised as important when there is a (potential) conflict of interests between the child and the parent(s). Specifically, in the ECECR, the CoE Guidelines and the IAYFJM Guidelines this right to legal representation and certain features thereof, such as free legal aid, are emphasised. Finally, although the UNCRC does not provide children with the right to party status in proceedings, the ACRWC, ECECR and both Guidelines do lean in that direction. It remains unclear, however, when and how the right to commence proceedings, file an appeal or have access to relevant files should be implemented in domestic law. Only the IAYFJM Guidelines are unambiguous in stressing that children must have the right to appeal decisions.

5. CONDITIONS FOR PARTICIPATION

Participation in family law proceedings is not an absolute right for children. Conditions are applied, mostly through the application of maturity requirements.

Article 12 UNCRC contains two conditions. The first is that the 'child capable of forming his or her own views' has the right to express views; the second, that these views should be given due weight 'in accordance with the age and maturity of the child'. While there is some contention regarding whether these conditions are separate conditions or overlap to form one condition, this debate is bypassed in this chapter except to say that the current interpretation tends to lean towards the conditions as separate.[82]

---

82 See C.R. Mol, 'Maturity and the Child's Right to be Heard in Family Law Proceedings: Article 12 UNCRC and Case Law of the ECtHR Compared' in K. Boele-Woelki and D. Martiny (eds.), *Plurality and Diversity of Family Relations in Europe*, Intersentia, Cambridge 2019, pp. 237–254, pp. 241–243; M.-F. Lücker-Babel, 'The right of the child to express views and to be heard: An attempt to interpret Article 12 of the UN Convention on the Rights of the Child', *The International Journal of Children's Rights*, Vol. 3, 1995, pp. 391–404, pp. 397 and 399; R. Thorburn Stern, *Implementing Article 12 of the UN Convention on the Rights of the Child: Participation, Power and Attitudes*, Brill/Nijhoff, Leiden 2017, pp. 56–58 and 62–64; A. Daly, 'No Weight for "Due Weight"? A Children's

So what do these two conditions refer to? The explanatory remarks of the UNCRC Committee provide some answers. With regard to the first condition, that the child is 'capable of forming his or her own views', the Committee provides five insights. Firstly, this is not meant as a limitation according to the Committee, but should be understood as an 'obligation for States parties to assess the capacity of the child to form an autonomous opinion.'[83] Subsequently, the Committee introduces a presumption of capacity for the child – placing the burden on states to assess whether a child is not capable of forming views.[84] How to determine a child's capacity to form an autonomous opinion, or to refute the presumption of capacity, is not further clarified. The UNCRC Committee furthermore discourages states from using the capability condition to introduce age limits 'either in law or in practice'.[85] The Committee adds that young children can be capable of forming views, even if they are not yet able to express them verbally.[86] Finally, it is clarified that the child should have 'sufficient understanding' to be capable of forming views, but that the child does not need to have 'comprehensive knowledge of all aspects of the matter'.[87]

The second condition concerns the due weight to be given to the child's views, which ought to occur 'in accordance with the age and maturity of the child'. The dual nature of the condition should emphasise that 'age alone cannot determine the significance of a child's views' according to the UNCRC Committee.[88] Instead, other factors drawn from research should also be considered, such as information provided to the child, experience, environment, social and cultural expectations and levels of support.[89] It is interesting to note that the Committee does not further elaborate on these factors nor does it make reference to the research mentioned. Age has to be considered together with maturity, neither of which can be determinative 'in isolation of the other'.[90] The views of the child are to be 'assessed on a case-by-case examination'.[91] The UNCRC Committee also

---

Autonomy Principle in Best Interest Proceedings', *The International Journal of Children's Rights*, Vol. 26, 2018, pp. 61–92, p. 68; and E.K.M. Tisdall, 'Challenging Competency and Capacity? Due Weight to Children's Views in Family Law Proceedings', *The International Journal of Children's Rights*, Vol. 26, 2018, pp. 159–182, p. 165.

83 General Comment No. 12, above n. 7, para. 20.

84 General Comment No. 12, above n. 7, para. 20; see also P. Alderson, Giving Children's Views "Due Weight" in Medical Law', *The International Journal of Children's Rights*, Vol. 26, 2018, pp. 16–37, p. 21; and C.R. Mol, above n. 82, p. 239.

85 General Comment No. 12, above n. 7, para. 21. It is interesting to note, however, that the Committee does accept fixed age limits with regard to the right to consent in healthcare matters so long as children under the age limit are allowed to express their views if they demonstrate the capacity to do so. See General Comment No. 12, above n. 7, para. 102.

86 General Comment No. 12, above n. 7, para. 21.

87 General Comment No. 12, above n. 7, para. 21.

88 General Comment No. 12, above n. 7, para. 29.

89 General Comment No. 12, above n. 7, para. 29.

90 See A. Parkes, above n. 38, p. 36.

91 General Comment No. 12, above n. 7, para. 29.

provides some guidance as to how 'maturity' should be understood, explaining it as 'the ability to understand and assess the implications of a particular matter'.[92] The Committee accepts that the term is 'difficult to define', but in the context of Article 12 it should be understood as 'the capacity of a child to express her or his views on the issues in a reasonable and independent manner'.[93]

How one should understand all these different comments, and the phrases used, remains a fertile topic for academic comment and discussion.[94]

In Article 4(2) ACRWC, the right for children to be heard in judicial or administrative proceedings is provided for 'a child who is capable of communicating his/her own views'. This phrasing is generally understood as being more restrictive than the phrasing used in Article 12(2) UNCRC.[95] Requiring capability to 'communicate' views instead of capability to 'form' views appears to imply a need for the child to be able to verbally communicate their views.[96] On the other hand, some argue that the threshold for children is lower in Article 4(2) ACRWC compared to Article 12(2) UNCRC. Article 4(2) does not make the weight given to the views of the child contingent on the 'age and maturity' of the child; instead the views 'shall be taken into consideration'.[97]

The mandatory procedural rights provided in the ECECR are (or may be if states so wish) limited to children with 'sufficient understanding'.[98] The Explanatory Report clarifies that the interpretation and implementation of this standard is left to states, who should define criteria to be able to evaluate 'whether or not children are capable of forming and expressing their own views'.[99] The Explanatory Report subsequently allows states to use age as a

---

92 General Comment No. 12, above n. 7, para. 30.

93 General Comment No. 12, above n. 7, para. 30.

94 See, amongst others, M.-F. Lücker-Babel, above n. 82, p. 397; R. Thorburn Stern, above n. 82, p. 63; E.K.M. Tisdall, above n. 82, pp. 162–166; P. Alderson, above n. 84, p. 21; L. Lundy, '"Voice" is not enough: conceptualizing Article 12 of the United Nations Convention on the Rights of the Child', *British Educational Research Journal*, Vol. 33, No. 6, 2007, pp. 927–942, pp. 937–938; D. Archard and M. Skivenes, 'Balancing a Child's Best Interests and a Child's Views', *The International Journal of Children's Rights*, Vol. 17, No. 1, 2009, pp. 1–21, p. 10; E.K.M. Tisdall, 'Children and Young People's Participation: A critical consideration of Article 12' in W. Vandenhole et al. (eds.), *Routledge International Handbook of Children's Rights Studies*, Routledge, London 2015, pp. 185–200; A. Daly, *Children, Autonomy and the Courts: Beyond the Right to Be Heard*, Brill, Leiden 2018, p. 47; and L. Lundy, J. Tobin and A. Parkes, 'Art. 12 The Right to Respect for the Views of the Child' in J. Tobin (ed.), *The UN Convention on the Rights of the Child: A Commentary*, Oxford University Press, Oxford 2019, pp. 397–434, pp. 405–406.

95 D.M. Chirwa, above n. 51, p. 161; M. Gose, above n. 50, p. 125; and K.-A. Cleophas and U.M. Assim, above n. 53, p. 296.

96 See M. Gose, above n. 50, p. 125; and K.-A. Cleophas and U.M. Assim, above n. 53, p. 296.

97 C. Du Toit, 'Legal Representation of Children' in T. Boezaart (ed.), *Child Law in South Africa*, JUTA Law, Claremont 2009, pp. 93–111, p. 95; and T. Boezaart, 'Listening to the Child's Objection', *New Zealand Law Review*, Vol. 26, No. 3, 2013, pp. 357–372, p. 361.

98 See Arts. 3, 6(b), 10(a) and (b) ECECR for the mandatory rights and Art. 4 ECECR for the mandatory right in which states are free to opt for this limitation.

99 ECECR Explanatory Report, above n. 27, para. 35.

criterion and notes that if states have not 'fixed a specific age' then the authorities will need to determine 'sufficient understanding' per case.[100] It is relevant to note that for the appointment of a special representative by the judicial authority 'sufficient understanding' is not required in Article 9 ECECR. In comparison to the UNCRC, the ECECR appears to include a more restrictive maturity condition.[101] Even though reference is made to the phrasing of the UNCRC in the Explanatory Report, the option of fixed age limits contradicts the UNCRC Committee's remarks. However, the UNCRC Committee itself has included 'sufficient understanding' in explaining the capability of children to form views.

The ECtHR has commented on the age and maturity for children's participation in its case law, specifically with regard to being heard directly. More generally, the ECtHR has found that whether a child ought to be heard directly depends 'on the specific circumstance of each case, having due regard to the age and maturity of the child concerned.'[102] Additionally, the ECtHR specified in *Płaza v Poland* that 'as children mature and become, with the passage of time, able to formulate their own opinion on their contact with the parents, the courts should give due weight also to their views and feelings as well as to their right to respect for their private life.'[103] The ECtHR therefore considers age and maturity to be relevant conditions regarding whether a child should be heard and how much weight should be given to the expressed views. How these conditions should be interpreted requires putting all the pieces from a range of case law together. In *M and M v Croatia* the ECtHR refers to and affirms the presumption of capacity as stipulated by the UNCRC Committee, thereby signalling an interpretation in conformance with the UNCRC.[104] However, the ECtHR does not adopt the duality of age and maturity in its case law, instead focusing mostly on the age of the child. The only other factors referred to are the intellectual capacities of the child,[105] the consistency of the views over time,[106] and whether the child is able to 'appreciate' or 'understand' the consequences of the decision.[107] Mol has previously analysed the case law of the ECtHR to determine the ages considered sufficient or insufficient by the ECtHR for both the child's participation and for

100 ECECR Explanatory Report, above n. 27, para. 36. See also I. Jansen, above n. 29, p. 134; and C. Sawyer, 'One step forward, two steps back – The European Convention on the Exercise of Children's Rights', *Child and Family Law Quarterly*, Vol. 11, 1999, pp. 151–166, p. 156.

101 See C. Sawyer, above n. 100, pp. 155–156.

102 ECtHR *Sahin v Germany* [GC] (Appl. No. 30943/96), 8 July 2003, para. 73; and ECtHR *Sommerfeld v Germany* [GC] (Appl. No. 31871/96), 8 July 2003, para. 71.

103 ECtHR *Płaza v Poland* (Appl. No. 18830/07), 25 January 2011, para. 71.

104 ECtHR *M and M v Croatia* (Appl. No. 10161/13), 3 September 2015, para. 184. See also C.R. Mol, above n. 82, p. 245.

105 ECtHR *M and M v Croatia* (Appl. No. 10161/13), 3 September 2015, para. 186.

106 ECtHR *Płaza v Poland* (Appl. No. 18830/07), 25 January 2011, para. 86; and ECtHR *Glesmann v Germany* (Appl. No. 25706/03), 10 January 2008, para. 110.

107 ECtHR *Döring v Germany* (dec.) (Appl. No. 50216/09), 21 February 2012; and ECtHR *Gobec v Slovenia* (Appl. No. 7233/04), 3 October 2013, paras. 137–138.

due weight to be given to the child's views.[108] She identified very general age ranges in the case law of the ECtHR: children under six years of age are generally considered insufficiently mature to be heard, while children above the age of 11 are mostly considered sufficiently mature.[109] Additionally, there appears to be a very rudimentary age split as to when the ECtHR finds children sufficiently mature for their views to be given due weight around the age of nine years.[110] These age ranges, however, ought to be considered with great caution as the ECtHR is a subsidiary supervisory court. This means that it reviews domestic proceedings, but does not reassess the evidence or facts – that remains the task of the national courts. Thus the age ranges may be mostly indicative of the age ranges adhered to in European states.[111]

The CoE Guidelines do not set any age limits, but instead use the notion of a certain discernment, maturity or level of understanding; age limits tend to be too rigid and arbitrary and can have truly unjust consequences.[112] According to the Guidelines, capability, maturity and level of understanding are more representative of a child's real capacities than their age. The CoE Guidelines thus follow the UNCRC approach in this regard, although mention is made of the risks due to the wide margin of appreciation left to the judge in question to assess the child's capability. However, it is emphasised that concepts such as 'age and maturity' and 'sufficient understanding' imply a certain level of comprehension, but do not go as far as to demand, from the child, full comprehensive knowledge of all aspects of the matters at hand.[113]

The CoE Guidelines, comparable to the UNCRC, mention that the child's right to participate in proceedings includes hearing the child who is deemed to have sufficient understanding of the matters in question and giving due weight to the child's views in accordance with their age and maturity.[114] However, 'a child should not be precluded from being heard solely on the basis of age; whenever a child takes the initiative to be heard in a case that affects him or her, the judge should not, unless it is in the child's best interests, refuse to hear the child and should listen to his or her views and opinion on matters concerning him or her in the case'.[115] Access to court should be facilitated 'for children who have sufficient understanding of their rights and of the use of remedies to protect those rights'.[116] The CoE Guidelines thus choose concepts such as 'maturity'

108 See C.R. Mol, above n. 82.
109 C.R. Mol, above n. 82, pp. 245–247.
110 C.R. Mol, above n. 82, pp. 247–249.
111 C.R. Mol, above n. 82, p. 250.
112 CoE Guidelines, above n. 5, para. 96.
113 CoE Guidelines, above n. 5, para. 108.
114 CoE Guidelines, above n. 5, paras. 44 and 46.
115 CoE Guidelines, above n. 5, para. 47.
116 CoE Guidelines, above n. 5, para. 34.

and 'capacity' and age as determining factors in realising the child's right to participate in proceedings, thereby optimising the child's effective participation.

Children who are capable of forming their own views have the right to participate according to the IAYFJM Guidelines. Their views must be given due weight in accordance with their age and maturity.[117] Comparable to the CoE Guidelines, both age and the concept of 'maturity' are used as defining elements for children's participation. An assessment should not be made solely on the basis of age: the individual child's maturity must be assessed on a case-by-case basis to see how capable the child is of forming their own views, according to the explanatory comments.[118] However, when children are too young or too immature to form and express their own views, independent representatives should be designated to bring forward their best interests and respect for their rights.[119]

All six international and regional human rights sources show that the core condition applied to children with respect to participation is one of maturity. The phrasing and packaging of the respective conditions vary greatly. Regarding the issue of participation itself, children ought to be 'capable of forming their own views', be 'capable of communicating' views, or have 'sufficient understanding', 'discernment', or 'age and maturity'. Subsequently, for the issue of affording due weight, 'age and maturity' are common factors (except in the ACRWC). Further specification of these requirements tends to be lacking. Although age limits are generally disapproved of, the ECECR and the ECtHR do appear to accept age limits as a practicality.

6. LOCATION OF PARTICIPATION AND METHOD OF COMMUNICATION

An important element of participation of children in legal proceedings concerns the context and location of their participation. In several sources this element is addressed in detail; in others it is more limited.

Article 12 UNCRC does not mention anything about the location, but General Comment No. 12 stresses that no effective hearing can be realised for the child where the environment is intimidating, hostile, insensitive or inappropriate for their age.[120] Therefore, accessible and child-friendly proceedings are necessary, but what this entails is not specified. However, the provision and delivery of child-friendly information, adequate support for self-advocacy, appropriately

117 IAYFJM Guidelines, above n. 6, para. 2.3.1.
118 IAYFJM Guidelines, above n. 6, pp. 16–17.
119 IAYFJM Guidelines, above n. 6, para 2.3.2.
120 General Comment No. 12, above n. 7, paras. 34 and 134.

trained staff, courtroom design, judges' and lawyers' clothing, sight screens and separate waiting rooms are mentioned as core elements of accessible and child-friendly proceedings. Furthermore, the context in which the child exercises their right to be heard has to be enabling and encouraging,[121] and, preferably, a child should not be heard in open court, but under conditions of confidentiality.[122]

With regard to the method of communication the UNCRC Committee encourages the format of a talk, rather than a one-sided examination.[123] Children are able to form views from the youngest age, even when they may be unable to express them verbally. Hence non-verbal forms of communication including play, body language, facial expressions, and drawing and painting should be recognised as modes of communication.[124] Training to acquire skills to effectively listen to, and engage with, children to facilitate their participation is essential.[125]

The ACRWC and the ECECR (or its Explanatory Report) do not provide any specifics on where participation should take place. Similarly, the case law of the ECtHR does not provide any clear guidance regarding the location of children's participation. The ECtHR also provides no additional information in its case law with regard to the method of communication. The other two instruments do.

In light of the phrasing in Article 4(2) ACRWC referring to the capability of communicating views, a number of authors infer that the ACRWC requires children to communicate verbally in judicial and administrative proceedings.[126] This is more limited than the UNCRC Committee's understanding.

Although the ECECR does not speak of how the child may communicate their views, the Explanatory Report does provide some information. Considering Article 10 ECECR on the role of the representative, the Explanatory Report clarifies that 'determining the views of the child' should not be interpreted strictly.[127] A child may express their views verbally, but determining the views can also be done through 'observations' of the child by the representative.

The CoE Guidelines address the need for a child-friendly environment in a separate paragraph,[128] which underscores that cases involving children should be dealt with in non-intimidating and child-sensitive settings. Furthermore, 'as far as appropriate and possible', interviewing and waiting rooms should be child-friendly. This framing seems to give some leeway to environments (interview location, waiting room) that are not child-friendly. The architectural

121 General Comment No. 12, above n. 7, para. 42.
122 General Comment No. 12, above n. 7, para. 43.
123 General Comment No. 12, above n. 7, para. 43.
124 General Comment No. 12, above n. 7, para. 21.
125 General Comment No. 12, above n. 7, para. 134.
126 See M. Gose, above n. 50, p. 125; and K.-A. Cleophas and U.M. Assim, above n. 53, p. 296.
127 ECECR Explanatory Report, above n. 27, para. 55.
128 CoE Guidelines, above n. 5, IV(D), para. 5.

surroundings of a courthouse can make children very uncomfortable; therefore, where possible, special interview rooms should be included.[129] Furthermore, child-friendly court settings may mean that no wigs or gowns or other official uniforms are worn. It is interesting that the CoE Guidelines specify that for some children the use of uniforms may have relevance and could enhance the child feeling that the matters affecting them are being taken seriously by the competent authority.[130] This could be applicable to many (older) adolescents who want to be taken seriously and would feel ridiculed in childish child-friendly interview rooms with judges without gowns. In other words, the specific nature of a child-friendly environment could be different for younger and older children. The CoE Guidelines point out that the setting could, depending on the child, be relatively formal but the behaviour of the officials should be less formal.

The CoE Guidelines also address the method of communication with children. Even young children can state their views clearly; the means to hear children should be adapted to the child's level of understanding of the matters in question and children should be consulted on the manner in which they wish to be heard.[131] Children can be heard by the judge or an appointed expert, depending on the child's wishes and interests. Language appropriate to children's age and level of understanding should be used and training for judges is vital. Besides this, children should have the opportunity to be accompanied by their parents or an adult of their choice, unless a reasoned decision has been made to the contrary.[132] Furthermore, court sessions should be adapted to the child's pace and attention span; regular breaks should be planned and the hearing should not last too long.

The IAYFJM Guidelines also address the context in which children exercise their right to participate; this context should be enabling and encouraging.[133] The explanations and comments refer to General Comment No. 12, paragraph 34 (discussed above). Children should have the free assistance of an interpreter if needed and children with communication disabilities should be provided with adequate and effective assistance by well-trained professionals (for example, in sign language).[134]

When hearing the child, language should be used that is easily understood by the child and at a speed that can be followed, keeping in mind the child's age and maturity.[135] Similar to the CoE Guidelines, it is further stated that children should have the possibility of being accompanied by their parents unless a

---

129 Explanatory Memorandum CoE Guidelines, para. 123.
130 Explanatory Memorandum CoE Guidelines, para. 123.
131 CoE Guidelines, above n. 5, IV(D), para. 44, and Explanatory Memorandum, para. 114.
132 CoE Guidelines, above n. 5, IV(D), para. 58.
133 IAYFJM Guidelines, above n. 6, para. 2.3.4.
134 IAYFJM Guidelines, above n. 6, paras. 3.6.1 and 3.6.2.
135 IAYFJM Guidelines, above n. 6, para. 3.4.2.

reasoned decision is made to the contrary, since this may be a reassuring factor for children.[136]

In implementing the right to participation, the location and method of communication are relevant aspects for making the procedure child-friendly. However, it is a topic that is covered only minimally in the binding sources of human rights law – except by the UNCRC Committee itself in the General Comment. The binding sources leave more leeway to states regarding how to implement the rights granted. In contrast, non-binding guidelines lend themselves better to providing details, suggestions and best practices. Both sets of Guidelines discussed also provide more input, considering amongst other things the 'child-friendly environment' of a courtroom and waiting room, appropriate language, the clothing of lawyers and judges and the possibility of the child bringing someone to support them during the hearing. The training of judges on listening and engagement skills are also considered vital.

7. INFORMATION AND FEEDBACK

A final important element of the child's right to participate in legal proceedings concerns the child's right to information and feedback. This is comprehensively addressed in various sources.

According to the UNCRC Committee, the realisation of the child's right to express their views requires that the child be informed about the decisions to be taken and their consequences by those who are responsible for the child. The child must also be informed about the conditions under which they will be asked to express their views. The child's right to information is essential, because it is the precondition for the child's clarified decisions.[137] Those responsible for hearing the child have to ensure that the child is informed about their right to express their opinion and about the impact that their expressed views will have on the outcome.[138] The child must be informed about the option of either communicating directly or through a representative and must be aware of the possible consequences of this choice. The child must be informed about how, when and where the hearing will take place and who the participants will be. Furthermore, those responsible for hearing the child have to inform the child of the outcome of the process and explain how their views were considered.[139] The feedback is a guarantee that the child's views are not only heard as a formality, but are taken seriously. Children are entitled to be provided with clear feedback on how their participation has influenced any outcomes.

136 IAYFJM Guidelines, above n. 6, para. 3.4.3.
137 General Comment No. 12, above n. 7, para. 25.
138 General Comment No. 12, above n. 7, para. 41.
139 General Comment No. 12, above n. 7, para. 45.

The right to information has a prominent position within the ECECR. Within the right to express views provided in Article 3, the child is provided with the right to receive all relevant information, together with the right to 'be informed of the possible consequences of compliance' with the views of the child and the 'possible consequences of any decision'. This information must either be provided by the appointed representative or the judicial authorities themselves.[140] The Convention defines 'relevant information' as 'information which is appropriate to the age and understanding of the child, and which will be given to enable the child to exercise his or her rights fully unless the provision of such information were contrary to the welfare of the child'.[141] The Explanatory Report adds two important reflections. The right to information does not mean that all information needs to be shared with the child, but the information that will be shared with the child must 'be adapted, both in form and content, to the age and understanding of the child'.[142]

Both the CoE Guidelines and the IAYFJM Guidelines extensively address the child's right to information and feedback. According to the CoE Guidelines, children and their parents should be promptly and adequately informed of, for example, their rights, the procedures involved and the role of the child and the different procedural steps, the existing support mechanisms and the availability of the services which can provide support.[143] This information should be provided to children in a manner adapted to their age and maturity in a language that they can understand and which is gender and culture sensitive. The CoE Guidelines underscore that provision of the information to the parents should not be an alternative to communicating the information to the child.[144] Independently of their parents, children should be provided with all necessary information on how effectively to use the right to be heard. Judgments affecting children should be duly reasoned and explained to them in child-friendly language, particularly those decisions in which the child's views and opinions have not been followed.[145] As regards family law cases, the CoE Guidelines emphasise that courts should exercise exceptional diligence to avoid any risk of adverse consequences on the family relations.[146] The child's lawyer, guardian ad litem or legal representative should communicate and explain the given judgment to the child in a language adapted to the child's level of understanding.[147] Children need to understand the nature and scope of the decision taken and its effects.

140 Art. 6(b) and 10 ECECR. See also K. Herbots, above n. 12, p. 1777.
141 Art. 2(d) ECECR.
142 ECECR Explanatory Report, above n. 27, para. 28.
143 CoE Guidelines, above n. 5, IV(A), para. 1.
144 CoE Guidelines, above n. 5, IV(A), para. 3.
145 CoE Guidelines, above n. 5, IV(D), para. 49.
146 CoE Guidelines, above n. 5, IV(D), para. 49.
147 CoE Guidelines, above n. 5, IV(E), para. 75.

While the judgment and the motivation thereof cannot always be recorded and explained in child-friendly wording, due to legal requirements, children should have those decisions explained to them, either by their lawyer or another appropriate person, such as a parent or a social worker.[148]

The IAYFJM Guidelines include similar provisions and standards and stress that in order to participate adequately, children must be provided with all necessary information.[149] When decisions are made, they should be explained to children in a language that they can understand, particularly when they conflict with their expressed wishes or views. Section 3.1 addresses information and advice and mentions this must be given about the same elements as those that are mentioned in the CoE Guidelines (as discussed above). The IAYFJM Guidelines are, to a large extent, similar to the relevant provisions in the CoE Guidelines, but remarkably no mention is made about giving feedback to the child after their views have been expressed.

Neither the ACRWC nor the case law of the ECtHR provide any clear guidelines for the information or feedback to be given to the child in light of their participation.[150] However, recently in *C v Croatia* the complaint was brought on behalf of the child that he was never 'informed in an appropriate manner' about the court proceedings, the opportunity to participate, nor the potential impact of these proceedings on his life.[151] The ECtHR does not directly respond to this complaint, but does note that a representative should have been appointed who could have explained the proceedings to the child.[152]

The final theme addressed in this chapter concerns the information and feedback given to the child when participating in family law proceedings. The UNCRC, ECECR and both Guidelines provide clear standards that require children to be informed before and after their participation. The child has the right to receive feedback about the extent to which their views and opinions were taken into account and what the nature and scope of the decision, and its effects, are. In that regard it is important to note that these instruments highlight the need for the information to be delivered in a fitting manner consistent with the child's age and maturity.

---

148 Explanatory Memorandum CoE Guidelines, para. 121.

149 IAYFJM Guidelines, above n. 6, para. 2.3.3.

150 Liefaard and Bruning argue, however, that Art. 6 ECHR and the right to a fair trial – which includes the equality of arms principle – should apply *mutatis mutandis* to children in child protection proceedings. See T. Liefaard and M. Bruning, 'Commentary on the Judgment of the *Hoge Raad* of the 5th December 2014' in H. Stalford et al. (eds.), *Rewriting Children's Rights Judgments: From Academic Vision to New Practice*, Hart Publishing, Oxford 2017, pp. 173–191.

151 ECtHR *C v Croatia* (Appl. No. 80117/17), 8 October 2020, para. 65.

152 ECtHR *C v Croatia* (Appl. No. 80117/17), 8 October 2020, para. 77.

8. CONCLUSIONS

Children have the right to participate in family law proceedings, such as separation, adoption, custody and access, international child abduction and relocation proceedings. In a number of sources, they also have the right to participate in alternative dispute mechanisms such as mediation and arbitration on these topics. The child's right to participate in legal proceedings encompasses the right to be heard directly, or indirectly through a right to representation, and procedural rights such as the right to commence proceedings, access to all relevant files or to appeal – as an independent party to the proceedings with legal status or indirectly via legal or other forms of representation. These elements of the child's right to procedural inclusion have been discussed in relation to the six human and regional human rights sources.

Keeping children out of family law proceedings is not ideal; they have the right to be heard directly or indirectly. Preferably they are heard directly by the court, but there should also be an option for them to be heard via a representative, ideally one specialised in hearing children. More specifically, children should be supported by legal representation or other professional support whenever there is a possible conflict of interests between parent(s) and the child. It is important to note that in family law proceedings, which can be prone to high conflict and parental animosity, possible conflicts of interest are likely. Furthermore, according to some of the relevant sources, children also have the right to commence proceedings, file an appeal and have access to all relevant files. However, with regard to these procedural rights, much greater leeway is granted to states. In most sources the child's right to legal representation or professional support seems to be primarily aimed at supporting children in family law proceedings that are initiated by others (often their parents). However, the importance of independent representation or support is just as important in situations in which the child wants to initiate proceedings, file an appeal or have access to all relevant files.

The standard condition applied to the child's right to participate concerns their maturity, although this is phrased in differing ways in the different instruments. Relying solely on age limits is not endorsed by the sources cited, although it is permitted by the ECECR and relied on by the ECtHR. In denouncing age limits, more open norms are presented such as 'capacity', 'maturity' or 'discernment'. This provides discretion for those who ought to decide on the child's right to participate on the individual level but, given the lack of guidance, it can raise more questions than effectively offering children a right to participate. Practically, therefore, a recommendation could be to use flexible age limits – by which the possibility of younger children participating remains available.

Turning to the more practical issues of the location of the child's participation, the method of communication, and the right to information and feedback, it becomes clear that, while the UNCRC Committee provides some direction, reliance must be mostly placed on both sets of Guidelines for input, as they outline a great number of factors to assist in providing child-friendly participation rights.

Of course, this may have been expected as there is a clear difference between the types of sources reviewed in this chapter. The binding conventions – the UNCRC, ACRWC and ECECR – required broad political agreement and thus could not be as specific as soft law instruments like the CoE and IAYFJM Guidelines.[153] Furthermore, all sources published after the UNCRC – including the UNCRC Committee's General Comment No. 12 – had the opportunity to build upon the general principle of Article 12 UNCRC and further explicate it.

More generally, we can conclude that these six international and regional human rights instruments send the clear message that children have the right to participate in family law proceedings that concern them. A blueprint for how to realise children's procedural inclusion is lacking, but the incentive to effectively include children is present. Much more remains to be achieved: the right of children to participate may be unambiguous from a human rights point of view, but the practical, effective and optimal implementation of child participation remains a work in progress.

153 Note, however, that broad political agreement appears to be lacking with regard to the ECECR if we consider its ratification status.

CHILD PARTICIPATION IN FAMILY LAW PROCEEDINGS

Pedagogical Insights on Why and How to Involve Children

Daisy J.H. SMEETS and Stephanie RAP

1. INTRODUCTION

Today, an increasing number of children are growing up in single-parent families. For example, in the Netherlands, one fifth of all minor children have parents who are separated or divorced (i.e. 727,000 children).[1] In the European Union, 17% of children live in a single parent household.[2] Parental separation is predominantly a Western phenomenon. In countries such as South Korea, Nepal and Ethiopia, children primarily report that they always (or usually)

1 Centraal Bureau voor de Statistiek (CBS), *Jaarrapport Landelijke Jeugdmonitor 2019*, CBS, The Hague/Heerlen/Bonaire 2019.

2 D. KUTSAR and K. RAID, 'When traditional measurement practices fail: who are the child's family?' in D. KUTSAR and K. RAID (eds.), *Children's subjective well-being in local and international perspectives*, Statistikaamet (Statistics Estonia), Tallinn 2019, pp. 85–93.

live in one home and not regularly in two homes.[3] As will be discussed below, parental separation may involve conflicts that put children in a vulnerable and sometimes threatening position. Consequently, the question regarding why and how to involve children in post-separation decisions (such as custody, care and contact arrangements) often arises in these kinds of family law proceedings in particular. Therefore, the focus of this contribution will be narrowed to judicial proceedings in the context of divorce. However, the pedagogical insights that we provide in this contribution are not exclusively relevant for cases of divorce. Rather, we will discuss general theories and principles that are important for other family law proceedings as well (such as legal parentage, international child abduction and adoption).

Numerous studies have shown that parental separation is associated with lower levels of child wellbeing after the separation of the parents. A lack of resources, both emotional and financial, due to living with one parent after separation has been found to be one of the most important factors contributing to lower levels of child wellbeing, next to parental conflicts.[4] For example, an important consequence of parental separation is that children have a higher likelihood of growing up in poverty. Specifically, single mothers more often depend on social welfare, compared to single fathers.[5] Steinbach concludes from a meta-analysis on custody arrangements after divorce that children are slightly better off in joint physical custody arrangements with regard to their overall wellbeing (i.e. emotional and financial resources), compared to children living with only one parent (i.e. sole physical custody).[6] Parental separation can also have negative effects on children's school achievement, self-esteem and psychological adjustment.[7] Parental conflict (pre- and post-separation) is considered a key stressor for children and negatively affects their wellbeing.[8] This is even more predictive of children's wellbeing than parental separation alone.[9]

---

3 A. Ben-Arieh, 'The well-being of the world's children: lessons from the International Survey of Children's Well-Being' in D. Kutsar and K. Raid (eds.), *Children's subjective well-being in local and international perspectives*, Statistikaamet (Statistics Estonia), Tallinn 2019, pp. 18–29.

4 A. Steinbach, 'Children's and parents' well-being in joint physical custody: A literature review' (2019) 58 *Family Process* 353–369.

5 Sociaal en Cultureel Planbureau (SCP), *Armoede in kaart 2019*, SCP, The Hague 2019, pp. 22–23; CBS, *Wonen en opgroeien*, https://longreads.cbs.nl/jeugdmonitor-2018/wonen-en-opgroeien/.

6 A. Steinbach, above n. 4.

7 K.A. Clarke-Stewart, D.L. Vandell, K. McCartney, M.T. Owen and C. Booth, 'Effects of parental separation and divorce on very young children' (2000) 14(2) *Journal of Family Psychology* 304–326.

8 P.R. Amato, 'Research on divorce: Continuing trends and new developments' (2010) 72(3) *Journal of Marriage and Family* 650–666; K. Musick and A. Meier, 'Are both parents always better than one? Parental conflict and young adult well-being' (2010) 39(5) *Social Science Research* 814–830.

9 P.R. Amato and B. Keith, 'Parental divorce and the well-being of children: A meta-analysis' (1991) 110(1) *Psychological Bulletin* 26–46.

Research has not only shown that parental separation is negatively associated with children's developmental outcomes and feelings of wellbeing, but has also demonstrated risks regarding parent–child attachment. According to the dominant attachment theory in education and child studies developed by Bowlby,[10] all children become attached to their parents (or primary carers) in the first year of life. When parents are sufficiently emotionally available to children and respond both adequately as well as positively (also known as 'sensitive parenting behaviour'), children will regard parents as a secure base to whom they can turn in times of distress.[11] Parental separation or divorce may threaten this secure attachment basis.[12] First, children have to cope with reduced contact with the non-residential parent, often the father. Second, the residential parent may become less emotionally available to the child, being preoccupied with his/her own experiences of loss during the separation.[13]

During a separation, most children express the wish to increase contact with the non-residential parent.[14] Stimulating a positive relationship with *both* parents is also important to value and maintain parent–child attachment, yet in conflictual separations this is often problematic. Children often find themselves caught in loyalty binds, asking themselves whether a fun time with dad will hurt mum, or if they can tell one parent about activities with the other.[15] In cases involving extremely high levels of conflict, the parent with whom the child resides may share his/her negative views on the ex-partner with the child.[16] Consequently, children may find themselves in a vulnerable position[17] and due

10 J. Bowlby, *Attachment and loss. Vol. I: Attachment*, Basic, New York 1969.

11 J. Bowlby, *A secure base. Clinical applications of attachment theory*, Routledge, London 1988; M.D.S. Ainsworth et al., *Patterns of attachment: A psychological study of the strange situation*, Erlbaum, Hillsdale NY 1978.

12 J.G. Byrne, T.G. O'Connor, R.S. Marvin and W.F. Whelan, 'Practitioner Review: The contribution of attachment theory to child custody assessments' (2005) 46 *Journal of Child Psychology and Psychiatry* 115–127; F. Juffer, *Beslissingen over kinderen in problematische opvoedingssituaties*, Raad voor de Rechtspraak, The Hague 2010.

13 G. Gloger-Tippelt and L. König, 'Attachment representations in 6-year-old children from one and two parent families in Germany' (2007) 28(3) *School Psychology International* 313–330.

14 C. Brand, G. Howcroft and C.N. Hoelson, 'The voice of the child in parental divorce: implications for clinical practice and mental health practitioners' (2017) 29(2) *Journal of Child & Adolescent Mental Health* 169–178.

15 E. Dowling and G. Gorell-Barnes, 'Children of divorcing families: A clinical perspective' (1999) 4(1) *Clinical Child Psychology and Psychiatry* 39–50.

16 S.R. Anderson, S.A. Anderson, K.L. Palmer, M.S. Mutchler and L.K. Baker, 'Defining high conflict' (2010) 39(1) *The American Journal of Family Therapy* 11–27; J.G. Moné and Z. Birigen, 'Perceived parent-child alienation: Empirical assessment of parent-child relationships within divorced and intact families' (2006) 4(3/4) *Journal of Divorce & Remarriage* 131–156.

17 K. Schoemaker, M. Visser, J. van Lawick and C. Finkenauer, *Vechtscheidingen: Beleving en ervaringen van ouders en kinderen en verandering na kinderen uit de knel*, Kinderen uit de Knel/Vrije Universiteit Amsterdam/Academische werkplaats kindermishandeling, Amsterdam 2017.

to loyalty conflicts, these children may be afraid to express positive affection to one of the parents in the presence of the other. In addition, children might feel reluctant to express a wish that contradicts one of the parents.

In this contribution the involvement of children in family law proceedings will be discussed. This means that the focus of this contribution will be narrowed to children whose married parents separate through a legal divorce and who are consequently involved in judicial proceedings, concerning for example custody and care and contact arrangements. The involvement of children in these judicial proceedings has its basis in the right to be heard (Article 12 UN Convention on the Rights of the Child (UNCRC)), which gives children the right to give their views in all matters affecting their life, specifically also in judicial proceedings.[18] For the reasons described above, hearing the views of children in these cases is particularly complex. The interests of parents and children do often not align and conflictual and stressful situations can substantially harm children's development. Before going into detail regarding the involvement of children in these judicial proceedings, a step back will be taken by looking at the historical background of the increased attention and presumed importance of child participation in judicial proceedings (section 2). Furthermore, the dominant theoretical underpinnings of child participation will be discussed in section 3. In section 4, an overview of empirical research outcomes of studies on child participation in family law proceedings will be presented. These studies are mainly socio-legal by nature and consist of interviews with children, parents and (legal) professionals about their experiences with the procedures and of observations of court hearings. On the basis of these research outcomes, in section 5 guidance will be given on how child participation can effectively be facilitated in family law proceedings, given the particular challenges these procedures present in relation to hearing children's views.

2. BRIEF HISTORICAL PERSPECTIVE ON CHILDHOOD AND CHILD PARTICIPATION

How the concepts of children, childhood and children's rights are defined varies greatly across time and place; they are defined by, among other things, the social, economic and cultural circumstances in a given time and place.[19]

---

18 See for more the contribution by M. Bruning and C. Mol in this Handbook.

19 D. Reynaert, E. Desmet, S. Lembrechts and W. Vandenhole, 'Introduction: A critical approach to children's rights' in W. Vandenhole, E. Desmet, D. Reynaert and S. Lembrechts (eds.), *Routledge International Handbook of Children's Rights Studies*, Routledge, London 2015, pp. 1–24; E. Verhellen, 'The Convention on the Rights of the Child: Reflections from a historical, social policy and educational perspective' in W. Vandenhole, E. Desmet, D. Reynaert and S. Lembrechts (eds.), *Routledge International Handbook of Children's Rights Studies*, Routledge, London 2015, pp. 43–59; P. Alderson, *Childhoods Real*

In past centuries, the Western conceptualisation of childhood has changed markedly. How we regard children and their capacities changed from seeing them as 'mini-adults', who were responsible for their actions from a young age, to individuals who had to be educated and prepared for adulthood, through increasingly humane, psychosocial interventions (as opposed to using for example corporal punishment).[20] An important element in defining childhood is the separation between children and adults based on child-specific biological and psychological traits. With the emergence of developmental psychology (starting in the 17th century) and the Enlightenment in the 18th century, children were increasingly seen as 'adults in waiting'. This meant that children were primarily regarded as objects of protection, because of their inherent vulnerability. This vulnerability was based on the biological and psychological immaturity of children.[21]

This view on children has been criticised and countered with the image of the *autonomous child*. Specifically, in the second half of the 20th century and in the global North (i.e. Western, developed countries), children were increasingly considered as active agents and independent human beings rather than as *human becomings*.[22] This child image has been adopted by the child rights movement, challenging the paternalistic treatment of children and 'advocating for the recognition of the participation rights of children'.[23] With the drafting and subsequent adoption of the UN Convention on the Rights of the Child, the view of children changed gradually from paternalistic perceptions of children to seeing them as active bearers of rights, while at the same time proclaiming both the importance of children's dependency and autonomy.[24] This development should be seen in the context of the emancipation of

---

and Imagined. Vol. 1: An introduction to critical realism and childhood studies, Routledge, London 2013, pp. 11–13; K. Hanson, 'Schools of Thought in Children's Rights' in M. Liebel, K. Hanson, I. Saadi and W. Vandenhole (eds.), *Children's Rights from Below: Cross-Cultural Perspectives*, Palgrave Macmillan, London 2012, pp. 63–79.

20 J. Junger-Tas, 'Youth justice in the Netherlands' in M. Tonry and A.N. Doob (eds.), *Youth crime and youth justice. Comparative and cross-national perspectives*, The University of Chicago Press, Chicago 2004, pp. 300–301; E. Verhellen, above n. 19; A. Ben-Arieh and N. Tarshish, 'Children's rights and well-being' in M.D. Ruck, M. Peterson-Badali and M. Freeman (eds.), *Handbook of children's rights. Global and multidisciplinary perspectives*, Routledge, New York 2017, pp. 68–79.

21 D. Reynaert et al., above n. 19, p. 3; K. Hanson, above n. 19, p. 63.

22 D. Reynaert et al., above n. 19; E. Verhellen, above n. 19; A. Invernizzi and J. Williams, 'Introduction' in A. Invernizzi and J. Williams (eds.), *Children and Citizenship*, Sage, London 2008, pp. 1–7. See also E.S. Scott and C. Huntington, 'Conceptualizing Legal Childhood in the Twenty-First Century' (2020) 118(7) *Michigan Law Review* 1371–1458.

23 D. Reynaert et al., above n. 19, p. 3.

24 E. Verhellen, above n. 19; See also M. Freeman, 'Why It Remains Important to Take Children's Rights Seriously' (2007) 15(5) *The International Journal of Children's Rights* 5–23; M. Freeman, 'Taking Children's Rights More Seriously' (1992) 6 *International Journal of Law and the Family* 52–71.

several groups of people, such as women, indigenous people and people with disabilities, and the acknowledgement of their fundamental rights as a group in society.[25] Verhellen points out that Article 12 UNCRC was key in this evolving child image and referring to children as subjects of rights. On the one hand, the dominant view of children is still that they are in need of protection and are human becomings.[26] Scott and Huntington point to the fact that parental rights are justified by the fact that they promote child wellbeing, because of the mere fact that stable parent–child relationships (and minimal state intervention) are beneficial to the child's development (see also above).[27] On the other hand, seeing children as a separate social category and as active agents has played an important role in the implementation of children's rights, as enshrined in the UNCRC.[28] The concept of participation has challenged traditional views and hierarchical structures and relations, among others in relation to children (i.e. as being dependent and vulnerable human beings).[29] Hanson places participation rights in his *schools of thought in children's rights* in the categories of welfare, emancipation and liberation. The liberal view on children's rights is most far reaching in this regard, stating that children 'have the right to autonomy and to full participation in society, in the same way as adults'.[30] Vanobbergen, in addition, argues that defining children as *non-adults* is problematic in light of the agency and autonomy that we accord to children at the same time, so we should regard children as individuals in their own right, rather than as 'not yet' adults. This places the rights of children in opposition to the rights of parents, which hampers their full participation. Vanobbergen proposes that '[c]hildren must be accepted as co-authors in dialogue about their best interests.'[31] Bosisio explains that Article 12 UNCRC presupposes that adults should be able to change their opinion and decisions on the basis of the views and opinion expressed by the child. The child's views should be seen as worthy of consideration.[32]

From this brief historical overview it can be concluded that the normative view that children should be able to give their views and opinions in important

25 See C.W. Henderson, *Understanding International Law*, Wiley-Blackwell, Chichester 2010, pp. 300–307.
26 E. Verhellen, above n. 19, pp. 51–52.
27 E.S. Scott and C. Huntington, above n. 22.
28 B. Vanobbergen, 'Children's rights and childhood studies: From living apart together to a happy marriage' in W. Vandenhole, E. Desmet, D. Reynaert and S. Lembrechts (eds.), *Routledge International Handbook of Children's Rights Studies*, Routledge, London 2015, pp. 60–76; M. Freeman, 2007, 1992, above n. 24; E.S. Scott and C. Huntington, above n. 22.
29 K. Tisdall, 'Children and young people's participation: A critical consideration of article 12' in W. Vandenhole, E. Desmet, D. Reynaert and S. Lembrechts (eds.), *Routledge International Handbook of Children's Rights Studies*, Routledge, London 2015, pp. 185–200.
30 K. Hanson, above n. 19, p. 74.
31 B. Vanobbergen, above n. 28, p. 73.
32 R. Bosisio, 'Children's right to be heard: What children think' (2012) 20 *International Journal of Children's Rights* 141–154.

decisions affecting their lives stems from the development of seeing children increasingly as capable of giving their views and as worthy of listening to. However, protecting children's interests is also an important pillar of the UNCRC, and particularly in family law cases involving parental divorce a tension can arise between protecting children and involving them.[33] In the next section, therefore, the theoretical underpinnings of child participation will be discussed, to come to a more nuanced understanding of how children can be involved in a meaningful manner, while at the same time protecting their rights and interest.

3. THEORETICAL PERSPECTIVES ON CHILD PARTICIPATION

Child participation is often used as an umbrella term under which different rights and concepts are placed. With the adoption of the UNCRC, children have been given the explicit *right* to participate. Participation is often advocated 'as an inherently good thing';[34] it improves decision-making, promotes children's protection, enhances their skills, empowers them and enhances their self-esteem.[35] However, participation may not always have positive results for children, depending on the situation in which children's views are sought and the manner in which this is done. Definitions of participation vary widely; these incorporate both individual as well as collective elements, participation as a process or an outcome, and participation as an end in itself or as a means to achieve other goals (i.e. the possibility of having an impact on decisions through participating).[36] Several scholars have developed typologies of participation, in order to theorise participation and to evaluate practice on the basis of different levels of participation.

The most widely known typology of child participation was developed by Roger Hart (1992), in his essay written for UNICEF, entitled *Children's Participation. From tokenism to citizenship*.[37] Hart developed the *ladder of participation*,

---

33 See for example T. Liefaard, 'Child-friendly justice: protection and participation of children in the justice system' (2016) 88 *Temple Law Review* 905–927; V.M. Smits, *Participatie van het kind bij het ouderschapsplan*, Maklu Uitgevers, Apeldoorn/Antwerp 2015.

34 K. Tisdall, above n. 29, p. 194.

35 R. Sinclair, 'Participation in practice: Making it meaningful, effective and sustainable' (2004) 18(2) *Children and Society* 106–118.

36 N. Thomas, 'Towards a theory of children's participation' (2007) 15(2) *International Journal of Children's Rights* 199–218; K. Herbots and J. Put, 'The Participation Disc: A Concept Analysis of (a) Child ('s Right to) Participation' (2015) 23 *International Journal of Children's Rights* 154; K. Tisdall, above n. 29.

37 R.A. Hart, *Children's Participation. From tokenism to citizenship*, UNICEF, Florence 1992. Hart was inspired by the ladder of citizen participation developed by Arnstein (S.R. Arnstein, 'A Ladder of Citizen Participation' (1969) 35(4) *Journal of the American Institute of Planners* 216–224.

a typology of children's participation in social movements and projects concerning children. The ladder consists of eight rungs, the lowest three of which refer to levels of non-participation, i.e. manipulation, decoration and tokenism. *Manipulation* refers to the situation where adults use children's participation to make their own point, but where children do not understand the event and their involvement in it. Hart gives the example of pre-school children carrying political posters concerning the impact of policies on children. If children do not understand the issue and their involvement therein, this is called manipulation. *Decoration* means that children are present at an event, but they do not know why or what the cause is of the event. Their presence, however, is not orchestrated by adults to show that children support the cause and 'adults do not pretend that the cause is inspired by children', but children are present and are for example asked to wear a t-shirt of the event.[38] *Tokenism* refers to 'those instances in which children are apparently given a voice, but in fact have little or no choice about the subject or the style of communicating it, and little or no opportunity to formulate their own opinions'.[39] The upper five rungs refer to increasingly effective and genuine forms of participation. These rungs refer to actual levels of child participation, ranging from *assigned but informed participation* – meaning that children at least know what they are participating voluntarily in and have a meaningful role – to *child-initiated shared decisions with adults*.

Harry Shier developed an alternative model based on Hart's ladder of participation, as an additional tool for practitioners to explore the different aspects of the participation process.[40] Shier identified five levels of participation, namely: (1) children are listened to; (2) children are supported in expressing their views; (3) children's views are taken into account; (4) children are involved in decision-making processes; and (5) children share power and responsibility for decision-making.[41] The final level was added because Shier argues that adults often deny children 'developmentally appropriate degrees of responsibility', but at the same time they should be careful not to force too much responsibility onto children in the decision-making process.[42] This, again, relates to the dichotomy between protection and participation and the extent to which children should be protected against potential harmful effects of participating in judicial proceedings.

A third model of child participation that is worth mentioning here is the one developed by Laura Lundy, to conceptualise the child's right to participation and to provide guidance to decision-makers on how to implement this right.

---

38 R.A. Hart, above n. 37, p. 9.

39 R.A. Hart, above n. 37.

40 H. Shier, 'Pathways to participation: openings, opportunities and obligations' (2001) 15(2) *Children & Society* 107–117.

41 H. Shier, above n. 40, p. 110.

42 H. Shier, above n. 40, p. 115.

She departs from the point of view that the child's right to be heard runs counter to the instinct and interests of adults and that conditions should be created which make it impossible for adults to ignore the views of children in decision-making. Lundy distinguishes four elements of child participation: space, voice, audience and influence. Safe *spaces* must be created for children to give their views, children must be given information and must be facilitated in giving their views (i.e. *voice*), the views must be listened to by someone (i.e. *audience*), and the views must be taken seriously and acted upon (i.e. *influence*).[43]

Hart's typology has had a profound influence on how practitioners and policy-makers regard and implement children's participation in decision-making.[44] However, several scholars have also criticised this model and made adaptations to it, such as removing the lower rungs and/or the hierarchical order, shifting rungs or adding new ones.[45] Thomas has identified two developments in this regard: (1) the hierarchical element is removed to adapt the type of participation to suit the type of setting or circumstance in which participation takes place, instead of presenting an hierarchical order of participation that is applicable in all kinds of settings; and (2) the participation typology shows the degree to which power is transferred from adults to children and the willingness of adults to share their power in the process. These developments in thinking about child participation may coexist in practice.[46]

A persistent criticism of child participation is the tokenistic nature of many forms of involvement by children. Lundy has further clarified the concept of *tokenism* in stating that it is unacceptable to state that participation should be denied completely, when it is considered tokenistic to involve children: '[i]f it cannot be achieved meaningfully, then it appears to be considered legitimate to not do it at all.'[47] Lundy argues that tokenistic ways of participating can sometimes be a starting point and are better than not involving children at all. Tisdall points out that participation models often depart from the notion of a dichotomy between children and adults, 'and thus ignore the diversity of individuals and relationships'[48] that exist between adults and children. According to Lundy dialogue between adults and children, feedback to children on their views and giving due weight to their views are important elements of participation and these should be encouraged by decision-makers and authorities, to prevent participation from becoming tokenistic.[49]

---

43 L. Lundy, '"Voice" is not enough: Conceptualising article 12 of the United Nations Convention on the Rights of the Child' (2007) 33(6) *British Educational Research Journal* 932–933.

44 N. Thomas, above n. 36; L. Lundy, 'In defence of tokenism? Children's right to participate in collective decision-making' (2018) 25(3) *Childhood* 340–354.

45 See N. Thomas, above n. 36.

46 N. Thomas, above n. 36.

47 L. Lundy, above n. 43.

48 K. Tisdall, above n. 29, p. 188.

49 L. Lundy, above n. 43.

The models presented here aim to conceptualise the notion of child participation and to give meaning to different types of involvement of children in decision-making in diverse contexts, such as at home, at school and in formal legal procedures. The increased attention drawn to child participation, as shown in section 2, has led to the development of various definitions and typologies which, in turn, highlight the challenges that are attached to implementation in practice. The models show that children do not always have the opportunity to participate genuinely, i.e. their views are actually taken into account in decision-making, irrespective of the context. However, it is acknowledged that the space and setting in which children participate play an important role, because the setting needs to provide a safe space in which the child is informed and enabled to give his/her views. The importance of the setting and contextual factors that help facilitate participation will be further discussed in the following section. It will be shown that judicial proceedings present particular challenges regarding the participation of children.

4. THE ROLE OF CHILDREN IN FAMILY LAW PROCEEDINGS

4.1. CHILDREN'S VIEWS ON PARTICIPATION

Decisions that are made in family law proceedings can have great impact on children's lives. In cases of parental separation, this can include a change in residence or reduced contact with one of the parents, for instance. The latter in particular is experienced as a great loss by children.[50] For the most part, such decisions are made by parents.[51] However, in their review on the voices of children in the context of child custody disputes, Birnbaum and Saini conclude that children prefer to be included in such decision-making processes.[52] Children wish to consider the parent–child relationship to be *bi*directional, as it makes them feel respected.[53] In addition, they want to feel acknowledged that *their lives* are affected by the court decision.[54] Yet at the

50 C. Brand, G. Howcroft and C.N. Hoelson, above n. 14.

51 A.B. Smith, N.J. Taylor and P. Tapp, 'Rethinking children's involvement in decision-making after parental separation' (2003) 10(2) *Childhood* 201–216.

52 R. Birnbaum and M. Saini, 'A qualitative synthesis of children's participation in custody disputes' (2012) 22(4) *Research on Social Work Practice* 400–409.

53 S.D. Maes, J. de Mol and A. Buysse, 'Children's experiences and meaning construction on parental divorce: A focus group study' (2012) 19(2) *Childhood* 266–279.

54 J. Cashmore and P. Parkinson, 'Children's participation in family law disputes: The views of children, parents, lawyers and counsellors' (2009) 82 *Family Matters* 15–21; C. Quigl and F. Cyr, 'The voice of the child in parenting coordination: Views of children, parents, and parenting coordinators' (2018) 59(6) *Journal of Divorce & Remarriage* 501–527.

same time, Birnbaum and Saini's review shows that some children express worries about participating. These feelings of ambivalence create the difficult task for professionals of balancing children's right to participate in important decisions about their lives and protecting them from being in the middle of their parents' conflicts.[55]

Children acknowledge that participation can put them in a difficult position. A study by Cashmore and Parkinson shows that children worry about the consequences of their court involvement for their parents (such as parents feeling hurt).[56] Such reasoning also became apparent in a more recent study by Holt, in which a child had concerns about expressing where he would like to live (i.e. either with mum or dad), because living with the one parent would have consequences for contact with the other parent.[57] Furthermore, children indicate that participation can cause stress because it may feel like 'choosing' between parents.[58] Interestingly, a recent study by Smeets, Bruning, de Boer and Bolscher demonstrated that a lack of information seems to be even more stressful. Not knowing what to expect and what is expected from children can cause feelings of anxiety towards participation.[59]

Despite these possible barriers to participation, children's desire to be included in the decision-making process seems to outweigh their concerns.[60] For a minority of children, however, it does not. A small proportion of children mention that participation could be traumatising.[61] This might especially be the case for children who have experienced a highly conflictual divorce and/or abuse (either direct or indirect through domestic violence). These children have shared their stories so many times and with so many different people and organisations (e.g. family, school, doctors, police, child protection workers, therapists) that it could be traumatising to repeat this.[62] In line with this, studies on the effects of

---

55 M. Hayes and R. Birnbaum, 'Voice of the child reports in Ontario: A content analysis of interviews with children' (2019) 60 *Journal of Divorce & Remarriage* 1–19.

56 J. Cashmore and P. Parkinson, above n. 54.

57 S. Holt, 'A voice or a choice? Children's views on participating in decisions about post-separation contact with domestically abusive fathers' (2018) 40(4) *Journal of Social Welfare and Family Law* 459–476.

58 J. Cashmore and P. Parkinson, above n. 54; S.D. Maes, J. de Mol and A. Buysse, above n. 53; M.M. Gollop, A.B. Smith and N.J. Taylor, 'Children's involvement in custody and access arrangements after parental separation' (2000) 12 *Child & Family Law Quarterly* 383–399.

59 D.J.H. Smeets, M.R. Bruning, R. de Boer and K.G.A. Bolscher, 'Praktijkonderzoek naar ervaringen met de civiele procespositie van minderjarigen' in M.R. Bruning et al., *Kind in proces: van communicatie naar effectieve participatie*, Meijers-reeks no. 335, Wolf Legal Publishers, Nijmegen 2020, pp. 161–234.

60 R. Birnbaum and N. Bala, 'Views of the child reports: The Ontario pilot project' (2017) 31(3) *International Journal of Law, Policy and the Family* 344–362; J. Cashmore and P. Parkinson, above n. 54; D.J.H. Smeets et al., above n. 59.

61 M.M. Gollop, A.B. Smith and N.J. Taylor, above n. 58.

62 K. Beckhouse, 'Laying the guideposts for participatory practice' (2016) 98 *Family Matters* 27.

adverse childhood experiences such as parental divorce, domestic violence and abuse have shown that the risk of trauma increases when exposed to multiple adverse childhood experiences.[63] In some cases, this can result in extreme, also called *toxic*, stress, in which children's (biological) stress response is highly sensitive, over-activated and results in extremely high levels of distress, which may impair functioning.[64] Professionals who interview children in family law disputes confirm that traumatising effects of repetitive interviewing can occur, in particular in cases of abuse allegations or police involvement.[65]

It is important to note, however, that not all adverse childhood experiences result in toxic stress or trauma.[66] In line with this, there are studies showing that children who experienced a highly conflictual divorce were able to participate in the judicial proceedings despite the potential stress of participating.[67] A literature review by Birnbaum and Saini including 35 studies confirms that the majority of children who participated in post-separation arrangements feel good about being consulted and considered.[68] Children value being included in the decision-making process as it makes them feel respected as an autonomous person.[69] Self-determination theory proposes that autonomy – the extent to which a person's behaviour is (perceived as being) self-determined rather than being coerced[70] – is one of the basic human psychological needs.[71]

---

63 M. Dong, R.F. Anda, V.J. Felitti, S.R. Dube, D.F. Williamson, T.J. Thompson, C.M. Loo and W.H. Giles, 'The interrelatedness of multiple forms of childhood abuse, neglect, and household dysfunction' (2004) 28(7) *Child Abuse & Neglect* 771–784; V.J. Felitti, R.F. Anda, D. Nordenberg, D.F. Williamson, A.M. Spitz, V. Edwards, M.P. Koss and J.S. Marks, 'Relationship of childhood abuse and household dysfunction to many of the leading causes of death in adults: The Adverse Childhood Experiences (ACE) Study' (2019) 56(6) *American Journal of Preventive Medicine* 774–786.

64 G. Hornor, 'Childhood trauma exposure and toxic stress: What the PNP needs to know' (2015) 29(2) *Journal of Pediatric Health Care* 191–198.

65 K.M. Turoy-Smith, M.B. Powell and S.P. Brubacher, 'Professionals' views about child interviews for family law assessments' (2018) (56(4) *Family Court Review* 607–622.

66 M. Dong et al., above n. 63; S.L. Lancaster, S.E. Melka, B.F. Rodriguez and A.R. Bryant, 'PTSD symptom patterns following traumatic and nontraumatic events' (2014) 23(4) *Journal of Aggression, Maltreatment & Trauma* 414–429.

67 J. Cashmore and P. Parkinson, above n. 54; B. Neale, 'Dialogues with children: Children, divorce and citizenship' (2002) 9(4) *Childhood* 455–475.

68 R. Birnbaum and M. Saini, above n. 52.

69 J. Cashmore and P. Parkinson, above n. 54; M.M. Gollop, A.B. Smith and N.J. Taylor, above n. 58; T. Morag, D. Rivkin and Y. Sorek, 'Child participation in the family courts – Lessons from the Israeli pilot project' (2012) 26(1) *International Journal of Law, Policy and the Family* 1–30; S. Holt, above n. 57; D.J.H. Smeets et al., above n. 59.

70 Y.L. Su and J. Reeve, 'A meta-analysis of the effectiveness of intervention programs designed to support autonomy' (2011) 23(1) *Educational Psychology Review* 159–188.

71 E.L. Deci and R.M. Ryan, 'Self-determination theory: A macrotheory of human motivation, development, and health' (2008) 49(3) *Canadian Psychology/Psychologie canadienne* 182–185.

Consistent with this theory, an autonomy-supportive environment has been demonstrated to benefit children in many ways. In educational settings, for instance, an autonomy-supportive teaching style stimulates engagement, motivation and achievement.[72] Similar benefits have been found when autonomy is supported by parents or in (mental) health care.[73] A lack of (perceived) autonomy on the other hand decreases self-esteem (as has been described above) and negatively affects the development of children's reasoning skills and their ability to express their own views:[74] children 'learn' not to have a say and, as a consequence, do not develop trust in their abilities to make decisions on their own.[75] Studies on children in child care and protection have shown that repeatedly being excluded from participation can result in feelings of frustration, desperation and powerlessness, and even problem behaviour.[76] This shows that the development of children's autonomy is at risk when children are repeatedly denied to participate.[77]

In line with these positive findings, Vis and colleagues have mentioned that child participation has a 'therapeutic effect' of being respected and acknowledged.[78] Judges in different jurisdictions seem to be aware of this as they report that participation is generally more important to children than to the court.[79] However, children's right to be heard does create an opportunity to gather information about the child and his/her current situation.[80]

72 J. Reeve, H. Jang, D. Carrell, S. Jeon and J. Barch, 'Enhancing students' engagement by increasing teachers' autonomy support' (2004) 28(2) *Motivation and Emotion* 147–169.

73 Y.L. Su and J. Reeve, above n. 70.

74 P.A. Klaczynski, J.P. Byrnes and J.E. Jacobs, 'Introduction to the special issue: The development of decision making' (2001) 22(3) *Journal of Applied Developmental Psychology* 225–236.

75 C. Leeson, 'My life in care: Experiences of non-participation in decision-making processes' (2007) 12(3) *Child & Family Social Work* 268–277.

76 S. Bessell, 'Participation in decision-making in out-of-home care in Australia: what do young people say?' (2011) 33(4) *Children and Youth Services Review* 496–501, 498; V. Barnes, 'Social work and advocacy with young people: Rights and care in practice' (2012) 42(7) *British Journal of Social Work* 1275–1292; K. Winter, 'The perspectives of young children in care about their circumstances and implications for social work practice' (2010) 15(2) *Child & Family Social Work* 186–195.

77 C. Leeson, above n. 75.

78 S.A. Vis, A. Stranbu, A. Holtan and N. Thomas, 'Participation and health – a research review of child participation in planning and decision-making' (2011) 16(3) *Child & Family Social Work* 325–335.

79 T. Morag, D. Rivkin and Y. Sorek, above n. 69; D.J.H. Smeets et al., above n. 59; M. Fernando, 'Children's Direct Participation and the Views of Australian Judges' (2013) 92 *Family Matters* 41–47.

80 K.A.M. van der Zon and M.P. de Jong-de Kruijf, 'Hoger beroep tegen een uithuisplaatsingsbeslissing en de rol van de minderjarige' (2015) 3 *TREMA* 298–307; M. Hayes and R. Birnbaum, above n. 55; F.E. Raitt, 'Hearing Children in Family Law Proceedings: Can Judges Make a Difference' (2007) 19 *Child & Family Law Quarterly* 204.

Letting children share their experiences, feelings and wishes creates an opportunity to make a more responsive decision that fits the child's needs.[81] A perfect fit with the child's wishes does not seem to be necessary, though.[82] As Cashmore states: 'children want to have a say, rather than their own way'.[83] In line with this, research has shown that participation increases the chance that children will accept a decision, even when the decision is not in line with the child's own wishes.[84] Furthermore, participation has been related to better outcomes after decision-making. In the case of separation and divorce, custody and contact arrangements can benefit from child participation.[85] Such benefits will also apply to children involved in other family law proceedings concerning adoption, legal parentage or international child abduction: involving children creates an opportunity to better fit the decision with the child's wishes or to explain why this is not possible.[86]

4.2. BARRIERS TO CHILD PARTICIPATION

Despite the benefits child participation can have for children and decision-makers in judicial proceedings, extensive research has shown that children's right to participate is not always fully satisfied.[87] Rap and colleagues discuss research showing that children do not feel heard and are not informed sufficiently and adequately.[88] This has been demonstrated in many different countries, such as

---

81 S.A. Vis, A. Stranbu, A. Holtan and N. Thomas, above n. 78.

82 A. Graham and R. Fitzgerald, 'Progressing children's participation: Exploring the potential of a dialogical turn' (2010) 17(3) *Childhood* 343–359.

83 J. Cashmore, 'Promoting the participation of children and young people in care' (2002) 26(8) *Child Abuse & Neglect* 837–847.

84 See also K. Saywitz, L.B. Camparo and A. Romanoff, 'Interviewing children in custody cases: Implications of research and policy for practice' (2010) 28(4) *Behavioral Sciences and the Law* 542–562.

85 J. Cashmore, above n. 83; V.M. Smits, above n. 33.

86 S.A. Vis et al., above n. 78.

87 B. Arad-Davidzon and R. Benbenishty, 'The role of workers' attitudes and parent and child wishes in child protection workers' assessments and recommendation regarding removal and reunification' (2008) 30(1) *Children and Youth Services Review* 107–121; M.D. ten Brummelaar, A.T. Harder, M.E. Kalverboer, W.J. Post and E.J. Knorth, 'Participation of youth in decision-making procedures during residential care: A narrative review' (2018) 23(1) *Child & Family Social Work* 33–44; G.G. van Bijleveld, C.W.M. Dedding and J.G.F. Bunders-Aelen, 'Children's and young people's participation within child welfare and child protection services: a state-of-the-art review' (2015) 20(2) *Child and Family Social Work* 129–138.

88 S.E. Rap, D.S. Verkroost and M.R. Bruning, 'Children's participation in Dutch youth care practice: an exploratory study into the opportunities for child participation in youth care from professionals' perspective' (2018) 24 *Child Care in Practice* 1–15.

the US,[89] Sweden,[90] Ireland,[91] England,[92] Australia[93] and the Netherlands.[94] Partly, the lack of child participation may be explained by the specific laws and procedures that apply in a particular country. In the Netherlands, for instance, a lack of participation of children under 12 years of age can partly be explained by the age limit of 12 years that the Dutch law applies for children to be heard in civil law proceedings.[95] However, since feelings of not being heard or not being able to participate are found among children across the world this seems to be a more general phenomenon, not caused only by legal restrictions on the right to be heard.

Research shows that professionals' lack of skills and time are major barriers to child participation.[96] In the studies by Van Bijleveld and colleagues, procedural aspects such as high caseloads were mentioned as obstacles by professionals in different countries.[97] These reasons have been reported not only by social workers

---

89 S.D. Block, H. Oran, D. Oran, N. Baumrind and G.S. Goodman, 'Abused and neglected children in court: Knowledge and attitudes' (2010) 34 *Child Abuse & Neglect* 659–670.

90 P. Leviner, 'Child Participation in the Swedish Child Protection System. Child-Friendly Focus but Limited Child Influence on Outcomes' (2018) 26(1) *International Journal of Children's Rights* 136–158; P. Pölkki, R. Vornanen, M. Pursiainen and M. Riikonen, 'Children's participation in child-protection processes as experienced by foster children and social workers' (2012) 18(2) *Child Care in Practice* 107–125.

91 U. Kilkelly, 'The CRC in Litigation Under the ECHR' in T. Liefaard and J.E. Doek (eds.), *Litigating the Rights of the Child. The UN Convention on the Rights of the Child in Domestic and International Jurisprudence*, Springer, Dordrecht 2015, pp. 193–209.

92 J. Cossar, M. Brandon and P. Jordan, *Don't make assumptions*': *Children and young people's views of the child protection system and messages for change*, The Office of the Children's Commissioner, London 2011; K. Muench, C. Diaz and R. Wright, 'Children and parent participation in Child Protection Conferences: A study in one English Local Authority' (2017) 23(1) *Child Care in Practice* 49–63.

93 J. Cashmore, above n. 83; R. Fitzgerald and A. Graham, '"Something Amazing I Guess": Children's Views on Having A Say About Supervised Contact' (2011) 64 *Australian Social Work* 487–501.

94 A.G. de Jong, J.B. van der Kooi and M.N. Barcas, *De zorg waar ze recht op hebben. Onderzoek naar de toegang tot en de kwaliteit van de jeugdhulp na decentralisatie*, De Kinderombudsman, The Hague 2016; M.R. Bruning et al., *Kind in proces: van communicatie naar effectieve participatie,* Meijers-reeks no. 335, Wolf Legal Publishers, Nijmegen 2020; M.J. Steketee, A.M. Overgaag and K.D Lünnemann, *Minderjarigen als procespartij? Een onderzoek naar de bijzondere curator en formele rechtsingang voor minderjarigen* Verwey-Jonker Instituut, Utrecht 2003.

95 K.A.M. van der Zon and M.P. de Jong-de Kruijf, above n. 80; V.M. Smits, above n. 33; A. van Triest, 'Het kinderverhoor in het ressort Den Bosch onder de loep' (2004) 26 *Tijdschrift voor Familie en Jeugdrecht* 16–26; Art. 809 Rechtsvordering (Rv) (Dutch Code of Civil Procedure).

96 S.E. Rap, D.S. Verkroost and M.R. Bruning, above n. 88; see also H. Stalford and K. Hollingsworth, 'Towards Judgments for Children' (2020) 83(5) *Modern Law Review* 1–29.

97 G.G. van Bijleveld, C.W.M. Dedding and J.G.F. Bunders-Aelen, above n. 87; G.G. van Bijleveld, *Dealing with the interplay of child image, protection and participation. A critical reflection on the essence of child participation in child protection services*, diss. Vrije Universiteit Amsterdam, 2019.

but also by judges. They report that in court there is no time to build rapport and establish a relationship of trust that benefits children in expressing their views.[98] This is especially important because children involved in family law proceedings experience loyalty conflicts, which can result in anxiety about expressing an opinion that contradicts one of the parents.[99] Consequently, professionals fear that this may restrict children from providing their own authentic opinion.[100]

Especially when cases include younger children, expectations regarding loyalty conflicts and related fears may form a barrier to child participation.[101] For instance, judges fear that young children in particular will feel responsible for the decision made by the judge.[102] In addition, it has been posited that the process of being interviewed by a judge might be harmful for children.[103] In general, an image seems to exist of participation being stressful for children and that they should be protected against it.[104] Thus, decisions to *deny* children to participate are often based on preventing (further) problems, whereas the potential harmful effects that are associated with excluding children (as described in section 4.1) are overlooked.[105]

The decision to deny children the option to participate may also be based on views regarding children's cognitive capacities. Predominantly, professionals consider that young children are not capable of verbalising their point of view and providing relevant information for decision-making.[106] In their literature study on skills that are relevant for child participation in judicial proceedings, Peper and Smeets conclude that children aged eight are sufficiently competent to talk to judges. At this age, children are not only capable of forming and verbalising their opinions, but their cognitive development allows for somewhat abstract and hypothetical reasoning, as is often necessary in family law proceedings

98 P. Tapp, 'Judges are human too: Conversation between the judge and a child as a means of giving effect to section 6 of the Care of Children Act 2004' (2006) 35 *New Zealand Law Review* 35–74.

99 J. Cashmore, above n. 83.

100 S.A. Vis, A. Holtan and N. Thomas, 'Obstacles for child participation in care and protection cases – why Norwegian social workers find it difficult' (2012) 21(1) *Child Abuse Review* 7–23.

101 F. Bell, 'Barriers to empowering children in private family law proceedings' (2016) 30(3) *International Journal of Law, Policy and the Family* 225–247.

102 P. Tapp, above n. 98.

103 P. Parkinson and J. Cashmore, 'Judicial conversations with children in parenting disputes: The views of Australian judges' (2007) 21(2) *International Journal of Law, Policy and the Family* 160–189.

104 G.G. van Bijleveld, C.W.M. Dedding and J.G.F. Bunders-Aelen, above n. 87; I.B. Jensen, I. Studsrød and I.T. Ellingsen, 'Child protection social workers' constructions of children and childhood: An integrative review' (2019) *Child & Family Social Work* 1–14.

105 F. Bell, above n. 101; A. Skelton, 'Balancing Autonomy and Protection in Children's Rights: A South African Account' (2015) 88 *Temple Law Review* 887–904.

106 G.G. van Bijleveld, C.W.M. Dedding and J.G.F. Bunders-Aelen, above n. 87; I.B. Jensen, I. Studsrød and I.T. Ellingsen, above n. 104.

(e.g. thinking about consequences of reduced parental contact or a change of residence). Emphasising the importance of child participation, the authors note that four- to five-year-olds could even be involved in decision-making through conversations with pedagogical or psychological experts.[107] However, judges seem to underestimate children's capacities or find it difficult to assess the child's competences.[108] Consequently, this may deny the child who is capable of being heard his/her right to participation, because he/she is wrongly found to be incapable of being heard. Therefore, it is important to increase judges' knowledge about child development,[109] as adequate knowledge and awareness-raising may reduce this barrier to children's participation.

In addition to general views on children's capacities, there are case-specific barriers as well. Van Bijleveld and colleagues have described how social workers are less inclined to invite children to participate when the case is 'more serious'.[110] For instance, children are more often excluded in cases of child abuse. A plausible explanation could be that professionals prioritise the child's physical safety over involving children in the process.[111] This dilemma has also been described by judges in family law proceedings.[112] Worries may involve domestic violence, but – especially in the case of highly conflictual divorces – the child's emotional safety can also be a concern. Furthermore, worries may exist regarding the authenticity of children's wishes and opinions. As mentioned above (section 4.1), children experience loyalty conflicts that could form a barrier to expressing their own wishes – being afraid of hurting one of the parents. Some judges may feel insecure about interviewing children in these circumstances because they may lack adequate communication and pedagogical skills in such a sensitive context or are unable to ascertain when children are being manipulated by their parents.[113] When facing the dilemma of interviewing a child in such conditions or not, the balance between protection and participation will probably tip towards protection.[114]

---

107 J.S. Peper and D.J.H. Smeets, 'Inzichten vanuit de pedagogische wetenschappen en de neuropsychologie' in M.R. Bruning et al., *Kind in proces: van communicatie naar effectieve participatie*, Meijers-reeks no. 335, Wolf Legal Publishers, Nijmegen 2020, pp. 123–160.

108 E. Burke, 'Family Court Judges' Training, Background, and Child Development Knowledge: Associations with Child Custody Decision Making' (2005) *Honors Scholar Theses*; W.J. Mlyniec, 'A Judge's Ethical Dilemma: Assessing a Child's Capacity to Choose' (1995) 64 *Fordham Law Review* 1873–1915.

109 T.M. Collins, 'A child's right to participate: Implications for international child protection' (2017) 21(1) *The International Journal of Human Rights* 14–46; E. Munro, 'Empowering looked-after children' (2001) 6(2) *Child & Family Social Work* 129–137.

110 G.G. van Bijleveld, C.W.M. Dedding and J.G.F. Bunders-Aelen, above n. 87.

111 B. Arad-Davidzon and R. Benbenishty, above n. 87; D. Archard and M. Skivenes, 'Hearing the child' (2009) 14(4) *Child & Family Social Work* 391–399.

112 W.J. Mlyniec, above n. 108.

113 P. Tapp, above n. 98.

114 V.M. Smits, above n. 33.

5. CONDITIONS FOR EFFECTIVE CHILD PARTICIPATION

It is important to recognise that child participation and protecting children involved in judicial proceedings are not mutually exclusive. Under the right circumstances, the benefits of participation can overrule the possible disadvantages. In this section, we will discuss some key aspects that should be taken into account when including children in the decision-making process. These aspects are based on pedagogical and psychological knowledge on how to involve and talk to children, which is used in practice by social professionals such as psychologists and social workers. It is not aimed at providing a complete set of conditions that will allow effective participation,[115] but at stressing the importance of these contextual aspects when speaking to children in judicial proceedings.

In some countries, children participate through talking to social workers, trained child advocates or a guardian ad litem. In many countries, though, it is standard practice that legal professionals such as judges or lawyers interview the child. Given that the latter group of professionals is generally not trained in talking to children, the call to protect children may be loudest in these situations. Therefore, this section takes the perspective of legal professionals talking to children, focusing on three important conditions that allow effective child participation: (1) access to legal procedures and informing children; (2) creating a safe environment; and (3) communication skills.

5.1. ACCESS AND INFORMATION

According to the UN Committee on the Rights of the Child (UNCRC Committee), every judicial procedure concerning minors should be both 'accessible and child-appropriate'.[116] Even when access to participation is available for children, participation is only possible when minors are made aware of this.[117] Research has shown, however, that children have little knowledge of their rights and ways to participate;[118] thus, informing children adequately may increase their level

---

115 See for example S.E. Rap, *The participation of juvenile defendants in the youth court: A comparative study of juvenile justice procedures in Europe*, Pallas Publications, Amsterdam 2013 (doctoral diss. Utrecht University).

116 UN Committee on the Rights of the Child, *General Comment No. 12: The Right of the Child to be Heard*, CRC/C/GC/12, 20 July 2009, para. 34.

117 A. Graham and R. Fitzgerald, above n. 82.

118 S.D. Block et al., above n. 89; H. Bouma, M.L. López, E.J. Knorth and H. Grietens, 'Meaningful participation for children in the Dutch child protection system: A critical analysis of relevant provisions in policy documents' (2018) 79 *Child Abuse & Neglect* 279–292; U. Kilkelly, *Listening to children about justice: Report of the Council of Europe consultation*

of participation. Importantly, it is often questionable whether information provided to children is 'child-appropriate', as the UNCRC Committee emphasises. Research has shown that legal terms are regularly used in communication with children, which can be intimidating and can decrease their motivation to participate.[119] In addition, confusion exists among professionals about who is responsible for providing the child with information, and about when and how that should happen.[120] Research on children who have to undergo medical treatment has shown that when they have more knowledge about what will happen to them, they also experience less anxiety.[121] Similarly, not knowing what to expect seems to be one of the main reasons why children in family law proceedings experience anxiety or stress.[122] Furthermore, when children have more knowledge and understanding of judicial proceedings, they also have a more positive opinion about how the process went and about the conduct of professionals.[123] In sum, informing children adequately is expected to have positive effects on the level of stress that children experience when participating.

Another important aspect of child participation is that children are informed about the outcome of the procedure and the extent to which their views have been taken into account in the final decision.[124] This may help children to understand and accept the decision, because the reasons for taking the decision should be explained and are consequently better understood by the child.[125] Judges have reported finding this important,[126] but it may be challenging to use child-friendly

with children on child-friendly justice, Council of Europe, Strasbourg 2010; K. van Hoorde et al., *Bouncing Back. The wellbeing of children in international child abduction cases*, EU-funded research project 'Enhancing the Well-being of Children in Cases of International Child Abduction' (eWELL), 2018.

119 M.D. ten Brummelaar, A.T. Harder, M.E. Kalverboer, W.J. Post and E.J. Knorth, above n. 87; K.M. Turoy-Smith, M.B. Powel and S.P. Brubacher, above n. 65.

120 S.E. Rap, D.S. Verkroost and M.R. Bruning, above n. 88.

121 J.A. Quas, A.R. Wallin, B. Horwitz, E. Davis and T.D. Lyon, 'Maltreated children's understanding of and emotional reactions to dependency court involvement' (2009) 27 *Behavioral Sciences and the Law* 97–117; U. Kilkelly and M. Donnelly, 'Participation in healthcare: the views and experiences of children and young people' (2011) 19(1) *International Journal of Children's Rights* 107–125.

122 D.J.H. Smeets et al., above n. 59.

123 S.D. Block et al., above n. 89; European Union Agency for Fundamental Rights (FRA), *Child-friendly justice. Perspectives and experiences of children involved in judicial proceedings as victims, witnesses or parties in nine EU Member States*, Publications Office of the European Union 2017.

124 UN Committee on the Rights of the Child, above n. 116, paras. 28, 45; See also UN Committee on the Rights of the Child, *General Comment No. 14: The right of the child to have his or her best interests taken as a primary consideration (Art. 3, para. 1)*, CRC/C/GC/14, 29 May 2013, para. 6

125 T. Collins, above n. 109; G. Schofield, 'The voice of the child in family placement decision-making: A developmental model' (2005) 29(1) *Adoption and Fostering* 29–43; G.G. van Bijleveld, C.W.M. Dedding and J.G.F. Bunders-Aelen, above n. 87.

126 P. Parkinson and J. Cashmore, above n. 103.

language in communicating court decisions.[127] In the Netherlands and in the UK, some courts have experimented with child-friendly judgments.[128] Stalford and Hollingsworth argue that 'the precise role of judges in communicating their decisions to children' is largely underdeveloped and generally other adult professionals are required to explain the judgment to the child and to consider the next steps to take.[129] In a similar vein, Lieber has suggested that 'simplifying' a court judgment is detrimental for the precision of the decision and proposes that children are informed about the judgment through a third party that 'translates' the decision.[130] Importantly, such an alternative finds support among judges[131] and children.[132]

5.2. CREATING A SAFE ENVIRONMENT

Another important implication of the UNCRC Committee's comment that participation should be 'child-appropriate' concerns the environment in which children are heard. General Comment No. 12 states that 'a child cannot be heard effectively when the environment is intimidating, hostile, insensitive or inappropriate for her or his age'.[133] Rather, the Committee stresses that dialogue should take place in 'an environment in which the child feels safe and respected'.[134] This notion is also very important according to attachment theory, which stresses the importance of children feeling safe and secure.[135] As discussed above, attachment refers to the bond between a child and his/her parent. Ideally, parents form a secure base on which children can count in times of distress. Children in family law proceedings, however, are at risk of developing an insecure attachment relationship with their parents. The term insecurity refers to children not being able to trust that their parents are the safe and secure base that they need. This feeling can also have consequences for their interaction with

---

127 A. Vandekerckhove and K. O'Brien, 'Child-Friendly Justice: turning law into reality' (2013) 14 *Era Forum* 523–541

128 M.H.L. van den Hoogen and P.J. Montanus, 'Hoe staat het anno 2017 met de informele rechtsingang?' (2017) 62(11) *Tijdschrift voor Familie- en jeugdrecht* 286–289; T. Liefaard and S.E. Rap, 'Hoezo kindvriendelijk? Over "child-friendly justice" ter bevordering van effectieve participatie van kinderen in juridische procedures en besluitvorming' (2018) 41(6) *Tijdschrift voor Familie- en jeugdrecht* 180–186.

129 H. Stalford and K. Hollingsworth, above n. 96, p. 9.

130 J.H. Lieber, 'De rechter en de taal van het kind' (2018) 41(6) *Tijdschrift voor Familie- en jeugdrecht* 172–179.

131 D.J.H. Smeets et al., above n. 59.

132 R. Fitzgerald and A. Graham, above n. 93.

133 UN Committee on the Rights of the Child, above n. 116, para. 34.

134 UN Committee on the Rights of the Child, above n. 116, para. 23.

135 J. Bowlby, above n. 10.

others; for instance, these children may be distrustful towards other adults – even the ones who try to help them (such as youth care professionals or judges). Although a safe and encouraging environment is important for all children, this is especially important for children who are involved in family law proceedings.

An important question is how courts can ensure that an environment encourages children to 'feel safe and respected'. First, the physical environment that the child is exposed to should be considered. In a short period of time, children are asked to tell the judge about their personal feelings, so it is important that the atmosphere of a room invites children to disclose.[136] From a pedagogical point of view, it is recommended that the level of formality be decreased when children are heard,[137] because this can be experienced as intimidating by both younger and older children.[138] In a courtroom in which children have to look up towards the judge, they may feel subordinate to the judge, which feeling may also arise when judges wear a gown when speaking to a child. In some cases, multiple judges may be present in the room when the child is heard, which can also be stressful for children. De Jong-de Kruijf and Van der Zon quote a child who experienced this and 'felt like a criminal'.[139] In sum, aspects such as clothing, seating position or number of judges in the room can emphasise authority and thus be intimidating for children. This should be avoided, because only when children feel comfortable and safe do they feel free to express their personal experiences, opinions and wishes to a stranger (i.e. the judge). Feeling intimidated hampers children in giving their own view on the case (i.e. the child's authentic voice).[140] The level of formality can also be decreased by hearing children outside the formal courtroom and in for example the judge's office. These settings provide a more informal atmosphere, smaller physical distances between the participants and usually a limited number of people being present.[141] This contributes, among other things, to making eye contact, which encourages children to be at ease and to feel free to give their views.[142]

Another way to compensate for the authoritative environment at court could be to allow children to bring a support person to court. The literature review by Kennan and colleagues has confirmed that an advocate can help to 'redress the power imbalances at play' and can 'give young people the confidence to infiltrate

136 C. van Nijnatten and E. Jongen, 'Professional conversations with children in divorce-related child welfare inquiries' (2011) 18(4) *Childhood* 540–555.

137 M.F. Delfos, *Luister je wel naar mij? Gespreksvoering met kinderen tussen vier en twaalf jaar oud*, SWP Uitgeverij, Amsterdam 2009.

138 K. Dekens and J. van der Sleen, *Handleiding het kind als getuige,* Stapel en De Koning, Amsterdam 2013.

139 K.A.M. van der Zon and M.P. de Jong-de Kruijf, above n. 80.

140 D. Archard and M. Skivenes, above n. 111.

141 S.E. Rap, above n. 115.

142 K. Saywitz et al., above n. 84.

an adult-dominated decision-making process'.[143] Especially for children who experience stress, a support person could be useful. It has been proposed that stress is less likely to become toxic when a supportive adult who forms a buffer against stress is present.[144] Judges, however, prefer to talk to a child alone – mainly to avoid children being influenced by the support person they brought.[145] This could mean that judges lack knowledge concerning the positive effects of an advocate or whether the applicable rules allow for the presence of a support person. In addition, it stresses the importance of setting ground rules regarding the tasks and responsibilities of a child advocate (when allowed).

Another factor that influences whether or not children feel at ease in a room is the way the room is decorated. A room that is somewhat cosy can also creating a safe and encouraging environment,[146] meaning that a room could benefit from some paintings, plants, drinks, coloured walls, and objects for children (e.g. books, pencils, etc.). Finally, it is also important to consider entrances and waiting rooms when creating a child-friendly physical environment. Children can experience stress when they see judges and lawyers, formally dressed, passing by.[147] They may also encounter a parent in the hall or waiting room, or feel stressed anticipating that this may happen, which can form a barrier to children participating and expressing their views freely.[148] Additionally, this can increase anxiety about expressing a wish that does not correspond with their parents' due to children's loyalty conflicts.[149]

5.3. COMMUNICATION SKILLS

A conversation between a professional and a child inherently involves an unequal power relationship.[150] For children to feel comfortable expressing their personal feelings and opinions, it is important to use appropriate communication skills. As Smith and colleagues argue, 'the issue of children of any age expressing their views is not so much one of the child's ability to provide information, as it is

---

143 D. Kennan, B. Brady and C. Florkan, 'Supporting children's participation in decision making: A systematic literature review exploring the effectiveness of participatory processes' (2018) 48(7) *British Journal of Social Work* 1985–2002.

144 S.B. Johnson, A.W. Riley, D.A. Granger and J. Riis, 'The science of early life toxic stress for pediatric practice and advocacy' (2013) 131(2) *Pediatrics* 319–327.

145 D.J.H. Smeets et al., above n. 59.

146 A. van Teijlingen-Pover, 'De gerechtelijke procedure in jeugd- en familiezaken door de ogen van de kinderen' (2019) 2 *TREMA*.

147 A. van Teijlingen-Pover, above n. 146.

148 K.A.M. van der Zon and M.P. de Jong-de Kruijf, above n. 80; FRA, above n. 123.

149 J. Cashmore and P. Parkinson, above n. 54.

150 M.D. Casley, *Conversations between Children and Adults*, doctoral diss. Griffith University, 2017.

of the adult's competence to elicit (or observe) it in the context of a trusting, supportive and reciprocal relationship'.[151]

Ideally, children should be able to share their experiences, feelings and wishes with a professional they trust. Studies on decisions made by youth care professionals have shown that a more positive relationship between a child and a professional helps the child to express his/her authentic opinion – even when this contradicts the parents' view.[152] Given that many countries conceptualise the right to be heard as a conversation with a judge, who is a stranger to the child, this finding could be interpreted as an advice against judges interviewing children directly. However, studies have shown that children prefer to speak to the person who will be making the decision about their lives – even if they do not know him/her.[153] Consequently, judges have to be aware that their communication skills are crucial in creating a safe and encouraging environment.

As mentioned before, some judges may question whether they are the best person to be interviewing children.[154] Judges acknowledge that the children they speak to find themselves in difficult and vulnerable positions. Given this context, judges feel that a high level of skill and specialisation is required to talk to children.[155] In jurisdictions that require judges or lawyers to talk to children, training on communication skills is necessary, given the fact that communication skills vary between individual judges or lawyers.[156] First, it may be important to recognise that children in divorce cases usually have no previous experience of visiting the court or speaking to a judge, which can be different from children in child protection cases. This lack of experience with the judicial system requires some explaining and taking the time to make the child feel at ease.[157] This could for example mean that courts should consider extending the time available for each case and in which judges can talk to children.

Furthermore, training should be focused on the appropriateness of some general communication techniques when talking to children, such as explaining the goal and the ground rules of the conversation. It is important that children know what is expected of them and what they can expect from the interviewer.[158] An important aspect to explain is confidentiality. When judges or lawyers talk to children, children should know whether the information will be shared with their parents.[159] In fact, children have reported breaches of confidentiality as a

---

151 A.B. Smith, N.J. Taylor and P. Tapp, above n. 51, p. 212.

152 S.A. Vis, A. Holtan and N. Thomas, above n. 100; G.G. van Bijleveld, C.W.M. Dedding and J.G.F. Bunders-Aelen, above n. 87.

153 D.J.H. Smeets et al., above n. 59; J. Cashmore and P. Parkinson, above n. 54.

154 P. Tapp, above n. 98; P. Parkinson and J. Cashmore, above n. 103.

155 K.M. Turoy-Smith, M.B. Powel and S.P. Brubacher, above n. 65.

156 K.A.M. van der Zon and M.P. de Jong-de Kruijf, above n. 80; F.E. Raitt, above n. 80.

157 F. Bell, 'Meetings between Children's Lawyers and Children Involved in Private Family Law Disputes' (2016) 28(1) *Child & Family Law Quarterly* 5–24.

158 C. van Nijnatten and E. Jongen, above n. 136.

159 P. Parkinson and J. Cashmore, above n. 103.

negative aspect of talking to lawyers,[160] which could be avoided when children are properly informed about what the interviewer will do with the information shared. To make sure children understand this, it is important to use simple and clear language and explain legal jargon.[161]

During the conversation, it is important to listen carefully and show understanding.[162] The latter is accomplished through asking questions, which should be open-ended and non-suggestive to stimulate free recall.[163] As communication is part of our daily lives, asking questions may seem 'easy', yet interviewing children requires some specific training. For instance, an intuitive technique when a conversational partner does not give a response is to repeat or rephrase the question. For children, this approach can be counter-productive because children interpret this to mean that an answer *must* follow. This can feel like pressure to provide an answer and could result in an answer that does not reflect the child's authentic wishes, but an answer that the child thinks will be approved of by the adult.[164] In addition, some questions are not appropriate for all developmental levels. 'Why' questions, for instance, are often used to investigate causes and motives, but such questions are not suited for young children who have difficulties with causal relationships.[165] Furthermore, the specific topic that is discussed during interviews in the context of family law proceedings is better not approached directly. Rather than directly asking a child whether he/she likes to visit his/her father, it is advisable to gather information more indirectly by asking what the child does when he/she visits father, for instance.[166] Thus, when talking to children, child-appropriate communication skills and knowledge about appropriate questioning techniques are necessary to encourage children to express their opinions and wishes freely.

A final concern when speaking to children in divorce cases is loyalty conflicts. When children are hesitant or anxious about expressing an opinion that contradicts one of the parents,[167] appropriate communication skills are required

160 M.M. Gollop, A.B. Smith and N.J. Taylor, above n. 58.

161 M.F. Delfos, above n. 137; K.M. Turoy-Smith, M.B. Powel and S.P. Brubacher, above n. 65.

162 M.D. ten Brummelaar, A.T. Harder, M.E. Kalverboer, W.J. Post and E.J. Knorth, above n. 87.

163 M.E. Lamb and M.P.Y Sim, 'Developmental factors affecting children in legal contexts' (2013) 13(2) *Youth Justice* 131–144; A.C. Cederborg, Y. Orbach, K.J. Sternberg and M.E. Lamb, 'Investigative interviews of child witnesses in Sweden' (2000) 24(10) *Child Abuse & Neglect* 1355–1361; J.Z. Klemfuss and S.J. Ceci, 'Legal and psychological perspectives on children's competence to testify in court' (2012) 32 *Developmental Review* 268–286.

164 K. Dekens and J. van der Sleen, above n. 138.

165 M.F. Delfos, above n. 137.

166 N. Bala, R. Birnbaum, F. Cyr and D. McColley, 'Children's voices in family court: Guidelines for judges meeting children' (2013) 47(3) *Family Law Quarterly* 379–408.

167 J. Cashmore, 'Children's participation in family law decision-making: Theoretical approaches to understanding children's views' (2011) 33(4) *Children and Youth Services Review*, 515–520; J. Cashmore and P. Parkinson, above n. 54.

to invite children to talk about their *own* feelings.[168] In highly conflictual divorces in which the residential parent speaks negatively about the other in front of the child, it may be particularly difficult to assess this. Because children are highly suggestible,[169] they may actually adopt negative affections towards the other parent. The term parental alienation has been used to refer to children becoming alienated from one of the parents due to such manipulations.[170] It should be noted that the notion of parental alienation is highly contested in academic literature and should therefore be regarded with much caution.[171] However, this does create a challenge for judges in determining how much weight to accord to the child's wishes in these situations.[172] Although judges seem to have a good sense of when a child's views are affected by one of the parents, figuring out what is in the best interests of the child may require more than a short interview with a judge or lawyer.[173] In these cases, a guardian ad litem can be appointed to investigate this in detail.

To conclude, talking with children requires specific knowledge and training, which judges or lawyers do not have compared to social workers with a pedagogical education. However, this does not mean that they are not the right person to talk to a child. A majority of children actually prefer talking to the judge as this is the person who makes the decision. Moreover, judges' communication skills are generally evaluated positively.[174] Even in jurisdictions where it is rare to speak to children, judges value this option.[175] Proper guidance for judges who talk to children should thus be available for them.

6. CONCLUSIONS

In recent decades, child participation has increasingly received attention, influenced among other things by the adoption of the UNCRC, and specifically the right to be heard that is accorded to children. Excluding children from being involved in judicial proceedings is not consistent with their right and preference

168 M.F. Delfos, above n. 137; C. van Nijnatten and E. Jongen, above n. 136; P. Tapp, above n. 98.

169 M. Bruck and S.J. Ceci, 'The suggestibility of children's memory' (1999) 50(1) *Annual Review of Psychology* 419–439.

170 R.A. Gardner, 'Recent trends in divorce and custody litigation' (1985) 29(2) *Academy Forum* 3–7; J.R. Johnston, 'Parental Alignments and Rejection: An Empirical Study of Alienation in Children of Divorce' (2003) 31 *Journal of the American Academy on Psychiatry Law* 158–170.

171 C. Migchels and D. de Walter, 'Ouderverstotingssyndroom en de controverse rond psychiatrische diagnostiek' (2017) *Tijdschrift voor Psychiatrie* 482–488.

172 F.E. Raitt, above n. 80; P. Parkinson and J. Cashmore, above n. 103.

173 D.J.H. Smeets et al., above n. 59; A. van Teijlingen-Pover, above n. 145.

174 D.J.H. Smeets et al., above n. 59.

175 M. Fernando, above n. 79.

to participate and the positive effects of participation on their development. At the same time, the conditions should be designed in such a way that children are not harmed by participating in judicial proceedings.

Research has shown, however, that there are many barriers for professionals to include children in judicial decisions that concern them. Moreover, when children do participate in private family law proceedings, the conditions are not always sufficiently child-appropriate or child-friendly. Ways of enhancing children's effective participation have been discussed, such as providing sufficient information in a child-friendly manner, providing a safe and encouraging environment for children (such as a child-friendly physical environment and the opportunity to bring a child advocate or support person) and using skills to communicate with children in an age-appropriate fashion. The decisions about children that are made by judges, or other professionals, have far-reaching consequences (such as reduced contact with a parent or a change of residence). It is therefore important to consider the pedagogical conditions that will enable the child to participate effectively in the decision-making process. This will, in turn, increase the likelihood of positive effects on both the quality of the decision-making and the child's development and wellbeing.

PART II

CHILD PARTICIPATION IN PRIVATE INTERNATIONAL LAW

THE HAGUE CONVENTIONS AND EU INSTRUMENTS IN PRIVATE INTERNATIONAL LAW

Thalia Kruger and Francesca Maoli*

1. INTRODUCTION

In this chapter, we will explain the role of private international law instruments in seeking to ensure children's right to participation.

---

* This chapter is the result of a collaboration between both authors. Sections 2.2 and 2.3 are attributed to Thalia Kruger and sections 2.1, 3.1 and 3.2 are attributed to Francesca Maoli. The introduction and the conclusions are attributed to both authors. The authors wish to acknowledge their colleagues, with whom they participated in an EU-co-funded research project, VOICE: Laura Carpaneto and Giovanni Sciaccaluga (University of Genoa) and Sara Lembrechts, Tine Van Hof and Wouter Vandenhole (University of Antwerp). Many of the ideas in this chapter have been developed from our common research and conversations.

Private international law instruments most often do not impose direct duties to hear the child or do not address the opportunity or the methods for child participation in judicial proceedings. This branch of law addresses four issues: which court has jurisdiction to hear disputes linked to two or more legal systems, what the applicable law is, what the conditions for the recognition and enforcement of foreign judgments are, and how authorities can cooperate across borders to solve disputes between individuals. In other words, private international law comprises road signs pointing the way to the legal system within which a certain case should be settled, not detailed traffic rules. Therefore, how children should participate in proceedings is generally a matter for national procedural law.

The fundamental rights of the child must be respected in all actions concerning the child, transnational cases included. This includes children's right to participate in all proceedings concerning them. In this context, the borders between private international law and human rights law are slowly fading, in the sense that the second influences the functioning of the first.

Supranational legislators of private international law are not blind to the importance of child participation, especially when their instruments have as a fundamental objective the protection of the best interests of the child. As will become apparent in this chapter, legislation on private international law more and more frequently makes explicit reference to the protection of the fundamental rights of the child as a primary concern and (at the same time) as a principle inspiring the interpretation and application of its rules.

In this chapter we identify indirect duties and careful nudges by supranational legislators to better respect children's right to participation. This includes explaining the role of private international law instruments like the 1980 Hague Convention on the Civil Aspects of International Child Abduction, the 1996 Hague Child Protection Convention, the Brussels II*bis* and *ter* Regulations and maintenance conventions and Regulation.

2. CHILD PROTECTION

2.1. 1980 HAGUE CONVENTION ON THE CIVIL ASPECTS OF INTERNATIONAL CHILD ABDUCTION

One of the areas in which the issue of child participation has emerged is international child abduction, a phenomenon that has become one of the most important concerns for public institutions since the second half of the 20th century.[1] The 1980 Hague Convention on the Civil Aspects of International

1 L. Silberman, 'Co-Operative Efforts in Private International Law on Behalf of Children: The Hague Children's Conventions' (2006) 323 *Recueil des cours/Académie de droit international de la Haye* 261, 300.

Child Abduction (HCCA)[2] represents one of the oldest instruments adopted in the field of children's protection at the international level, predating by a few years the 1989 United Nations Convention on the Rights of the Child (UNCRC).[3] The 1980 Hague Convention has been, and continues to be, a great success. It is now in force in 101 states and still gaining adherents.[4] As concerns child participation, the approach of the Convention will be examined, taking into account the evolution in the interpretation of the original text due to the obligations arising from Article 12 UNCRC and to the influence of the case law of the European Court of Human Rights (ECtHR).

The Convention takes a unique approach to the problem of international child abduction,[5] providing – as a general rule – for the immediate return of the child to the state of habitual residence. At the same time, the Convention also gives relevance to the voice of the child in these proceedings, although in a limited and indirect way (section 2.1.1 below). Moreover, the legal framework of the Convention has to be interpreted in light of the evolutions in human rights law over the years, with particular reference to Article 12 UNCRC and the case law of the ECtHR. These evolutions (discussed in section 2.1.2 below) include the obligation to give the child the opportunity to be heard gradually becoming a principle of universal application:[6] reference is made here to the widespread ratification of the UNCRC (although with the notable exception of the United States), which makes it the most successful human rights treaty in the world. If courts apply the legal frameworks coherently, the desired result of child participation can be reached (section 2.1.3).

---

2 Hague Convention of 25 October 1980 on civil aspects of international child abduction, http://www.hcch.net. For a complete and in-depth analysis of the Convention, see P.R. Beaumont and P.E. McEleavy, *The Hague Convention on International Child Abduction*, Oxford University Press, Oxford 1999; R. Schuz, *The Hague Child Abduction Convention: A Critical Analysis*, Hart Publishing, Oxford 2013. On the topic see also C. Gonzalez Beilfuss, 'Child Abduction' in J. Basedow et al., *Encyclopedia of Private International Law*, Edward Elgar Publishing, Cheltenham 2017, pp. 297–304; M. Freeman, 'International Child Abduction: Is It All Back to Normal Once the Child Returns Home?' (2001) *International Family Law* 39; M. Freeman, 'International Family Mobility: Relocation and Abduction: Links and Lessons' (2013) *International Family Law* 41; T. Kruger, *International Child Abduction – The Inadequacies of the Law*, Hart Publishing, Oxford 2011; S Vigers, *Mediating international child abduction cases: the Hague Convention*, Hart Publishing, Oxford 2011.

3 United Nations Convention on the Rights of the Child, New York, 20 November 1989.

4 The updated status table of the Convention is available at: http://www.hcch.net.

5 L. Silberman, above n. 1, pp. 308, 465; W. Duncan, 'Conclusions on the Globalization of Child Law and the Role of the Hague Conventions' in S. Detrick and P. Vlaardingerbroek (eds.), *Globalization of Child Law: The Role of the Hague Conventions*, Martinus Nijhoff Publishers, The Hague 1999, p. 90.

6 In the words of Lady Hale in the House of Lords' decision *Re D (A Child) (Abductions: Rights of Custody)* [2006] UKHL 51, at [58]. See H. Stalford and K. Hollingsworth, 'Towards a Children's Rights-Based Approach to Judging Child's Objections Cases (2018) *The Judge's Newsletter on International Child Protection* 50.

2.1.1. *The HCCA's Provisions and Child Participation*

The summary return mechanism established by the Hague Convention has the aim of preventing and discouraging the removal or retention of a child under the age of 16 when this is wrongful as a result of the violation of rights of custody.[7] In the spirit of the Convention, the best interests of the child wrongfully removed or retained are better served through the prompt return to their country of habitual residence, considered as the place in which the child has settled and has their social and family ties.[8] The general rule of immediate return is subject to a limited number of exceptions.[9] The authorities of the state in which the child has been wrongfully conducted may refuse to order the return when: (i) more than one year has elapsed between the date of the abduction and the initiation of proceedings (Art. 12(1) HCCA); (ii) the child is settled in their new environment (Art. 12(2) HCCA); (iii) custody rights were not exercised at the time of the abduction and the abduction was consented to or acquiesced in (Art. 13(1)(a) HCCA); (iv) there is a grave risk that return would expose the child to physical or psychological harm or otherwise place the child in an intolerable situation (Art. 13(1)(b) HCCA); (v) the child objects to return and has attained an age and maturity at which it is appropriate to take these views into account (Art. 13(2) HCCA); or (vi) return would not be permitted by the protection of human rights and fundamental freedoms (Art. 20 HCCA).

The exception laid down by Article 13(2) is relevant for the scope of the current chapter[10] and will be discussed further. The first element that the court has to consider is whether the child has expressed an objection to return. It is interesting to note that the HCCA does not oblige courts to hear the child or even to investigate whether the child objects. It must merely take into account an objection of which it is aware. It can become aware of the objection through statements made by the parties or by the child themselves. The Convention in itself thus does not greatly enhance child participation.

---

7 Art. 3 of the 1980 Hague Convention.

8 On the concept of habitual residence T. Kruger, 'Habitual Residence: The Factors that Courts Consider' in P. Beaumont, M. Danov, K. Trimmings and B. Yüksel (eds.), *Cross-border litigation in Europe*, Hart Publishing, Oxford 2017, pp. 741 ff.; A. Fiorini, 'The Protection of the Best Interests of Migrant Children Through Private International Law and Habitual Residence', in F. Ippolito and G. Biagioni (eds.), *Migrant Children: Challenges for Public and Private International Law*, Editoriale Scientifica, Napoli 2016, pp. 379 ff.; E. Di Napoli, 'A place called home: Il principio di territorialità e la localizzazione dei rapporti familiari nel diritto internazionale privato post-moderno' (2013) *Rivista di Diritto Internazionale Privato e Processuale* 899, 907; R. Lamont, 'Habitual Residence and Brussels IIbis: Developing Concepts for European Private International Family Law' (2007) *Journal of Private International Law* 261.

9 Laid down in Arts. 12(2), 13 and 20.

10 See R. Schuz, above n. 2, p. 317; L.D. Elrod, '"Please Let Me Stay": Hearing the Voice of the Child in Hague Abduction Cases' (2011) 63 *Oklahoma Law Review* 663.

This ground for refusal applies when the child has attained an age and degree of maturity at which it is appropriate to take into account their views. Therefore, the second element that needs the attention of the court is the assessment of age and maturity. The Convention does not provide for a minimum age threshold[11] and does not give further indications on how to conduct the assessment. Therefore, the age and maturity test depends on the domestic law of each court considered and on the approach of the judge regarding the application of these parameters. Several studies have highlighted different approaches by courts according to the geographical area, the culture and the individual perception.[12]

As a third element in the decision-making process, even when it has been established that the child is of an age and degree of maturity at which it is appropriate to take account of their views, the court still has a certain degree of discretion regarding whether to order the return. Therefore, the child's objection does not automatically result in a rejection of the return application. In origin, this approach was perfectly integrated into the overall objectives and structure of the Convention. The ground for refusal on the basis of the objection by the child was inspired mainly by pragmatism and in order to avoid the return of children of 14 or 15 years old against their will.[13] However, the objection should now be seen in a context where the child's views have assumed a central role in the assessment of their best interests, including in return proceedings. Even if the latter are not concerned with the merits of custody rights – and do not have to take a final decision on the future of the child in respect of their best interests – the valorisation of the best interests principle within return proceedings has resulted in a more respectful consideration of the child's opinion. Thus, in exercising its discretion, the court should find a balance between the strict application of the ground for non-return and respect for the child's right to be heard, which does not imply that the opinion of the child should always be followed by the judge, but merely that the child's views should be carefully evaluated.

---

11 Due to the impossibility of establishing an age that could be valid in every situation: see E. Pérez-Vera, *Explanatory Report on the 1980 Hague Child Abduction Convention*, 1982, https://assets.hcch.net/docs/a5fb103c-2ceb-4d17-87e3-a7528a0d368c.pdf, para. 30. Indeed, the practice of courts in different countries concerning the hearing of children in general also shows that a common solution in this regard is unlikely to be found, it being understood that, when it comes to children, a case-by-case assessment is desirable.

12 R. Schuz, above n. 2, p. 349. For an extensive analysis of the topic, concerning 17 countries, see the research carried out by L. Carpaneto, T. Kruger W. Vandenhole, F. Maoli, S. Lembrechts, G. Sciaccaluga and T. Van Hof, within the EU-co-funded project VOICE, 'The VOICE of the child in international child abduction proceedings in Europe', JUST-AG-2016/JUST-AG-2016-02/764206. The research report (2018) can be consulted at: https://repository.uantwerpen.be/docman/irua/b0c972/157267.pdf See also H. Stalford, K. Hollingsworth and S. Gilmore, *Rewriting Children's Rights Judgments – From Academic Vision to New Practice*, Hart Publishing, Oxford 2017.

13 E. Pérez-Vera, above n. 11, §30.

Indeed, research has shown a wide divergence in the decisions of judges in refusing return orders on the basis of the child's objection. Firstly, the exception seems to be applied less frequently than the other grounds for non-return: as highlighted by Lowe and Stephens, among the decisions of non-return adopted in 2015, only 15% of applications were based on the child's objection under Article 13(2) of the Convention.[14] Even if the application of the provision at hand depends to a large extent on the age and maturity of the children involved and on the factual background of each individual case, this data may indicate that (i) judges are reluctant to hear children, (ii) children are heard but their objections are not taken in to account, or (iii) the children do not object to return. Moreover, different approaches among judges have been highlighted in terms of how to consider the weight which should be given to the child's views,[15] and of the role of the latter in interpreting the best interests of children involved in abduction procedures:[16] these considerations do not necessarily result in a negative impact on the situation of children, but may be an indicator of the inconsistent application of Article 13(2) of the Convention and of the principles enshrined in Article 12 UNCRC.

2.1.2. The HCCA under the Influence of Children's and Human Rights Law

Underlying the ground for refusal based on the child's objection, one can read a concern that the opinion of the child should be given due weight in accordance with their age and maturity.[17] Those proceedings are linked to the fundamental right of the child to be heard, as stated by Article 12 UNCRC and the European Convention for the Protection of Human Rights and Fundamental Freedoms (ECHR).

---

14 See N. Lowe and V. Stephens, *A statistical analysis of applications made in 2015 under the Hague Convention of 25 October 1980 on the Civil Aspects of International Child Abduction – Global report*, Prel. Doc. No 11 A of September 2017 – Part I, 3, 15, available on the official website of the Hague Conference on Private International Law: http://hcch.net. According to the research, 'In 2015, 243 applications ended in a judicial refusal. Some cases were refused for more than one reason and if all reasons are combined, the most frequently relied upon ground for refusal was Article 13(1)(b) (47 applications, 25%) and the child not being habitually resident in the Requested State (46 applications, 25%). Article 12 was a reason for refusal in 32 applications (17%) and the child's objections in 27 applications (15%).'

15 On this topic see the research of N.J. Taylor and M. Freeman, 'Outcomes for objecting children under the 1980 Hague Convention on the Civil Aspects of International Child Abduction' (2018) XXII(Summer-Fall) *The Judges' Newsletter* (Special Focus: The Child's Voice – 16 Years Later) 8–12.

16 See L. Carpaneto et al., above n. 12.

17 T. Kruger, above n. 2, p. 36; B. Ubertazzi, 'The Hearing of the Child in the Brussels IIa Regulation and its Recast Proposal' (2017) *Journal of Private International Law* 568, 583.

This is increasingly recognised by the (national and international) case law and the legal literature.[18]

The child's participation has a greater relevance than only assessing whether they actually object to returning. Their views may be relevant even if they do not object. They can help the court to determine their habitual residence or to verify the preconditions for the application of other grounds for non-return.[19] For instance, by talking to the child, a judge may be able to better assess whether the child would face a risk if returned. In addition, there might be beneficial effects that the hearing has on the child, and the corresponding harm that may result from excluding the child from participation, as revealed by recent research.[20]

In the EU, Article 24 of the Charter of Fundamental Rights (Charter)[21] echoes the UNCRC's participation right for children. The Charter applies when national courts or EU institutions have to apply EU law.[22] The HCCA has been drawn into EU law by the fact that the EU legislated on the matter (see the discussion of Brussels II*bis* in section 2.3.1 below).[23] Thus, when courts in EU Member States apply the HCCA, they have to also respect the Charter.

A different but equally relevant issue is the interaction with Article 8 ECHR and how it is interpreted by the ECtHR. The obligation to hear the child in return proceedings under the 1980 Hague Convention has become even more stringent in light of the different understanding of such proceedings by the ECtHR. Assessing alleged violations under Article 8 ECHR, the Court has required judicial authorities to conduct an effective examination of the situation of the child involved in each particular case, in order to also take into account the child's best interests in the context of return proceedings.[24]

---

18 UN Committee on the Rights of the Child, *General Comment No. 12: The Right of the Child to be Heard*, CRC/C/GC/12, 20 July 2009, https://www2.ohchr.org/english/bodies/crc/docs/AdvanceVersions/CRC-C-GC-12.pdf, §32.

19 See e.g. *Re LC (Children)* [2014] UKSC 1; Italian Corte di cassazione, sez. I, 5 December 2017, no. 29118.

20 On this topic see the contribution by D.J.H. Smeets and S. Rap in this Handbook.

21 The Charter entered into force on 1 December 2009, as part of the Treaty of Lisbon amending the Treaty on European Union and the Treaty establishing the European Community, signed at Lisbon, 13 December 2007, *OJ C* 306, 17 December 2007, 1.

22 This limitation is expressed in Art. 51 of the Charter.

23 See CJEU Opinion 2/13 of 14 October 2014, ECLI:EU:C:2014:2303.

24 The ECtHR in *Neulinger and Shuruk v Switzerland* [GC] (Appl. No. 41615/07), 6 July 2010, favoured an in-depth analysis of the child's best interests. This approach has been nuanced in *X v Latvia* [GC] (Appl. No. 27853/09), 26 November 2013, where the ECtHR explained how the best interests analysis can be done in the return procedure, even though this procedure

2.1.3. *Coherent Interpretation of the HCCA and Children's and Human Rights Instruments*

While Article 13(2) of the Hague Child Abduction Convention applies where the child objects to return and it prescribes the conditions under which the judge may take into account (but not necessarily follow) the child's views, Article 12 UNCRC states the general duty for the court to give, on its own initiative, the child the opportunity to be heard and explains how to take into consideration the child's perspective.[25]

Hearing the child – as well as the necessary procedural guarantees – may be difficult in the context of child abduction proceedings, where the court has to act expeditiously and must take a decision on (non-)return within six weeks.[26] Moreover, the court must refrain from entering into the merits of the case, as the court of the habitual residence of the child will decide on this.[27] Therefore, a tension may arise between the summary nature of return proceedings and the child's right to participate. How the judiciary deals with this tension varies significantly between states.[28]

The human rights standards that national courts must follow in addressing child abduction cases, as well as the duty to find a solution that is respectful of the child's best interests in each case, implies that the obligation to hear the child has become even more stringent and advisable, as underlined by the ECtHR itself in more recent judgments.[29] This is in line with the duty under the UNCRC.

In conclusion, we are of the view that a coherent interpretation of the HCCA with the UNCRC and, in the states where they apply, with the ECHR and the EU's Charter[30] guarantees children's participation rights. If all applicable legal

---

does not relate to the merits. On the topic P. McEleavy, 'The European Court of Human Rights and the Hague Child Abduction Convention: Prioritising Return or Reflection?' (2015) 62 *Netherlands International Law Review* 365; P. Beaumont, K. Trimmings, L. Walker and J. Holliday, 'Child Abduction: Recent Jurisprudence of the European Court of Human Rights' (2015) *International and Comparative Law Quarterly* 39.

25 On Art. 12 UNCRC and on child participation in other international human rights instruments see the contribution by M. Bruning and C. Mol in this Handbook. On the importance of the child's participation and views in international abduction proceedings, see also J. Tobin, N. Lowe and E. Luke, 'Article 11' in J. Tobin (ed.), *The UN Convention on the Rights of the Child: A Commentary*, Oxford University Press, Oxford 2019, p. 385; E. Sthoeger, 'International child abduction and children's rights: two means to the same end' (2011) *Michigan Journal of International Law* 511, 528; L.D Elrod, above n. 10; R. Schuz, 'The Hague Child Abduction Convention and Children's Rights' (2002) 12(2) *Transnational Law and Contemporary Problems* 393, 422–423.

26 Arts. 2 and 11 of the 1980 Hague Convention.

27 E. Pérez-Vera, above n. 11, §16.

28 L. Carpaneto et al., above n. 12, p. 86.

29 ECtHR *MK v Greece* (Appl. No. 51312/16), 1 February 2018, para. 75.

30 States outside Europe could rely on other human rights instruments to the same effect.

frameworks are respected, there is no need to amend the HCCA. The HCCA can be applied in a way that is respectful of children's participation rights.

2.2. 1996 HAGUE CHILD PROTECTION CONVENTION

The Hague Child Protection Convention of 1996[31] regulates private international law matters in child protection more generally, complementing the system of the HCCA. The Child Protection Convention took some time to gain support, but is now in force in 52 states, including all EU Member States.[32]

This Convention is a traditional private international law instrument concerned with jurisdiction, applicable law, recognition and enforcement, and cross-border administrative cooperation. Such cooperation includes for instance attempting to find amicable solutions for the protection of children in cross-border family conflicts, or assisting in finding the whereabouts of a child who might be in need of protection while present in a contracting state other than that of their habitual residence.[33] Like the HCCA, it was set up with the aim of protecting children.[34] The preamble affirms that the best interests of the child are a primary consideration and refers explicitly to the UNCRC.

The Hague Child Protection Convention mentions the child's right to be heard only once, in the chapter on recognition and enforcement:[35] if the child has not been given the opportunity to be heard, recognition and enforcement of the decision may be refused. The yardstick to apply this ground for refusal is the 'fundamental principles of procedure of the requested State'. This is a classical private international law approach: public policy as a ground for refusal also uses the fundamental principles of the requested state as yardstick. The Convention does not introduce or refer to an international standard for child participation. Such a standard would probably have been very difficult to agree on between the negotiators. It would also have gone beyond the mandate and core business of the Hague Conference on Private International Law.[36] However, the explicit reference to the child's right to participate in this manner is positive for the evolution of this right. The knowledge that a judgment may be refused recognition and enforcement serves as a reminder to judges to grant children

---

31 Hague Convention of 19 October 1996 on Jurisdiction, Applicable Law, Recognition, Enforcement and Co-operation in Respect of Parental Responsibility and Measures for the Protection of Children.

32 https://www.hcch.net/en/instruments/conventions/status-table/?cid=70.

33 Arts. 31 et seq. Hague Child Protection Convention.

34 See the Preamble of the Hague Child Protection Convention.

35 Art. 23(2)(b) Hague Child Protection Convention.

36 This intergovernmental organisation's purpose is the progressive unification of rules of private international law: see Art. 1 of its Statute, https://www.hcch.net/en/instruments/conventions/full-text.

the opportunity to be heard. It is not known whether the Convention in fact has this effect, although the similar provision in Brussels II*bis* does (see below). It furthermore encourages judges to express in their judgments whether the child has been given such opportunity and if not why not. This could lead to convergence on children's participation rights. Even if such development is slow, small steps forward are happening, as discussed in the next section.

2.3. EU REGULATIONS ON PARENTAL RESPONSIBILITY: BRUSSELS II*BIS* AND *TER*

In 2000 the European Union legislator moved into the area of international family law, first with the Brussels II Regulation,[37] replaced in 2003 by the Brussels II*bis* Regulation,[38] and in 2019 by the Brussels II*ter* Regulation.[39] Brussels II*ter* will enter into force on 1 August 2022.[40] This section therefore considers both Brussels II*bis* and *ter*. These pieces of EU legislation cover jurisdiction in cross-border matters and the recognition and enforcement of judgments on divorce and on parental responsibility, including international child abduction.[41] It will for instance determine whether a Spanish court can hear a dispute on where the children will live after their French and Spanish parents divorce.

*2.3.1. Brussels II*bis

Brussels II*bis* addresses child participation explicitly in two provisions. The first concerns international child abduction, on which the Regulation aimed to strengthen within the European Union the legal framework created by the HCCA.[42] One of the modifications that Brussels II*bis* made to child abduction law relates to the child's objection as a ground for refusal of return. Brussels II*bis*

---

37 Council Regulation 1347/2000 of 29 May 2000 on jurisdiction and the recognition and enforcement of judgments in matrimonial matters and in matters of parental responsibility for children of both spouses, *OJ L* 160, 30 June 2000, 19. This Regulation became fully applicable on 1 March 2001 (Art. 46).

38 Council Regulation 2201/2003 of 27 November 2003 concerning jurisdiction and the recognition and enforcement of judgments in matrimonial matters and the matters of parental responsibility, *OJ L* 338, 23 December 2003, 1. This Regulation has been applicable since 1 March 2005 (Art. 72).

39 Council Regulation 2019/1111 of 25 June 2019 on jurisdiction, the recognition and enforcement of decisions in matrimonial matters and the matters of parental responsibility, and on international child abduction, *OJ L* 178, 2 July 2019, 1.

40 Art. 105(2) Brussels II*ter*.

41 Art. 1 determines the scope of each Regulation. The first version, Brussels II, dealt only with parental responsibility disputes that were related to a divorce, while Brussels II*bis* and *ter* cover all cross-border parental responsibility disputes.

42 See P. McEleavy, 'The new child-abduction regime in the European Union: symbiotic relationship or forced partnership?' (2005) 1 *Journal of Private International Law* 5, 15.

provides that in child abduction cases the child must be given the opportunity to be heard '*unless* this appears inappropriate having regard to his or her age or degree of maturity' (emphasis added).[43] This is a different approach to that in the HCCA, where a court may refuse the return if the child objects '*if* it finds that the child objects to being returned and has attained an age and degree of maturity at which it is appropriate to take account of its views' (emphasis added).[44] Brussels II*bis* imposed a duty on courts to give children the opportunity to participate regardless of the fact that they object to return, which was not the case under the HCCA.

This duty in Brussels II*bis* is more of a reminder than a new obligation, as the UNCRC already imposes this duty on states.[45] However, a reminder in a piece of EU legislation has proved to be useful, as EU law is directly applicable in the Member States and judges receive training on it.

The second explicit reference to child participation in Brussels II*bis* is the same as that in the Hague Child Protection Convention (discussed above): the fact that the child has not been given the opportunity to be heard, in violation of the fundamental principles of the requested Member State, is a ground for refusal of recognition and enforcement.[46] This reference applies to all cases of parental responsibility, and is not restricted to child abduction cases. As explained above, this provision allows diversity in legal systems and does not harmonise child participation. However, it is an encouragement for courts to grant this opportunity to children or to explain why they have not heard the children involved. For instance, German law requires the participation of children from a very young age.[47] Judges often know this German requirement. Thus, when realising that their judgment might at a later stage require recognition in that country, they sometimes consider child participation more explicitly. If they do not hear the child, they have to explain the reasons why they did not hear them.[48]

Apart from these two rules, Brussels II*bis*'s recitals also make reference to the important role of hearing the child. This is qualified, however, by the statement that the Regulation does not aim to modify national procedures.[49] Such a specification is not surprising in a private international law Regulation, as procedural law mostly remains national. This concerns issues such as who hears the child (judges themselves or social or welfare workers who then report to the judge), where the child is heard (in open court or in the judge's chambers),

---

43 Art. 11(2) Brussels II*bis*.

44 Art. 13(2) Hague Child Abduction Convention; see the discussion above.

45 Art. 12 UNCRC, which applies to all EU Member States.

46 Art. 23(b) Brussels II*bis*.

47 See the chapter by N. Dethloff and D. Schröder on Germany in this Handbook.

48 See I. Viarengo and F. Villata (eds.), *Planning the Future of Cross Border Families: A Path through Coordination. Final Study*, http://www.eufams.unimi.it/wp-content/uploads/2017/12/EUFams-Final-Study-v1.0.pdf, p. 222.

49 Recital 19 Brussels II*bis*.

how the child is summoned or informed of the hearing and whether the child is afforded independent legal representation. The age at which a child is given the opportunity to be heard is a grey area. At first sight, an age requirement is a matter of national law. However, as is discussed in other chapters in this Handbook, there is relevant international law.

It should be recalled here, as noted above, that Member States have to abide by the Charter when implementing EU law.[50] The Charter provides that children may express their views freely and that those views 'shall be taken into consideration on matters which concern them in accordance with their age and maturity'.[51] This of course applies whenever Brussels II*bis* is applicable.

2.3.2. *Improvements Made by Brussels II*ter

Brussels II*ter* has taken various steps forward concerning children's rights.[52] It is relevant that this piece of legislation was drafted after the Charter came into existence. This means that the legislator knew that the new Regulation would operate under the auspices of the Charter. The initial proposal for the new Regulation, drafted by the European Commission, explicitly mentioned respect for the rights set out in the Charter.[53] Brussels II*ter*'s recitals mention not only the Charter,[54] but also the UNCRC[55] and the ECHR.[56] There is thus an explicit concern for children's rights from the legislator's side.

It is significant to note that the Brussels II*ter* Regulation was passed by unanimity in the Council (where all Member States are represented).[57] This shows that there was broad support for the solidification of children's rights, at least to the extent of the accepted amendments, discussed below.

The issues with the wording of the child's objection and whether the child must get the opportunity to be heard only *if* mature or *unless* not mature have been fixed. Brussels II*ter* uses the language of the UNCRC: courts must give children capable of forming their own views the opportunity to express those views and give due weight to these views in accordance with their age

---

50 Art. 51(1) Charter.

51 Art. 24(1) Charter.

52 See also L. Carpaneto, 'Impact of the Best Interests of the Child on the Brussels II ter Regulation' in E. Bergamini and C. Ragni, *Fundamental Rights and Best Interests of the Child in Transnational Families*, Intersentia, Cambridge 2019, pp. 265–286.

53 Commission's Proposal for the Recast of Brussels II*bis*, 30 June 2016, COM(2016) 411 final, p. 12.

54 Recitals 19, 39 and 71 Brussels II*ter*.

55 Recitals 19, 39, 71 and 84 Brussels II*ter*.

56 Recital 83 Brussels II*ter*.

57 Except for Denmark, which does not participate in this chapter of EU law. See Protocol No. 22 to the Treaty on the EU and to the Treaty on the Functioning of the EU on the position of Denmark, and Recital 96 Brussels II*ter*.

and maturity.[58] In other words, a court deciding whether to hear a child must assess the child's capability of forming their own views and not their maturity to form an opinion that should be taken into account for the decision.[59] Only when considering the weight that the court will give to the child's views do the age and degree of maturity become relevant.

The EU legislator has enhanced children's rights further by providing that the opportunity must be 'genuine and effective'.[60] The provision applies to all cases that fall within the scope of Brussels II*ter* and is not restricted to child abduction cases, as it was under Brussels II*bis*.

As under Brussels II*bis*, the EU legislator steered clear of national procedural law. The opportunity to be heard must be given 'in accordance with national law and procedure'. That law still determines whether the child is heard directly or indirectly. The European Parliament's Committee on Petitions for the Committee on Legal Affairs (PETI) was the only EU organ in the legislative procedure that proposed age limits.[61] This was not taken over by the European Parliament or in the text of the Regulation. As stated earlier, introducing an age limit is not only difficult in an international setting where negotiators from different legal systems have to agree, but also controversial.[62]

2.3.3. *What Brussels II*ter *did not Improve*

While taking several positive steps to enhance child participation, the EU legislator has removed the ground for refusal of recognition and enforcement in cases where the child has not been given the opportunity to be heard. The idea is that all Member States respect children's rights and trust each other to respect children's rights. From an EU law point of view, this makes sense, but its impact on children's rights on the ground remains to be seen. The previous ground for refusal did have some impact on child participation. In EUfams, an EU-co-funded research project, researchers found for instance that the Tribunal of Bolzano, in the north of Italy and close to the German border, was more inclined to hear small children due to the influence of the extensive child participation practices in Germany.[63] The Italian Central Authority moreover told the researchers that

---

58 Art. 21 Brussels II*ter*.

59 The issue of capability under the UNCRC has been discussed in the chapter of this Handbook by M. Bruning and C. Mol. See also S. Lembrechts, M. Putters, K. Van Hoorde, T. Kruger, K. Ponnet and W. Vandenhole, 'Conversations between children and judges in child abduction cases in Belgium and the Netherlands' *Family & Law*, February 2019, DOI: 10.5553/FenR/.000039.

60 Art. 21(1) Brussels II*ter*.

61 Opinion of the Committee on Petitions for the Committee on Legal Affairs, 15 January 2017, 2016/0190(CNS), proposed Amendment 18, pp. 13–14.

62 See the chapter by M. Bruning and C. Mol in this Handbook.

63 See I. Viarengo and F. Villata (eds.), above n. 48, p. 222.

abductions involving northern European countries were problematic and that there was a need in such cases to show that hearing the child was impossible.[64] The research report also indicates that 64% of surveyed experts responded 'yes' to the question whether 'a higher degree of harmonization at the EU level would prove useful in order to minimize the recourse of the ground of non-recognition provided in Article 23 (b).'[65]

Another element of concern is the so-called 'second chance procedure' or 'trumping order'. This is a custody procedure on the merits after an order for non-return in a child abduction case.[66] If the return is refused on the basis of the objection of the child, this is not the end of the matter. The court of the former habitual residence of the child maintains jurisdiction to decide on the custody dispute (i.e. with which parent and where the child will live in the future and what the contact arrangement with the other parent will be). This procedure encompasses an amendment to the mechanism of the HCCA and a different version of it was introduced by Brussels II*bis*.[67] Whether one regards this as a positive or a negative modification of the Hague system,[68] there is concern for child participation. It is not only the judge deciding on the return that will have to assess the child's objection, but the judge in the second chance procedure will have to do this again. The court has to make this assessment while the child is at that moment in a different country. The judge can use the Evidence Regulation to either organise a video conference with the child or ask a judge in the country where the child is present to hear the child and send a report or recording.[69] Asking a judge in the country where the child is might be a bit awkward, because a judge in that country might have already heard the child in the initial return proceedings and is now asked to do so again with the explicit object of achieving the opposite result.

Assessing the objection can be difficult, as the judge has to determine whether it is a true objection or merely a preference concerning where to live.

---

64 I. Viarengo and F. Villata (eds.), above n. 48, p. 222.

65 I. Viarengo and F. Villata (eds.), above n. 48, p. 222.

66 Art. 29 Brussels II*ter*.

67 Art. 11(6)–(8) Brussels II*bis*. Under this provision it was not explicit that second chance proceedings may only be custody proceedings. It might have been the initial intention of the legislator, but did not function in this way in practice.

68 For criticism of this procedure, see P. Beaumont, L. Walker and J. Holliday, 'Conflicts of EU Courts on Child Abduction: The Reality of Article 11(6)-(8) Brussels IIa proceedings across the EU', https://www.abdn.ac.uk/law/documents/CPIL_Working_Paper_No_2016_1.pdf; for a more positive view, see L. Carpaneto, 'In-depth Consideration of Family Life v Immediate Return of the Child in Child Abduction Proceedings within the EU' (2014) *Rivista di diritto internazionale privato e processuale*, 931, 943.

69 Council Regulation 1206/2001 of 28 May 2001 on cooperation between the courts of the Member States in the taking of evidence in civil or commercial matters, *OJ L* 174, 27 June 2001, 1. The Brussels II*bis* and II*ter* Regulations refer to the Evidence Regulation in their Recitals 20 and 39 respectively.

An objection falls within the ambit of the return procedure, while a preference is something that should be taken into account by the judge assessing the custody. This is a very fine line, which is difficult enough for judges and lawyers, but which they moreover have to explain to the child in order to respect participation rights fully. If children do not receive a proper explanation, they might get the impression that judges are not listening to them and that they have to tell the same story twice.[70]

All in all, with Brussels II*ter* the EU legislator has made important progress in the assurance of children's right to participation, but the legal framework is not yet perfect. It gives important nudges to national judges, but a lot is still in their hands. As explained above, private international law cannot encroach on national procedural law. The EU legislator is pushing the boundaries, and has done so in a good way. Whether subsequent versions of the Regulation will push further remains to be seen. But for now, the proof of the pudding is in the application of Brussels II*ter* as from August 2022.

3. MAINTENANCE

3.1. HAGUE CONVENTIONS AND PROTOCOL

The general obligation to enable children's participation in all proceedings affecting them, as stated by Article 12 UNCRC, is also relevant in the context of support and family maintenance. However, as in other contexts, it is always necessary to ascertain whether the matter under discussion 'affects' the child and, subsequently, that the child is capable of forming their own views. Under these conditions, Article 12 UNCRC also applies in cases of maintenance. This seems to be the position of the Committee on the Rights of the Child within the General Comment No. 12 to the UNCRC, which states that '[i]n cases of separation and divorce, the children of the relationship are unequivocally affected by decisions of the courts. Issues of maintenance for the child as well as custody and access are determined by the judge either at trial or through court directed mediation'.[71] It is not uncommon for issues on maintenance to heard by the court in the context of a family dispute in a broader sense, i.e. in the context of divorce, separation or parental responsibility: in this case, the participation of

70 See S. Lembrechts et al., above n. 59, giving this quote from an interview with a child: 'I mean, I could indeed say something to the judge, but I do not know what the judge will then say, he can say whatever he wants, isn't it.' See also K. Van Hoorde, M. Putters et al., 'Bouncing Back. The wellbeing of children in international child abduction cases', Research Report of the EU-co-funded research project EWELL, https://biblio.ugent.be/publication/8561029/file/8561030.pdf, p. 101.

71 General Comment No. 12, above n. 18, §51.

the child has its legal basis in the relevant legislation examined in the previous sections. Indeed, when considered as a part of the judicial determinations issued within a proceeding of this kind, a decision on maintenance contributes to affecting the child's living conditions, health, education or general well-being.

The Hague Convention of 2007 on child support and family maintenance[72] and the Hague Protocol on the law applicable to maintenance obligations[73] do not explicitly address the issue of child participation in legal proceedings. Indeed, the main objective of these instruments is to ensure the swift administration of maintenance obligations in cross-border cases, in particular when the creditor and debtor are in different countries. They focus on child support and seek to ensure respect for the best interests of the child.[74] For this purpose, the Convention and the Protocol aim at making effective the recovery of maintenance at the international level through accessible, efficient and cost-effective procedures and clear rules.[75]

The Convention has a general public policy ground for the refusal of recognition and enforcement.[76] Unlike the Hague Child Protection Convention discussed above, this provision does not explicitly refer to the child's participation rights. This silence is interesting: it does not mean that the fact that a child was not heard is excluded as a fundamental principle (a state would still be able to invoke it). The reason for the silence is not apparent.

In any event, it is for national law to determine the modalities and the conditions of child participation, while respecting the state's duties under the UNCRC.

3.2. MAINTENANCE REGULATION

The conclusions reached for the Hague Convention on 2007 and its Protocol are also valid for the Maintenance Regulation.[77] This Regulation does not contain

72 Hague Convention of 23 November 2007 on the International Recovery of Child Support and Other Forms of Family Maintenance, entered into force on 1 January 2013.

73 Protocol of 23 November 2007 on the Law Applicable to Maintenance Obligations, available at: http://www.hcch.net.

74 See the Preamble of the Convention, where it states that 'in all actions concerning children the best interests of the child shall be a primary consideration', as well as the *Explanatory Report* by A. Borrás and J. Degeling, 2013, §§36–41.

75 Preamble of the 2007 Hague Convention.

76 Art. 22(a) Hague Maintenance Convention.

77 Council Regulation 4/2009 of 18 December 2008 on jurisdiction, applicable law, recognition and enforcement of decisions and cooperation in matters relating to maintenance obligations, *OJ L* 7, 10 January 2009, 1. On the Regulation F. Gascón Inchausti, 'Le recouvrement des aliments en Europe' in M. Douchy-Oudout and E. Guinchard (eds.), *La justice civile europeénne en marche*, Dalloz, Paris 2012, p. 147; F.C. Villata, 'Obblighi alimentari e rapporti di famiglia secondo il regolamento n. 4/2009' (2011) *Rivista di Diritto Internazionale* 731; H. Muir Watt, 'Aliments sans frontiéres. Le reglément CE n° 4/2009

any specific reference to child participation in legal proceedings and it does not prescribe the duty for judicial authorities of the Member States to hear the child before issuing a decision on maintenance. It does not provide for a specific ground for refusal if the child was denied a right to participate.[78]

Nevertheless, national authorities are bound by Article 24 of the EU Charter of Fundamental Rights and thus have the duty to listen to children and take into consideration their views in accordance with their age and maturity. Indeed, Article 24 of the EU Charter has a broad scope of application and is relevant in every proceedings that affects the child. In any event, the decision of the European legislator to adopt a specific Regulation on maintenance obligations, separating the subject from the general legal framework provided for civil and commercial matters,[79] was motivated by (and resulted in) greater attention to the rights of the child. The Maintenance Regulation is inspired, inter alia, by the objective of protecting the child from the difficulties that may arise in the recovery of maintenance obligations within the European Union.[80] This means that the proceedings within the scope of the Regulation are subject to the legal framework that protects the best interests and the fundamental rights of the child, including the promotion of child's participation and the right of the child to express their opinion in matters affecting them.

Moreover, specific obligations concerning the child's participation may derive from other instruments applicable to a dispute on family issues as a whole.

4. CONCLUSION

This brief overview of private international law shows that while some international conventions and EU regulations make reference to child participation, few hard rules exist. Some instruments contain provisions that address possible grounds for refusal or they contain nudges for national courts to take into account the views of the child.

Private international law conventions and regulations do not function on their own: they interact with national law, especially procedural law.

du 18 décembre 2008 relatif à la compétence, la loi applicable, la reconnaissance et l'exécution des décisions et la coopération en matière d'obligations alimentaires' (2020) *Revue Critique du Droit International Privé* 457; P. Beaumont, B. Hess. L. Walker and S. Spancken (eds.), *The Recovery of Maintenance in the EU and Worldwide*, Hart Publishing, Oxford 2014.

78 Art. 24 of the Maintenance Regulation contains the grounds for refusal, but makes no mention of the child's right to participation.

79 Previously maintenance was covered by Council Regulation 44/2001 of 22 December 2000 on jurisdiction and the recognition and enforcement of judgments in civil and commercial matters, *OJ L* 12, 16 January 2001, 1.

80 An indication in this sense derives from Art. 4 of the Regulation, which excludes the possibility of concluding choice-of-court agreements in disputes relating to a maintenance obligation towards a child under the age of 18.

National law determines the modalities of how children will be made aware of the proceedings, how and by whom they will be listened to and whether they will have a right to separate legal representation.

Private international law instruments can cautiously move national procedural law in the right direction. They can for instance contain grounds for refusal if the child has not been heard. This can lead to a race to the top: if judges know that a judgment might be refused recognition in a state that takes a more stringent stance on child participation, they might consider such participation more carefully, and if they do not hear the child, at least explain why they do not.

Brussels II*ter*, which will only enter into force on 1 August 2022, has made significant progress: it contains a general obligation for courts to give the child the opportunity to be heard. The obligation is phrased in clear children's rights language. This is a step forward from older conventions and regulations that made children's right to participation conditional upon their age and maturity. The fact that the EU Member States all agreed on the amendments shows a great commitment to children's rights. It is appropriate that children will have the right to participate, with their age and maturity only becoming relevant when a court assesses the weight it will give to their views.

Some difficulties regarding guaranteeing child participation are particular to cross-border cases. Sometimes the judge is in a different country from the child. There are instruments that can be used to overcome this challenge, such as the Evidence Regulation. However, judges can be in a difficult position when they have to rely on colleagues in a different country who might have a different view on the case and children might find it strange that a judge in a different place decides about them.

Other difficulties regarding child participation are equally present in domestic procedures: gaining the trust of children, finding enough time for a meaningful conversation, showing children that they are really listened to and giving feedback. A cross-border element to a case might enhance such difficulties of trust and time.

Private international law instruments can regulate the cross-border elements and create incentives for better national procedures.

PART III

NATIONAL PERSPECTIVES

AUSTRALIA

Felicity Bell, Judy Cashmore and Joe Harman

1. INTRODUCTION

Australia is a large island continent with a relatively small population of approximately 26 million people. Children comprise just under 19% of the population, which is an aging one.[1] Approximately one in four children will experience the permanent separation or divorce of their parents.[2] Australia is an ethnically diverse nation with more than a quarter of the population born

[1] Australian Bureau of Statistics, *Australian Demographic Statistics*, June 2019 (3101.0). https://www.abs.gov.au/AUSSTATS/abs@.nsf/DetailsPage/3101.0Jun%202019.

[2] In 2018, 47.3% of divorces involved children (42,523 children): Australian Bureau of Statistics, *Marriages and Divorces, Australia, 2018*, Catalogue No. 3310.0, https://www.abs.gov.au/AUSSTATS/abs@.nsf/DetailsPage/3310.02018?OpenDocument; and 'Parental Divorce or Death during Childhood', *Australian Social Trends*, September 2010, Catalogue No. 4102.0, https://www.abs.gov.au/ausstats/abs@.nsf/lookup/4102.0main+features40sep+2010.

overseas.[3] Approximately 3% of the population are Aboriginal or Torres Strait Islander.[4]

Australia is a Federation, with six states and two territories. Pursuant to the Constitution, private family law matters (typically disputes between those having or seeking parental responsibility for children) are a Commonwealth responsibility and governed by the Family Law Act 1975 (Cth) (FLA). These matters are heard by the Family Court of Australia and the Federal Circuit Court of Australia (collectively 'the family law courts'). Care and protection matters (disputes between the carers of a child and the state) and adoption are a state and territory responsibility and dealt with in Children's Courts, or in the case of adoption, in the Supreme Court in some states.

In private law matters, children may be consulted in the course of negotiations between their parents on the arrangements and the amount of time they will spend with each parent; they might be interviewed by a counsellor and their views fed back to their parents in the course of mediation; they might have their views included in a family report; and they might be involved in the trial process as well, at least through having an independent lawyer to represent them, and also (though uncommonly in Australia) by having the opportunity to talk with the judge.

2. STATUTORY PROVISIONS

Children's wishes or views have typically been one of the factors that courts are required to consider in many jurisdictions in making determinations about children's welfare. The family law courts have jurisdiction over children's living arrangements in the event of the divorce or separation of their parents, including relocation matters, and international child abduction.[5] In determining a child's best interests under the FLA, the court is required to consider 'any views expressed by the child and any factors (such as the child's maturity or level of understanding) that the court thinks are relevant to the weight it should give to

[3] The 2016 census reported that the five most common birthplaces of those born overseas were England (14.7%), New Zealand (8.4%), China (8.3%), India (7.4%), and the Philippines (3.8%): Australian Bureau of Statistics, Census of Population and Housing: Reflecting Australia – Stories from the Census, 2016, 'Cultural Diversity in Australia, 2016', Catalogue No. 2071.0, https://www.abs.gov.au/ausstats/abs@.nsf/Lookup/by%20Subject/2071.0~2016~Main%20Features~Cultural%20Diversity%20Article~60.

[4] Australian Institute of Health and Welfare, 'Profile of Indigenous Australians', 11 September 2019, https://www.aihw.gov.au/reports/australias-welfare/profile-of-indigenous-australians.

[5] Family Court only. The Hague Convention on the Civil Aspects of International Child Abduction is incorporated into Australian law by way of the Family Law (Child Abduction Convention) Regulations 1986 (Cth) made pursuant to FLA s 111B.

the child's views'.[6] A means of appointing a legal representative for children has always been provided for under the FLA.[7]

The totality of the Convention on the Rights of the Child 1989 (UNCRC), which Australia ratified in 1990, is incorporated as an 'additional object' of the FLA.[8] Consistent with Article 12 of the UNCRC, children have a right to be heard in judicial proceedings affecting them.[9] In determining what is in a child's best interests, a court is entitled to take into account any view expressed by a child. The weight that is 'attached to a child's views is subject to any factors (such as the child's maturity or level of understanding) that the court thinks are relevant'.[10]

Mechanisms enabling the child's voice to be heard in court proceedings are generally limited to one or both of:

- The appointment of an Independent Children's Lawyer (ICL) to represent the child's best interests.[11] An ICL must advance the child's views[12] but is not bound by them;
- The preparation of reports by court-employed Family Consultants[13] or external report writers.[14] Such reports typically include interviews with and observations of children, and report as to their views and the weight to be attached to those views.[15]

However, a child cannot be required to express his or her views in relation to any matter.[16]

Research has generally found that ICLs are more focused on obtaining and presenting evidence of children's views rather than facilitating direct participation.[17] As explained below, while it is possible for children to directly participate in proceedings as parties in their own right or through judicial

6 FLA s 60CC(3)(a).
7 Family Law Act, No. 53 of 1975, s 65 (the original provision).
8 FLA s 60B(4).
9 Art. 12 of the UN Convention on the Rights of the Child; United Nations Committee on the Rights of the Child, *General Comment No. 12, The Right of the Child to be Heard*, CRC/C/GC/12, 20 July 2009, https://www2.ohchr.org/english/bodies/crc/docs/AdvanceVersions/CRC-C-GC-12.pdf. For a comprehensive commentary, see L. Lundy, J. Tobin and A. Parkes, 'Article 12. The Right to Respect for the Views of the Child' in J. Tobin (ed.), *United Nations Convention on the Rights of the Child. A Commentary*, Oxford University Press, Oxford 2019.
10 FLA s 60CC(3)(a).
11 FLA s 68L.
12 FLA s 68LA(5)(b).
13 FLA ss 11F and 62G.
14 Family Law Rules 1984, pt 15; Federal Circuit Court Rules 2001, r 15.
15 FLA s 60CD. See below section 3.2.
16 FLA s 60CE.
17 See further section 4 below.

meetings, these modes of participation are rare and, in relation to judicial meetings, have been cautioned against.[18]

A child's views are only one element for the court to consider as part of the best interests determination. For all children, other considerations include factors such as ensuring, where possible, that children maintain a meaningful relationship with both their parents and that children are protected from harm.[19] In relation to Aboriginal and Torres Strait Islander children, the court must also consider the child's rights to maintain, explore and develop a positive appreciation for his or her culture with people of that culture.[20] This may necessitate the use of report writers who are themselves Indigenous or have some expertise in relation to Indigenous families.[21] Indigenous children and families tend to be under-represented in private family law proceedings[22] and over-represented in care and protection matters.[23]

Finally, children's views may be considered, in limited circumstances, within international child abduction proceedings which also fall within the jurisdiction of the Family Court of Australia. The Hague Convention on the Civil Aspects of International Child Abduction is incorporated into Australian law.[24] As proceedings pursuant to the Convention are primarily concerned with returning children to the country deemed the most appropriate forum to determine parenting matters, children's ability to be heard is more circumscribed. Their views will likely be sought where the parent resisting return claims that the child or children have an unusually strong objection to return.[25] An ICL is only to be appointed in such matters in 'exceptional circumstances'.[26]

---

18 D. Bryant, 'Children's Participation in Decision Making in Relation to their Post Separation Living Arrangements', Australian Institute of Family Studies Conference, 30 July 2014. The current Chief Justice of the Family Court/Chief Judge of the Federal Circuit Court has not had cause to make any comment on this issue.

19 FLA s 60CC.

20 FLA s 60CC(6).

21 S. Ralph, *Indigenous Australians and Family Law Litigation: Indigenous perspectives on access to justice*, Commonwealth of Australia, October 2011, pp. 32–33. See below section 3.2.

22 S. Ralph, above n. 21, p. 9 (Table 1) (1–2.3% of applications for final orders involved an Indigenous party in the years 2004–2011).

23 For instance, Aboriginal and Torres Strait Islander children comprised 36.9% of children placed in out-of-home care (OOHC) in 2016/2017, yet only 5.5% of the total population of children: Australian Institute of Family Studies, 'Children in care', September 2018, https://aifs.gov.au/cfca/publications/children-care. The national rate of Indigenous children in OOHC is more than 10 times that of non-Indigenous children: Australian Institute of Health and Welfare, *Child protection Australia 2016–2017*, Child Welfare Series No. 68, 2018.

24 See above n. 5.

25 Family Law (Child Abduction Convention) Regulations 1986 (Cth), reg. 16(3)(c) (Art. 13.2 of the Hague Convention).

26 FLA s 68L(3).

3. MODES OF CHILD PARTICIPATION

3.1. OUT-OF-COURT OPPORTUNITIES

Outside of court proceedings, the extent of a child's participation in decision-making is determined by the persons with parental responsibility for the child. Subject to any court order in force, the people with parental responsibility for a child are typically the child's parents.

The FLA requires that parents consider participating in Family Dispute Resolution (FDR) or mediation prior to commencing court proceedings.[27] However, the actual rate of attendance at FDR prior to court filing would seem to be low.[28] In certain cases, such as those involving allegations of family violence or child abuse, parties are exempted from attendance.[29]

FDR may comprise 'child-inclusive' as well as 'child-focused' processes. In child-inclusive processes, the child participates in FDR by meeting with and being represented in the FDR process by a child consultant. The role of the child consultant is to meet with the child, explore the child's views and feelings about their living and visiting arrangements, and discuss how and what the consultant can feed back to the parents from their conversation or activities. Child-inclusive practice can occur only with parental consent and generally involves school-aged children. The aim is 'not to ascertain the "wishes" of the children but to explore more widely their perspectives and experiences of the current living and visiting arrangements and the conflict between the parents, as well as their hopes for the future'.[30] Child-focused mediation does not directly include children, but involves group parental educational sessions to help parents reflect upon their children's needs and experiences as a result of the changed living arrangements and circumstances as a result of the parents' separation from each other.

3.2. INDIRECT FORMS OF PARTICIPATION: EXPERT REPORTS

Where court proceedings have commenced, an expert's report may be prepared by a social science trained professional, most frequently a psychologist, on the family situation, making recommendations about what he or she considers is in the best interests of the child.

---

27 FLA s 60I.

28 J. Harman, 'The intersection of family violence and family dispute resolution: Implications for evidence gathering and mediation confidentiality' (2019) 33(1) *Australian Journal of Family Law* 1–28.

29 FLA s 60I(9)(b).

30 F. Bell, J. Cashmore, P. Parkinson and J. Single, 'Outcomes of Child-Inclusive Mediation' (2013) 27(1) *International Journal of Law, Policy and the Family* 116–142.

Family Consultants are based within the courts, though external private practitioners may also fill their role.[31] They may undertake child and family assessments and, if directed by the court, prepare 'Family Reports'.[32] One study reported that a Family Report was on file in 23% of children's cases judicially determined or settled by consent after proceedings had commenced.[33]

The court can decide to involve a Family Consultant at any time in the proceedings and can at any time (though this usually occurs at an early stage) order parties to attend a meeting with the consultant.[34] There are different types of meeting: a Child Dispute Conference (in which only adults are present); or a Child Inclusive Conference (in which children are seen, though separately from their parents).[35] In the Family Court, a Child Responsive Report may also be used: though not a full assessment, this report by the Family Consultant is intended to flag issues for the judicial officer and prioritise children's needs. The court may also order a Family Consultant to supervise compliance with an order once made.[36]

Family Reports, when ordered, address inter alia children's views, though a child cannot be required to express a view to the Family Consultant.[37] This prohibition applies notwithstanding that, in preparing reports, Family Consultants are required to 'ascertain the views of the child in relation to that matter and include the views of the child on that matter in the report'.[38] Communications between Family Consultants and children are not confidential.[39]

If a case raises issues that are beyond the expertise of a Family Consultant, an independent expert, such as a psychiatrist or other specialist, may be engaged to prepare a report in addition to, or instead of, a Family Report.[40] While Family Consultants are allocated to a matter, independent experts are usually agreed upon by the parties and the ICL and appointed by consent, though the court appoints them.

---

31 Federal Circuit Court Rules 2001 (Cth), rr 15.09, 23.01A; Family Law Rules 2004 (Cth), pt 15.5; FLA s 11B. Private counsellors or psychologists may be appointed to fill this role pursuant to the Family Law Regulations 1984 (Cth), reg. 7.

32 FLA ss 62G or 55A(2). See also s 11A; Family Law Courts, 'Fact Sheet: Family Consultants'; M. Foster, 'The Powers and Responsibilities of the Family Consultant' (2011) 21(3) *Australian Family Lawyer* 16–19.

33 R. Kaspiew, R. Carson, S. Moore, J. De Maio, J. Deblaquiere and B. Horsfall, *Independent Children's Lawyers Study: Final Report*, Australian Institute of Family Studies, May 2013, p. 36 (Box 2).

34 FLA ss 69ZS, 11F.

35 Following these meetings, the Family Consultant would prepare a memorandum for the Court.

36 FLA s 65L(1)(a).

37 FLA s 60CE.

38 FLA s 62G(3A).

39 FLA s 11C(1).

40 Family Law Rules 2004 (Cth), pt 15.5; Federal Circuit Court Rules 2001 (Cth), r 15.09.

3.3. REPRESENTATION FORMS OF PARTICIPATION: INDEPENDENT CHILDREN'S LAWYERS

Lawyers titled Independent Children's Lawyers may be appointed by court order, with the Legal Aid Commission (LAC) in the relevant state or territory administering the appointment. ICLs may be employed by the LAC or be private family lawyers who have undertaken training in child representation. They are remunerated by the LAC, though some of these costs can be sought from the parties in limited circumstances. Appointment of an ICL has never been across the board: the types of cases in which they should be appointed has been the subject of court guidance[41] but is left to judicial officers and/or the LAC, which determines whether appointment will be funded.[42]

The qualifications needed to become an ICL vary from state to state, but generally involve a minimum of five years' experience as a lawyer working predominantly in family law and attendance at ICL training In some states additional qualifications may be set.[43] The ICL's appointment ceases only when the initiating application is determined or withdrawn; or, if there is an appeal, when the appeal is determined or withdrawn;[44] or if discharged by the court. A child cannot remove his or her ICL.[45] The court can to some extent control and direct the ICL in relation to certain events and judicial officers can also complain about ICLs to Legal Aid or the legal services regulatory body.

ICLs are 'best interests' representatives. The FLA contains statements that the ICL is *not* the representative of the child and is *not* bound to act on the child's instructions.[46] However, the ICL 'must … ensure that any views expressed by the child in relation to the matters to which the proceedings relate are fully put before the court'.[47] As with expert reports, though, the child cannot be required to express a view.[48] However, both ICLs and Family Consultants must ensure that any views expressed by a child in relation to the matters to which the proceedings relate are fully put before the court.[49] This is so, as regards ICLs, notwithstanding that an ICL is not under an obligation, and cannot be required,

41 *Re K* (1994) FLC 92-461, 80,773–80,775.
42 *Re JJT; Ex parte Victoria Legal Aid* (1998) 195 CLR 184.
43 See e.g. Victoria Legal Aid, 'Independent Children's Lawyer Panel Information Package', https://www.legalaid.vic.gov.au/sites/www.legalaid.vic.gov.au/files/vla-independent-children s-lawyer-panel-information-package-accessible-jan-2019.docx.
44 Family Law Rules 2004, r 8.02(5).
45 *Dylan & Dylan* [2007] FamCA 842 (21 August 2007) [187].
46 FLA s 68LA.
47 FLA s 68LA(5)(b).
48 FLA s 60CE.
49 FLA s 68LA(5)(b) for ICLs and s 62G(3A) in relation to Family Consultants.

to disclose to the court any information that the child communicates to the ICL.[50] These provisions potentially create ethical difficulties as they require that a child be effectively cautioned before any discussion, placing the child in a position where they must safeguard their own confidentiality and determine for themselves what is 'safe' for them to disclose.

Whether or not ICLs meet with the children for whom they are appointed varies based on local practices. In Queensland, South Australia and Western Australia, for example, meeting children is seen as the role of the expert or Family Consultant, rather than the ICL.[51]

3.4. DIRECT FORMS OF PARTICIPATION

3.4.1. *Judicial Meeting with the Child*

As noted, it is possible for a child to meet with the judicial officer who is determining proceedings. That this occurs infrequently is, no doubt, informed by considerations of due process that require any such meeting be 'transparent' and the content of what transpires be disclosed to the parties.[52] Judges are generally reluctant to meet with children, citing concerns about due process[53] and about their expertise to do so. Further, a focus upon forensically gathering evidence of the child's views by commissioning a report from a Family Consultant or other expert is generally seen by judges as preferable to or obviating against the need for such meetings. There are, however, instances in which judges have detailed the process they used when meeting with children and noted that such meetings have tended to be desired by the children.[54]

3.4.2. *Child Litigating on Own Behalf*

The FLA has always provided that a child has standing to bring parenting proceedings.[55] In the 2003 case *B v Minister for Immigration*, children held in immigration detention commenced proceedings (by their mother as next friend)

50 FLA s 68LA(6). Subsection (7) permissively allows an ICL to disclose anything communicated by the child if the ICL considers this disclosure to be in the child's best interests. The FLA provides no guidance as to the criteria that might be considered in forming such a view and the disclosure may be made by the ICL against the child's wishes (subsection (8)).

51 R. Kaspiew et al., above n. 33, pp. 43, 47–49, 55 (Table 3.6).

52 See J. Harman, above n. 28 and M. Fernando, 'Proposed Guidelines for Judges Meeting with Children in Family Law Proceedings' (2012) 2 *Family Law Review* 213–224.

53 *R v Kirby; Ex parte Boilermakers' Society of Australia* (1956) 94 CLR 254.

54 See e.g. R. Benjamin, 'Judges Receiving Evidence Directly from Children' (2012) 2 *Family Law Review* 99–107; *Duffy v Gomes No. 2* (2015) FCCA 1757 (21 May 2015).

55 FLA s 65C(b).

seeking they be released in furtherance of their best interests.[56] In two, more recent, cases, female children represented by the LAC commenced proceedings under the FLA seeking that they be placed on the Airport Watch List, in order to prevent their families taking them overseas for the purpose of marriage.[57]

These cases can, however, be regarded as extraordinary. Australian courts have generally held that it is undesirable for children to be joined as parties or directly participate in their parents' family law dispute, though this has occurred.[58] As parties, children have access to relevant documents and evidence. A child may also appeal from a decision to which they were a party, though not otherwise. There are court filing fees, but a child would usually qualify for an exemption on the basis of not being employed.

In 2012, four children brought an application to Australia's highest court challenging a Family Court decision which had determined they should not have a case guardian appointed to represent them 'directly'.[59] Rejecting their application, the High Court clarified that there is no recognised right on the part of children to be 'directly' represented (nor to have an ICL appointed). The case in question involved proceedings pursuant to the Hague Convention on the Civil Aspects of International Child Abduction, but it seems likely that this applies also to other family law proceedings.[60]

4. RESEARCH

There is a substantial body of research in Australia conducted over the last 20 years by the Australian Institute of Family Studies (an independent, government-funded research body), and by academics, in relation to children's views and experiences of parents' and judicial decision-making as well as the role of ICLs. Research has also explored the views of parents, mediators, lawyers, counsellors and judges about the best ways to involve children. A consistent finding in this research, and consistent too with international research, is that children generally want their views to be heard and taken into account in decisions affecting them – as long as this does not upset their parents or jeopardise their relationship with them.[61] Children's concerns about being caught in the middle

---

56 *B v Minister for Immigration and Multicultural and Indigenous Affairs* (2003) 199 ALR 604 (Nicholson CJ and O'Ryan J). This decision was overturned by the High Court of Australia: *Minister for Immigration and Multicultural and Indigenous Affairs v B* (2004) 206 ALR 130.

57 *Kandal v Khyatt* (2010) 43 Fam LR 344; *Madley* (2011) FLC 94-000.

58 E.g. *Pagliarella* (1993) FLC 92-40.

59 *RCB as Litigation Guardian of EKV, CEV, CIV and LRV v Hon Justice Colin James Forrest* (2012) 247 CLR 304 (*RCB v Forrest*).

60 *RCB v Forrest* (2012) 247 CLR 304, 321 (French CJ, Hayne, Crennan, Kiefel and Bell JJ).

61 J. Cashmore and P. Parkinson, 'Children's and Parents' Perceptions on Children's Participation in Decision Making after Parental Separation and Divorce' (2008) 46(1)

of a dispute between their parents were also expressed by parents, lawyers, and non-legal professionals.[62] These same groups have also expressed concerns about undue pressure on children and the possible manipulation of their views, and the difficulty of determining the 'authentic' view of the child. These concerns can act as barriers to children being involved as they would wish to be.[63]

While children involved in mediation and in contested matters were often not clear which professionals they had engaged with, some children indicated that those professionals had acknowledged their views and that they had been helpful in facilitating their input into the decision-making process.[64] A substantial proportion of children, however, were unsure whether report writers or their ICL had accurately 'represented' their views in court or that it had had any effect. Some were disappointed that their views had been 'interpreted' or misinterpreted, or distressed by what they saw as a betrayal of trust when parents were upset or angry by what children were reported to have said in reports.[65]

A recent survey of 55 children and young people aged seven to 16 in one state (NSW), following their meeting with the ICL, indicated a higher level of trust and satisfaction with ICLs, with most children reporting that they generally felt listened to and heard, and trusted their lawyer to speak for them. They were less sure about the lawyer having told them about the limits of confidentiality and checking what was OK for them to say in court.[66] This survey was part of a comprehensive legal education process for lawyers in NSW representing children in family law and also in care and protection matters, to overcome lawyers' reluctance to meet with the children they

---

Family Court Review 91–104; A. Graham and R. Fitzgerald, 'The Changing Landscape of Family Law: Exploring the Promises and Possibilities for Children's Participation in Australian Family Relationship Centres' (2010) 53 *Family Matters* 53–60; J. Lodge and M. Alexander, *Views of Adolescents in Separated Families: A Study of Adolescents' Experiences after the 2006 Reforms to the Family Law System,* Australian Institute of Family Studies, Melbourne 2010; L. Qu and R. Weston, 'Children's views about parental separation' in *The Longitudinal Study of Australian Children Annual Statistical Report 2014,* Australian Institute of Family Studies, Melbourne 2015, pp. 13–37.

62 J. Cashmore and P. Parkinson, above n. 61; P. Parkinson and J. Cashmore, *The Voice of a Child in Family Law Disputes*, Oxford University Press, Oxford 2008.

63 F. Bell, 'Barriers to Empowering Children in Private Family Law Proceedings' (2016) 30 *International Journal of Law, Policy and the Family* 225–247.

64 R. Carson, E. Dunstan, J. Dunstan and D. Roopani, *Children and Young People in Separated Families: Family Law System Experiences and Needs*, Australian Institute of Family Studies, Melbourne 2018, pp. 44, 92: about a third of the 61 children and adolescents in this study could recall engaging with Family Consultants or report writers (20/61), and half of them indicated that their views had not been acknowledged in the process.

65 R. Carson et al., above n. 64; P. Parkinson and J. Cashmore, above n. 62.

66 D. Anderson, A. Graham, J. Cashmore, F. Bell, K. Beckhouse and M. Alex, *Legal Aid NSW Independent Children's Lawyers: Survey of Children and Young People*, Southern Cross University, 2016.

represent and some of the difficulties in talking with and facilitating children's participation.[67]

Children involved in contested matters where there were high levels of conflict or violence were more likely to want their views to be heard directly by the judge, without interpretation, even though most had already engaged with a Family Consultant/report writer and had an independent child lawyer.[68] Yet judges in Australia are, as noted, generally reluctant to speak with children because of their concerns about due process and transparency, their expertise and training to do so, and the impact on children or their family relationships.[69]

There are two marked gaps in Australian research in relation to children's participation in family law decision-making. The first concerns children's involvement in out-of-court processes and particularly mediation and alternative dispute resolution processes. Child-focused and child-inclusive mediation has been operating in Australia for over a decade, but there has been no independent research to evaluate children's satisfaction with the processes or, importantly, the appropriateness of the arrangements and outcomes for children and their families. The second concerns the preparation of Family Reports. The FLA and privacy law as well as ethical constraints[70] have restricted research on Family Reports, in contrast with the research on custody assessments in the United States.[71] There has been no systematic research in Australia on the methods, substance and quality of these family and expert reports and the extent to which they influence judicial determinations, though they are allegedly very influential and were rated positively in general terms by family lawyers, ICLs, judicial officers and psychologists in one study.[72] Some of the children and parents in

67 K. Beckhouse, 'Laying the Guideposts for Participatory Practice: Children's Participation in Family Law Matters' (2016) 98 *Family Matters* 26–33; F. Bell, above n. 63; N. Ross, 'Children's Lawyers: "Seeing" Children' (2013) 3 *New Zealand Law Review* 409–427.

68 P. Parkinson and J. Cashmore, above n. 61.

69 P. Parkinson and J. Cashmore, 'Judicial Conversations with Children in Parenting Disputes: The Views of Australian Judges' (2007) 21 *International Journal of Law, Policy and the Family* 160–189; M. Fernando, 'Children's Direct Participation and the Views of Australian Judges' (2013) 92 *Family Matters* 41–47.

70 R. Carson et al., above n. 64, reported that the ethical requirements of six different ethics committees which imposed strict age limits and a 12-month waiting period from the date of finalising any proceedings constrained children's participation in their study and caused disappointment and distress for children and young people excluded from the study 'arising from the screen-outs due to age and stage of proceedings' (p. 11). The selection bias in participants is an ongoing concern in research in this area.

71 L. Drozd, M. Saini and N. Olesen, *Parenting Plan Evaluations: Applied Research for the Family Court,* 2nd ed., Oxford University Press, Oxford 2016; J. Zumbach and U. Koglin, 'Psychological Evaluations in Family Law Proceedings: A Systematic Review of the Contemporary Literature' (2015) 46(4) *Professional Psychology: Research and Practice* 221–234.

72 A.T. O'Neill, K. Bussey, C.J. Lennings and K.M. Seidler, 'The Views of Psychologists, Lawyers, and Judges on Key Components and the Quality of Child Custody Evaluations in Australia' (2018) 56(1) *Family Court Review* 64–78.

Carson et al.'s study, however, were discomfited by the artificiality of the context and the process, particularly being observed by people behind a glass screen in a one-off, unnatural environment.[73] Moreover, a majority of Indigenous participants in one study were critical of the Family Report writer's capacity to deal with Indigenous cultural issues.[74]

5. CONCLUSION

The Family Law jurisdiction in Australia has been the subject of significant and ongoing review since its introduction in 1975, when children's participation and their views, as opposed to considerations of their 'best interests' in parental disputes, were largely absent from thinking and processes. In an explicit recognition of this change, section 60B(4) of the FLA was amended in 2011, in a somewhat awkwardly worded statement, to include as an 'additional object' of the Act 'to give effect to the Convention on the Rights of the Child done at New York on 20 November 1989'.[75] A recent, extensive review of the jurisdiction by the Australian Law Reform Commission (ALRC) in its final report indicates, however, that there is still some way to go to give real effect to this object in relation to Article 12 of the UNCRC.[76] Citing a number of submissions to the inquiry and the report by Carson et al., the ALRC concluded that children's and young people's

> desire to participate is often not realised. The [Carson et al. study] found that, for a substantial proportion of children and young people:
>
> *the approaches adopted by the service professionals with whom they interacted operated in a way that limited their practical impact or effectively marginalised the child or young person's involvement in decision making about parenting arrangements.*[77]

This conclusion was supported by an influential submission by the Australian Human Rights Commission and the Children's Commissioner, which stated that:

> The National Children's Commissioner has received numerous representations from children and young people, and their advocates, about failures by courts and agencies

---

73 R. Carson et al., above n. 64, pp. 55–56, 93.

74 S. Ralph, above n. 21, p. 32.

75 Family Law Legislation Amendment (Family Violence and Other Measures) Act 2011.

76 Australian Law Reform Commission, 'Family Law for the Future – An Inquiry into the Family Law System', ALRC Report 135, Commonwealth of Australia 2019, https://www.alrc.gov.au/wp-content/uploads/2019/08/alrc_report_135_final_report_web-min_12_optimized_1-1.pdf.

77 Australian Law Reform Commission, above n. 76, 12.29; citing R. Carson et al., above n. 64.

> within the family law system to solicit their views in the context of decision making, and to provide them with accessible information about processes and outcomes.[78]

Concerns also relate to out-of-court processes and family services, and systems responses. The ALRC recommended that:

> The Family Law Council should establish a Children and Young People's Advisory Board in order to receive feedback on children's experiences of the family law system and incorporate children's views into policy and practice development.[79]

In its recent Concluding Observations for Australia, the UN Committee on the Rights of the Child also recommended that Australia should:

> Amend the Family Law Act of 1975 (Cth) to provide all children, in accordance with their age and maturity, the opportunity to have their views heard in all matters concerning them, including in 'non-court based family services'.[80]

A response is yet to be provided by government to the ALRC report or to the UN Committee's recommendations. Further, ongoing inquiries into the family law system and other changes to the court are unlikely to do anything positive as regards the child's voice.[81]

---

78 Australian Law Reform Commission, above n. 76, para. 12.31.

79 Australian Law Reform Commission, above n. 76, para. 13.2.

80 UN Committee on the Rights of the Child, *Concluding Observations on the Combined Fifth and Sixth Periodic Reports of Australia*, CRC/C/AUS/CO/5-6, 30 September 2019, https://tbinternet.ohchr.org/Treaties/CRC/Shared%20Documents/AUS/CRC_C_AUS_CO_5-6_37291_E.pdf. See also Australian Child Rights Taskforce, *Australia's NGO Coalition report to the United Nations Committee on the Rights of the Child*, UNICEF Australia, November 2018.

81 In September 2019, a Joint Select Committee on Australia's Family Law System was established (see https://www.aph.gov.au/Parliamentary_Business/Committees/Joint/Family_Law_System/FamilyLaw). The Committee published its first report in December 2020 and Parliament has recently agreed to extend the presentation of the final report until 30 June 2021. In addition, on 17 February 2021, the Australian Parliament passed the Federal Circuit and Family Court of Australia Bill 2019, and its supplementary legislation, allowing for the merger of the Federal Circuit Court and the Family Court to create the Federal Circuit and Family Court of Australia (FCFC). This move has been strongly and widely criticised by former judges, legal experts and the law Council of Australia.

BELGIUM

Ingrid BOONE, Charlotte DECLERCK and Eva VERTOMMEN

1. INTRODUCTION

This chapter provides an overview of child participation in the legal context of post-separation family proceedings according to Belgian law. In the Belgian family justice system, disputes during or after a separation or divorce in which children are involved fall under the competence of the family courts.[1] The family courts consist of family chambers and chambers of friendly settlement, in which the judge seeks to bring the parties to an agreement. The family courts are

[1] Belgium is a federal state, with a complex institutional structure. It is divided into three regions (the Flemish Region, the Walloon Region and the Brussels-Capital Region) and into three communities (the Flemish Community, the French-speaking Community and the German-speaking Community). Family law and judicial law fall under the competence of the federal legislature.

competent for a variety of matters, which include adoption and filiation matters, proceedings concerning parental authority, residence arrangements, contact with the child and alimony.[2]

About 36% of the Belgian population consists of married men and women, while 9% are divorced.[3] 20% of the Belgian population are minors.[4] In 2018, 45,059 marriages were registered in Belgium, as well as 23,135 divorces.[5] In the same year, in the Flemish Region, nine out of 1,000 couples divorced. In the Walloon Region, this number was 12 out of 1,000, and in the Brussels Region 29 out of 1,000. The numbers were higher in 2000 and 2010.[6] In 2014, it was estimated that in Belgium, children were involved in two out of three divorces.[7]

Furthermore, in 2018, 38,921 partnerships were registered and 25,852 registered partnerships were dissolved.[8] There are no reliable statistics on the number of non-registered relationships that came to an end, nor on the number of children involved in these separations.

In this chapter, firstly, the different modes of child participation according to Belgian law will be presented. In the second part, the focus is on the right of the child to be heard in the Belgian family justice system. Lastly, the representation of the child in family proceedings and the possibility for the child to initiate proceedings will be discussed. In this chapter, 'child' means a person who is a minor, i.e. who is not yet 18 years old.[9]

2. STATUTORY PROVISIONS

There are different ways in which children can participate in family law proceedings. Children can have a substantive right to determine the outcome of the case, they can participate in judicial proceedings through the hearing of

---

2 Art. 572*bis* of the Judicial Code.

3 In 2019, there were 4,178,161 married men and women out a population of 11,431,406 people. 1,049,336 men and women were divorced. See https://statbel.fgov.be/nl/themas/bevolking/structuur-van-de-bevolking#panel-14.

4 https://bestat.statbel.fgov.be/bestat/crosstable.xhtml?view=5fee32f5-29b0-40df-9fb9-af43d1ac9032.

5 https://statbel.fgov.be/nl/themas/bevolking/partnerschap/huwelijken; https://statbel.fgov.be/nl/themas/bevolking/partnerschap/echtscheidingen#figures.

6 https://www.statistiekvlaanderen.be/sites/default/files/atoms/files/2019-02-sv-rapport-echtscheidingen-3-OK.pdf, p. 5.

7 https://www.statistiekvlaanderen.be/sites/default/files/atoms/files/svr-verkenning2016-4-echtscheiding_0.pdf.

8 https://statbel.fgov.be/nl/themas/bevolking/partnerschap/wettelijke-samenwoning#panel-13. It should be noted that the dissolution of a registered partnership does not necessarily mean that the partners separated. A marriage or the death of (one of) the partners also leads to the dissolution of the registered partnership.

9 Art. 388 of the Old Civil Code.

the child, and finally, they can be involved as a party to certain proceedings. The various modes of child participation are regulated by the Old Civil Code[10] and the Judicial Code. The right of the child to be heard is also enshrined in the Constitution.

First of all, a child may have a substantive right to determine the outcome of the case. For example, in adoption cases, if the child has reached the age of 12, the child's consent to the adoption is required (Art. 348-1 of the Old Civil Code). If the child does not consent, this is a veto and the adoption will not proceed. Similarly, in filiation cases, a child who has reached the age of 12 can oppose the judicial determination of parenthood.[11] However, the child has no veto right against this determination of parenthood. If the child opposes, the family court will only reject the claim if the court finds that the determination of parenthood is contrary to the best interests of the child (Art. 332*quinquies*, §2 of the Old Civil Code).

Secondly, children can participate in judicial proceedings that concern them, by being heard by the court. The right of the child to be heard of Article 12 of the Convention on the Rights of the Child (UNCRC) is encompassed in the Constitution and in the Judicial Code. Article 22*bis*, second paragraph of the Constitution states that every child has the right to express his/her opinion in all matters that concern him/her and that due weight should be given to his/her views in accordance with the age and maturity of the child. In cases concerning the exercise of parental authority, residence arrangements and the right to personal contact, the hearing of the child is regulated by Articles 1004/1 and 1004/2 of the Judicial Code, introduced by the Act of 30 July 2013 on the family and juvenile courts. In matters of youth protection, Article 52*ter* of the Youth Protection Act[12] regulates the hearing of the child.[13] The hearing of the child in adoption proceedings is covered by Articles 1231-10 and 1231-11 of the Judicial Code. The personal hearing of the child by a mediator is not provided for by law, but is generally accepted. This is, however, more a meeting between the child and the mediator than a hearing.[14] Since the focus of this chapter is on

---

10 The Act of 13 April 2019 established a new Civil Code, which entered into force on 1 November 2020. Since then, the Civil Code of 21 March 1804 is referred to as the 'Old Civil Code' (Art. 2 of the Act of 13 April 2019 to establish a Civil Code and to insert Book 8 'Evidence' into it, *BS* 14 May 2019). At the time of writing (February 2021), the provisions of family law in the Old Civil Code are still in force.

11 This is the determination of legal parenthood (motherhood, fatherhood or co-motherhood) by a judge. In filiation cases the child is a party to the proceedings (Art. 332*bis*–332*ter* of the Old Civil Code).

12 Act of 8 April 1965, *BS* 15 April 1965. The organisation of the juvenile courts and the legal procedure are a federal competence (Art. 5, §1, II, 6° of the Act of 8 August 1980 for Institutional Reform).

13 Since the Act of 19 March 2017, juvenile courts can order measures concerning parental authority, as far as these measures are related to youth protection measures.

14 L. Jacobs, 'La parole de l'enfant face à la séparation parentale: regards croisés sur les pratiques d'audition', *RTDF* 2017, 649, 670.

child participation in the context of post-separation family proceedings, only the hearing of the child regulated by Articles 1004/1 and 1004/2 of the Judicial Code will be discussed below.

Finally, a child may be involved as a party in judicial proceedings, for example in filiation cases or disputes concerning assets, or in proceedings for compensation for damage suffered by the child. As a rule, the child is considered incapable of taking legal action him/herself and defending his/her interests independently. The child is represented as a party in the proceedings by the person indicated by law (parents or guardian; see below, section 3.2.1). Only in exceptional cases can the minor take legal action him/herself, independently (see below, section 3.2.2).[15]

3. MODES OF CHILD PARTICIPATION

3.1. THE RIGHT OF THE CHILD TO BE HEARD

The fundamental idea of Articles 1004/1 and 1004/2 of the Judicial Code is that every child has the right to be heard in proceedings before Belgian family courts, regardless of his/her nationality or place of residence.[16] In accordance with General Comment No. 12 of the UNCRC, there is no obligation for the child to express his/her views.[17]

3.1.1. Types of Proceedings

The child's right to be heard is limited to matters that concern the child with regard to the exercise of parental authority, residence arrangements and the right to personal contact. This means that the child has no right to be heard in, for example, disputes about child alimony. This limitation is criticised in Belgian doctrine.[18] Within the matters in which the child has the right to be heard, there

---

15 See a recent overview in P. Senaeve and C. Declerck, *Compendium van het personen- en familierecht*, Acco, Leuven 2020, p. 559.

16 P. Senaeve, 'Het hoorrecht van minderjarigen' in P. Senaeve (ed.), *Handboek familieprocesrecht*, Kluwer, Mechelen 2020, p. 475.

17 UN Committee on the Rights of the Child (UNCRC), *General Comment No. 12: The Right of the Child to be Heard*, CRC/C/GC/12, 20 July 2009, https://www.refworld.org/docid/4ae562c52.html; J.M. Thiery, 'Les nouvelles dispositions du Code judiciaire relatives à l'audition de l'enfant mineur dans les matières familiales: une petite révolution', *Le Pli Juridique* 2014, 23.

18 L. Dreser, 'Uitdagingen bij de toepassing van het hoorrecht bij minderjarige kinderen' in I. Boone and C. Declerck (eds.), *Actualia Familierecht. Co-ouderschap vandaag en morgen*, die Keure, Bruges 2017, p. 36; P. Senaeve, 'Het hoorrecht van minderjarigen sinds de wet op de familie- en jeugdrechtbank', *T.Fam.* 2014, 176, 185–186. *Contra*: Van Gysel states that children should not be involved in financial disputes. A.C. Van Gysel (ed.), *Traité de droit civil Belge. Les personnes*, Bruylant, Brussels 2015, p. 1346, nr. 1379.

are no exceptions for disputes which are of little importance. For example, when parents do not agree on the exact time of picking up the child on Sunday evening at one parent's home (i.e. 7 pm or 7.30 pm), Article 1004/1 of the Judicial Code is fully applicable.[19] Disputes about the relocation of one of the parents with the child,[20] as well as proceedings in international child abduction cases before Belgian courts,[21] fall under the scope of Article 1004/1 of the Judicial Code.

There is uncertainty about whether the child has a right to be heard in proceedings in the family courts' chambers of friendly settlement,[22] and in proceedings of a divorce by mutual consent. As the original proposal of the law to amend various provisions on the right of minors to be heard stated that the minor should only be heard in *disputes* that concern him/her, one could argue that the child has no right to be heard in proceedings where there is no real dispute.[23]

The doctrine accepts that, although there is no right of the child to be heard in the chambers of friendly settlement, the child *can* be heard when all parties agree upon it. There is, however, no consensus about the confidentiality of this hearing. Some authors maintain the hearing is covered by the rule of confidentiality of the chambers of friendly settlement,[24] while others state that

---

19 P. Senaeve, 'Het hoorrecht van minderjarigen sinds de wet op de familie- en jeugdrechtbank', *T.Fam.* 2014, 176, 183.

20 Art. 1004/1 of the Judicial Code is only applicable when the parents do not agree on the relocation of one of the parents with the child, as this is an aspect of the exercise of parental authority.

21 On the hearing of children in Belgian and Dutch courts in cases of international child abduction, see S. Lembrechts, M. Putters, K. Van Hoorde, T. Kruger, K. Ponnet and W. Vandenhole, 'Conversations between children and judges in child abduction cases in Belgium and the Netherlands', *Family & Law*, http://www.familyandlaw.eu/tijdschrift/fenr/2019/02/FENR-D-18-00007.

22 Belgian family courts consist of family chambers, for regular judicial proceedings, and chambers of friendly settlement. In the chambers of friendly settlement, a judge will help the parties to reconcile and find a solution to their dispute. The family judge can send the case to the chambers of friendly settlement on the parties' request or when the judge deems it appropriate (Art. 1253*ter*/1, §2 of the Judicial Code). Everything that has been said or written during the proceedings in the chambers of friendly settlement is confidential and cannot be used afterwards in the regular proceedings in the family chambers, in the event that no agreement has been reached (S. De Bauw and G. Verschelden, 'De kamer voor minnelijke schikking en de bevordering van een minnelijke oplossing van familiale geschillen' in P. Senaeve (ed.), *Handboek familieprocesrecht*, Kluwer, Mechelen 2020, pp. 222–223).

23 Proposal of law to amend various provisions on the right of minors to be heard by the judge (S. De Bethune and M. Taelman), *Parl.St. Senate* (BZ) 2010, nr. 115/1, 11; P. Senaeve, 'Het hoorrecht van minderjarigen' in P. Senaeve (ed.), *Handboek familieprocesrecht*, Kluwer, Mechelen 2020, p. 488.

24 L. Dreser, 'Uitdagingen bij de toepassing van het hoorrecht bij minderjarige kinderen' in I. Boone and C. Declerck (eds.), *Actualia Familierecht. Co-ouderschap vandaag en morgen*, die Keure, Bruges 2017, p. 45; L. Jacobs, 'La parole de l'enfant face à la séparation parentale: regards croisés sur les pratiques d'audition', *RTDF* 2017, 649, 664.

the report of the hearing should be included in the file of the proceedings, as the confidentiality is only applicable to what has been said or written by the parties themselves. If the report of the hearing is included in the file of the proceedings, the family judge, who has to decide on the matter if no agreement between the parties has been reached, as well as the parties have access to the report of the hearing.[25]

In proceedings of a divorce by mutual consent, parents have to reach an agreement about the consequences of the divorce.[26] The child will not receive a letter or invitation to be heard, but it is possible for the judge to hear the child if the child, one of the parents or the public prosecutor requests to do so.[27] The 2018–19 report of the Flemish Children's Rights Commission rightly states that the lack of clarity in these kinds of proceedings is a shortfall of the right of the child to be heard and that there should be an opportunity for children to speak out in all types of proceedings.[28]

3.1.2. A Distinction Based on Age

In Article 1004/1 of the Judicial Code, a distinction is made between a hearing of children below the age of 12 and children who have reached that age. All children have the right to be heard, but only children who have reached 12 years of age are informed about this right by the family court registry.[29] On the one hand, this distinction based on age is criticised, as it is not the age of the child that should matter, but the child's maturity and discernment.[30] On the other hand, it is argued that a clear distinction based on age is needed to make the

25 S. De Bauw and G. Verschelden, 'De kamer voor minnelijke schikking en de bevordering van een minnelijke oplossing van familiale geschillen' in P. Senaeve (ed.), *Handboek familieprocesrecht*, Kluwer, Mechelen 2020, p. 200; P. Senaeve, 'Het hoorrecht van minderjarigen' in P. Senaeve (ed.), *Handboek familieprocesrecht*, Kluwer, Mechelen 2020, p. 514.

26 In 2013, 57% of the divorces in the Flemish Region were divorces by mutual consent. In the Walloon Region, this was 40%. See https://www.statistiekvlaanderen.be/sites/default/files/atoms/files/svr-verkenning2016-4-echtscheiding_0.pdf, p. 4.

27 P. Senaeve, 'Het hoorrecht van minderjarigen sinds de wet op de familie- en jeugdrechtbank', *T.Fam.* 2014, 176, 184; G. Verschelden, *Handboek Belgisch Personen, familie- en relatievermogensrecht*, die Keure, Bruges 2021, p. 459, nr. 948.

28 Children's Rights Commission, *Annual Report 18–19*, https://www.kinderrechtencommissariaat.be/sites/default/files/bestanden/book_jaarverslag_krc_2018-19_volledig_def_lr.pdf, p. 189.

29 P. Senaeve, 'Het hoorrecht van minderjarigen' in P. Senaeve (ed.), *Handboek familieprocesrecht*, Kluwer, Mechelen 2020, pp. 475, 477.

30 A.C. Van Gysel (ed.), *Traité de droit civil Belge. Les personnes*, Bruylant, Brussels 2015, p. 1347, nr. 1379; L. Jacobs, 'La parole de l'enfant face à la séparation parentale: regards croisés sur les pratiques d'audition', *RTDF* 2017, 649, 652; P. Senaeve, 'Het hoorrecht van minderjarigen' in P. Senaeve (ed.), *Handboek familieprocesrecht*, Kluwer, Mechelen 2020, p. 476.

family court registry's obligation to provide information to the child practically feasible.[31]

3.1.3. *Children Who have Reached the Age of 12*

Children who have reached the age of 12 are informed about their right to be heard. At the start of the proceedings, the family court registry sends a letter to the address of each of the child's parents or to the child's residence when the child does not reside with the parents (Art. 1004/2 of the Judicial Code).

In this letter, the judge informs the child about his/her right to be heard, the way in which the hearing will take place and how the child can accept or decline to be heard. In addition, the letter should mention that the report of the hearing will be included in the file of the proceedings, that the parties to the proceedings can take note of the report's content and that it can be used in the proceedings. In other words, the judge must make clear that there is no confidentiality of the information provided by the child to the court. Finally, the letter should clarify that the hearing of the child does not mean the judge is obliged to comply with what the child wants (Art. 1004/2 of the Judicial Code).

The letter sent to the child also has a reply form, which the child can send to the family court registry, or the child can send an e-mail with his/her response to the judge. Possibly, more modern communication techniques should be available to children to contact the court, for example via social media or WhatsApp.[32]

To ensure that the letter is easy for children to understand, two model letters were drawn up with the help of the Flemish Children's Rights Commission and the General Delegate for Children's Rights of the French Community.[33] The first model includes the time and place of the hearing of the child. On the reply form, the child can indicate whether he/she does, or does not, want to talk to the judge, or that he/she wishes to talk to the judge but not at the stated time and/or place. The second model does not mention the time and place of the hearing of the child. On the reply form, the child can only indicate whether he/she wants to talk to the judge or not. When he/she does want to talk to the judge, the family court registry will send the child another letter with the time and place of the hearing.

---

31 P. Senaeve, 'Het hoorrecht van minderjarigen sinds de wet op de familie- en jeugdrechtbank', *T.Fam.* 2014, 176, 179.

32 J. De Mets, 'Kinderen worden gehoord, maar wordt er ook geluisterd?' *De Juristenkrant* 2018, 10.

33 Royal Decree of 23 August 2014 establishing the model of information form referred to in Article 1004/2 of the Judicial Code, *BS* 29 August 2014. In 2017, the letter was updated to become even more accessible (Royal Decree of 28 April 2017 establishing the model of information form referred to in Article 1004/2 of the Judicial Code, *BS* 22 May 2017); Report on the speeches in the Commission for Justice of 30 May 2017, *Parl.St. Chamber* 2016–2017, 54/677, 11; E. Merckx, 'Sociaalwetenschappelijk onderzoek als leidraad bij het vormgeven van kinderrechten in de wet', *TJK* 2019, 10, 15.

The use of these models is recommended, yet not mandatory.[34] Every family court can use its own letter as long as the letter contains the elements mentioned in Article 1004/2 of the Judicial Code.[35]

3.1.4. Children under the Age of 12

Children under the age of 12 are not informed by the court about their right to be heard. The child him/herself, the parties to the proceedings or the public prosecutor can however request the hearing of the child (Art. 1004/1, §2 of the Judicial Code). The question arises as to how the child will be aware of his/her right to be heard when he/she is not informed by the court. It is assumed that it is part of the parental responsibilities to tell the child about his/her right to be heard. However, it cannot be ruled out that parents themselves may not know of the child's right to be heard, or that they may not tell the child about this right or even pressure their child not to exercise it.[36]

According to Article 1004/1, §2 of the Judicial Code, the family court can refuse to hear the child by a well-motivated decision, unless the request is made by the child or by the public prosecutor. There is no legal remedy against the refusal of the family court to hear the child. The child is not a party to the proceedings between the parents and, according to Belgian law, does not have the legal capacity to be a party to judicial proceedings.[37] However, the child has a right to be heard, and when this right is unlawfully denied by a judge, it is argued in doctrine that a child should have the possibility of appealing the judge's decision to refuse to hear the child.[38] Furthermore, the Constitutional Court ruled on the previous provision on the right of the child to be heard (old Art. 941 of the Judicial Code) that the absence of a right of the child to appeal the court's decision to decline the child's request to be heard on other grounds than a lack of maturity is contrary to the Constitution and to Article 12 UNCRC.[39]

---

34 Report on the speeches in the Commission for Justice of 30 May 2017, *Parl.St. Chamber* 2016–2017, 54/677, 11.

35 L. Dreser, 'Uitdagingen bij de toepassing van het hoorrecht bij minderjarige kinderen' in I. Boone and C. Declerck (eds.), *Actualia Familierecht. Co-ouderschap vandaag en morgen*, die Keure, Bruges 2017, p. 43.

36 L. Dreser, 'Uitdagingen bij de toepassing van het hoorrecht bij minderjarige kinderen' in I. Boone and C. Declerck (eds.), *Actualia Familierecht. Co-ouderschap vandaag en morgen*, die Keure, Bruges 2017, p. 46.

37 Cass. 10 February 2020, *T.Fam.* 2020, 198, note P. Senaeve. C. Van Roy, 'Artikel 374 BW – Mama en papa, of mama, papa en kind?' in I. Boone, J. Put, F. Swennen and G. Verschelden (eds.), *Liber Amicorum Patrick Senaeve*, Kluwer, Mechelen 2017, p. 246.

38 E. Merckx, 'Sociaalwetenschappelijk onderzoek als leidraad bij het vormgeven van kinderrechten in de wet', *TJK* 2019, 10, 15; P. Senaeve, 'Het hoorrecht van minderjarigen' in P. Senaeve (ed.), *Handboek familieprocesrecht*, Kluwer, Mechelen 2020, pp. 483–484.

39 GwH 4 February 2010, no. 9/2010.

3.1.5. *The Exception of a Previous Hearing*

Article 1004/1, §4 of the Judicial Code states that if the child has already been heard in the course of the proceedings or in a previous instance, even before another court, the court is not obliged to grant the request to hear the child if there is no new element to justify an additional hearing.

The family chambers of the courts of appeal do not have to send another letter with information and an invitation to a hearing to the child, but they can.[40] In addition, some authors believe that when a child who has reached the age of 12 requests another hearing, the judge should accept this request,[41] as refusing to hear the child would be contrary to the constitutional right of the child to be heard and to Article 12 of the UNCRC.[42]

3.1.6. *The Course of the Hearing*

According to Article 1004/1, §5 of the Judicial Code, the judge hears the child in a place he/she deems suitable. First of all, this means that only the judge him/herself can hear the child. When the judge wishes to know the child's opinion, but does not want to hear the child him/herself, the only other option is to order an expert opinion or social study.[43] Family judges receive special training on how to hear the child.[44] However, in interviews on the hearing of children, judges have stated that this training is too limited and that they only really learned to hear the child by doing so.[45] Therefore, some authors state that there should be more attention given to this training,[46] or that it should be possible for the judge to delegate the hearing of the child to a professional.[47] For the child, the wording of Article 1004/1, §5 of the Judicial Code means that he/she must *talk* to the judge. The judge should not accept written documents as a preparation or as a replacement for the hearing. When the judge does accept

---

40 P. Senaeve, 'Het hoorrecht van minderjarigen' in P. Senaeve (ed.), *Handboek familieprocesrecht*, Kluwer, Mechelen 2020, p. 484.

41 D. Pire, 'La loi du 30 juillet 2013 portant création d'un tribunal de la famille et de la jeunesse', *Act.dr.fam.* 2013, 170, 192.

42 L. Dreser, 'Uitdagingen bij de toepassing van het hoorrecht bij minderjarige kinderen' in I. Boone and C. Declerck (eds.), *Actualia Familierecht. Co-ouderschap vandaag en morgen*, die Keure, Bruges 2017, p. 45.

43 L. Jacobs, 'La parole de l'enfant face à la séparation parentale: regards croisés sur les pratiques d'audition', *RTDF* 2017, 649, 661.

44 Art. 259*sexies*, 1° of the Judicial Code.

45 L. Jacobs, 'La parole de l'enfant face à la séparation parentale: regards croisés sur les pratiques d'audition', *RTDF* 2017, 649, 655.

46 B. Vanobbergen, 'Naar een (nog meer) kindvriendelijke justitie', *T.Fam.* 2018, 146.

47 L. Jacobs, 'La parole de l'enfant face à la séparation parentale: regards croisés sur les pratiques d'audition', *RTDF* 2017, 649, 687.

a document written by the child, he/she should add this document to the report of the hearing.[48]

It is important that the hearing takes place somewhere the child feels confident and is at ease to speak freely.[49] Therefore, the hearing can occur outside of the courthouse (e.g. at the child's school).[50] Interviews with judges, however, show that mostly the hearings take place in the courthouse, in the office of the family judge.[51]

The hearing should take place without anyone else present, unless the judge decides otherwise (Art. 1004/1, §5 of the Judicial Code). For example, the judge can allow the child to be accompanied by a confidant, like an adult member of the family. The law does not specify whether (minor) brothers and sisters should be heard separately or together.[52]

The presence of the registrar is not undisputed, as the law clearly states that the hearing should take place 'without the presence of anyone else'. Nevertheless, legal doctrine nowadays accepts that the registrar can be present during the hearing of the child.[53] The registrar's presence has the advantage of allowing the judge to focus on the conversation with the child while the registrar takes notes. Depending on their personal preference, some judges allow their registrar to be present and take notes, while others do not.[54]

The child does not have the right to an attorney during the hearing. When the judge allows a lawyer to be present during the hearing, the lawyer can only be present as a confidant of the child, not as an attorney.[55] The representatives of the bar of lawyers and the Flemish Children's Rights Commission believe that the presence of a professionally trained juvenile lawyer could have added value, as he/she could guarantee the minor's right to express him/herself and reduce the risk of parental manipulation.[56] Interviews with judges, however, have

---

48 P. Senaeve, 'Het hoorrecht van minderjarigen' in P. Senaeve (ed.), *Handboek familieprocesrecht*, Kluwer, Mechelen 2020, p. 513.

49 P. Senaeve, 'Het hoorrecht van minderjarigen sinds de wet op de familie- en jeugdrechtbank', *T.Fam.* 2014, 176, 187.

50 J. Mahieu, 'Een blik in het hoofd en het hart van een familierechter', *T.Fam.* 2020, 2, 10.

51 L. Jacobs, 'La parole de l'enfant face à la séparation parentale: regards croisés sur les pratiques d'audition', *RTDF* 2017, 649, 656.

52 P. Senaeve, 'Het hoorrecht van minderjarigen sinds de wet op de familie- en jeugdrechtbank', *T.Fam.* 2014, 176, 191.

53 D. Pire, 'La loi du 30 juillet 2013 portant création d'un tribunal de la famille et de la jeunesse', *Act.dr.fam.* 2013, 170, 192; P. Senaeve, 'Het hoorrecht van minderjarigen' in P. Senaeve (ed.), *Handboek familieprocesrecht*, Kluwer, Mechelen 2020, p. 504; G. Verschelden, *Handboek Belgisch Personen-, familie en relatievermogensrecht*, die Keure, Bruges 2021, p. 460, nr. 951.

54 L. Jacobs, 'La parole de l'enfant face à la séparation parentale: regards croisés sur les pratiques d'audition', *RTDF* 2017, 649, 660. Also P. Senaeve, 'Het hoorrecht van minderjarigen sinds de wet op de familie- en jeugdrechtbank', *T.Fam.* 2014, 176, 190.

55 Cass. 10 February 2020, *T.Fam.* 2020, 198, note P. Senaeve.

56 *Parl.St. Senate* 2010–2011, nr. 5-115/4, report on behalf of the Justice Committee, 18 and 20 (Vander Stock, Ordre des barreaux francophones et germanophone); P. Senaeve,

shown that the majority of the judges were opposed to the presence of a lawyer, as the hearing involves no risks for the child and their presence would be quite costly.[57]

3.1.7. *The Report of the Hearing*

The judge or the family court registrar will write a report on the hearing of the child. This report should reflect the child's opinions on the matter of the dispute. The judge informs the child about the content of the report and checks whether the report truly expresses his/her opinions (Art. 1004/1, §5 of the Judicial Code). This report should not be a verbatim copy of the hearing, but the law does not specify whether this report can be a summary of the hearing,[58] or whether it must be quite detailed.[59]

The judge has to inform the child at the start of the hearing about the fact that the parties to the proceedings (the child's parents) can take note of the report.[60] The parties have access to the report and can even get a copy of it. This should guarantee their rights of defence.[61]

A counterargument to the non-confidential character of the hearing, is that children might feel less comfortable to speak freely.[62] In addition, one can claim that a parent does not have to 'defend' him/herself against the views of the

'Het hoorrecht van minderjarigen' in P. SENAEVE (ed.), *Handboek familieprocesrecht*, Kluwer, Mechelen 2020, p. 505; E. DEBUSSCHER, 'Het informatieformulier betreffende het hoorrecht van minderjarigen', *NNK* 2015, 59, 60. B. VANOBBERGEN, 'Naar een (nog meer) kindvriendelijke justitie', *T.Fam.* 2018, 146.

57 L. JACOBS, 'La parole de l'enfant face à la séparation parentale: regards croisés sur les pratiques d'audition', *RTDF* 2017, 649, 658.

58 P. SENAEVE, 'Het hoorrecht van minderjarigen' in P. SENAEVE (ed.), *Handboek familieprocesrecht*, Kluwer, Mechelen 2020, p. 509.

59 Pire states that the report should be detailed, so that in the event of appeal, the judge of appeal does not have to hear the child again (D. PIRE, 'La loi du 30 juillet 2013 portant création d'un tribunal de la famille et de la jeunesse', *Act.dr.fam.* 2013, 170, 193). Counterarguments to this are that the court of appeal can always decide to conduct another hearing and that non-verbal information can also be very useful, which a judge can only obtain by hearing the child him/herself (E. MERCKX, 'Vertrouwelijke informatie bij het horen van minderjarigen in zaken van gezag en verblijf of contact: schending van de rechten van verdediging of in het belang van het kind?', *T.Fam.* 2019, 203, 212).

60 Art. 1004/1, §5 of the Judicial Code; P. SENAEVE, 'Het hoorrecht van minderjarigen' in P. SENAEVE (ed.), *Handboek familieprocesrecht*, Kluwer, Mechelen 2020, p. 515.

61 P. SENAEVE, 'Het hoorrecht van minderjarigen' in P. SENAEVE (ed.), *Handboek familieprocesrecht*, Kluwer, Mechelen 2020, pp. 510, 513.

62 E. MERCKX, 'Vertrouwelijke informatie bij het horen van minderjarigen in zaken van gezag en verblijf of contact: schending van de rechten van verdediging of in het belang van het kind?', *T.Fam.* 2019, 203, 207; P. SENAEVE, 'Het hoorrecht van minderjarigen' in P. SENAEVE (ed.), *Handboek familieprocesrecht*, Kluwer, Mechelen 2020, p. 514.

child.[63] Some authors therefore defend absolute confidentiality of the hearing of the child,[64] while others argue for an assessment *in concreto* of the balance between the interests of the child and the confidentiality of the report versus the rights of defence of the parties and their right to have access to the information of the case.[65]

The child does not sign the report. If, during the hearing, the judge finds that the child does not have the necessary maturity or discernment, he/she mentions this in the report of the hearing (Art. 1004/1, §5 of the Judicial Code).

3.1.8. The Consequences of the Hearing

By hearing the child, the child does not become a party to the proceedings (Art. 1004/1, §6 of the Judicial Code). The child does not receive any information about the decision of the family court. The feedback on the court's decision to the child is considered to be a task for the parents, as a part of their parental responsibilities.[66]

The judge should give due weight to the opinion of the child, in accordance with his/her age and maturity (Art. 1004/1, §6 of the Judicial Code). As mentioned in the model letter, hearing the child does not mean that the judge is obliged to comply with what the child wants.

3.2. REPRESENTATION AND INITIATING PROCEEDINGS

3.2.1. Representation

In principle, the child is not capable of litigating and is therefore generally not able to take legal action independently. The legal incompetence of children also applies to proceedings concerning their residence arrangements. The child may not intervene as a party in these proceedings nor may he/she initiate such proceedings.[67]

---

63 C. Van Roy, 'Artikel 374 BW – Mama en papa, of mama, papa en kind?' in I. Boone, J. Put, F. Swennen and G. Verschelden (eds.), *Liber Amicorum Patrick Senaeve*, Kluwer, Mechelen 2017, p. 243.

64 C. Declerck, 'Het ondergesneeuwde belang van het kind tijdens een scheiding', *T.Fam.* 2016, 2.

65 E. Merckx, 'Vertrouwelijke informatie bij het horen van minderjarigen in zaken van gezag en verblijf of contact: schending van de rechten van verdediging of in het belang van het kind?', *T.Fam.* 2019, 203, 212.

66 L. Dreser, 'Uitdagingen bij de toepassing van het hoorrecht bij minderjarige kinderen' in I. Boone and C. Declerck (eds.), *Actualia Familierecht. Co-ouderschap vandaag en morgen*, die Keure, Bruges 2017, pp. 40 and 51.

67 Cass. 10 February 2020, *T.Fam.* 2020, 198, note P. Senaeve.

When the child is involved as a party in judicial proceedings, for example in filiation cases or disputes concerning assets, the child is represented by the person appointed by law for that purpose. This is based on the idea of protection. The child must be protected from his/her ignorance and lack of experience.[68]

In principle, the parent(s) represent their child in court to the extent of the exercise of their parental authority (Art. 376 of the Old Civil Code).[69] In this regard a distinction must be made in terms of whether the parents live together or not. If the parents live together, they jointly exercise parental authority and therefore act jointly as representatives of the minor child (Art. 376, paragraph 1 of the Old Civil Code). They have no separate authority to represent their child. If the parents disagree, either parent may apply to the family court. The latter may then authorise a parent to act alone. If this does not happen and the parent acting alone cannot prove the consent of the other parent, he/she does not have the required capacity to take legal action. In cases where the parents do not live together, the power of representation depends on who is exercising parental authority (Art. 376, paragraph 3 of the Old Civil Code). When the parents jointly exercise parental authority, they act together as representatives of their child. If one of the parents exercises parental authority exclusively, the power of representation belongs exclusively to that parent and does not require the consent of the other parent. The parent who does not exercise parental authority cannot validly represent the child. Within the framework of his/her right of supervision, this parent may, however, apply to the family court (Art. 376, paragraph 4 of the Old Civil Code).

If there is only one available parent, he/she shall exercise the power of representation alone.

The parent(s) is/are the formal *litigating* party taking all legal actions for the child. They shall carry out the legal proceedings in the best interest of the child and in the name and on behalf of the child.[70] The parent(s) do(es) not have to request prior special authorisation from the justice of the peace to represent the child as a plaintiff in judicial proceedings (Art. 378, §1, paragraph 1 of the Old Civil Code in conjunction with Art. 410, §1, 7° of the Old Civil Code). In this way, the rights and duties of the child are assessed and determined without the child being involved.

In the event of a conflict of interests between the child and his/her parents or the only available parent, the law requires the appointment of an *ad hoc* guardian (Art. 378, §1, paragraph 6 of the Old Civil Code). The *ad hoc* guardian represents the child in the legal action or in legal proceedings in which his/her

---

68 C. De Boe, 'La place de l'enfant dans le procès civil', *JT* 2009, 485, 486, nr. 3; E. De Kezel, 'Het recht op rechtsingang van de minderjarige: een nieuwe lente in zicht?', *TJK* 2002, 129.

69 The representation of the child in legal proceedings concerning filiation is regulated by a special provision, namely Art. 331*sexies* of the Old Civil Code.

70 C. De Boe, 'La place de l'enfant dans le procès civil', *JT* 2009, 485, 486, nr. 3.

parents' interests conflict with his/hers (Art. 378, §1, paragraph 6 of the Old Civil Code).[71] A *real* conflict of interest is required.[72] It is therefore not because both parents and child take part in the same legal proceedings that there is a conflict of interest between them; they might possibly have concurrent interests. The question arises as to whether there is an actual conflict of interest when the parent(s) simply do(es) not take action when needed. Legal doctrine predominantly assumes that there is *not necessarily always*, but *possibly*, a conflict of interest that can justify the appointment of an *ad hoc* guardian in the event of mere inaction on the part of the legal representative(s).[73] However, this requires an appreciation in concrete terms.

The initiative for the appointment of the *ad hoc* guardian can be taken by any party involved (e.g. parent, grandparent, third party), as well as by the judge of his/her own motion. It is disputed whether the child him/herself should be able to request the appointment of the guardian on an *ad hoc* basis in the event of inertia, inaction or unwillingness on the part of his/her parents.[74] Certain authors assume this should be considered as an act of preservation so the child him/herself can request the appointment of the *ad hoc* guardian.[75] The Public Prosecutor has no direct right of initiative to request the appointment of the guardian on an *ad hoc* basis.[76] However, at the request of the Public Prosecutor's Office, the family court may, in the interests of the child, impose or amend all orders relating to parental authority, and therefore also relating to the power of representation (Art. 387*bis* of the Old Civil Code). The Public Prosecutor's Office may also, in cases of absolute necessity, address the president of the court of first instance, who may subsequently take measures to safeguard the rights of the child (Art. 584, fourth and fifth paragraph of the Judicial Code).

In the absence of an available parent, guardianship is created and the guardian represents the child (Art. 389 of the Old Civil Code). Unlike the parent(s), the guardian needs the authorisation of the justice of the peace to represent the child in court as the plaintiff, except for representing the child as a civil party in criminal proceedings (Art. 410, §1, 7° of the Old Civil Code). It is assumed that

---

71 E.g. Vred. Roeselare 15 November 2001, *T.Vred.* 2002, 395.

72 P. Senaeve and C. Declerck, *Compendium van het personen- en familierecht*, Acco, Leuven 2020, p. 450, nr. 1519. For an application see Rb. Veurne 14 June 2007, *T.Fam.* 2011, 11; Vred. Fontaine-l'Evêque 22 August 2011, *T.Vred.* 2013, 426.

73 Vred. Westerlo 18 April 2005, *RABG* 2005, 1819; Vred. Brasschaat 18 November 2008, *RABG* 2009, 849; D. Ballet and A. Wylleman, 'Proceswaarborgen voor minderjarigen in procedures die hen aanbelangen', *RW* 1989–1990, 804–805, nrs. 33–34; A. Van Thienen, 'Justice must also be enabled to be done', *T.Fam.* 2015, 116, 121, nr. 10; G. Verschelden, 'De aanstelling van een voogd ad hoc en andere remedies tegen ouderlijk wanbeheer', *T.Fam.* 2011, 13, 14–16, nrs. 4 and 8–9. Compare Rb. Veurne 14 June 2007, *T.Fam.* 2011, 11, note G. Verschelden.

74 *Contra* Ghent 19 December 2013, *T.Fam.* 2015, 115, note A. Van Thienen.

75 A. Van Thienen, 'Justice must also be enabled to be done', *T.Fam.* 2015, 116, 122, nr. 13.

76 S. Mosselmans, 'Voogdij' in *APR*, Kluwer, Mechelen 2004, p. 409, nr. 688; A. Van Thienen, 'Justice must also be enabled to be done', *T.Fam.* 2015, 116, 123, nr. 14.

an authorisation is required not only for preliminary, and even intermediate, claims, but also for appeals.[77]

When the interests of the guardian conflict with the interests of the child, the supervisory guardian shall act as representative (Art. 404 of the Old Civil Code). If the interests of the supervisory guardian also conflict with those of the child, the justice of the peace shall appoint an *ad hoc* guardian and an *ad hoc* supervisory guardian (Art. 404 of the Old Civil Code). The justice of the peace may do so of his/her own motion or at the request of a party involved.

3.2.2. Initiation of Proceedings by the Child

If the child takes legal action him/herself, the defendant may raise a suspensory objection, which obliges the child to summon his/her legal representative to intervene.[78] The child's own and independent action in violation of his/her legal incapacity thus does not lead to the nullity of the procedural act. The exception suspends the proceedings until the proceedings have been regularised. The suspensive effect shall continue until the child is lawfully involved in the proceedings, either through the intervention of his/her legal representative or until he/she reaches 18 years of age. It is disputed whether the judge can or should raise this objection ex officio. Certain jurisprudence and legal doctrine are of the opinion that the issue is not of public order, so the judge cannot raise it ex officio.[79] Other authors, however, are of the opinion that the court can do this because it concerns a mandatory protection on the part of the child.[80] If a court decision is reached without the prior intervention of the legal representative of the at least partly unsuccessful plaintiff or defendant, the ordinary remedies of opposition and appeal are available.[81]

Legislation and case law, both in civil and administrative matters, formulate exceptions to the principle of the child's legal incapacity to initiate proceedings.

As far as the legal exceptions are concerned, they usually concern rights linked to the person of the child, such as the status of parent or spouse.

---

77 T. Robert, 'De burgerrechtelijke procesbekwaamheid van de minderjarige' in Centrum voor Beroepsvervolmaking in de Rechten (ed.), *De procesbekwaamheid van minderjarigen*, Intersentia, Antwerp 2006, p. 47, nr. 23.

78 Application: Brussels 28 June 1988, *RTDF* 1988, 565.

79 See e.g. Luik 17 December 2002, *JLMB* 2003, 1577; C. De Boe, 'La place de l'enfant dans le procès civil', *JT* 2009, 485, 487, nr. 6; Y.H. Leleu, *Droit des personnes et des familles*, Larcier, Brussels 2020, p. 264, nr. 257; P. Senaeve and C. Declerck, *Compendium van het personen- en familierecht*, Acco, Leuven 2020, p. 454, nr. 1539; A. Van Thienen, 'Justice must also be enabled to be done', *T.Fam.* 2015, 116, 118, nr. 5.

80 F. Swennen, 'Vertegenwoordiging in rechte als eiser van een onbekwame: gevolgen van de afwezigheid van machtiging' in *Liber amicorum Pierre Marchal*, De Boeck&Larcier, Brussels 2003, pp. 394–398, nrs. 14–16.

81 T. Robert, 'De burgerrechtelijke procesbekwaamheid van de minderjarige' in Centrum voor Beroepsvervolmaking in de Rechten (ed.), *De procesbekwaamheid van minderjarigen*, Intersentia, Antwerp 2006, p. 50, nr. 29.

For example, the child has his/her own right of action regarding the application for dispensation from the age requirement when entering into a marriage (Art. 145 of the Old Civil Code).

In addition, jurisprudence and legal doctrine accept that the child who has sufficient discernment can take protective measures him/herself independently, such as filing a claim for sealing of goods or a claim in preliminary relief proceedings.[82] Similarly, certain case law of lower courts sometimes allows the child to bring an action for maintenance against his/her parents.[83] The conditions that must be met in order for the court to allow the child to take legal action vary from case to case. Sometimes reference is made to the protective nature of the measures claimed, sometimes to the strictly personal nature of the right which is the subject matter of the proceedings. In Belgian law, there is no clear demarcation as to when a child can act independently.[84] In a judgment of 10 February 2020, the Court of Cassation ruled that neither Articles 3, 9 and 12 UNCRC nor Article 8 ECHR nor Article 22*bis* of the Constitution require the child to be given the opportunity to intervene as a party in proceedings concerning his/her residence arrangements or to initiate such proceedings.[85]

In cases where the child is considered capable of taking legal action him/herself independently, it is logical that he/she also has the possibility to be assisted by a lawyer. Every child has the right to legal advice through free first-line assistance and free second-line assistance.[86] There is an irrefutable presumption that the child does not have a sufficient income. Sometimes the law explicitly provides for the obligation to appoint a lawyer for the child. One example is when a child has to appear before the juvenile court and is without representation. In this case, he/she is automatically assigned legal representation (Art. 54*bis* of the Youth Protection Act of 8 April 1965).

Legal practice and doctrine have for some time advocated for generalised independent access to justice for children in civil cases, but to date this has remained without further effect.[87]

---

82 P. Senaeve and C. Declerck, *Compendium van het personen- en familierecht*, Acco, Leuven 2020, p. 457, nr. 1545; A. Van Thienen, 'Justice must also be enabled to be done', *T.Fam.* 2015, 116, 118, nr. 5; G. Verschelden, *Handboek Belgisch Personen-, familie- en relatievermogensrecht*, die Keure, Bruges 2021, p. 426, nr. 879.

83 See e.g. Vred. Bergen 19 April 1989, *JDJ* 1989, 34.

84 E. De Kezel, 'Het recht op rechtsingang van de minderjarige: een nieuwe lente in het zicht?', *TJK* 2002, 129, 130, nr. 3; A. Van Thienen, 'Justice must also be enabled to be done', *T.Fam.* 2015, 116, 118, nr. 5.

85 Cass. 10 February 2020, *T.Fam.* 2020, 198, note P. Senaeve.

86 First-line assistance implies free legal advice; second-line assistance refers to free legal representation by a pro deo lawyer; T. Robert, 'De burgerrechtelijke procesbekwaamheid van de minderjarige' in Centrum voor Beroepsvervolmaking in de Rechten (ed.), *De procesbekwaamheid van minderjarigen*, Intersentia, Antwerp 2006, p. 71, nrs. 102–103.

87 E. De Kezel, 'Naar een veralgemeende procesbekwaamheid van minderjarigen in burgerrechtelijke zaken?', *TJK* 2001, 51–57; E. De Kezel, 'Het recht op rechtsingang van de

4. RESEARCH

Not much research has been carried out on the practice of child participation. However, the court statistics show that the number of children that are heard by the family courts has increased in recent years. In 2014, 2,617 hearings were registered.[88] In 2017, three years after implementation of the Family Courts Act and the new regulation on the hearing of the child, 5,381 reports of hearings were registered.[89]

Moreover, a large empirical study found that in cases concerning the residence arrangements of children, the courts very often decide in accordance with the wishes of the child. Van Roy examined 1,069 published and unpublished court decisions from 2013 on the residence arrangements of children after a separation or a divorce.[90] In 23% of the examined cases, the child was heard by the judge. In 82% of these cases, the court's decision was in accordance with the child's wishes.[91]

Nevertheless, the application of the law in practice is not flawless. The 2017–18 report of the Flemish Children's Rights Commission shows that some children experience the hearing as a performance *pro forma*.[92] In its 2018–19 report, the Flemish Children's Rights Commission mentions complaints from children who did not receive any response from the court to their request to be heard.[93] Thus, in practice, the child's request to be heard is sometimes ignored.

5. CONCLUSION

In Belgian law, the legal position of the child can be improved. As a rule, the child does not have the possibility of going to court independently. Thus, the child is

minderjarige: een nieuwe lente in het zicht?', *TJK* 2002, 129–131; B. Vanobbergen, 'Naar een (nog meer) kindvriendelijke justitie', *T.Fam.* 2018, 146–147. More reticent: C. De Boe, 'La place de l'enfant dans le procès civil', *JT* 2009, 485, 493, nr. 27.

88 P. Senaeve, 'Het hoorrecht van minderjarigen' in P. Senaeve (ed.), *Handboek familieprocesrecht*, Kluwer, Mechelen 2020, p. 472

89 Steundienst van het College van de hoven en rechtbanken, *De jaarlijkse statistieken van de hoven en rechtbanken*, https://www.rechtbanken-tribunaux.be/sites/default/files/college/files/pub_2018_rea_familie_nl.pdf. Note that the statistics for the resort of Mons and the jurisdictions of Namur and Dinant are not available.

90 C. Van Roy, *De (on)deelbaarheid van het kind*, Intersentia, Antwerp 2021, p. 123.

91 C. Van Roy, *De (on)deelbaarheid van het kind*, Intersentia, Antwerp 2021, p. 180. Note that the family courts were not yet established at the time of the research.

92 Flemish Children's Rights Commission, *Annual Report 2017–18*, https://www.kinderrechtencommissariaat.be/sites/default/files/bestanden/jaarverslag_krc_2017-2018_webversie_def.pdf, p. 153. Also C. Declerck and T. Wuyts, 'Anders omgaan met scheidings conflicten', *T.Fam.* 2019, 178, 181.

93 Children's Rights Commission, *Annual Report 18–19*, https://www.kinderrechtencommissariaat.be/sites/default/files/bestanden/book_jaarverslag_krc_2018-19_volledig_def_lr.pdf, p. 190.

dependent on his/her legal representative(s). In the case of inertia or refusal by the legal representative, it is highly disputed whether the appointment of an *ad hoc* guardian is justified and whether the child can request the appointment of an *ad hoc* guardian. This means that the child is often formally powerless and the question arises as to what extent this is compatible with the right of access to justice under Article 6 ECHR. Both the legislator and the case law have formulated exceptions to the legal incapacity of the child. The legal exceptions are not very coherently defined. As far as jurisprudential exceptions are concerned, much depends on the willingness of the judge. For some time now, there has been a plea for the generalised introduction of independent access to justice for children, but to date without any successful outcome.

In accordance with Article 12 UNCRC and Article 22*bis*, second paragraph of the Constitution, the child has the right to be heard in all proceedings concerning him/her, including, for example, in disputes between his/her parents concerning the exercise of parental authority over him/her as a person, the residence arrangements or the exercise of the right to personal contact by the parent not exercising parental authority. However, with regard to the hearing of children by the family court, there are a number of bottlenecks in Belgian law at different levels, ranging from poor application of the law to gaps in the law. There are also major differences in the application of children's hearing rights by the various family courts.[94] This problem should also be addressed.

94 Children's Rights Commission, *Annual Report 18–19*, https://www.kinderrechtencommissariaat.be/sites/default/files/bestanden/book_jaarverslag_krc_2018-19_volledig_def_lr.pdf, pp. 190–191.

CANADA

Rachel BIRNBAUM and Nicholas BALA

1. INTRODUCTION

While traditionally Canadian courts and legislatures discouraged involvement of children in family proceedings, there is growing acceptance that children's views and wishes must be considered by decision-makers in these proceedings. However, while Canadian law now requires that the perspectives and preferences of children 'shall' be considered, children do not have a 'right of participation', and there is great variation in how, and indeed whether, their views are considered in family proceedings.

Canada has 10 provinces and three territories with an estimated population of 38,008,005 people as of 31 December 2020.[1] There are no national statistics on the number of marriages, divorces or parental separations in Canada, or

1 Statistics Canada at: https://www.statcan.gc.ca/eng/subjects-start/population_and_demography.

regarding the number of children involved in family disputes, and only limited provincial data on family proceedings, with no systemic information about how children's views are considered.[2] However, census and tax data reveals that the marriage and divorce rates have been falling and that over one fifth of couples cohabit outside of marriage rather than marrying.[3] While the number of children affected by parental separation is not known, a 2011 General Social Survey (GSS) found that 24% of separated or divorced parents in Canada had children under the age of 18 years.[4]

In an 18-month longitudinal study of parents in Ontario and Quebec involved in family proceedings involving children (both represented by legal counsel and self-represented), researchers found that approximately 12 months after an initial in-person survey, only 13 out of 113 cases had an assessment by a mental health professional, a report from a social worker on the child's views, or child legal representation ordered by the court. In other words, only 12% of parenting disputes that resulted in continued court proceedings had a mental health professional or lawyer obtain children's views and preferences.[5]

Another Ontario study of 1,000 court files involving parental disputes found that the Ontario Office of the Children's Lawyer[6] was only involved in 3.1% of court cases, which resulted in child legal representation being provided in 2.2% of cases and a clinical investigation report (e.g. publicly paid report) in 0.9% of cases. Mental health professionals in private practice prepared evaluation reports in only 0.5% of cases in the court sample.[7]

In another Canadian study, researchers reported on court decisions on relocation between 2000 and 2010 and found that the wishes or perceptions of children, as reported to the court in any way, including testimony from parents, were only mentioned in 25% of the court decisions. They also found that where children expressed a clear view about moving or not moving, judges tended to

---

2 See e.g. the Ministry of Attorney General, Ontario website, which lists annual statistics on solely court filings: https://www.ontariocourts.ca/ocj/stats-fam/.

3 R. Margolis, Y. Choi, F. Hou and M. Haan, 'Capturing trends in Canadian divorce in an era without vital statistics' (2019) 41 *Demographic Research* 1453–1478, https://www.demographic-research.org/Volumes/Vol41/52/.

4 Statistics Canada, 2021 at: https://www150.statcan.gc.ca/n1/pub/89f0115x/89f0115x2019001-eng.htm.

5 R. Birnbaum, K. Poitras, M. Saini, N. Bala and F. Cyr, 'Views and Experiences of Parents in the Family Justice Systems in Ontario and Quebec: Report on First Stage of a Longitudinal Research Project' (forthcoming) *Journal of Marriage & Divorce.*

6 The Ontario Office of the Children's Lawyer is an independent government agency that provides child legal representation in parenting disputes, child protection matters and estate matters. Some of the representation is provided by staff lawyers, but much is provided by lawyers in private practice who have had some training for this type of work.

7 M. Saini, R. Birnbaum, N. Bala and B. McLarty, 'Understanding Pathways to Family Dispute Resolution and Justice Reforms: Ontario Court File Analysis and Survey of Professionals' (2018) 54(3) *Family Court Review* 382–397.

give considerable weight to their wishes: in 94 of the 124 cases (76%) in which children expressed clear views, the court's decision accorded with those wishes.[8]

This chapter begins with a discussion of the legislative framework and resources related to children's participation in family law proceedings in Canada,[9] reviewing the different forms of children's participation post-separation in court and out-of-court processes, and outlines the empirical research about the experiences of children and professionals with child involvement in family justice processes in Canada.[10] We conclude that while the requirements of Article 12 of the *UN Convention on the Rights of the Child* (UNCRC) are in theory being met by legislation, in practice the extent of children's participation varies greatly across the country, not only because of differences in legislation, government funding and support for services, but also as a result of differences in attitudes of the family justice professionals who remain the gatekeepers to children's participation.

2. STATUTORY PROVISIONS

In Canada, provincial and territorial legislation and case law have long required courts to consider the views and preferences of children as a factor in making 'best interests' decisions about parenting arrangements, generally based on the dated concepts of 'custody' and 'access'.[11] Canada's *Divorce Act* amendments, in force 1 March 2021, introduced new concepts, including parenting time,

---

8 N. Bala, L. Bertrand, A. Wheeler, J. Paetsch and E. Holder, *A Study of Postseparation/divorce Parental Relocation Family*, Children and Youth Section, Department of Justice, Canada 2012, https://www.justice.gc.ca/eng/rp-pr/fl-lf/divorce/spsdpr-edpads/spsdpr-edpads.pdf.

9 There are different statutes, resources and considerations that apply to children's involvement in other types of proceedings in Canada, in particular in child welfare proceedings, where the Charter of Rights may apply because the state is a party and children may have greater rights of participation, including for mature children the right to state-funded counsel in appropriate cases: see *AC v Manitoba (Director of Child and Family Services)*, 2009 SCC 30.

10 R. Birnbaum, *The Voice of the Child in Separation/divorce Mediation and Other Alternative Dispute Resolution Processes: A Literature Review*, Family, Children and Youth Section, Department of Justice, Canada 2009, https://www.justice.gc.ca/eng/rp-pr/fl-lf/divorce/vcsdm-pvem/pdf/vcsdm-pvem.pdf; R. Birnbaum, N. Bala and F. Cyr, 'Children's Experiences with Family Justice Professionals and Judges in Ontario and Ohio' (2011) 25(3) *International Journal of Law, Policy and the Family* 398–422.

11 The federal Divorce Act applies across Canada to parenting disputes when the parents were legally married and are obtaining a divorce. If the parents are not obtaining a divorce, usually because they were cohabiting without marrying or never cohabited, then the legislation of the child's province or territory applies to their dispute. As discussed in this chapter, there is now consistency in the federal and provincial/territorial laws requiring consideration of the views and perspectives of children. However, the manner in which this is done, even in cases under the federal Divorce Act, is the responsibility of the provincial and territorial governments, which have varying legislation, resources and programmes for child participation.

parental decision-making and parenting plans. These amendments also require that in making 'best interests' decisions the courts shall consider 'the child's views and preferences, giving due weight to the child's age and maturity, unless they cannot be ascertained.'[12] This legislation does not, however, provide any mechanism for ascertaining the child's views. Rather, children's participation remains dependent on provincial laws and services, and on the gatekeepers of the family justice system (e.g. lawyers, mental health professionals and judges) as well as parents.[13]

Our central thesis in this chapter is that if there is litigation between separated parents, children should be involved in the process in a way that respects their needs, interests and wishes. Including children promotes their long-term welfare and provides their sense of involvement, respects their rights as recognised in the UNCRC, results in improved decision-making, and may also facilitate settlement of disputes by parents themselves. Individual children, however, also must have a central role in deciding whether and how they will participate.

3. MODES OF CHILD PARTICIPATION

3.1. INDIRECT FORMS OF CHILD PARTICIPATION

3.1.1. Parents, Guardians and Professionals

Parents, guardians and professionals in family cases may be permitted to testify about what children told them about their views and preferences.

However, judges in litigated family disputes are concerned about parents manipulating their children and, if there is conflicting evidence from parents, may put little or no weight on such evidence. Canadian judges discourage parents from presenting recordings of statements from their children, now typically made on smartphones, and often refuse to admit this evidence in family proceedings.[14]

It is more acceptable to Canadian courts to admit testimony from an independent professional, like a school teacher, who may have spoken to a child and can share the child's views with the court.

12 S.C. 2019, c. 16, in force 1 March 2021. See N. Bala, 'Bill C-78: *The 2020 Reforms to the Parenting Provisions of Canada's Divorce Act*' (2020) 39 *Canadian Family Law* Quarterly 45–74.

13 R. Birnbaum and N. Bala, *Making Parenting Plans in Canada's Family Justice System: Challenges, Controversies and the Role of Mental Health Professionals*, Thomson Reuters Publishing, Toronto 2019.

14 See e.g. *Whidden v Ellwood*, 2016 ONSC 6938; *Maharaj v Wilfred-Jacob*, 2016 ONSC 7925.

3.1.2. *Parenting Assessments*

For parents who have the financial resources, the court has the authority to order them to pay for a parenting assessment by a mental health professional (e.g. psychologist, social worker, psychiatrist). These assessments typically report on interviews with each parent and other significant figures, as well as interviews with the child, and they include parenting recommendations about a plan that would promote the best interests of the child. However, these private assessments are expensive, and many parents cannot afford them. In some jurisdictions in Canada there are limited government-funded programmes to prepare for an assessment report by a social worker or psychologist (e.g. British Columbia, Alberta, Saskatchewan, Manitoba, Ontario, Quebec, Nova Scotia), though these programmes do not have sufficient funding to allow an assessment in most litigated cases. In some parts of the country these programmes are unavailable (e.g. Yukon, Nunavut, Northwest Territories, New Brunswick, Newfoundland and Labrador), or publicly funded assessment reports are available for only a very small portion of cases.

3.1.3. *Child Legal Representation*

In some Canadian jurisdictions, including Ontario, Quebec, Alberta, Yukon and the Northwest Territories, there is a possibility that a government-paid lawyer may be appointed to represent the child whose parents are litigating about parenting arrangements. While judges may request the involvement of a lawyer for a child, judges generally do not have the authority to require the government to provide counsel for a child in a family proceeding.[15] Even in jurisdictions with established offices of child legal representation, resource restraints result in many parenting cases being resolved without a lawyer for a child, even if requested by the court.[16]

It is accepted that one of the roles of counsel appointed for children is to ensure that the views and preferences of the child are before the court. In some cases, this may be done by having a mental health professional retained by the child's lawyer interview the child and report about the child's statements. It is generally accepted in Canada that a lawyer for the child may tell the court about a child's wishes and preferences, including telling the court about 'the clarity, consistency, and independence of the children's views [as the basis] to inform the [child's lawyer's] own assessment of what position to take on behalf of

15 *B(AC) v B(R)*, 2010 ONCA 714; *JESD v YEP*, 2018 BCCA 286. In most provinces, judges can order representation for a child in child welfare proceedings.

16 N. Bala and R. Birnbaum, 'Preferences and Perspectives of Children in Family Cases: Rethinking the Role of Children's Lawyers' (2018) 59(4) *Les Cahiers de droit* 787–829.

the children'.[17] However, there are judicial concerns about lawyers appointed for children 'giving evidence from counsel table' about statements from the child, for example, about alleged abuse or not wanting to visit with the other parent, because the lawyer is not subject to cross-examination.

There is variation in policy and practice between provinces about the extent to which lawyers appointed for children will advocate a position based on the child's wishes, or whether counsel for child will advocate a position based on their own assessment of the child's interests, though also ensuring that the court is aware of the child's preferences. There are particular concerns about a lawyer 'acting on a child's instructions' if the child appears to be unduly influenced by one of the parents, such as when there are concerns about alienation, though even in alienation cases it is important for children's views to be known to the court and parents. In practice, lawyers appointed for children often try to promote a settlement that is consistent with the child's wishes.[18]

3.2. DIRECT FORMS OF CHILD PARTICIPATION

3.2.1. Judicial Interviews with the Child

Although children now regularly testify in criminal proceedings in Canada, and are occasionally witnesses in child protection cases, they almost never testify in parenting disputes. If a parent (usually acting without a lawyer) wants to call a child as witness, with the possibility of being subject to cross-examination, there will be concerns about the effect this will have on the child. Judges have the authority to refuse to allow a parent to have a minor child testify as a witness in a family proceeding. However, judges have the authority to conduct a judicial interview with a child in a parenting dispute.[19] In some provinces, such as Quebec, judicial interviews with children who are the subject of parenting disputes are common. In most parts of Canada, there is wide variation in practice, with some judges doing this regularly, and others not at all. Some judges feel that it is not their role to be gathering evidence in the parenting dispute and are concerned that they are not properly trained in interviewing children, but other judges are willing to interview children, without having had formal training.[20]

---

17 *Ludwig v Ludwig*, 2019 ONCA 680.

18 N. Bala and R. Birnbaum, above n. 16, pp. 787–829.

19 Legislation in most provinces and territories allow judges to interview children who are involved in their parental disputes: Newfoundland and Labrador, Prince Edward Island, Ontario, the Northwest Territories, and Nunavut, while in most other provinces, case law recognises that this can be done. In Quebec, Art. 34 of the Civil Code establishes a presumption that judges will hear directly from children. R. Birnbaum and N. Bala, 'Judicial Interviewing with Children in Custody and Access Cases: Comparing Experiences in Ontario and Ohio' (2010) 24(3) *International Journal of Law, Policy and the Family* 300–337.

20 R. Birnbaum and N. Bala, above n. 13, pp. 300–337.

It is generally accepted in Canada that judicial interviews with children should not be forensic; in particular, they should not be intended to ascertain the truth of a child's allegations of abuse or witnessing spousal violence. While children's testimony in court about abuse is common in criminal cases, in parenting disputes, evidence of the child's reports about abuse or neglect is rarely if ever introduced by having the child testify, and never by having a child meet with the judge outside of court.[21]

3.2.2. *Voice of the Child Reports*

There is a growing use of Voice of the Child Reports in some parts of Canada, including in British Columbia, Saskatchewan, Manitoba, Ontario, Nova Scotia and New Brunswick.[22] These reports are short, focused reports about what the child says about their views and preferences in a parenting dispute. A social worker or lawyer with training interviews only the child and prepares a report for the court about what the child said. The interviews typically take about one hour. There are generally two interviews, with the child brought to each interview by a different parent. No other information is collected about the child and no parenting recommendations are made. These reports are much less expensive than a full assessment, as only a few hours of professional time are required, and they can be prepared much more quickly. In some provinces, such as British Columbia, Ontario, Manitoba and Nova Scotia, the government may pay for such a report in some cases.

3.2.3. *Children in Mediation*

While children have not regularly been involved in mediation in Canada, the practice is becoming more common.[23] Whitehead and Birnbaum[24] surveyed family law mediators in Ontario about a range of issues related to working with children and families in mediation. Some reported that they incorporate the child's perspective into the mediation process regularly (15%), and others reported they do this sometimes (34%). Several commented that the age of the child and whether parents had differing views about their children's perspective are important factors in deciding whether to involve the child in the mediation process in some way. Several mediators reported that they would use another child specialist to hear from the child and bring those views into the mediation process.

---

21 R. Birnbaum and N. Bala, above n. 13, pp. 300–337.

22 These reports are also called Views of the Child Reports and Hear the Child Reports.

23 L.A. Yasenik and J.M. Graham, 'The Continuum of Including Children in ADR Processes: A Child-centered Continuum Model' (2016) 54(2) *Family Court Review* 186–202.

24 D. Whitehead and R. Birnbaum, 'Ontario's Publicly Funded Family Mediation Services: Exploring what influences uptake' (2020) 39 *Canadian Family Law Quarterly* 109–148.

3.3. SUMMARY OF DIRECT AND INDIRECT MODES OF PARTICIPATION

There is no 'best way' to hear from children and there is no research to date in Canada that demonstrates that any one method or any one family justice professional (e.g. judge, lawyer, social worker, psychologist, psychiatrist) is 'better' than another for involving children. The method used in an individual case will depend on the stage of the process, the issues in dispute, the resources available, the age and communication abilities of the child, and the views of the child about how to be involved. In practice, often more than one method is used over the course of a parenting dispute. There are advantages and disadvantages to each of these methods, and which method or combination of methods is used may depend on a number of factors such as:

- the matter at issue;
- the resources available (e.g. private or publicly funded);
- the child's age and capacity (e.g. whether the child has any special needs, such as learning problems, foetal alcohol syndrome disorder (FASD), autism spectrum disorder (ASD) and epilepsy);
- whether the child wishes to participate and, if so, how;
- the stage of process (e.g. case conference, interim hearing, trial);
- the nature of the dispute resolution process (e.g. mediation, negotiation, arbitration, litigation);
- concerns about fairness to parents and the child;
- the attitude of the family justice professionals (e.g. whether they are focused on children as objects or subjects); and
- the legal framework and attitude of the decision-maker.[25]

In deciding about how children's views should be received, there also needs to be a balancing of a number of competing factors, including:

- providing the court with as much information as necessary;
- minimising the trauma or distress to the child;
- ensuring a fair process for the parents;
- ensuring a fair process for the child; and
- resolving the dispute in a way that is as cost-effective as possible for the parents, the child and the family justice system.[26]

---

25 J. Cashmore and P. Parkinson, 'Children's and Parents' Perceptions on Children's Participation in Decision Making After Parental Separation and Divorce' (2008) 46(1) *Family Court Review* 91–104.

26 N. Bala, R. Birnbaum and F. Cyr, 'Judicial Interviews of Children in Canada's Family Courts: Growing Acceptance But Still Controversial' in T. Gal and B.F. Duramy (eds.),

An important distinction must also be made between evidence about the preferences of children and their statements about factual issues that may be in dispute. For example, hearing from children about where they want to live and how often they want to visit a parent is different from hearing about their own maltreatment or witnessing family violence. While children's preferences are related to their experiences, there are significant differences about how these types of views and preferences are expressed and how the court will deal with them, with greater expectations for parental due process if children are providing evidence of factual matters in dispute.[27]

4. RESEARCH

There is a growing body of empirical research that explores children's experiences and the perceptions of professionals with the different ways that children's views may be considered in the family justice process in Canada.

4.1. HEARING CHILDREN DIRECTLY

In 2002, Birnbaum and Bala interviewed 11 young adults (aged 19–21 years) who had been represented as a child by a lawyer in a family dispute in Ontario.[28] These young people reported having felt divided loyalties as a result of their parents' separation, particularly feeling that they were caught in the middle of their parents' dispute. They reported both benefits and concerns about their lawyers. While the majority (7/11) were satisfied with their lawyer as they had someone to talk to who reassured them that their views would be communicated to the court, they (7/11) also expressed the need for more information from their lawyer, a follow-up with them after court appearances, and more explanation of the process to them in child-friendlier language.

Birnbaum, Bala and Cyr (2011) interviewed 32 children aged 7–17 years in Ontario and Ohio who had either met with a judge, had a lawyer represent them, or spoke to a mental health professional in a parenting assessment.[29] Regardless of which family justice professional the children spoke to, they all reported that they wanted to be involved in the decision-making process in some way, but most did not want to decide parenting arrangements. None reported negative

Promoting the Participation of Children across the Globe: From Social Exclusion to Child-Inclusive Policies, Oxford University Press, Oxford UK 2015, pp. 135–157.

27 N. Bala and R. Birnbaum, above n. 16, pp. 787–829.

28 R. Birnbaum and N. Bala, 'The Child's Perspective on Legal Representation: Young People Report on Their Experiences with Child Lawyers' (2009) 25(1) *Canadian Journal of Family Law* 11–71.

29 R. Birnbaum, N. Bala and F. Cyr, above n. 10, pp. 398–422.

effects as a result of their interviews with judges or other professionals. All of those interviewed by a judge reported that they appreciated having had an opportunity to be heard by the judge, even those who did not get the outcome they wanted.

As part of a pilot project, Voice of the Child Reports in Ontario, Birnbaum and Bala (2017) interviewed 33 children, 37 parents, 27 social workers, 31 parents' lawyers and 27 judges.[30] The majority of the parents, parents' lawyers, judges, and most notably the children involved, believed that having children's views reported was a positive, and believed that these reports were a valuable way to do this. Further, a majority of the cases settled soon after the report was provided, generally in a way consistent with the views expressed by the child. It is clear that most parents were often not fully aware of their children's views and that, once the parents were provided with accurate information, many were able to settle their disputes. Certain caveats were raised by some parents and professionals about the use of this type of report. For example, cases involving children who do not wish to visit with the other parent (e.g. where a child refuses to visit the other parent), have special learning needs or have not had contact with the other parent for a long period of time may require a more detailed parenting assessment. As a result of this study, since July 2018, the Ontario Office of the Children's Lawyer added Voice of the Child Reports to the other services it provides: focused investigations, full investigations and child legal representation.

4.2. HEARING FROM PROFESSIONALS ABOUT CHILDREN'S PARTICIPATION

Birnbaum and Bala (2010) interviewed 16 judges in Ohio and 30 judges in Ontario in 2009.[31] The interviews revealed a broad range of differing opinions across and within jurisdictions. Unlike Ohio judges, who are encouraged by legislation in that state to regularly interview children, Ontario judges (12/30) reported that they rarely interview children. In Ontario, the legislation permits judges to interview children, but does not encourage this. Most of the Ontario judges (18/30) reported that they had never done so, but several indicated that if they had training, they would be willing to do so.

Five years later, Birnbaum and Bala[32] found increased use of judicial interviewing in Canada, but still significant variation across the country,

---

[30] This study was funded by the Law Foundation of Ontario.

[31] R. Birnbaum, and N. Bala, above n. 13, pp. 300–337.

[32] R. Birnbaum and N. Bala, 'A Survey of Canadian Judges About Their Meetings with Children: Becoming More Common But Still Contentious' (2014) 91 *Canadian Bar Review* 637–655.

with the highest rates in Quebec,[33] where the Civil Code[34] establishes a presumption of judges interviewing children. In their survey of 62 judges from across Canada, over half of the judges had experience with interviewing children.

In 2016, the Canadian Research Institute for Law and the Family conducted a survey of family justice professionals (lawyers and judges) which found that judges (36%) more often than lawyers for parents (20%) seek the views of children. Lawyers obtained children's views most often through the use of mental health professionals (63%) or a non-evaluative Voice of the Child Report prepared by a lawyer or mental health professional (41%).[35]

In 2017, the Canadian Research Institute for Law and the Family conducted another survey of family justice professionals about children's participation in the family justice process.[36] The lawyers surveyed reported frequent use of:

- children being represented by a lawyer (59%);
- parenting assessments prepared by mental health professionals (56%);
- lawyer for a child meeting with the child and providing a report (44%);
- a Voice of the Child Report prepared by a mental health professional or lawyer (31%);
- a mental health professional meeting with the child and reporting back to parents (28%); and
- a child meeting with a judge in a judicial interview (9%).[37]

It is clear that obtaining evidence about children's views and preferences is constrained by the services actually available, the financial cost of services to parents and whether they can afford them.

5. CONCLUSION

In this chapter we discussed the different ways in which children are heard across Canada, and provided a summary of the growing body of empirical research

[33] In Quebec, Art. 34 Civil Code states: 'The court shall, in every application brought before it is affecting the interest of a child, give the child an opportunity to be heard if his age and power of discernment permit it.'

[34] See s 394.1 of the Code de procédure civile, RLRQ c C-25 and s 203(1) of the Family Law Act, SBC 2011, c 25.

[35] L. Bertrand, J. Paetsch, J.P. Boyd and N. Bala, 'The Practice of Family Law in Canada: Results from a Survey of Participants at the 2016 National Family Law Program', Canadian Research Institute for Law and the Family, 2016, https://prism.ucalgary.ca/handle/1880/107202.

[36] The conference was comprised of a majority of family justice professionals from Western Canada (especially Alberta) and the results need to be cautiously interpreted.

[37] J. Paetsch, L. Bertrand and J.P. Boyd, 'Children's Participation in Justice Processes: Finding the Best Ways Forward, Results from the Survey of Symposium Participants', Canadian Research Institute for Law and the Family, 2017, https://prism.ucalgary.ca/handle/1880/107587.

from this country that examines what children and family justice professionals have to say about children's participation in family disputes. While the UNCRC, which Canada ratified in 1991, promotes children as rights-bearing individuals who should be consulted about plans for their care in the context of parental separation and divorce, there remains wide discretion about whether and how children are really being heard in Canada. It is hoped the *new Divorce Act* amendments will result in more opportunities for children to be heard. However, much is dependent on the financial supports and policies of governments, and the attitudes of family justice professionals, including lawyers, judges and mental health professionals.

CHINA

Ningning ZHAO

1. INTRODUCTION

The National Bureau of Statistics of the People's Republic of China (NBS) publishes precise statistical data about the population of Chinese children and young people. For instance, as of 2019, the population aged 0–14 years was 234,920,000, comprising roughly 16.78% of the entire population of Mainland China in the same year. According to statistical data from the NBS, the past decade, from 2009 to 2018, has seen a distinct and continuous increase, from 1.85% to 3.20%,[1] in the crude divorce rate,[2] from which a corresponding increase in the number of minor children (younger than 18 years old) involved in these family conflicts may be predicted. The China Justice Big Data Service Platform also released nationwide statistics[3] revealing that 96% of divorce litigation cases from 2014 to 2016 were child custody disputes. In addition to

[1] National Bureau of Statistics of China, 'Crude Divorce Rate', http://data.stats.gov.cn/easyquery.htm?cn=C01&zb=A0P0C&sj=2018.

[2] The crude divorce rate refers to the ratio of divorced couples to the annual average population for the reference year. The formula is: crude divorce rate = number of couples divorced for the reference year/annual average population * 100. The crude divorce rates for 2009 to 2018 respectively are 1.85%, 2.00%, 2.13%, 2.29%, 2.57%, 2.67%, 2.79%, 3.02%, 3.15%, and 3.20%.

[3] China Justice Big Data Service Platform, 'Judicial Data Special Report of Divorce Disputes', http://data.court.gov.cn/pages/categoryBrowse.html?keyword=离婚.

marriage dissolution through a judicial process, under which child-related issues would be settled, a minor child can initiate litigation pertaining to child issues as the subject of the litigation, represented by his/her guardian. As a matter of procedure, as part of the in-depth reform of the mode of hearing family disputes, children can participate both in and out of court verbally or in writing, and, where necessary, children's opinions and views can be represented by an independent legal proxy, as explained below.

2. STATUTORY PROVISIONS

In judicial practice in China, children involved in family disputes keep their own independent personality rather than being accessories of the parents or the family. Since China became a member of the United Nations Convention on the Rights of the Child (UNCRC) in 1992, the principle of the child's best interests, which is the overarching principle in family dispute resolutions set out in Article 3(1) UNCRC, has been adopted. This principle states that: 'In all actions concerning children, whether undertaken by public or private social welfare situations, courts of law, administrative authorities or legislative bodies, the best interests of the child shall be a primary consideration.' The overarching principle is also stipulated by many domestic laws of the People's Republic of China (PRC), such as Chapter Five of the Civil Code on Marriage and Family, the Law on the Protection of Minors, the Civil Procedure Law, etc. However, in various circumstances, the application standards vary. Therefore, when deciding what is in the best interests of the minor child, courts look into not only the material support but also the psychological benefits for the child in his/her growth. When a child over eight years of age is involved in a dispute concerning child-related issues, the child's views should be considered. With the guidance of the international consensus, in China, with respect to family disputes, the welfare of children shall be the first and paramount consideration of the court when determining child-related issues.

3. MODES OF CHILD PARTICIPATION

3.1. DIRECT FORMS OF PARTICIPATION

In the Chinese tribunal system, the judge is the authority who ultimately decides whether the child may participate in the proceedings. Pursuant to the latest Opinion of the Supreme People's Court of the PRC,[4] people's courts, when hearing

[4] Art. 28 of Opinions of the Supreme People's Court regarding Further Deeping the Hearing Forms and Working Mechanics of Family Cases (for Trial Implementation), No. 12 (2018) of the Supreme People's Court, effective on 18 July 2018.

family cases involving child custody, shall adequately listen to the thoughts and views of children over the age of eight, which means minor children may be included in trials in order to give their views, so that they can be taken into account by judges in the decision-making process. Moreover, according to this Opinion, people's courts can, if necessary, provide an appropriate environment for children when making enquiries of them, separate from the hearing proceedings. When deciding whether a child can participate in the proceedings, the child's age, awareness and understanding are always considered, as well as the child's wish to participate.

However, in practical terms, the preferences and opinions of a child shall never be the sole and determinative factor when adjudicating on custody issues. According to trial guidance[5] and judicial precedents,[6] and having in mind acting in the best interests of the child, in divorce cases involving domestic violence, for example, the violent conduct shall be the overriding concern as courts examine the risk to the child in the custody dispute. This is the case even if the child prefers to live with the 'violent parent', so it is generally inadvisable for people's courts to grant physical custody to the parent who committed the violence. That being said, in non-domestic violence cases, the preferences and views expressed by a minor child over eight years old shall be as a critical consideration when deciding on physical custody. Under these circumstances, the people's courts exercise their discretion to make a judgment in the best interests of the child.

According to the provisions of the Law of the People's Republic of China on the Protection of Minors (revised in 2012),[7] if a dispute arises in a divorce case between the two parties concerning custody arrangements for their minor child, the people's court shall adequately listen to the opinions of the child if he/she is capable of expressing his/her thoughts or wishes, and make a decision based on the principle of protecting the interests and rights of the child and the circumstances specific to the disputing parents. The age threshold for hearing the opinions of the minor child is eight years, according to above-mentioned laws.

In practice, the child can participate separately at the judge's request. In this case, the child directly expresses his/her views verbally to the judge or other experts/psychologists involved in the court case. Additionally, the child can file his/her views with the people's court in writing or on a video recording instead of being interviewed by the judge, but it remains for the court to decide whether

5 The Eighth People's Courts Conference Summary of Trials of Civil and Commercial Cases, issued on 30 November 2016 by the Supreme People's Court.

6 Ten Typical Ruling Cases involving Domestic Violence Released by the Supreme People's Court, Bulletin of the Supreme People's Court No. 2, 2015 (No. 220).

7 Art. 52 section II of the Law of the People's Republic of China on the Protection of Minors (revised in 2012), effective on 1 January 2013, promulgated by the Standing Committee of the National People's Congress.

the views reflect the genuine wishes of the child. In effect, pursuant to established practices and principles on written opinions or evidence, the child, if eligible, who has filed written views would be required to appear to be interviewed by the judge.

In summary, a child over eight years of age can express his/her views directly to the judge or the mediator. Meanwhile, as stated above, the child's views could be listened to and recorded by the court judge, if necessary, and all the content would be analysed and considered in combination with the child's living conditions, mental health, family circumstances, etc., in the decision-making process. To protect the privacy of minors, the views expressed by the child are kept confidential.

3.2. INDIRECT FORMS OF PARTICIPATION

In addition to the aforesaid methods of direct communication/participation, in some family disputes where the courts deem it necessary to hear from other perspectives than the parties themselves, a report presented by an independent third party (e.g. family issues investigators, psychologists, law experts) will be required. In practice, the independent third party should have engaged in in-depth discussions with the parents, the child him/herself and other relevant persons. Careful observations of the relationship between all the persons concerned, or even comprehensive visits to survey the child's living conditions, can effectively allow the child to participate in the proceedings in an indirect way. Using these various methods, a child over the age of eight years can pass on his/her views and preferences regarding custody and visitation issues through the investigators, who file a 'social care investigation report' with the people's court for reference during the decision-making process.[8]

As mentioned above, in principle a child willing to express his/her views or opinions is interviewed by the judge or the family issues investigator (if the court deems it necessary) about his/her views or opinions prior to, or during, the trial. As a consequence, what the child has expressed will be written down in the record of inquiries which will be taken into consideration while deciding child-related issues and the people's court will examine or look into this later on in combination with evidence, testimony, statements, investigation reports, etc. The detailed information about what is said in the interview is not disclosed to the parties to the case, but the judge should make his/her decision on custody based on the views of the child.

[8] Art. 22(3) of the Supreme People's Court Opinions regarding Deepening the Reform of the Family Trial Mode and Working Mechanism (Trial Implementation), No. 12 (2018) of the Supreme People's Court, effective on 18 July 2018.

Some people's courts in China have a system of 'family issues investigators' who play a role in providing psychological counselling for children and assist the people's court with disputes regarding children.

In accordance with the current laws,[9] the people's courts may invite the National People's Congress deputies, the Chinese People Political Consultative Conference members, people's jurors, people's mediators, experts and scholars, lawyers, grassroots legal service workers, arbitrators, retired legal workers, professionals at grassroot-level and other personnel with expertise in sociology, humanities, law, education, psychology, marriage, etc. to join the roster of 'family issues investigators'. At least two investigators in every case are entitled or authorised by the people's court to obtain evidence through their investigation and submit a written investigation report to the people's court. The investigators are obliged to report to the people's courts anything that they learn during their investigation about domestic violence or other conduct that violates the child's legal rights and interests. Besides reporting to the people's courts, they also can report the situation to relevant departments of government and relief organisations, thus bringing these institutions into the dispute resolution process. In the process, family issues investigation reports can be considered by the courts and the parties to the case are entitled to present views on this report. Additionally, the Anti-domestic Violence Law of the People's Republic of China grants people's courts the authority to issue a writ of habeas corpus to the applicant who is suffering domestic violence or a real risk of it. If a child is experiencing such violence in family disputes, his/her close relatives, public security bureaus, the Women's Federation, neighbourhood committees, or aid and relief management institutions may apply for a writ of habeas corpus on the child's behalf.[10] Due to the emphasis placed on the psychological wellbeing of children, psychologists or psychology organisations appointed by the people's courts[11] can provide psychological counselling for the child if the child consents. The specific information and form of psychological counselling is decided on a case-by-case basis by the court and psychology organisation. The 'psychological counselling report'[12] filed with the court should be considered while dealing

9 Arts. 17, 22, 23, 24 and 25 of the Supreme People's Court Opinions regarding Deepening the Reform of the Family Trial Mode and Working Mechanism (Trial Implementation), No. 12 (2018) of the Supreme People's Court, effective on 18 July 2018.

10 Article 23 of the Anti-domestic Violence Law of the People's Republic of China, effective on 27 December 2015, promulgated by Standing of Committee of the National People's Congress.

11 Arts. 29 and 31 of the Supreme People's Court Opinions regarding Deepening the Reform of the Family Trial Mode and Working Mechanism (Trial Implementation), No. 12 (2018) of the Supreme People's Court, effective on 18 July 2018.

12 Art. 34 of the Supreme People's Court Opinions regarding Deepening the Reform of the Family Trial Mode and Working Mechanism (Trial Implementation), No. 12 (2018) of the Supreme People's Court, effective on 18 July 2018.

with the case, but any information in the report should remain confidential and not be disclosed to the parties to the case. Ultimately, the psychologists follow up and review the child's living conditions regularly, according to any additional requirements set out by some people's courts.

3.3. REPRESENTATION FORMS OF PARTICIPATION

Subject to the PRC Civil Procedure Law, a child with no legal capacity to participate in a case shall be represented by his/her legal representative if he/she commences or participates in a case. Classified by the litigation status of children, there are two broad categories of proceedings pertaining to child-related issues. The first category is litigation initiated by a child whose parent acts as the child's legal representative against the other parent or whose guardian, who is someone other than either parent, acts as the child's legal representative against both parents, for example in disputes regarding maintenance In the other category of litigation, the parents are respectively the plaintiff (petitioner) and the defendant (respondent), and the child participates in the case as the person concerned, for example in disputes over child custody, visitation, etc.

Generally, the parties to the litigation are informed by the people's court's service. A child could be the subject of litigation represented by his/her guardian or legal representative, rather than engaging in litigation on his/her own. The legal representative, acting as the agent of the child, would have substantive as well as procedural rights and obligations. Accordingly, as the litigating party, the child who does not have legal capacity to bring a litigation receives the service of process like an adult party, but through his/her legal representative.

Similarly, a child who does not have legal capacity is informed of the outcome of the proceedings by the court through his/her guardian or legal representative.

In general, a minor's guardians are his/her legal representatives, acting on behalf of the him/her in the proceedings. Where the guardians try to shirk their responsibilities, the people's court will appoint one of them to participate in the proceedings.[13] Furthermore, the legal representative of the child can also entrust, in the name and for the sake of the child, one or two agent(s) ad litem and pay the representation fees. An example may be seen in maintenance cases, where one parent who has custody of the child can, as the child's legal representative, hire a lawyer, for the sake of the minor child's interest, to represent the child in the court proceedings to sue the other parent for maintenance. Pursuant to the law,[14] lawyers, grassroots legal service workers, close relatives of the minor

13 Art. 57 of the Civil Procedure Law of the People's Republic of China (revised in 2017), effective on 1 July 2018, promulgated by the Standing Committee of National People's Congress.

14 Art. 58 of the Civil Procedure Law of the People's Republic of China (revised in 2017), effective on 1 July 2018, promulgated by the Standing Committee of National People's Congress.

litigant, and citizens recommended by the relevant social organisation and the community where the minor litigant lives can be entrusted as agents ad litem. The agents perform their duties within the scope of power as well as in the best interests of the child.

In addition to the traditional forms of representation, people's courts throughout China have been advocating for a reform of family case hearings since 2016.[15] It is notable that Shanghai Putuo District People's Court has borrowed from the successful overseas experience of the 'independent representative'[16] to introduce the scheme of 'proxy for children's rights and best interests' (hereinafter the 'child's proxy scheme') in order to better safeguard the interests of the children involved in the cases where the traditional forms of representation cannot help.

Regarding the situations in which the child's proxy scheme could be introduced, Shanghai Putuo District People's Court entertains the following four types of cases:[17] where minor children are abandoned or abused by parents; where parents insist on giving up custody of their children; where property rights under the names of the children may be infringed; or where the children are suffering from mental or physical illnesses. A proxy can participate throughout the entire proceedings, including: prior to the trial, communicating with the minor child and carrying out relevant investigations to find out the real needs and best interests of the child; representing the child in the mediation process and during the course of hearing of the case; in certain family cases concerning enforcement, bringing up specific plans to deal with enforcement issues; and, even afterwards, paying a return visit, keeping the focus on the child's happiness and development. Similarly, one of the pilot areas for family trials reform, Nanjing Intermediate People's Court, has been promoting the system of 'representatives of minors' interests'[18] consisting of two aspects of protection. One is the system

---

15 In April 2016, the Supreme People's Court issued its Opinions Regarding Developing a Pilot Project for Reform of the Family Trial Mode and Working Mechanism and Notification of Developing a Pilot Project for Reform of the Family Trial Mode and Working Mechanism in Some People's Courts, specifying that the Reform would be implemented formally on 1 June 2016 in 118 people's courts across the country. In July 2017, the Supreme People's Court and 15 other authorities jointly issued the Opinions Regarding Establishing the Joint Meeting Mechanism of Reform of the Family Trial Mode and Working Mechanism. Afterwards, Shanghai, Beijing, Guangdong, Guangxi, Henan, Jiangsu, Fujian, et al. successively released specific rules for family trials and opinions supporting measures. Then, in July 2018, summing up the reform experience over the two years in the pilot areas, the Supreme People's Court issued the Supreme People's Court Opinions regarding Deepening the Reform of the Family Trial Mode and Working Mechanism (Trial Implementation) and issued prescriptive guidance therein.

16 For example, the 'officer of the service' or 'Welsh family proceedings officer' appointed by courts under the UK Children Act 1989 (s 41).

17 N. Guo and Y. Gao, 'Shanghai's First Exploration of the System of Proxy for Children's Rights and Interests', *Labor Newspaper*, 1 December 2017, p. 11.

18 Nanjingshi Jianyequ Renminfayuan, 'Nanjing Intermediate People's Court Implementation Opinions regarding Promoting the Reform of Family Trial Mode', http://www.njjyfy.gov.cn/www/jyfy/2017/sfzw3_mb_a3916052425858.htm.

of 'litigation guardians', who act as the representatives during trials of minor litigants (plaintiffs) whose statutory guardians cannot appear at trial or where a conflict of interests exists. The other is the system of 'observation and care', which provides support to children who are involved in, or affected by, family disputes. Volunteers and social workers appointed by the court accompany the children during the proceedings, if necessary, to ensure that the children express themselves independently without being impacted on by any others present.

3.4. CHILD LITIGATING ON OWN BEHALF

As stated above, since minor children lack legal capacity, their guardians shall be their legal representatives in their litigation. Accordingly, they can be represented in order to exercise the conduct necessary for litigation. For example, according to Chapter Five of the Civil Code of the PRC on Marriage and Family, if parents fail to perform their duty to raise their children, those who are minors or who are incapable of living on their own shall have the right to demand the cost of their upbringing from their parents. In the relevant court proceedings for this claim, the children will be represented by their legal representatives, including when commencing a litigation, receiving service of process, etc. Simply put, in China, a child under the age of 18 who lacks legal capacity is represented by his/her legal representative if the child is the party to a case. Since a minor child has limited or no legal capacity, in the litigation it is the legal representative, on behalf of the child, who plays a decisive role in collecting, submitting and managing the relevant documents, reports or other evidence by law. Nevertheless, as the subject of the proceedings, the minor child's preferences and views could be adopted by his/her legal representative if the minor child is able to provide opinions or evidence within the reasonable scope of his/her level of knowledge and understanding. Precedents reveal that if the legal representative's claim conflicts with that of the child, and if the child is considered sufficiently mature, the courts would examine the claim taking into consideration the real wishes of the child. But obviously, due to the child's inability to conduct civil litigation, he/she cannot appeal a decision independently.

In terms of the payment for the cost of litigation, it is borne in advance by the plaintiff/applicant who initiates the litigation. When issuing its judgment, the court may shift a certain portion of the cost to the defendant, who is then obliged to pay his/her share. If the minor plaintiff or his/her legal representative cannot afford to pay the costs of litigation due to certain circumstances – for example being disabled without a fixed source of income, living in poverty as defined by the government, etc. – the court will allow him/her to make a reduced, deferred payment or will exempt him/her from payment. According to the regulations in the Measures for the Payment of Litigation Fees, if a party who applies for judicial reparation meets any of a particular set of circumstances,[19] for example, being disabled and lacking a stable income, applying for compensation for the suffering or damages caused by his/her act of protecting social or public interests, etc., the people's court shall approve the exemption, reduction[20] or postponement of payment[21] of the cost of litigation.

4. TYPES OF PROCEEDINGS

As previously discussed, litigation may be initiated before the Chinese court with jurisdiction over divorce, which covers child custody or child maintenance, alteration of child custody, child visitation and other cases concerning the legal rights and interests of children. Children can participate in these proceedings directly or indirectly. The relevant requirements of age/maturity/capability/capacity required for any type of proceedings concerning minors are the same as for the modes of participation.

Arbitration is a significant alternative dispute resolution process in China. It provides greater autonomy for the parties as compared to litigation. However, pursuant to the Arbitration Law of the People's Republic of China, disputes over marriage, adoption, guardianship, child maintenance and inheritance may not be submitted to arbitration.[22] Thus, family disputes are not dealt with by arbitration, and accordingly there is no opportunity for minor children involved in family cases to participate in arbitration.

In Chinese legal practice, mediation is a common process for dispute settlement in family cases. More specifically, mediation of family disputes forms part of the whole civil litigation process, including mediation prior to the formal acceptance of the case by the people's court and mediation during the whole course of the hearing. In disputes over issues concerning a minor child who is aged eight or over, that child's views should be considered, as mentioned above, and child participation is allowed, whether by appearing before the judge to express his/her views, submitting his/her own written statements, via reports filed by a designated third person, or any other format.

---

19 Art. 45 of the Measures for the Payment of Litigation Fees, effective on 1 April 2007, promulgated by the State Council.

20 Art. 46 of the Measures for the Payment of Litigation Fees, effective on 1 April 2007, promulgated by the State Council.

21 Art. 47 of the Measures for the Payment of Litigation Fees, effective on 1 April 2007, promulgated by the State Council.

22 Art. 3(1) of the Arbitration Law of the People's Republic of China (revised in 2017), effective on 1 January 2018, promulgated by the Standing Committee of the National People's Congress.

5. POLICY OR PRACTICE DEVELOPMENTS

In recent years, people's courts have created or introduced various forms of hearings to meet the needs of minor children in cases concerning them. For instance, some courts in China have adopted 'round table trials' to hear custody disputes involving minor children. In these trials, the judge and the parties are seated at a round table, which reduces the pressure arising from the judge sitting higher up and further away and the hostility created by both parties sitting opposite each other. Furthermore, the parties are referred to as 'the father' and 'the mother' instead of 'the plaintiff' and 'the defendant', in order to create a more comfortable and friendly environment for them. Additionally, some people's courts are trying out 'weekend courts' to resolve the problem of schoolchildren facing the stress of studying and finding it hard to participate in court hearings during schooltime. In judicial practice, in order to help the child to better express his/her true views and opinions and prevent any interference in the child's expression, in a variety of locations to suit the actual circumstances of the child, for example at school, at home, in court, or any other place that is convenient for the child to express themselves.

6. CONCLUSION

In China, the requirements of Article 12 of the UNCRC are being met and gradual developments in the reform of the hearing of family cases in China can be seen. However, due to regional differences and the complexity of family cases concerning children, there is still much room for improvement. Currently, people's courts throughout China are engaged in exploring and implementing methods of hearing or other forms of dispute resolution that are more appropriate to achieving the best interests of children.

On the one hand, judicial intervention and power is being exerted over issues concerning abuse and neglect, child support, evidence and the ascertainment of children's views, etc. On the other hand, the proceedings as a whole should involve a greater focus on children's feelings, i.e. not only taking children's opinions and views sufficiently into account where necessary, but also reducing to a minimum the harm to children, mentally or physically, whether from the family or the hearing process, by delivering warmth and care within the judicial process.

In view of the specific national conditions and extensive trial experience abroad, legal experts and scholars in China are calling for, and Chinese courts are trying for, more and greater opportunities for children's participation in family dispute proceedings.

CROATIA

Branka REŠETAR and Nataša LUCIĆ

1. INTRODUCTION

More than 40 years before the adoption of the UN Convention on the Rights of the Child (UNCRC),[1] the former Yugoslav, i.e. Croatian, Act on the Relationship between Parents and Children (1947) obliged social welfare centres to take account of the views of the child in divorce proceedings.

The right of the child to express their views was first incorporated into Croatian legislation in its current form in 1998. The incorporation resulted from an international responsibility laid down in the UNCRC.[2] However, research conducted at Croatian courts 10 years later revealed that despite their explicit right to be heard, children rarely participate in proceedings concerning parental responsibility or contact with their parents either directly or with the assistance of the competent social welfare centre.[3]

---

1 Convention on the Rights of the Child, 20 November 1989, United Nations, Treaty Series, vol. 1577.

2 B. REŠETAR, *Pravna zaštita prava na susrete i druženje*' ['Family Right to Contact concerning Children'], Josip Juraj Strossmayer University, Faculty of Law Osijek, Osijek 2011, pp. 202–208.

3 B. REŠETAR and R.E. EMERY, 'Children's Rights in European Legal Proceedings: Why are Family Practices So Different from Legal Theories?' (2008) 46 *Family Court Review* 165–177.

In addition the hearing of children, the concept of a special guardian for children has been introduced into a number of Family Acts since 1947. The special guardian's tasks include child representation and the protection of their interests when the interests of children and parents collide. Yet a number of recent studies have demonstrated that special guardians for children have often only formally represented the child, without being truly interested in their concerns. Hearing the child's views on their concerns and needs has almost been completely avoided.[4]

According to its latest Concluding Observations (2014), the Committee on the Rights of the Child is concerned about the fact that hearing children's views is not adequately implemented in practice in all matters affecting them, including judicial and administrative proceedings, and that there is insufficient training of experts working with children in the Croatian legal system.[5]

Croatia's international and European responsibilities have pushed the Croatian legislator into stronger regulation of the protection of children's procedural rights in family proceedings with the aim of achieving their full protection in practice.[6] The strengthening of children's procedural rights in family proceedings has also been influenced by recent judgements of the European Court of Human Rights in this field, particularly by those referring to Croatia.[7] Child participation in judicial and extrajudicial decision-making pertaining to family matters represents an important part of the Croatian legislative reform which resulted in the adoption of the 2015 Family Act (FA 2015).[8] Family matters include: divorce

---

4 B. Rešetar and D. Rupić, 'Posebni skrbnik za dijete u hrvatskom i njemačkom obiteljskopravnom sustavu' ['Child's Special Guardian under the Croatian and German Legal System'], *Zbornik Pravnog fakulteta Sveučilišta u Rijeci*, 37 (2016/3), 1175, 1196; A. Radina, 'Praksa suda i posebnog skrbnika u postupcima radi odlučivanja o mjerama zaštite osobnih prava i dobrobiti djeteta' ['Case-Law in Regard to Proceedings Revolving around Measures for the Protection of the Personal Rights and Wellbeing of the Child'] in B. Rešetar and S. Aras (eds.), *Represivne mjere za zaštitu osobnih prava i dobrobiti djeteta. Interdisciplinarni, komparativni i međunarodni osvrti* ['Repressive Measures to Protect the Personal Rights and Wellbeing of the Child. Interdisciplinary, Comparative and International Reviews'], Josip Juraj Strossmayer University, Faculty of Law Osijek, Osijek 2014, pp. 23–39.

5 UN Committee on the Rights of the Child (2014), *Concluding observations on the combined third and fourth periodic reports of Croatia*, adopted by the Committee at its 67th session (1–19 September 2014), CRC/C/HRV/CO/3-4; I. Majstorović, 'The Realization of the Right of the Child to Express His/Her Views – How "Visible" are Children in Croatian Family Judicial Proceedings?', *Ljetopis socijalnog rada*, 24 (2017/1), 55, 62.

6 The UN Convention on the Rights of the Child (Official Gazette of the Socialist Federal Republic of Yugoslavia no. 14/1990; Official Gazette – International Treaties no. 12/93, 20/97); European Convention on the Exercise of Children's Rights (Official Gazette – International Treaties no. 1/2010), which came into force in the Republic of Croatia on 1 July 2010; and Regulation (EC) No. 2201/2003 on jurisdiction, recognition and enforcement of matrimonial and parental judgments, which has applied since Croatia became a Member State.

7 ECtHR *M and M v Croatia* (Appl. No. 10161/13), 3 September 2015; ECtHR *Adžić v Croatia* (Appl. No. 22643/14), 12 March 2015.

8 Family Act (Official Gazette no. 103/15, 98/19).

or separation, parentage, parental responsibility, contact concerning the child, relocation, child protection, adoption, guardianship and maintenance. Child abduction also falls within family matters, although it is not regulated by the FA 2015. According to the FA 2015, the child's right to participate in family proceedings is exercised in several different forms: (1) the child is a party in all proceedings where their rights and interests are decided upon; (2) the child has the procedural capacity to litigate; (3) the child has the right to express their opinion; and (4) the child has the right to a special guardian who represents their interests in the proceedings.

According to the 2011 census, 4,284,889 people lived in Croatia, out of which 896,605 people aged 0–19.[9] Pursuant to an estimate of the Central Bureau of Statistics, in 2019 the total Croatian population fell to 4,067,500 and the population aged 0–19 to 785,700.[10]

In the last 10 years, the average number of marriages concluded per year has been 20,000, while 6,000 marriages have been dissolved on average annually.[11] There are no official statistical data on the number of divorces involving minor children, so it is unknown how many children have been affected by divorce and how many children have participated in other types of family proceedings.

2. STATUTORY PROVISIONS

According to the FA 2015, parents and other children's guardians are obliged to respect the child's views in accordance with their age and maturity (see Art. 86 paragraph 1). This parents' liability refers to making decisions affecting the child. In all proceedings affecting any right or interest of the child, the child has the right to find out, in an appropriate way, about relevant circumstances of the case, get advice, express their views and obtain information on the possible consequences of the respect for their opinion (see Art. 86 paragraph 2 of the FA 2015). Family proceedings mean all judicial and extrajudicial proceedings dealing with divorce or separation, parentage, parental responsibility, contact concerning the child, relocation, child protection, adoption, guardianship and maintenance. Pursuant to the Act on the Implementation of the Hague Convention on the Civil Aspects of International Child Abduction (Implementation Act),[12] the child has the right

9 Croatian Bureau of Statistics, *Census of Population, Households and Dwellings 2011*, https://www.dzs.hr/default_e.htm.

10 Croatian Bureau of Statistics, *Population Estimate 2019*, https://www.dzs.hr/default.htm.

11 Accurate data of the Croatian Bureau of Statistics on the natural change in population are available at: https://www.dzs.hr/.

12 Act on the Implementation of Hague Convention on the Civil Aspects of International Child Abduction (Official Gazette no. 99/18).

to express their views and the right to a special guardian in cases handling child abduction. In addition, the child shall be heard in accordance with their age and maturity (see Art. 86 of the FA 2015 and Art. 7 of the Implementation Act).

The right of the child to be heard corresponds to the obligation of the court to enable the child to exercise this right. If there are justified reasons for which the court does not have to provide the child with this right (e.g. the child refuses to express their views or is too young), the court shall give the reasons why in its reasoning (see Art. 360 paragraph 4 of the FA 2015).

The child is now provided with the status of a party in all family proceedings, with the right to directly or indirectly express their views in all extrajudicial and judicial family proceedings and with a special guardian whose duties are clearly prescribed by the law.[13] In fact, in the period prior to the adoption of the FA 2015, the child had not been regarded as a party to divorce proceedings despite the fact that their rights were decided upon.

With respect to child participation in *extrajudicial proceedings*, it is necessary to emphasise that the FA 2015 requires spouses with minor children to undertake a mandatory step before initiating divorce proceedings at the court, namely participation in mandatory counselling at social welfare centres. Mandatory counselling also precedes any court proceedings concerning a dispute over parental responsibility and contact concerning the child. Mandatory counselling is conducted by a team of experts working in social welfare centres (social worker, psychologist and lawyer). With the parents' consent, the child is already allowed to express their views in the mandatory counselling procedure (Arts. 321, 325 and 327 of the FA 2015).[14]

Apart from mandatory counselling, the FA 2015 envisages family mediation where family members strive to resolve a family dispute with the help of one or more family mediators. According to Article 339 paragraph 2 of the FA 2015, in the process of family mediation, a family mediator can enable the child to express their opinion with their parents' consent. This is a right of the child, not a duty.

In terms of child participation in *family proceedings* according to Article 358 of the FA 2015, the child is a party in all proceedings before the court where their rights and interests are decided upon. In the period prior to the adoption of the FA 2015, the child had not been deemed a party to divorce proceedings, but this is not the case with the FA 2015, which sees the child as a party before the court and provides them with a special guardian who represents them in divorce proceedings. This includes different types of family proceedings.

13 B. Rešetar, 'New Divorce Legislation in the Republic of Croatia' (2018) 32(1) *International Journal of Law, Policy and the Family* 63–79.

14 B. Rešetar, 'New Divorce Legislation in the Republic of Croatia' (2018) 32(1) *International Journal of Law, Policy and the Family* 63–79.

Contentious family proceedings in which the child has the right to participate are as follows: contentious divorce of the child's parents, litigation in regard to determining or contesting the parentage, and litigation concerning parental responsibility, contact with the child and child maintenance (Art. 368 of the FA 2015). The right to participate implies that the child, besides the right to express their views, shall have the right to a special guardian and if they are over 14, they can actively participate in judicial proceedings (state facts, produce evidence, lodge legal remedies).

The child's participation rights are recognised not only in contentious proceedings but also in non-contentious ones where private family matters are decided upon. This concerns: issuing permission for marriage to a minor, consensual divorce of the child's parents, approval of a parental responsibility agreement by the court, determining child maintenance, parental responsibility, and contact with the child (Art. 433 of the FA 2015).

3. MODES OF CHILD PARTICIPATION

3.1. EXTRAJUDICIAL PROCEEDINGS

Direct child participation in all extrajudicial proceedings depends on the parents' consent. While counselling is mandatory for parents or family members, family mediation is a procedure in which they take part voluntarily. Regardless of this difference, neither social welfare centres in the mandatory counselling procedure nor family mediators in the family mediation procedure can enable the child to express their views if they are not provided with prior consent of their parents. Even if an older child insists on expressing a view without their parents' consent, the competent social welfare centre cannot permit the child to do so, but it should register the child's intention in its report on completed mandatory counselling (though such a duty is not explicitly prescribed by the law). Considering that mandatory counselling precedes court proceedings, the court should certainly enable the child to provide their opinion in the courtroom. This results from a presumption that a parents' agreement is always considered to be in the best interests of the child. It is also presumed that before reaching an agreement the parents will have already talked with the child, which is one of the liabilities set forth by the FA 2015. Considering that every such agreement shall be approved by the court, there is always a possibility for the court to invite the child to express their views.

In the mandatory counselling procedure preceding divorce proceedings involving minor children, the competent social welfare centre should, if necessary, provide the parents with assistance in drawing up a Parental Responsibility Agreement (or Parenting Plan, PRA). A PRA is a written agreement between the parents on how they will exercise their shared parental responsibility after the separation.[15] The required form of a PRA encompasses the expression of the child's views and hence, the child will be given an opportunity to express their views about divorce-related issues affecting their position. The 2015 Family Act explicitly prescribes that parents are obliged to inform their child about the content of the PRA and provide the child with the possibility of expressing their opinion in accordance with their age and degree of maturity. The parents shall also respect their child's opinion in accordance with the wellbeing of the child standard (Art. 106 paragraph 4 of the FA 2015). A PRA template contains a field in which parents should indicate whether they have given their child an opportunity to express their views about the content of the PRA. If they have failed to do so, they shall give the reasons why. The template also includes a field in which parents should disclose whether or not they have taken their child's opinion into consideration. If they have not done so, they shall also give the reasons.[16]

As part of mandatory counselling, the competent social welfare centre shall inform spouses on the obligation to attend the first meeting within the framework of family mediation if they have not reached a PRA. Pursuant to the FA 2015, the main purpose of family mediation is to reach a PRA and other agreements relating to the child. In the family mediation procedure, all the other issues can be dealt with too. If parents do not reach a PRA in the mandatory counselling procedure and in the family mediation procedure, their marriage will be dissolved in contentious proceedings in which the child's views will be examined in an appropriate way, either directly by the judge (assisted by an expert) or through a special guardian for children.[17] Non-contentious divorce involving minor children can only be approved if spouses draw up a PRA. If there is no indication that the PRA is contrary to the interests of the child, the court shall not re-examine child's views and the PRA thus becomes effective.[18]

---

15 A PRA shall contain the following information: the child's post-divorce residence, time that the child is to spend with each parent (contact concerning the child), the manner of exchange of relevant information on the child, child maintenance, and the manner of resolving all possible controversial issues. In a PRA, parents may regulate other relevant issues relating to the exercise of parental responsibility (Art. 106 paragraphs 2 and 3 of the FA 2015).

16 N. Lucić, 'Protection of the Right of the Child to be Heard in Divorce Proceedings – Harmonization of Croatian Law with European Legal Standards' in D. Duić and T. Petrašević (eds.), *EU and Comparative Law Issues and Challenges Series*, Faculty of Law, Osijek 2017, pp. 391, 408.

17 If divorcing parents do not conclude a PRA, the competent social welfare centre shall warn them that the court will in contentious divorce proceedings make a decision ex officio on issues relevant for the child, enable the child to be heard and appoint a special guardian for the child.

18 The child is a party to the PRA reached by his/her parents and to the (adhesive, ancillary) procedure for approving the PRA, which accompanies consensual divorce. Therefore, a PRA approving decree acts prejudicially with respect to the child too. S. Aras Kramar, 'Novi pristup uređenju postupka radi razvoda braka u Hrvatskoj' ['New Approach to the Regulation of Divorce Proceedings in Croatia'], Collection of Contemporary Developments in Civil Procedure – achievements in national and comparative legal theory, Faculty of Law of the University of Split, Split 2015, pp. 235, 251.

3.2. JUDICIAL PROCEEDINGS

3.2.1. Hearing the Child

In judicial proceedings where the child's personal and property rights are decided upon, the court shall, unless the child opposes doing so, enable the child to express their opinion (Art. 360 of the FA 2015). The methods of communication as well as the choice of professionals who will communicate with the child depend on the type of proceedings, the child's age, maturity and ability to communicate. The court shall state the circumstances concerning the child's opinion in its reasoning (Art. 360 of the FA 2015). The way the court *obtains the opinion of the child* in family proceedings is regulated by the Bylaw on the Methods of Communication with the Child (2015 Bylaw).[19] A child aged 14 or older can express their opinion *independently* and *directly* to the court. The court shall enable children under 14 to express their opinion directly, or indirectly through *a special guardian or with the help of another expert.* An expert in this context means a psychologist and exceptionally another professional with corresponding qualifications, expert knowledge and skills needed for determining the child's opinion (Art. 2 of the 2015 Bylaw). When determining the child's opinion, a professional or special guardian shall apply expert procedures that will help the child to form and express their opinion (Art. 6 paragraph 2 of the 2015 Bylaw). Exceptionally, several professionals of different vocations can be included in determining the child's opinion if this is deemed necessary considering the developmental, health and disabilities or specificities of the child (Art. 6 paragraph 4 of the 2015 Bylaw).

According to Article 7 paragraph 1 of the 2015 Bylaw, determining the child's opinion consists of several steps: preparation of the child, assessment of their skills and maturity, and hearing their views. Preparation refers to informing the child about the right to express their views on all matters pertaining to the proceedings and on the consequences of their statement for the outcome of the proceedings. Assessment of the skills and maturity of the child means an assessment of the child's cognitive abilities to form and express an opinion in a reasonable and independent way and to understand the outcome thereof. There are no legal norms governing the manner of such assessment. It is up to the professional concerned to come up with an appropriate assessment method. The child should express their opinion in the form of a conversation conducted in an encouraging and stimulating atmosphere where the child will feel safe and respected. Such an expression should be seriously heard and taken into consideration. The court shall provide the child with an opportunity to express their views in an appropriate place (Art. 2 paragraphs 2 and 3 of the FA 2015).

---

19 Bylaw on the Methods of Communication with the Child (Official Gazette no. 123/2015).

This is not the courtroom, but for example the child's home, another room in the court, competent social welfare centre or special guardianship centre, or any other place determined by the court under the following conditions: that such a place is equipped and adapted for working with the child and that the child is ensured privacy and safety. The child's opinion can be heard through a video link (Art. 5 of the 2015 Bylaw) in their parents' home (with the consent of the parents), foster home or institution. A professional shall enable a child who cannot express their opinion through speech to express their views through non-verbal forms of communication such as games, body language, facial expressions, projective techniques and similar (Art. 7 paragraph 2 of the 2015 Bylaw). The child shall give their opinion in the absence of their parents or other carers (Art. 4 of the 2015 Bylaw). A special guardian or another expert shall present the child's option to the court orally or in writing, depending on the court's request (see Art. 8 of the 2015 Bylaw). The child's views shall be incorporated into a protocol into which parties (parents and other family members) to the proceedings can have an insight.

The FA 2015 obliges parents or special guardians (depending on the circumstances of a case) to *inform* the child not only on the course of the proceedings but also on its outcome and consequences and the possibility of submitting legal remedies. Article 361 of the FA 2015 stipulates that the decision of the court which governs the rights and interests of the child shall be delivered to the child's special guardian or legal representative. The child's special guardian or legal representative is obliged to inform the child about the content of the decision and their right, assisted by a professional, to lodge an appeal. The child shall have the right to an appeal whenever a court's decision affects their rights. Such an appeal can be lodged by a special guardian (see Art. 361 paragraph 2 of the FA 2015) or by children over 14 themselves if the court has recognised their procedural capacity (see Art. 359 of the FA 2015).

The child shall not be informed about the reasoning of the decision if doing so may have negative impact on their health and development.

3.2.2. Special Guardian

When it comes to divorces involving minor children, a failure to reach a PRA and, generally, a lack of will to cooperate on the part of the parents affect the child's position in court proceedings and the related costs. In fact, the court can establish that parents shall bear the costs of the services provided by a special guardian (Art. 366 paragraph 2 of the FA 2015). In the event of reaching, verifying and approving a PRA (consensual divorce), the child is represented by both parents, whereas in the event of a family dispute, the child is represented by a *special guardian for children*. For the sake of protection of the personal and property rights and interests of the child, the competent social welfare centre or court can appoint a special guardian in other family proceedings as well.[20] A special guardian in family proceedings must be a lawyer who has passed the bar exam and is employed at the Centre for Special Guardianship (Art. 240 paragraph 3 of the FA 2015). Special guardians for children shall complete interdisciplinary university education where they acquire the skills and competences required for communicating with children in legal matters.[21] Special guardians always have the option to ask for help from other experts when it is necessary to fully understand the child's family situation and opinion. Special guardians are obliged to respond to the invitation extended to a child to participate in the proceedings as the child's representative and to represent the interests of the child to whom they have been appointed. Furthermore, they are obliged to inform the child on the matter, course and outcome of the dispute in a way that is appropriate for their age. Special guardians have the responsibility to talk with the parent(s) or other persons closely related to the child if they find it necessary or if the court or social welfare centre obliges them to do so (Art. 240 paragraph 2 of the FA 2015).

The rights and duties of a child's special guardian cease to exist when the guardianship termination decree becomes effective. The decree is issued by the competent social welfare centre or court, whichever appointed the guardian in the first place (Art. 246 of the FA 2015).

3.2.3. *Children's Procedural Capacity to Litigate*

As holders of particular subjective rights, children should be able to independently initiate proceedings aimed at the exercise or protection of those rights. This concerns the rights guaranteed by the FA 2015. The FA 2015 grants, in certain circumstances, the child the right to independently initiate family proceedings and hence the child has the same procedural capacity as adults. Moreover, the FA 2015 explicitly permits a child who has turned 14 to independently initiate

20 In family disputes and procedures on parentage, parental responsibility, contact with the child, relocation, in child protection proceedings, on adoption; to a child in the event of a conflict between their interests and the interest of his/her legal representatives in property proceedings and disputes or when concluding a legal transaction; to children in case of a dispute or conclusion of a legal transaction between them when the same person is provided with the parental responsibility for them; to a child who is a foreign citizen or has no citizenship and who is currently on the territory on the Republic of Croatia; in other cases prescribed by the law or when it is necessary for protection of the right and interest of the child (Art. 240 paragraph 1 of the FA 2015) and child abduction (Art. 7 of the Implementation Act of the HCCA).

21 Interdisciplinary University Vocational Training Programme in the field of the protection of children's procedural rights and communication with the child, available at: http://www.pravos.unios.hr/katedra-obiteljsko-pravnihznanosti/program-strucnog-usavrsavanja. This lifelong vocational training programme intended for experts trained in communicating with children in the fields of law and psychology was adopted at the Faculty of Law Osijek, which is a member of the Children's Rights European Academic Network (CREAN).

proceedings before the competent bodies in regard to the exercise of their rights and interests (Art. 87 paragraph 1 of the FA 2015). In matters relating to the personal rights of the child, the court shall, upon a child's request, allow the child to state facts, propose evidence, file an appeal and carry out other acts in those proceedings if they are over 14 and being capable of understanding the meaning and legal consequences of those acts. Matters relating to the personal rights of the child include the right to life and healthcare, the right to safety and to be raised in a family in accordance with their physical, psychological and developmental needs, the right to live with their parents, the right to contact with the non-resident parent and other non-resident relatives, the right to choose education and the right to work in accordance with their abilities and wellbeing (Art. 84 of the FA 2015).

Before making a decision in which it acknowledges the child's procedural rights, the court shall ask the competent social welfare centre to give their opinion on it (Art. 359 of the FA 2015). The parent(s) are also authorised to carry out acts in the proceedings alongside the child. If the acts of the child and parents oppose each other, the court shall assess which acts it will take into account in accordance with the child's best interests.

Pursuant to Article 366 paragraph 1 of the FA 2015, the court shall, at its own discretion, make a decision on status issues, matters related to parental responsibility, personal relationships and measures for protection of the rights and wellbeing of the child, and child maintenance, without being influenced by the child's parents whatsoever and taking account of the circumstances and outcome of the case. As far as production of evidence proposed by the child is concerned, the related costs shall be, in accordance with Article 366 paragraph 4 of the FA 2015, borne by the child's parents in proportions determined by the court.[22]

4. RESEARCH

The largest research study on the exercise of the right of the child to be heard in divorce proceedings in Croatia has revealed disappointing results. At the biggest Croatian court (Municipal Civil Court of Zagreb), only 3.5% of children were given a chance to express their views in divorce proceedings in the period 2003–2004.[23]

---

22 S. Aras Kramar, 'Novi pristup uređenju postupka radi razvoda braka u Hrvatskoj' ['New Approach to the Regulation of Divorce Proceedings in Croatia'], Collection of Contemporary Developments in Civil Procedure – achievements in national and comparative legal theory, Faculty of Law of the University of Split, Split 2015, pp. 235, 245.

23 B. Rešetar and R.E. Emery, 'Children's Rights in European Legal Proceedings: Why are Family Practices So Different from Legal Theories?' (2008) 46 *Family Court Review* 165–177.

Two years after the family legislation reform, in 2017, a survey was held on child participation in the mandatory counselling procedure for spouses to attend before initiating divorce proceedings.[24] Since the FA 2015 requires the parents' consent for the child to participate, there is a question about how often children are heard within the mandatory counselling procedure. Do social welfare centres require the child to express their views? Are parents reluctant to give their consent to the child expressing their views? How often do they encourage the child to do so?

Essentially, the research based on the survey demonstrated the following:

1. The majority of the social welfare centres that responded to the survey never or hardly ever require the child to express their views within the mandatory counselling procedure prior to the initiation of divorce proceedings. Only 17% of the participating social welfare centres require the child to express their views in most cases and none of the centres ask the child to express their views in every case;
2. When social welfare centres require the child to express their views within the mandatory counselling procedure, the child's parents do not usually have any objections to the child doing so. Indeed, most respondents have confirmed that parents never oppose this possibility;
3. Within the mandatory counselling procedure, parents rarely invite their child to express their views to the social welfare centre directly.[25]

There is no research on child participation in judicial family proceedings. There are some studies indicating a drop in the number of contentious divorce proceedings involving minor children. This is a consequence of the fact that there is a growing number of parents who conclude a PRA.[26] Those studies imply that there is also a declining number of children who are invited to express their views before the court in divorce proceedings. This means, according to Aras Kramar, that the Croatian legislator has found efficient solutions for

24 The survey was conducted within the framework of a scientific paper. N. Lucić, 'Protection of the Right of the Child to be Heard in Divorce Proceedings – Harmonization of Croatian Law with European Legal Standards' in D. Duić and T. Petrašević (eds.), *EU and Comparative Law Issues and Challenges Series*, Faculty of Law, Osijek 2017, pp. 391–423.

25 N. Lucić, 'Protection of the Right of the Child to be Heard in Divorce Proceedings – Harmonization of Croatian Law with European Legal Standards' in D. Duić and T. Petrašević (eds.), *EU and Comparative Law Issues and Challenges Series*, Faculty of Law, Osijek 2017, pp. 391, 410–411.

26 See e.g. N. Lucić and K. Marošević, *Financial Aspects of Divorce Proceeding – Case Law Findings*, Economic and Social Development: Book of Proceedings, Split 2019, pp. 216–224; B. Rešetar, 'Growing Numbers of Parental Responsibility Agreements following the Divorce Reform in Croatia' in C. Rogers, M. Antokolskaia, J. Miles, P. Parkinson and M. Vonk (eds.), *Family Law and Family Realities*, Eleven International Publishing, The Hague 2019, pp. 367–380.

shifting the responsibility for deciding on the exercise of parental responsibility from the state to parents after the termination of their marital union. However, the Croatian legislator wants to keep the power of the state to intervene if the wellbeing of the child is in jeopardy.[27]

The relevant Croatian literature often points to the low level of protection of the child's right to express their views in judicial proceedings prior to the latest reform of the family legislation.[28] The recent literature warns that judges are not well trained in communicating with children[29] and indicates the importance of interdisciplinary education of judges, with a particular emphasis on their psychological education, which would lead to a 'constructive, non-stigmatising and non-victimising conversation with the child'. Finally, not every Croatian court has an adequate place for interviewing children. Most Croatian courts lack financial resources to implement these provisions in their daily work. This is likely the most important criticism regarding the Bylaw 2015, since it overlooks the fact that insufficient budgetary resources are available for these matters.[30]

5. POLICY OR PRACTICE DEVELOPMENTS

Considering the fact that it has been less than five years since the Croatian family legislation was last reformed, which has considerably enhanced the procedural position of the child in family proceedings, it is no wonder that at the moment there are no initiatives to amend family legislation in this area. Croatia is currently improving the existing mechanisms for efficient protection of children's procedural rights, primarily that of the special guardian for children. In that respect, the Government sent Parliament a Draft Act on the Centre for

---

27 S. Aras Kramar, 'Novi pristup uređenju postupka radi razvoda braka u Hrvatskoj' ['New Approach to the Regulation of Divorce Proceedings in Croatia'], Collection of Contemporary Developments in Civil Procedure – achievements in national and comparative legal theory, Faculty of Law of the University of Split, Split 2015, pp. 235, 266.

28 See e.g. D. Hrabar, 'Zastupanje djece i postupovna prava djeteta pred sudskim i upravnim tijelima u obiteljskopravnim stvarima' ['Representation of the Child and Its Procedural Rights before Judicial and Administrative Bodies in Family Matters'], *Hrvatska pravna revija*, 2 (2002/10), 46–53; A. Uzelac and B. Rešetar, 'Procesni položaj i zastupanje djeteta u sudskom postupku prema hrvatskom i komparativnom pravu – neka otvorena pitanja' ['Procedural Position of the Child before Judicial and Administrative Bodies in Family Matters – Some Open Issues'] in B. Rešetar (ed.), *Dijete i pravo* [Child and Law], Faculty of Law Osijek, Osijek 2009, pp. 163–194.

29 R. Šantek and M. Parać Garma, *Sudjelovanje djeteta u sudskim postupcima te zaštita prava i dobrobiti djeteta u tim postupcima* [The Participation of the Child in Court Proceedings and the Protection of the Rights and Wellbeing of the Child in These proceedings], Pravosudna akademija, Zagreb 2016, p. 43.

30 I. Majstorović, 'The Realization of the Right of the Child to Express His/Her Views – How "Visible" are Children in Croatian Family Judicial Proceedings?', *Ljetopis socijalnog rada*, 24 (2017/1), 55, 65–66.

Special Guardianship,[31] which sets out in detail the competences and internal organisation of that body. The Draft Act highlights the excessive workload of special guardians.[32] It also stresses that taking into consideration the growing specificities of cases in which a special guardian is appointed, particularly a special guardian for children, and the specific features of procedures for obtaining children's opinions, there is a need to employ other experts possessing the experience, knowledge, competencies and skills required for communication with children and obtaining their views. The Draft Act also sets forth that experts in this context mean lawyers who have passed the bar exam, social workers and psychologists who have passed the relevant professional exam. Beside this Draft Act, in Croatia there are currently neither policies nor practice initiatives related to children's procedural rights.

6. CONCLUSION

In compliance with Article 12 of the UNCRC, the FA 2015 provides promising mechanisms which enable the child to be heard in any judicial and extrajudicial family proceedings affecting them. The methods of communication as well as the choice of people who will communicate with the child depend on the type of proceedings and the child's age, maturity and ability to communicate. All the actors whose tasks include protection of the child in family proceedings (parents, child's special guardian, social welfare centre and the court) are obliged to respect children's views in line with their age, maturity and best interests. Participation not only includes the right to be heard but also the right to be informed on the case, its course and outcome, in accordance with the child's age and maturity. Moreover, in some legal matters, a child who has turned 14 can independently initiate family proceedings and file corresponding legal remedies and thus enjoy the same procedural position as adults have.

Croatia thus has created solid legal foundations for active child participation in family proceedings in terms of respect for their rights and interests. What needs to be improved are the mechanisms for effective implementation of standards relating to children's procedural rights. This primarily means efforts should be made to further develop the Centre for Special Guardianship and to organise systematic training for all experts who communicate with children in family proceedings and who are responsible for efficient protection of their procedural rights.

---

31 Draft Act on the Centre for Special Guardianship, https://www.sabor.hr/sites/default/files/uploads/sabor/2019-11-29/094804/PZ_804.pdf.

32 The Centre for Special Guardianship currently employs only 19 special guardians. In 2017, the Centre received 3,756 applications for a special guardian for children and 1,879 applications for a guardian for adults, while in 2018, there were 4,468 applications concerning children and 2,620 applications concerning adults.

DENMARK

Christina G. Jeppesen de Boer and Annette Kronborg

1. INTRODUCTION

Denmark has a child population of 1,165,500, amounting to 20% of the total population.[1] Most Danish children, 73%, live with both parents, 16% live with their mother, 6% live with their mother and her partner, and 4% live with their father. One per cent of children do not live with either of their parents. The number of children who live with both their parents decreases as children grow older. Amongst one-year-olds, 89% live with both parents, whereas this applies to only 57% of 17-year-olds.[2]

Children's participation rights are recognised in Danish law; however, there is no constitutional or overarching regulation of these rights. The right to participation is regulated in a piecemeal way in various statutes, for example

---

1 Denmark is an EU Member State, but has made a reservation to the Maastricht Treaty of 1992 concerning legal cooperation. The result is that certain international private law regulations such as the Brussels II*bis* Regulation concerning jurisdiction and the recognition and enforcement of judgments in matrimonial matters and the matters of parental responsibility (Regulation (EC) No. 2201/2003) are not applicable in Denmark. Denmark shares many legal and societal characteristics with the other Nordic countries.

2 Per 1 January 2018, Statistics Denmark, *Børn og deres familier*, 2018, pp. 7 and 43.

in the Parental Responsibility Act and the Social Services Act.[3] Generally, it is presumed in literature and the *travaux préparatoires* that in procedures that are relevant to the child, the child has the right to participate through a child hearing (*børnesamtale*), although the legal regulation does not always stipulate this. It may be stated more indirectly, as is the case for the Parental Responsibility Act, which mentions 'involvement' to allow the child's perspective and views to be expressed, for instance, but not only, through a hearing.

The participation rights of children have been strengthened in legislative reforms over the past decades. Most notably, the general age limit of 12 years for hearing children in family law procedures was abandoned in 2007 in favour of an individual assessment of the child's maturity by the relevant authority.[4] Further, the mode of hearing was amended in 2012 to allow only child professionals such as psychologists to hear children, so that judges and other lawyers cannot hear children without the presence of a child professional, who normally conducts the hearing.[5] Although the participation rights have been strengthened, it remains the general more formal legal position that the child who is a party to the case is represented by the holder(s) of parental authority, most often the child's parents, and only exceptionally has separate legal representation. Thus, the development is characterised not by independent rights of the child, but rather by parallel rights of the parents and the child.[6] Nonetheless, the presumed authority of the parents is challenged in a number of situations, for example when a child participates in a hearing without permission from the parents or accepts the assistance of a support person (*bisidder*) without such permission. In fact, administrative practice has been changed to not require parental permission[7] and children are addressed directly, for example, in the situation of divorce via a website of the main government family law authority, the Family Law House (*Familieretshuset*), '*Mig I midten*', which offers various forms of help and assistance directly to the child, such as participation in children's groups, talking to professionals, a helpline, and (from the age of 10) the right to initiate

3 Act on Parental Responsibility, Forældreansvarsloven, Act No. 776 of 07.08.2019 and Social Services Act, Serviceloven, Act No. 798 of 07.08.2019.

4 Act No. 499 of 06.06.2007, Art. 5.

5 Lov om ændring af forældreansvarsloven, retsplejeloven og lov om Det Centrale Personregister, Act No. 600 of 18.06.2012, Art. 450c. See also the website of the courts under 'Børnesamtale', www.domstol.dk.

6 Similar description: C. Adolphsen, 'Constitutional Rights for Danish Children' in T. Haugli, A. Nylund, R. Sigurdsen and L.R.L. Bendiksen (eds.), *Children's Constitutional Rights in the Nordic Countries*, Brill Nijhof, Leiden 2019, p. 130.

7 Administrative Ordinance on the Family Law House, Bekendtgørelse om Familieretshuset, No. 286 of 20.03.2019, Art. 4. According to this provision, the Family Law House must *inform* the parents about the purpose and importance of the hearing unless this is considered unnecessary.

a meeting concerning parental authority, the child's residence and contact with the parents and professionals from the Family Law House.[8]

In this chapter we address children's participation rights in Danish family law procedures. First, we will elaborate on the statutory provisions and consider the aim of child participation in the context of the Parental Responsibility Act (section 2). We will then examine the mode of hearing children, taking first an institutional perspective due to the very recent fundamental changes to the family law procedures and newly established authorities, before considering how children are practically involved in the procedure (section 3). We then look at research on child participation in family law procedures (section 4) and consider any pending changes (section 5). Finally, we conclude in section 6.

2. STATUTORY PROVISIONS

Various family law statutes regulate child participation, for example the Parental Responsibility Act and the Adoption Act, but participation is not mentioned in the Parentage Act.[9] There are also some provisions in the Procedural Act and the Act regulating the main family law authority, the Family Law House.[10] The regulations on child participation are not coherent in wording, but this does not necessarily mean that there are differences in their application. Rather, it reflects the legislative technique of separate acts for different private law areas rather than codification, the latter perhaps generally involving more coherence.[11] The regulation in the Parental Responsibility Act on child participation is more detailed than the other acts. First, this Act regulates matters involving older children, whereas the other acts typically concern infants. Secondly, the divorce context provides the obvious framework for the development of a new perspective on children's participation. The implementation of the 'child's perspective' was also an important part of the 2007 reform of this act, and this reform unquestionably has influenced child participation beyond this Act.

The aim of child participation in family law procedures is not explicitly mentioned in the legislation. On the website of the main government family authority, the Family Law House, it is addressed as a right of the child to be heard.

8 https://migimidten.dk/. An adolescent has his/her own digital mailbox to receive mail from public authorities from the age of 15. Currently, this mailbox is not used to invite the child to a hearing in family law matters.

9 Adoptionsloven, Act No. 775 of 07.08.2019, Art. 6, and Børneloven, Act No 772 of 07.08.2019.

10 Retsplejeloven, Act No. 938 of 10.09.2019, and Familieretshusloven, Act No 766 of 07.08.2019.

11 U. Bernitz, *What is Scandinavian Law? Concept, Characteristics, Future*, Stockholm Institute for Scandinavian Law, Stockholm 2007, pp. 20–21.

Nevertheless, the aim may be derived from legislation. It follows from the Parental Responsibility Act that the aim is not merely procedural but also substantive, given that the child's wishes shall be taken into consideration in the interpretation of substantive law. Section 5 of the Act states that in all aspects concerning the child, the child's views shall be taken into consideration depending on maturity. Section 4 states that decisions should be based on the best interests of the child. Sections 4 and 5 were implemented as part of a reform in 2007 and it follows from the *travaux préparatoires* that these provisions are fundamental elements of what is deemed the Act's 'child perspective' (*barnets perspektiv*). This child perspective thus incorporates best interests and the child's own views; however, it should be on a level with the individual child in question and concretely pertain to the views and perceptions of this individual child rather than pertain to more general notions of what is in the interests of children. It further follows from the *travaux préparatoires* that the rule takes its starting point in Article 12 of the UN Convention on the Rights of the Child (UNCRC).[12] Chapter 6 of the Act contains an ambiguous provision on the participation of the child. According to section 34, a child shall be involved in a case concerning parental authority, residence or contact to facilitate the expression of the child's perspective and possible views. The wording of the section points to the direct involvement of the child, but this is not necessarily required because it may happen either in a hearing or through a child professional investigation or in some other manner to discover the child's perspective to be determined by the relevant authority. It may be derived from the *travaux préparatoires* that the perspective may be covered by the parents or third parties such as the school or the general practitioner. Direct involvement may further be difficult for children under seven years of age, according to the *travaux préparatoires*, but the maturity of each child has to be individually assessed.[13] Thus, the child's perspective may be entangled with the perspective of the parents, as well as other third parties, and may even be based upon information from them only. Section 34 is designed to comprise the main rule and an exception. The wording of the latter is that the direct involvement of the child is not obligatory for the authorities if it may harm the child or if it is considered unnecessary under the specific circumstances. While it is not required to involve the child directly in the procedure, there must be a concrete assessment of the child's perspective. The Eastern Appeal Court found in 2015 that a decision not to hear a nine-year-old in a contact procedure

---

12 2006/1 LSF 133; comments to §5 in the draft act and Commission Report on the Child's Perspective, Barnets perspektiv, Forældremyndighed Barnets bopæl Samvær Tvangsfuldbyrdelse, Report No. 1474, 2006, pp. 21, 55.

13 2006/1 LSF 133; comments to §33 in the draft act and Commission Report on the Child's Perspective, Barnets perspektiv, Forældremyndighed Barnets bopæl Samvær Tvangsfuldbyrdelse, Report No. 1474, 2006, p. 94. It seems that the courts currently hear children from the (school-) age of six to seven. https://www.domstol.dk/alle-emner/familieret/boernesamtalen/.

did not render the administration's decision invalid. The child's perspective was informed through information from the parents, the school and the social services and the use of a child professional who presumably had talked to the boy. In consideration of this, the high level of conflict between the parents and the father's mental health problems, the Appeal Court considered the decision to protect the boy by not involving him directly to be legitimate [14] The boy, now aged 10, was also not involved directly in the subsequent court proceedings where the mother was granted sole parental authority due to the mental health problems of the father.[15]

3. MODES OF PARTICIPATION

Child participation usually takes the form of hearing the child (*børnesamtale*), although, as mentioned, the legal regulation does not always stipulate this. Essentially, the child's perspective must come to light. There is no formal legal institution of a 'child representative' granting a third person independent procedural capacity on behalf of the child. In parentage proceedings, the court has discretion to appoint a lawyer to represent the child.[16]

In recent decades, a system has developed providing the child with a support person (*bisidder*) in meetings with public authorities, such as a hearing in family law. Professional support persons are publicly funded and are provided through an NGO (*Børns Vilkår*) for free. The Family Law House is obliged to help the child find a support person, if needed, and it is not required that the parents consent. The support person has no independent rights and he/she may be excluded from meetings if his/her presence poses an obstacle to revealing the true wishes of the child. The function of the support person is only to support the child in the sense of being there as 'an extra pair of ears' and for the child to have someone to talk to, thereby improving the balance of power between the child and the professional. The support person cannot be a minor under the age of 15, but may be an adult the child already knows, for example a teacher or a professional from the NGO.[17]

Given the importance of administrative procedures in Danish family law and the 2019 changes to this system, we will first take an institutional perspective on the authorities and the family law system. The reform involved a revision of the interplay between the relevant authorities, state administration (family law), municipalities (social law and child protection) and the court. The aim of the reform was to establish a system that can facilitate children being brought

[14] TFA 2015.45Ø.
[15] TFA 2015.185Ø.
[16] Procedural Act, Art. 456g, and Adoption Act, Art. 15a.
[17] Family Law House Act, Arts. 15 and 18.

more gently through their parents' divorce or break-up. Although the system was presented as a 'new system for divorces', it applies to family law procedures generally, for example to matters of parentage and parental responsibility, maintenance, contact, etc. The Family Law House remains an administrative authority in line with Danish tradition, albeit with a redefined relationship to the court system and with the newly established Child Unit as a central unit within the authority. All cases must begin in the Family Law House, but the newly established Family Court is the authority competent to make decisions in all family law matters that are considered complex or burdensome to the child, including all cases on matters of parental responsibility (parental authority, residence and some but not all contact cases). The aim is to establish a unified and focused system with holistic procedures for families and a child-centred approach.[18]

The reform is implemented by the Family Law House Act, an Act that addresses procedural issues.[19] The Act implements a new mandatory digital screening system of applications (section 4). The general rule is that any application (divorce, parental authority, contact, parentage, maintenance) must be made digitally. On the basis of the information obtained from the applicant about the conflict and family circumstances, such as the level of conflict, respect of the other parent, vulnerabilities of the child and in some cases based upon information from the municipality, the Family Law House shall decide whether the case is simple, less simple or complex. These three options are named in the *travaux préparatoires* the green, yellow and red tracks, each with their own procedural trajectory. The green cases are cases where the parties agree but need a registration, such as concerning consensual divorce, parentage, sole/joint parental authority, residence or contact. The yellow cases are cases where a settlement is sought through a pedagogical and conflict-resolving approach, such as by using counselling and mediation. The Family Law House may grant a decision or submit the case to the Family Court if it is considered factually or legally complicated. The red cases are complex cases pertaining to the Parental Responsibility Act, and the Family Law House is obliged to contact the municipality and, if needed, initiate cooperation with them. All these 'red' complex cases shall be decided by the Family Court. Analogous to the different procedural regimes in the Family Law House, two different procedural regimes exist in the family court system implemented through a revision of chapter 42 of the Procedural Act: a simple regime where court decisions are made based on the case as received from the Family Law House, and a regime where the

---

18 'Nyt system for skilsmisser, Nyt og samlet familieretligt system: læs om familieretshuset, familieretten, børneenheden og refleksionsperiode mv', TEMA 27.03.2018, https://www.regeringen.dk/nyheder/2018/aftale-om-nyt-skilsmissesystem/.

19 Familieretshusloven Act No. 1702 of 27.12.2018.

Family Court holds an actual hearing. In the simple regime, children are not heard normally, but the court has discretion. In the latter case, the Child Unit in the Family Law House is still responsible for investigating the child perspective – normally through a hearing. Children who are old enough to attend school (aged six to seven) may be heard again in court though. Ideally, the same child professional that the child already knows from the hearing in the Family Law House will conduct the hearing together with the judge. However, the judge has discretion to decide to use a different child professional.[20]

3.1. THE CHILD UNIT

The primary consideration in the reform is the paramount interests of the child. The aim is to have the focus on the child during the entire process and to guarantee the child's safe and supported participation. There is a focus on the child's need for protection and simultaneously a recognition of the child's need to be heard. Therefore, a Child Unit has been established in the Family Law House. It supports the fundamental principle of the inclusion of a child perspective in the case. The child is offered a contact person (*kontaktperson*) to minimise the number of adults the child has contact with and a support person (*bisidder*) who may join the child in meetings. The child is also informed about their rights and the various support options available through the Child Unit, including children's support groups and a children's phone line.

According to chapter 5 of the Family Law House Act, the Child Unit has two main functions. One is to support and counsel the child. This includes children in general (not necessarily involved in a present case) and children older than 10 years of age, who can make use of their right to initiate a meeting with the Family Law House and the parents, as well as maintaining other functions in the case management. Secondly, the Child Unit is responsible for the investigation of the child's perspective. The Child Unit has child professionals[21] that hear children in administrative as well as court proceedings. In cases where the child is heard, the holders of parental authority receive a meeting request in their digital mailbox.[22] In cases where a child professional investigation (*børnesagkyndig undersøgelse*)[23] is made, the Child Unit does not necessarily carry out this investigation, but

20 https://www.domstol.dk/alle-emner/familieret/boernesamtalen/.

21 A child professional may be a psychologist, social worker or have other relevant education/experience, cf. n. 23 below on the requirement in child professional investigations.

22 A digital mailbox is used for all communication with public authorities. An adolescent child has his/her own digital mailbox from the age of 15. To our knowledge, this mailbox is not currently used to invite a child to a hearing in family law matters. It is used in health matters.

23 A child professional investigation is regulated in detail in the Guidance to Child Professional Investigations, Vejledning om børnesagkyndige undersøgelser, VEJ No. 9256 of 20.03.2019. It must be conducted by a psychologist, preferably one specialising in child psychiatry.

they are responsible for commissioning and planning it, and for communication with the child. Thus, the contact person has many functions. The contact person is the institutional means to ensure the child is protected against unnecessary involvement in the case and to manage all communication with the child. From a child's perspective, the institutional weakness of the contact person may be that the child might find it difficult to understand when the contact person is playing supportive role and when he/she has a function related to the case, such as in a hearing. These two different functions should be kept separate. The degree of confidentiality offered to the child differs: in the supportive function there is confidentiality, and in the case-related function there is not. However, this obligation is always overruled by the duty to inform the municipality if the child is in need of social support and/or child protection.[24]

In the following we will try to illustrate when and how children are involved in different types of proceedings, distinguishing matters of divorce/parental responsibility, parentage, adoption and child maintenance.

3.2. DIVORCE AND PARENTAL RESPONSIBILITY

Divorce proceedings must be initiated digitally on the website of the Family Law House using one's personal digital signature. When the spouses agree that they wish to divorce and do not require the settlement of disputes regarding parental responsibility (parental authority, the child's residence and contact with the child), the divorce takes place on a simple 'green' track whereby the divorce may be granted digitally.[25] There is no requirement to attend a hearing. In such cases, the minor child of the spouses is not granted an opportunity to be heard. This may also be the case when there are some differences between the parents and they make use of the option to receive counselling or, since 2019, a 'settlement session' at the Family Law House. So far, child participation has not been common and it is probable that this remains the case in the new system.

A child who is 10 years old may initiate a meeting with the parents and professionals at the Family Law House, whether there is an existing procedure or not.[26] Matters concerning parental responsibility can be discussed in this meeting where child professionals from the Child Unit assist the child in addressing

24 Family Law House Act chapter 5, and the Guidance to the Family Law House, Vejledning om Familieretshuset, VEJ No. 9253 of 20.03.2019.

25 The mandatory three-month waiting period for parents with minor children during which the parents received mandatory digital divorce education was abandoned only a little more than a year after its introduction in 2019 as it was considered to enhance conflicts rather than decrease such conflicts. Lov om ændring af lov om Familieretshuset og lov om ægteskabs indgåelse og opløsning (Afskaffelse af refleksionsperioden), Act No. 969 of 26.06.2020.

26 Parental Responsibility Act, Art. 35.

issues that are problematic for the child. However, the Family Law House, or for that matter the Family Court, cannot decide ex officio. Consequently, existing decisions or agreements cannot be changed without parental agreement or a request from one or both parents for a new decision. If the Family Law House is concerned about the safety of the child, they may inform the municipality, which handles child protection matters.

When the divorce is screened onto the yellow or red track, and there are issues that concern the child, the starting point is that a child with sufficient maturity will be given an opportunity to be heard. Spouses may in the course of the divorce procedure submit agreements on parental authority, for example an agreement giving one parent sole parental authority and/or agreements on residence or contact for registration. There is no substantive review of such agreements and therefore also no point at which children are heard.

The same is true for matters of parental responsibility (parental authority, residence and contact) outside the divorce procedure. The request must be made digitally, and the case is screened onto the green, yellow or red track. On the green track, children are not given an opportunity to be heard. Research carried out before the 2019 reform show that 25–30% of parents contact the administrative authority with issues concerning parental responsibility in connection with divorce or after divorce and relationship breakdown. This means that the majority of divorcing parents will not have procedures concerning their children. The cases that are raised can be divided into three main groups. In the first group the parents have minor differences (30%), in the second group the major problem is the conflict level and the parents' inability to cooperate (40%), and in the third group the cases have a higher degree of complexity (30%).[27]

It is characteristic of Danish family law concerning parental responsibility that cases are screened according to the parents' level of conflict and family circumstances onto tracks. In the simple 'green' cases children are not given an opportunity to be heard, whereas in the complex 'red' track they are. However, it is difficult to pinpoint at which point children are heard in the more complicated 'yellow' track cases, keeping in mind that there is a degree of discretion in hearing the child. It may further be that children are more likely to be heard when the case concerns an issue which has practical relevance to the child, such as his/her residence or a contact arrangement, rather than an issue which is considered primarily legal in nature, such as the allocation of joint or sole parental authority.[28]

In cases of international child abduction, execution of foreign decisions on parental responsibility, and the enforcement of national decisions on parental

---

27 M.H. Ottosen and K.M. Dahl, *Kategorisering af familieretlige sager i statsforvaltningen*, SFI, Copenhagen 2017, pp. 27–46.

28 Commission Report on the Child's Perspective, Barnets perspektiv, Forældremyndighed Barnets bopæl Samvær Tvangsfuldbyrdelse, Report No. 1474, 2006, p. 62

responsibility, the request must be made directly to the Family Court. The Family Court may ask a representative from the social services to be present to preserve the interests of the child, and the court hears the child who is of sufficient maturity, unless it is harmful to the child, in the presence of a child professional from the Child Unit of the Family Law House and/or a representative from the social authorities.[29]

3.3. PARENTAGE

Danish law provides for an obligation to establish parentage. This means that if no father or second parent has been registered within six months after the child's birth, the Family Law House will initiate proceedings to establish the parentage of the second parent. In such proceedings the mother is under an obligation to reveal the possible father(s). Consequently, the establishment of parentage takes place when the child is very young and unable to participate. When established parentage is challenged, or a case is reopened, the general procedural rules contained in the Family Law House Act apply (screening onto green or yellow tracks) and the child will be heard in more complicated cases depending upon maturity. The court has discretion to appoint a lawyer to represent the child in the procedure. This happens especially in situations where there may be a conflict of interest between the mother and the minor child.[30]

An adoption must not be granted if the minor child aged 12 years or older does not consent to the adoption, unless the obtainment of consent is considered harmful to the child. The views of a younger child must be obtained depending upon their maturity and the circumstances of the case. These views must be taken into account as much as possible in granting the adoption decree. The court has discretion to appoint a lawyer to represent the child.

3.4. CHILD MAINTENANCE

Proceedings concerning child maintenance follow the general trajectory of family law proceedings as regulated in the Family Law House Act. However, such proceedings are normally entirely written procedures and thus do not give children any opportunity to participate.

29 Procedural Act, Art. 456r, and Act on International Child Abduction, Børnebortførelsesloven, Act No. 768 of 07.08.2019, Art. 12.

30 For example, the decision of the Eastern Appeal Court, Østre Landsret, in a case where the mother had requested the reopening of the paternity case in respect of a two-year-old child, TFA 2016.24.

4. RESEARCH

There is no recent research on the involvement of children in family law procedures. Statistics concerning cases in a three-month period from February to April 2010 gathered for the purpose of evaluating the Act on Parental Responsibility concerned a total of 7,929 cases – 2,173 on matters of parental responsibility and 3,912 on contact. This research considers how the child perspective had been realised in the case.[31]

In cases concerning parental responsibility, the parents came to an agreement in approximately 30% of the cases at the administrative level (before the case was submitted to the court). Counselling (in various forms) and mediation were used in 1,642 cases at the administrative level. Of these cases, 702 were submitted to court.

The cases on contact were *at that time* primarily decided by the administrative authority. The parents reached an agreement in 1,920 of the total of 3,912 cases. Counselling and mediation were used in 1,841 of the cases. The way the child's perspective had been investigated in both types of cases at the administrative level[32] was examined and yielded the following results. Approximately 63% of the cases were decided on the basis of information provided by the parents; 12% on the basis of information stemming from the parents' previous agreement; 8% through statements from the child's day care/school; 8% through a child hearing; 4% on the basis of information from the social services; 3% on the basis of information from the general practitioner/psychologist; 2% through a child investigation; and less than 1% of cases through the child's use of the initiative right or through supervised contact.

A case study from 2004 dealing specifically with parent–child contact in complex contact procedures showed that children were practically invisible in a third of the cases.[33] In other cases, the children were represented indirectly through information stemming from the parents or from child professionals. The children were only direct actors in the sense that they were heard by legal or child professionals in a quarter of the cases. Children over the age of 12 seemed to be listened to and taken seriously, having an important influence upon the decision-making in the case. Sometimes, younger children, aged five to six years, seemed to have a participant's role in the case; however, the case study indicated that the family justice system is marked by ambivalence concerning the role of younger children and that, generally, younger children cannot be characterised

---

31 Justitsministeriet, Familiestyrelsen, *Statistik om forældreansvarslovens effekt i de sager, der behandles i statsforvaltningerne*, 2010, J.nr.: 2010-7200-00008.

32 Excluding the cases that were sent directly to the court or closed after only preliminary case handling.

33 M.H. Ottosen, *Samvær til barnets bedste*, Det Nationale Forskningscenter for Velfærd, Copenhagen 2004, p. 6.

as important actors in the procedure.[34] However, this research published in 2004 is not that relevant to the current situation as important developments, such as the abandonment of a general age limit from which children are heard and an increased focus upon the child's perspective, have occurred since then. It is likely that children have more of a participant's status now.

The 2019 changes to the family law authorities and the procedural system, including the establishment of the Child Unit, make it difficult to pinpoint the exact moment in time at which children are involved in the current procedures and to assess whether more children are involved more directly in the procedure.[35]

5. PENDING CHANGES

There are no pending changes to the rules on child participation in family law. The evaluation of the new 'divorce system' has resulted in the removal of the obligatory waiting period for consensual divorce of spouses with minor children. This means that spouses with minor children (again) can divorce directly and digitally without addressing parental responsibility matters and leaving no scope for the hearing of children.

6. CONCLUSION

The development of the past few decades has increased children's participation rights in Danish law. The child's perspective must be included in a family law procedure, typically, but not only, through hearing of children who are considered to have sufficient maturity. As such, children are viewed as participants rather than subjects to be decided upon. Nonetheless, the formal legal position remains that the child who is a party to the case is represented by the holders of parental authority, typically the parents. However, this position can be challenged in a number of situations where the child in fact acts independently, for example by requesting professional counselling or making use of a support person (*bisidder*) in a hearing without the consent of his/her parents. We conclude that the development is characteristic of there being parallel rights of the parents and the child without a clear demarcation between them, rather than independent rights of the child.

From a practical perspective, children are not necessarily heard or provided with the opportunity to be heard in the event of their parents' divorce or when

---

[34] M.H. Ottosen, *Samvær til barnets bedste*, Det Nationale Forskningscenter for Velfærd, Copenhagen 2004, p. 6.

[35] We contacted the Family Law House with several questions regarding the hearing of children in the current system. However, we did not receive an answer due to the Covid-19 lockdown.

the parents make or alter agreements concerning the child, such as agreements on parental responsibility, residence and contact. Rather, participation rights come into play when there is a dispute between the parents. The right of children aged 10 or older to initiate a meeting with the parents and professionals at the Family Law House does not provide independent access to a decision given the fact that the authorities, the Family Law House and the Family Court cannot decide ex officio, i.e. without a request from one of the parents.

Some differences can be attributed to the family law issue at hand. Some procedures are primarily written procedures, such as child maintenance procedures, and consequently children do not participate. In procedures concerning the establishment of parentage, the court has discretion to appoint a lawyer. Such representation is not provided for in other types of cases. Further, children's participation rights may have more weight when they concern an issue which has practical relevance to the child, such as his/her residence or a contact arrangement, rather than an issue which is primarily legal in nature, such as the allocation of joint or sole parental authority.

Article 12 UNCRC has been an important driver for the development of children's participation rights in Danish law. The point at which current Danish family law on children's participation is at odds with the UNCRC is the focal point of the parental dispute as a turning point for involving the child. This leaves children with limited opportunities to voice their opinion in matters that concern them, such as where they live and how they have contact with the parent they do not live with, when their parents agree or reach an agreement in the administrative procedure. This point was raised by the UN Committee on the Rights of the Child in its last report.[36]

---

36 Committee on the Rights of the Child, *Concluding observations on the fifth periodic report of Denmark*, 29.09.2017, p. 4.

ENGLAND AND WALES

Marilyn FREEMAN and Nigel LOWE

1. INTRODUCTION

In mid-2018 England and Wales had an estimated population of 59,115,800,[1] of which 12,584,403 (21%) were children aged 0–18 years.[2] In 2017 there were 101,669 divorces of opposite-sex couples in England and Wales (the lowest

1 Office for National Statistics, https://www.ons.gov.uk/peoplepopulationandcommunity/populationandmigration/populationestimates/bulletins/annualmidyearpopulationestimates/mid2018.

2 Population estimates: Persons by single year of age and sex for local authorities in the UK, mid 2018 MYE2-All; Office for National Statistics, above n. 1.

since 1973), 338 divorces of same-sex couples,[3] and 1,217 dissolutions of civil partnerships.[4] Between 2008 and 2018[5] there was a 25.8% increase in the number of people who live together as a family without being married to each other, making this the fastest-growing family type in England and Wales and, indeed, the UK as a whole. Given that there is an increased likelihood that such families will break down as against married couples,[6] the fact that there are less divorces does not necessarily mean there are less family breakdowns. Although there are no statistics on the breakdown of family relationships outside marriage or civil partnership, it is clear that the 3.9 million children who are part of the 2.5 million separated families in England, Wales and Scotland[7] are directly impacted by the decision-making processes which take place about their post-separation care arrangements. If those with parental responsibility for the children are unable to agree what these arrangements should be, the decisions will be made through agreement in mediation or some other form of dispute resolution, or by the court in judicial proceedings.

England and Wales has a Family Court which deals with all family cases, including *all* those concerning the upbringing and status of children except those invoking the inherent jurisdiction of the High Court[8] and international cases concerning applications relating to child abduction and matters of jurisdiction, recognition and enforcement under the 1996 Hague Protection of Children Convention. These latter cases are heard by the Family Division of the High Court. Whenever a court decides an issue relating to a child's upbringing, its paramount consideration is the child's welfare.[9]

---

3 Divorces in England and Wales: 2017. Annual divorce numbers and rates, by duration of marriage, sex, age, previous marital status, and to whom granted and reason.

4 Civil partnerships in England and Wales: 2017 Annual statistics on formations and dissolutions of civil partnerships analysed by the sex, age, and previous marital status of the couples and the place of registration.

5 https://www.ons.gov.uk/peoplepopulationandcommunity/birthsdeathsandmarriages/families/bulletins/familiesandhouseholds/2018.

6 HM Government, *State of the Nation Report: Poverty, Worklessness and Welfare Dependency in the UK*, May 2010, p. 50; A. Goodman and E. Greaves, 'Cohabitation, marriage and relationship stability', Institute for Fiscal Studies Briefing Note BN107, 2010, at [12]; Marriage Foundation (2015) *Get married BEFORE you have children*, https://marriagefoundation.org.uk/wp-content/uploads/2019/09/MF-paper-Get-married-before-children.pdf.

7 These statistics relate to 2016/17. In *Estimates of the separated family population statistics data for April 2014-March 2017* (17 April 2019), the Department for Work and Pensions defined a separated family as one resident parent, one non-resident parent and any biological or adopted children they have between them who are either under 16 or under 20 and in full-time non-tertiary education.

8 The inherent jurisdiction is based on the sovereign's power to protect those such as children who are unable to protect themselves. It has no statutory foundation and can be invoked as a supplementary jurisdiction.

9 Children Act 1989, s 1(1).

2. STATUTORY PROVISIONS

2.1. DOMESTIC PRIVATE CHILD LAW PROCEEDINGS

There is no mandatory provision governing children's participation in domestic private child law proceedings. However, by section 1(3)(a) Children Act 1989, the court must have regard to the 'ascertainable wishes and feelings of the child concerned (considered in the light of his age and understanding)'. The Act is silent on how these wishes and feelings should be ascertained. Furthermore, the *obligation* only arises in *contested* applications for section 8 orders[10] (principally those determining with whom the child should live and/or have contact), which means that, if the *adults* are agreed on such matters, there is no statutory compulsion to consult the children at all.

Absent any child-related proceedings, the court has no obligation to consider the child's position. This has a particular impact in the context of divorce, especially since the removal (by section 17 Children and Families Act 2014) of the divorce court's obligation to consider whether they should exercise any of their powers under the 1989 Act in relation to any children of the family. A similar gap exists in proceedings concerning parentage (though English law treats the genetic issue in parentage disputes as a matter of fact) and financial proceedings.

Under section 10 Children and Families Act 2014, save in cases of domestic violence, any person wishing to make a relevant family application must first attend a family mediation and assessment meeting (MIAM). However, there is no statutory requirement for children's views to be ascertained at these meetings. There is concern, too, that mediators do not always adopt a child-inclusive approach.[11] The evidence is that whilst mediation is child-focused, it is rarely child-inclusive.[12] There is no legislation controlling the practice and procedure of mediation in England and Wales[13] so, despite the Family Mediation Council's

10 Children Act 1989, s 1(4)(a).

11 See J. Walker, 'How Can We Ensure That Children's Voices are Heard in Mediation?' [2013] *Fam Law* 191. See also J. Norton, 'The Voice of the Child in Mediation in NFM Services' [2012] *Fam Law* 84. For an interesting discussion of engaging children in contact centres see L. Trinder, C. Jenks and A. Firth, 'Talking Children into Being *In Absentia*? Children as a Strategic and Contingent Resource in Family Court Dispute Resolution' [2010] *CFLQ* 234; L. Caffrey, 'Hearing the "Voice of the Child"? The Role of Child Contact Centres in the Family Justice System' [2013] *CFLQ* 357.

12 A. Barlow, J. Ewing, R. Hunter and J. Smithson, *Creating Paths to Family Justice Study – Briefing Paper and Report on Key Findings*, Universities of Exeter and Kent 2014, p. 18.

13 L. de Oliveira and C. Beckwith, 'Is there a need to regulate mediation? The English and Welsh Case Study' (2016) 42(3) *Commonwealth Law Bulletin* 327, 327.

Code of Practice[14] requiring all children and young people over the age of 10 years to be offered the opportunity to have their voices heard directly in the mediation, if they wish, the extent of children's actual involvement in family mediation remains inconsistent, varying according to the mediator.[15]

2.2. ADOPTION PROCEEDINGS

Since adoption was introduced into English law in 1927 courts have had to give due consideration to the wishes of the children concerned, having regard to their age and understanding.[16] Currently, the obligation, which lies on both courts *and* adoption agencies, is to have regard, whenever they are 'coming to decisions relating to the adoption of a child', to the child's ascertainable wishes and feelings considered in the light of the child's age and understanding.[17] A similar obligation applies when determining parental order applications.[18] There is no fixed age at which this obligation is triggered. It is a matter for the court's discretion in each case.

2.3. CROSS-BORDER PROCEEDINGS

Following *Re D (A Minor) (Abduction: Rights of Custody)*[19] children's views are commonly investigated in all Hague Abduction Convention cases. Children as young as six now routinely have their views investigated in all Hague abduction proceedings.[20] In *Re KP (A Child) (Abduction: Rights of Custody) (Practice Note)*[21] Moore-Bick LJ considered that there is a presumption that a child should

14 The Family Mediation Council comprises six family mediation organisations in England and Wales.

15 The Child Dispute Resolution Advisory Group report (March 2015) endorsed the principle of child inclusive practice, and recommended the adoption of a non-legal presumption that all children and young people aged 10 and above should be offered the opportunity to have their voices heard directly during dispute resolution processes, including mediation, if they wish. https://assets.publishing.service.gov.uk/government/uploads/system/uploads/attachment_data/file/421005/voice-of-the-child-advisory-group-report.pdf. See also J. Walker and A. Lake-Carroll, 'Hearing the Voices of Children and Young People in Dispute Resolution Processes: Promoting a Child-inclusive Approach' [2014] *Fam Law* 1577.

16 Adoption of Children Act 1926, s 3(b).

17 Adoption and Children Act 2002, ss 1(1) and (4)(a).

18 See the Human Fertilisation and Embryology (Parental Orders) Regulations 2010, reg. 2 and Sch. 1.

19 [2006] UKHL 51.

20 This seems to have become the general practice in *all* Hague abduction proceedings, following *Re W (Abduction) (Child's Objections)* [2010] EWCA Civ 520, in which the Court of Appeal made it clear that there was no 'age barrier' in relation to the child's objection defence.

21 [2014] EWCA Civ 554, at [53].

be heard during Hague Convention proceedings, unless it appears inappropriate (by 'hearing' is meant listening to the child's point of view independent of the abducting parent). The 2018 *President's Guidance* states (at 3.5):

> Where it is clear on the face of the application and supporting evidence that it will be appropriate for the child to be heard during the proceedings the court may give directions to facilitate this at a without notice hearing or by way of standard directions on issue. Where directions have not already been given, the question of whether the child is to be given an opportunity to be heard in proceedings having regard to his or her age and degree of maturity, and if so how, must be considered and determined at the first on notice hearing.

3. MODES OF CHILD PARTICIPATION

Children may participate in family proceedings in different ways. They can have their views conveyed to the court by reporting officers, they can talk to the judge directly, they can be formally represented in the proceedings and participate as a party, or they can bring proceedings in their own right.

3.1. REPRESENTATION FORMS OF PARTICIPATION

3.1.1. Domestic Proceedings

Even where their views, wishes and feelings must be taken into account, children are not usually made parties to private law proceedings (and will not therefore be separately represented), though the court has a general power to join them.[22] Normally, the court learns of the child's views, wishes and feelings via a court welfare report. Any court, when considering *any* question with respect to a child under the 1989 Act, can ask for a report to be made to the court 'on such matters relating to the welfare of that child as are required to be dealt with in the report'.[23] These reports are usually provided by officers appointed by the Children and Family Court Advisory and Support Service (Cafcass) known as Children and Family Reporters (CFRs). These officers are independent of the parties and are appointed by the court to investigate and report on the child's circumstances. In the words of Thorpe LJ:

> Both judge and CFR are united sharing the same ultimate objective, namely, the protection of children and the advancement of their welfare. In pursuit of

22 Family Procedure Rules (FPR) 2010, r 16.2.
23 Children Act 1989, s 7.

> that overriding objective each must be free to operate independently as well as collaboratively and independent operation includes the exercise of an independent discretion.[24]

The reporter's duty is to report on the child's welfare rather than on the child's wishes and feelings, although, in discharging this duty, the reporter will investigate those wishes and feelings and will likely comment on whether those are in the child's best interests. In other words, a welfare report provides a limited indirect voice in the proceedings for the child.

A report should not be ordered unless there is a contested issue under the Children Act or one which the court thinks should be investigated, and before one is ordered consideration should be given to the power to refer the parties (with their consent) to mediation. According to the Child Arrangements Programme,[25] the court should specifically consider whether there are welfare issues that need addressing and, in any event, consider whether there are alternative ways of working with the parties such as through mediation. At every First Hearing Dispute Resolution Appointment (FHDRA), a Cafcass officer is expected to be available to facilitate early dispute resolution rather than to prepare a formal report. Commonly, the court decision to order a report will be taken at the FHDRA, though there is power to order a report at any stage.

The officer must notify and explain to the child such contents as the officer considers appropriate to the child's age and understanding, including any reference to the child's own views and the recommendation.[26] Written reports, which are filed with the court, are confidential documents that should not be disclosed to anyone other than a party (which will normally include the parents of the child concerned), their legal representative, the Cafcass officer and the Legal Services Commission without court leave.[27] The court is not bound by any recommendations contained in the report, but reasons should be given if it departs from them.[28]

3.1.2. Cross-Border Proceedings

Any inquiry into the child's views is normally made by a Cafcass reporting officer (CRO).[29] That officer sees the child and reports upon that meeting as close to the final hearing as possible so as to ensure that the child's current position is being

24 *Re M (Disclosure: Children and Family Reporter)* [2002] EWCA Civ 1199, at [26].
25 (2014), para. 11.12.6(a).
26 *Practice Direction 16A*, para. 9.3.
27 FPR 2010, r 16.33.
28 See, for example, *Re M (Residence)* [2004] EWCA Civ 1574.
29 *Re M (A Minor) (Child Abduction)* [1994] 1 FLR 390.

reported to the court.[30] Reports usually take three weeks to prepare. The 2018 *President's Guidance* states:

> In most cases where it is appropriate for the child to be given an opportunity to be heard in proceedings an interview of the child by an officer of the Cafcass High Court Team will be sufficient to ensure that the child's wishes and feelings are placed before the court. In only a very few cases will party status be necessary. … The court should record on the face of any final order the manner in which the child has been heard in the proceedings.[31]

3.2. DIRECT FORMS OF PARTICIPATION

Children's direct involvement in private law proceedings is generally limited, their views either being conveyed to the court through a welfare report or via the parents. Nevertheless, children can have direct involvement in domestic private child law proceedings. Even where they are not parties, judges can, at their discretion, interview children in private. Furthermore, there are occasions when children can be made parties to proceedings brought by the parents. Finally, children of sufficient age and understanding can initiate proceedings themselves. Competence in this regard is based on an assessment (ultimately by the court) of whether the child has sufficient understanding, intelligence and maturity to instruct a solicitor to bring proceedings.[32]

3.2.1. Judicial Interviews with Children

3.2.1.1. Domestic Proceedings

The appropriateness of judges seeing children in private was referred to a sub-committee of the Family Justice Council, 'The Voice of the Child'. That committee was strongly in favour of judges seeing children. The resulting guidance from the Council, *Guidelines for Judges Meeting Children Who Are Subject to Family Proceedings* (2010) (hereafter Guidelines), states its purpose as being:

> to encourage judges to enable children to feel more involved and connected with proceedings in which important decisions are made in their lives and to give them

30 See *Re J (Children) (Abduction: Children's Objections to Return)* [2004] EWCA Civ 428, at [64], per Wall LJ.

31 Para. 3.5.

32 See *Re CS (Appeal FPR 2010, Rule 16.5: Sufficiency of Child's Understanding)* [2019] EWHC 634 (Fam).

> an opportunity to satisfy themselves that the judge has understood their wishes and feelings and to understand the nature of the judge's task.[33]

The Guidelines, which are not binding,[34] emphasise that the child's meeting with the judge is not for the purpose of obtaining evidence, which, instead, is the responsibility of the Cafcass officer. 'The purpose is to enable the child to gain some understanding of what is going on, and to be reassured that the judge has understood him/her.'[35] They provide that the judge is entitled to expect the child's lawyer, if there is one, and/or the Cafcass officer to advise on whether the child wishes to meet the judge and whether that accords with the child's welfare. If a judge decides not to meet the child, he/she should consider providing the child with a brief written explanation. The other parties are entitled to make representations about any proposed meeting. If the meeting takes place before the conclusion of proceedings, the judge should explain to the child that they cannot hold any secrets and discuss with the child how their decision (which they should explain is their responsibility) should be communicated. These Guidelines have been said to create dilemmas for judges about how to treat the information they inevitably obtain when meeting children face-to-face. The continuing lack of clarity regarding this issue has been identified as 'something that needs to be addressed for children involved in the proceedings.'[36]

3.2.1.2. Cross-Border Proceedings

Judges can see the child in private and, in appropriate cases, ask the child to expand on, and explain, their views.[37] In *Re J (Abduction: Children's Objections)*,[38] the trial judge was held to have erred by not raising with the parties upon his motion the need for him to meet the children (aged 15, 13 and 10) face-to-face. That case also established that the Guidelines (referred to above) apply to Hague abduction proceedings.

In *Re KP*[39] Moore-Bick LJ advised that in any meeting between a young person and judge, 'the judge's role should be largely that of a passive recipient of whatever communication the young person wishes to transmit', and that its

---

33 [2010] 2 FLR 1872 (Preamble).

34 '[T]he Guidelines are no more than they purport to be, namely guidelines', per Moore-Bick LJ in *Re KP*, above n. 21, at [52].

35 See Guidelines, para. [5].

36 Mr Justice MacDonald (Deputy Head of International Family Justice for England and Wales), 'Hearing the Children's Objections. Some Perspectives From a Judge Hearing Cases in England and Wales' (2018) XXII *Judges' Newsletter on International Child Protection – Special Focus. The Child's Voice – 15 Years Later*, p. 48, www.hcch.net.

37 See, for example, *Re G (Abduction: Child's Objections)* [2010] EWCA Civ 1232, at [15], per Thorpe LJ.

38 [2011] EWCA Civ 1448.

39 Above n. 21, at [56].

purpose is not to obtain evidence, but rather primarily for the benefit of the child. Its dual purpose is to allow the judge to hear what the young person may wish to volunteer and for the young person to hear the judge explain the nature of the court process. If the child volunteers evidence that would, or might be, relevant to the outcome of the proceedings, the judge should report back to the parties and determine whether, and how, that evidence should be adduced.

In *B v P (Hague Convention: Children's Objections)*[40] MacDonald J commented that where a judge considers that what they have heard in the meeting with the child has some relevance to the issues to be determined in the proceedings, 'it would be entirely artificial, and potentially unjust simply to banish those matters from his or her mind without more'. Parties or their representatives should therefore be given the opportunity to respond to the contents of the meeting.

3.2.2. *Children as Parties*

3.2.2.1. Domestic Proceedings

Children are not automatically parties to private law proceedings. Nevertheless rule 16.2 of the FPR 2010 allows a court to make a child a party if it considers it is in the child's best interests to do so.

Practice Direction 16A provides general guidance on when to make children parties to proceedings concerning them. Its basic premise is that making a child a party is 'a step that will be taken only in cases which involve an issue of significant difficulty and consequently will occur in only a minority of cases.' Before taking such a step, the court should consider whether an alternative route might be preferable, such as asking a Cafcass officer to make further enquiries or possibly by obtaining expert evidence. The court should also take into account the risk of delay that such an appointment will inevitably cause.

Upon being made a party, the court must appoint a children's guardian to act for the child, unless the child has obtained the court's permission to act without such a guardian or a solicitor considers that the child is able, having regard to his/her understanding, to give instructions (which the solicitor has accepted) in relation to the proceedings.[41] According to *Practice Direction 16A*, a 'children's guardian' should 'fairly and competently conduct proceedings on behalf of the child' such that all steps and decisions taken by the children's guardian 'are taken for the benefit of the child.' However, as Thorpe LJ said in *Mabon v Mabon*:[42]

> The guardian's first priority is to advocate the welfare of the child he represents. His second priority is to put before the court the child's wishes and feelings.

---

40 [2017] EWHC 3577 (Fam), at [45].
41 FPR 2010, rr 16.4 (c), 16.6 (3).
42 [2005] EWCA Civ 634, at [26].

3.2.2.2. Cross-Border Proceedings

In cross-border proceedings involving children, the court is obliged (FPR 2010, rule 12.48(1)(e)), as soon as practicable after the application has been made, to give directions as to whether the child should be made a party. However, by rule 16.2, the court may only make a child a party if it considers that it is in the child's best interests to do so.

In *Re C (Abduction: Separate Representation of Children)*[43] Ryder J held that the proper test for considering an application for the child's separate representation in Convention cases[44] is whether such representation 'will add enough to the court's understanding of the issues that arise under the Hague Convention to justify the intrusion and the expense and delay that may result'.

If a child is joined as a party, the court must appoint a children's guardian for the child and make directions for doing so as soon as practicable after the application has been made.[45] There is no power in Convention proceedings to permit children to participate in the proceedings without a representative.[46] A grant of party status leaves the court with a wide discretion to determine the extent of the role the child should play in the proceedings.[47]

3.2.3. Children as Litigants

Children's ability to seek section 8 orders in their own right was an innovation of the 1989 legislation. Court leave (which can only be granted where the court is satisfied that the child has sufficient understanding to make the application)[48] is a prerequisite to seeking an order.[49]

FPR rule 16.5 requires a child who is a party to, but not the subject of, proceedings to have a litigation friend to conduct proceedings on their behalf. A litigation friend is a disinterested person who can fairly and competently conduct proceedings on the child's behalf. However, as an exception, rule 16.6 enables a child to conduct proceedings under the 1989 Act and, under the High Court's inherent jurisdiction, without a litigation friend or children's guardian. By rule 16.6(3) a child may do so either where the court has given leave or where a solicitor considers that the child is able, having regard to their age and

43 [2008] EWHC 517 (Fam), [2008] 2 FLR 6, at [31]–[33].

44 Cf. in non-Convention applications in which the appropriate test is the child's best interests, see *Re C*, above n. 43, applying *Mabon v Mabon*.

45 See FPR 2010, rr 16.4 and 12.48(1)(g), respectively.

46 See *Re L (Children) (Reunite International Child Abduction Centre intervening)* [2014] UKSC 1, at [46], per Lord Wilson.

47 *Re L*, above n. 46, per Lord Wilson, at [55].

48 See s 10(8).

49 Section 10(1)(a)(ii).

understanding, to give instructions and has accepted instructions from the child to act for him/her in the proceedings.

Re T (A Minor) (Child: Representation)[50] established that where the court considers that the child does not have sufficient understanding, though the solicitor's assessment of the child's capacity to instruct him is otherwise, the court is the final arbiter and can appoint a litigation friend or guardian ad litem.

The required level of understanding of a child was considered in *Mabon v Mabon*,[51] in which the Court of Appeal overturned a refusal to grant three brothers, aged 17, 15 and 13, separate representation. In so concluding, Thorpe LJ recognised that there is now 'a keener appreciation of the autonomy of the child and the child's consequential right to participate in decision-making processes that fundamentally affect his family life'. Consequently, courts must accept that in the case of articulate teenagers 'the right to freedom of expression and participation outweighs the paternalistic judgment of welfare'.[52] However, this is not to say that welfare has no place. There are acknowledged limits to the willingness of the court to respect even an articulate teenager's desire for self-determination when this puts their welfare in jeopardy.[53] In this context,[54] Bridge argues that 'the law should openly declare that welfare reigns when grave decisions with momentous outcomes are considered and recognise that adolescent autonomy is, inevitably, circumscribed.'

4. RESEARCH

In the divorce context, research has found that welfare is the primary rationale for ordering separate representation and, in particular, 'a desire to ensure that a conflict of interests of the parents does not obscure the real needs of the child'.[55] The courts' overall concern, when ordering separate representation, is 'to obtain a complete picture of the situation, where necessary presented by someone who is independent of the parents' positions. This will often be motivated less by a concern to hear the child than to explore conflicts of evidence or to hear arguments that neither adult party wishes to put forward'. More generally, research suggests that many family practitioners lack the necessary skills for effective face-to-face work with children and that children may not be receiving

50 [1994] Fam 49.

51 Above n. 42.

52 *Mabon v Mabon*, above n. 42, at [28].

53 *An NHS Trust and Child B and Mr & Mrs B* [2014] EWHC 3486 (Fam).

54 C. Bridge, 'Religious Beliefs and Teenage Refusal of Medical Treatment' (1999) 62 *Modern Law Review* 585, 594.

55 G. Douglas, M. Murch, C. Miles and L. Scanlan, *Research into the Operation of Rule 9.5 of the Family Proceedings Rules 1991*, 2006, paras. 2.38 ff.; See also M. Murch, *Supporting Children When Parents Separate*, Policy Press, Bristol 2018, ch. 4.

information about judicial proceedings, the options available and the possible consequences that are compatible with their age and maturity, in a language that they understand, and in a manner sensitive to their culture and gender.[56]

5. CONCLUSION

The UK ratified the UNCRC in 1991, but has not incorporated it into domestic law despite continuing calls to do so, including in particular by the Children's Commissioners for England, Scotland, Wales and Northern Ireland, who commented:

> Wales has a legal requirement on government ministers to have due regard to the UNCRC, and in Scotland ministers must keep it under consideration. Northern Ireland and England do not have such requirements, although in England a template for Child Rights Impact Assessments is being introduced across government. Scotland is so far the only nation to have plans to incorporate the UNCRC into law, with a bill due to be introduced in 2020.[57]

James[58] expressed serious reservations about the extent to which the Children Act 1989 has delivered the level of participation by children in family proceedings that would be consistent with the provisions of the UNCRC. He suggested that this was connected to the traditional view of the role of parents in making decisions about their children:

> … the provisions of Article 12, which have in many ways proved to be more problematic than other provisions, not least because, in the context of family law, children's participation rights are necessarily juxtaposed with the long-standing and hitherto unchallenged rights of parents to make important decisions about family life.[59]

Aldridge[60] argued that, as Article 12(2) UNCRC states that children's opportunities to be heard should be in a manner consistent with procedural

---

[56] See, for example, J. Hunt and J. Lawson, *Crossing the Boundaries – The Views of Practitioners of Family Court Welfare and Guardian ad Litem Work on the Proposal to Create a Unified Court Welfare Service*, 1999; J. Beqiraj and L. McNamara, *Children and Access to Justice: National Practices, International Challenges*, Bingham Centre for the Rule of Law Report 02/2016, International Bar Association 2016.

[57] UK Children's Commissioners' UNCRC mid-term review, November 2019, p. 3.

[58] A. James, 'Children, The UNCRC, and Family Law in England and Wales' (2008) 46 *Family Court Review* 53–64.

[59] A. James, above n. 58, p. 53.

[60] J. Aldridge, *Introduction to the Issue: Promoting Children's Participation in Research, Policy and Practice*, Cogitatio Press, Lisbon 2019, p. 90.

rules of national law, it is questionable how children and young people can exercise their right to express their views contained within Article 12(1) if they have no legal standing or agency in their own country. She stated that this can only be achieved through the actions of both adults and children/young people, by continuing to promote children's right to participation in decisions which affect their lives, and by states and governments hearing their voices and acting according to children's expressed views and wishes.

An illustration of judges acting in a way which promotes children's right to participation in decisions affecting their lives may be seen in *Re A: Letter to a Young Person*[61] where Peter Jackson J gave his decision by letter to the child (addressing it 'Dear Sam'), read the judgment to the parents, and gave it to the child's solicitor to give to, and discuss with, the child. Interestingly, Peter Jackson J was the first judge to include emojis in a judgment.[62] There are other signs that child-friendly awareness might be gaining traction as, for example, when HHJ Lynch, in *Re X (A Child)*,[63] said that her judgment would be written so as to make sense to the parents and the adopted child, and abandoned legal jargon, using far greater colloquial language instead.

However, as encouraging as these are, such decisions remain uncommon. In view of the reports from the interviewees in the study by Lundy et al.[64] that incorporation of Article 12 into domestic law had had a strong impact on practice in their countries, it may be that incorporation of the UNCRC into domestic law would provide the additional impetus in England and Wales for more meaningful participation of children in decisions affecting their lives.

---

61 [2017] EWFC 48.

62 *Lancashire County Council and Mr A, Mr B, The Children (by their Children's Guardian)* [2016] EWFC 9.

63 [2018] EWFC B82.

64 L. Lundy, U. Kilkelly, B. Byrne and J. Kang, *The UN Convention on the Rights of the Child: A Study of Legal Implementation in 12 Countries*, Unicef, United Kingdom 2012, p. 101.

GERMANY

Nina DETHLOFF and Daniela SCHRÖDER

1. INTRODUCTION

In Germany, family procedural law is codified in the Family Procedure Act (*Gesetz über das Verfahren in Familiensachen und in den Angelegenheiten der Freiwilligen Gerichtsbarkeit*, FamFG).[1] Separate from the German Civil Code of Procedure (*Zivilprozessordnung*, ZPO), the FamFG intends to ensure that all matters relating to family law proceedings take place before one and the same 'large court' – the family court.[2] Family courts are part of the ordinary jurisdiction with special assignments.[3]

With a total of 13,504,000 minors in Germany in 2019,[4] the number of proceedings in parent and child issues as well as parentage and adoption matters before the local courts (*Amtsgericht*, AG), in which departments are competent as family courts of first instance, came to approximately 179,209.[5] Before the

1 From 17 December 2008, entered into force on 1 September 2009 (BGBl. I 2008, 2586).
2 BT-Drucksache 16/6308, pp. 1, 168.
3 N. DETHLOFF, *Familienrecht*, 32nd ed., C.H. Beck, Munich 2018, §1, No. 46.
4 https://de.statista.com/statistik/daten/studie/197783/umfrage/minderjaehrige-kinder-in-deutschland/.
5 Statistisches Bundesamt, *Rechtspflege Familiengerichte*, Fachserie 10, Reihe 2, July 2020, p. 18.

Higher Regional Courts (*Oberlandesgericht*, OLG), competent in the second instance, the number equalled approximately 6,261 in 2019.[6]

The provisions on family law in the German Civil Code (*Bürgerliches Gesetzbuch*, BGB)[7] and the ones in the FamFG provide various possibilities for the child's participation. In parent and child matters (§151 FamFG)[8] as well as parentage (§169 FamFG) and adoption matters (§186 FamFG), children are usually directly affected themselves, meaning that they must be involved as parties (§7 para. 2 No. 1 FamFG). In parent and child matters children must be heard from the age of 14 (§159 para. 1 FamFG). With the new law passed by the legislature on 25 March 2021, the mandatory child hearing under §159 para. 1 FamFG-New will be independent of the child's age.[9] In parentage matters the court should hear children from the age of 14 (§175 para. 2 FamFG). In adoption matters the hearing of the child is mandatory for all children (§192 para. 1 FamFG). However, they are only capable of participating themselves insofar as they have reached the age of 14 and are asserting one of the few rights of objection and participation granted under civil law[10] (§9 para. 1 No. 3 FamFG). Children who are incapable of participating in proceedings are represented by their parents.[11] In accordance with §§181, 1629 para. 2 and 1795 BGB, the parental representation of minors is excluded by law in certain cases of serious conflicts of interest, for example when contracting with the parent him/herself. The family court may also deprive the parents of their power of representation in other cases if there exists such a conflict.[12] In these cases, the family court appoints a supplementary curator for the child.[13]

---

6 Statistisches Bundesamt, *Rechtspflege Familiengerichte*, Fachserie 10, Reihe 2, July 2020, p. 72.

7 See for the provisions on family law, the 4th Book of the BGB, §§1297–1921 BGB.

8 Relating to: parental custody (includes care for the person of the child (also maintenance) and the property of the child, §1626 para. 1 s. 2 BGB; also includes determination of the existence or non-existence of parental custody, withdrawal of representation, transfer of parental custody, right of residence, child abduction); the right of contact and the right to information concerning the personal circumstances of the child (§§1684, 1685 BGB); request to return the child (§1632 para. 3 and 1 BGB, according to which care for the person of the child includes the right to require return of the child from any person who is unlawfully withholding the child from the parents or from one parent; in cross-border conflicts, the international conventions, in particular the Hague Convention on Child Abduction, must be observed); guardianship; curatorship; the approval of placement.

9 See for this 'Entwurf eines Gesetzes zur Bekämpfung sexualisierter Gewalt gegen Kinder', BT-Drucksache 19/23707, 27 October 2020, p. 15, new regulations from this law in the following FamFG-New. The Act will enter into force after its promulgation pursuant to Article 10.

10 In particular, this includes: the right of objection in custody proceedings according to §1671 para. 2 No. 1 BGB; the consent of the child to the adoption pursuant to §1746 para. 1 BGB; the contact of the child with its parents according to §1684 para. 1 BGB.

11 According to §1629 para. 1 BGB.

12 Pursuant to §1629 para. 2 s. 3 in conjunction with §1796 BGB.

13 Pursuant to §1909 BGB; see for more information about the appointment of curator, A. Schneider, *Münchener Kommentar zum Bürgerlichen Gesetzbuch,* 8th ed., C.H. Beck, Munich 2020, §1909, No. 7 et seq.

In parent and child matters concerning parental custody upon separation or divorce, the child's place of residence, the right of contact, and the return of the child,[14] the court shall facilitate agreement between participants at every phase of the proceedings.[15] For this, the court shall provide information on counselling options available from respective counselling offices as well as child and youth welfare services.[16] In accordance with §156 para. 1 s. 4 and s. 2 FamFG, the court may also order that the parents participate in such counselling.[17] Consequently, in addition to in-court proceedings, there are various out-of-court dispute resolution procedures that concern children.[18]

2. STATUTORY PROVISIONS

Substantive family law in particular provides for the child's right of objection in the case of transfer of sole custody where the parents live apart (§1671 para. 1 s. 2 No. 1; para. 2 s. 2 No. 1 BGB). Under this provision, and with the consent of the other parent, each parent may apply for the family court to fully or partially transfer parental custody to him/her alone – unless the child has reached the age of 14 and objects to the transfer. If the child objects, this removes the binding effect which normally arises for the court through parental consent.[19] However, the child does not have the right to veto; the child can only prevent the parental proposal from being implemented without any child welfare examination.[20]

Procedural law in particular provides for the hearing of the child. It primarily serves to clarify facts and enables the court to fulfil its inquiry ex officio (§26 FamFG) (*Amtsermittlungsgrundsatz*).[21] Besides this, it ensures the child's right

---

14 See above n. 8.

15 If this is not contrary to the child's best interest, §156 para. 1 s. 1 FamFG.

16 K. Tillmanns, *Münchener Kommentar zum Bürgerlichen Gesetzbuch*, 8th ed., C.H. Beck, Munich 2020, §17 SGB VIII, No. 16; D. Zorn, *Kommentar zum Gesetz über das Verfahren in Familiensachen und in den Angelegenheiten der freiwilligen Gerichtsbarkeit*, 3rd ed., Gieseking, Bielefeld 2018, §156 FamFG, No. 10.

17 S. Hammer, *FamFG Gesetz über das Verfahren in Familiensachen und in den Angelegenheiten der freiwilligen Gerichtsbarkeit*, 5th ed., Otto Schmidt, Cologne 2020, §156 FamFG, No. 28; K. Tillmanns, *Münchener Kommentar zum Bürgerlichen Gesetzbuch*, 8th ed., C.H. Beck, Munich 2020, §17 SGB VIII, No. 16.

18 R. Bastine, B. Römer-Wolf, F. Decker, A. Haid-Loh, S. Mayer and K. Normann, 'Praxis der Familienmediation in der Beratung' [2006] *Praxis der Kinderpsychologie und Kinderpsychiatrie* 584 et seq.

19 H. Hennemann, *Münchener Kommentar zum Bürgerlichen Gesetzbuch*, 8th ed., C.H. Beck, Munich 2020, §1671 BGB, No. 88.

20 See draft legislation on reforming parent and child matters (*Gesetzentwurf der Bundesregierung zur Reform des Kindschaftsrechts*) from 13 June 1996, BT-Drucksache 13/4899, p. 99; I. Götz in O. Palandt, *Bürgerliches Gesetzbuch*, 80th ed., C.H. Beck, Munich 2021, §1671 BGB, No. 9.

21 *Bundesgerichtshof* (Federal Court of Justice, BGH) 11 July 1984 – IV b ZB 73/83, *FamRZ (Zeitschrift für das gesamte Familienrecht)* 1985, 169, 172.

to be heard and allows him/her to exercise his/her right to self-determination.[22] The hearing of the child equally provides space for the child to express his/her will and motives, as well as to disclose his/her personal relationship to the parents.[23] To this purpose the child should be informed of the object, course and potential result of the proceedings in a manner suitable for his/her age (§159 para. 4 s. 1 FamFG). The hearing presents the singular opportunity for the court to obtain its own impression of the child, which is absolutely essential for the consideration of the child's welfare.[24] The child shall be given the opportunity to make a statement at the hearing (§159 para. 4 s. 2 FamFG). Instead of the child being asked directly about facts, he/she should be asked open-ended questions, and should – in colloquial terms – 'simply be able to narrate'.[25] With this method, the child expresses his/her interests and wishes primarily through words. In regard to younger children, in particular, the Federal Court of Justice has ruled the child's behaviour may also be used to derive conclusions about his/her wishes or relationships.[26] Thus, interests and wishes can also be expressed non-verbally. The concrete form of the hearing may be determined at the discretion of the court (§159 para. 4 s. 4 FamFG). Jurisprudence does not specify the exact requirements for non-verbal forms of communication. German literature, however, does provide some indication as to how the child's interests and wishes may be determined using non-verbal methods. This includes observing the child as well as his/her body language and facial expressions during the hearing; moreover, painting, drawing and playing with the child may allow for further conclusions to be drawn regarding his/her wishes and interests.[27] Suggestions

---

22 D. Zorn, *Kommentar zum Gesetz über das Verfahren in Familiensachen und in den Angelegenheiten der freiwilligen Gerichtsbarkeit*, 3rd ed., Gieseking, Bielefeld 2018, §159 FamFG, No. 2.

23 R. Balloff, *Kinder vor dem Familiengericht*, 3rd ed., Nomos, Baden-Baden 2018, p. 260; C. Krumm, 'Die wichtigsten Praxisprobleme der persönlichen Kindesanhörung nach §159 FamFG' [2013] *FamFR (Familienrecht und Familienverfahrensrecht)* 265, 268.

24 E. Carl, M. Clauss and M. Karle, *Kindesanhörung im Familienrecht, Rechtliche und psychologische Grundlagen sowie praktische Durchführung*, C.H. Beck, Munich 2015, p. 27.

25 S. Hammer, *FamFG Gesetz über das Verfahren in Familiensachen und in den Angelegenheiten der freiwilligen Gerichtsbarkeit*, 5th ed., Otto Schmidt, Cologne 2020, §159 FamFG, No. 21; D. Zorn, *Kommentar zum Gesetz über das Verfahren in Familiensachen und in den Angelegenheiten der freiwilligen Gerichtsbarkeit*, 3rd ed., Gieseking, Bielefeld 2018, §159 FamFG, No. 17.

26 BGH 5 October 2016 – XII ZB 280/15, *FamRZ* 2016, 2082, No. 46; H. Borth and M. Grandel, *Familiengerichtliches Verfahren*, 6th ed., C.H. Beck, Munich 2018, §159 FamFG, No. 3.

27 E. Carl, M. Clauss and M. Karle, *Kindesanhörung im Familienrecht, Rechtliche und psychologische Grundlagen sowie praktische Durchführung*, C.H. Beck, Munich 2015, p. 60; S. Hammer, *FamFG Gesetz über das Verfahren in Familiensachen und in den Angelegenheiten der freiwilligen Gerichtsbarkeit*, 5th ed., Otto Schmidt, Cologne 2020, §159 FamFG, No. 21; N. Ivanits, *Die Stellung des Kindes in auf Einvernehmen zielenden gerichtlichen und außergerichtlichen Verfahren in Kindschaftssachen*, Peter Lang, Frankfurt am Main 2012, p. 50; Bundesministerium für Familie, Senioren, Frauen und Jugend (BMFSFJ) & Deutsches Kinderhilfswerk, *Kindgerechte Justiz – Zugang zum Recht für Kinder*, Workshop 2018, p. 10.

concerning suitable locations are also plentiful in the literature; there is broad agreement that the child's hearing should take place at a neutral location, such as at the courthouse, youth welfare office, childcare centre or even school, which ensures the conversation will be free of disturbances.[28] In contrast, it is considered inappropriate to conduct the hearing at the child's home, since even the indirect presence of the parents could influence the child's statement and behaviour.[29] The location should also be chosen to reflect the child's age. It is preferable, for example, to hear children under the age of eight in a 'children's room', i.e. a room at the courthouse that has been furnished in a child-friendly manner, while older children should be heard in a sober atmosphere so they feel they are being taken seriously.[30] The Higher Regional Court of Frankfurt illustrates how courts endeavour to allocate suitable rooms for children. The Court has a spacious and bright children's room, equipped with games, painting materials, a football table and a dollhouse, where younger children are heard.[31] The court may forego hearing the child if there are substantial grounds to do so (§159 para. 3 s. 1 FamFG, §159 para. 2 No. 1 FamFG-New). This is the case if the hearing might result in a significant impairment of the child's physical and/or mental health.[32] In order to determine this, the judge must balance the interests of the child with the duty to clarify the facts (§26 FamFG).[33] Additionally, in cases subject to interim legal protection (*einstweiliger Rechtsschutz*), the court may make a decision without having heard the child.[34] These cases of interim legal protection are often caused by imminent danger (*Gefahr im Verzug*). If a hearing does not take place solely because of imminent danger, it shall be held as soon as possible thereafter.[35] However, courts rarely follow through with

---

28 R. Balloff, 'Anhörung und Kommunikation mit dem Kind im Familiengericht' [2017] *Justizministerialblatt für Schleswig-Holstein* 441, 444; E. Carl, M. Clauss and M. Karle, *Kindesanhörung im Familienrecht, Rechtliche und psychologische Grundlagen sowie praktische Durchführung*, C.H. Beck, Munich 2015, p. 65; J.A. Rohmann, 'Anhörung des Kindes und der Eltern sowie die Bekanntgabe der Entscheidung an das Kind als kommunikativer Prozess' [2013] *FPR (Familie Partnerschaft Recht)* 464 et seq.; T. Obermann, 'Kindesanhörung bei Einigung der Eltern' [2015] *NZFam (Neue Zeitschrift für Familienrecht)* 1129 et seq.

29 R. Balloff, 'Anhörung und Kommunikation mit dem Kind im Familiengericht' [2017] *Justizministerialblatt für Schleswig-Holstein* 441, 444.

30 H. Hennemann, 'Die Anhörung des Kindes in Kindschaftssachen, §159 FamFG' [2014] *NZFam* 871, 872.

31 Y. Gottschalk, 'Wie kindgerecht ist die Justiz?' [2018] *ZRP (Zeitschrift für Rechtspolitik)* 249.

32 BGH 31 October 2018 – XII ZB 411/18, *NJW (Neue Juristische Wochenzeitschrift)* 2019, 432; E. Schumann, *Münchener Kommentar zum FamFG*, 3rd ed., C.H. Beck, Munich 2018, §159 FamFG, No. 6 et seq.

33 BGH 31 October 2018 – XII ZB 411/18, *NJW* 2019, 432.

34 This occurs in custody and contact proceedings, where more than 20% of cases are impacted by interim legal protection, see Bundesministerium der Justiz und für Verbraucherschutz (BMJV) together with S. Ekert and B. Heiderhoff, 'Die Evaluierung der FGG-Reform', Abschlussbericht zum Forschungsvorhaben, Berlin 15 January 2018, p. 195.

35 Pursuant to §159 para. 3 s. 2 FamFG.

this step. Thus, in a considerable number of decisions involving interim legal protection, the child is not heard.[36]

The child's right to appeal (§60 FamFG) presents another procedural right of participation. Accordingly, a 14-year-old minor can personally complain in all matters concerning him/her[37] without his/her legal representative. As this is not an additional right, a general right to appeal must exist (§58 para. 1 FamFG).[38] By the age of 14, a child is usually mature enough to be able to understand the implications and significance of a court decision in personal matters; it is on this basis that the child is granted the right to complaint on appeal independently.[39]

Finally, the guardian ad litem for minors[40] should be noted. In contrast to the aforementioned rights, this is not a direct form of participation. Nevertheless, the guardian represents the minor's interests and wishes in proceedings that concern the person of the child, like proceedings relating to parental custody,[41] the return of the child[42] or personal contact.[43] The appointment of a guardian is required when the interests of the minor are significantly at odds with those of the child's legal representatives (§158 para. 2 No. 1 FamFG[44]). This is the case if the parents primarily pursue their own interests[45] or if, due to the intensity of the conflict, there is a threat that they will lose sight of the child's interests.[46] The appointment is also required in proceedings concerning the endangerment

---

36 In nearly 20% of interim legal protection proceedings, the child is not heard: Bundesministerium der Justiz und für Verbraucherschutz (BMJV) together with S. Ekert and B. Heiderhoff, 'Die Evaluierung der FGG-Reform', Abschlussbericht zum Forschungsvorhaben, Berlin 15 January 2018, p. 199; H. Roth, 'Die Evaluierung des FamFG' [2018] *FamRZ* 1637, 1642.

37 For example: matters concerning parentage (§169 FamFG); the return of the child (§1632 BGB); the withdrawal of the power of representation of the parents or the guardian (§§1629 para. 2 s. 3, 1796, 1915 para. 1 s. 1 BGB); see for more information U. Meyer-Holz, *FamFG Gesetz über das Verfahren in Familiensachen und in den Angelegenheiten der freiwilligen Gerichtsbarkeit,* 3rd ed., C.H. Beck, Munich 2018, §60 FamFG, No. 10.

38 OLG Düsseldorf 10 January 2011 – II-3 WF 148/10, *FamRB (Familienrechtsberater)* 2011, 172; OLG Nuremberg 8 September 2011–7 UF 883/11, *FamRZ* 2012, 804, 805.

39 A. Fischer, *Münchener Kommentar zum FamFG,* 3rd ed., C.H. Beck, Munich 2018, §60 FamFG, No. 2; in practice, however, the right of appeal has almost no effect, see H. Borth and M. Grandel, *Familiengerichtliches Verfahren,* 6th ed., C.H. Beck, Munich 2018, §60 FamFG, No. 1.

40 In the following 'guardian'.

41 §§1671, 1674, 1680 para. 2 BGB.

42 §1632 paras. 1, 4 BGB.

43 §§1684, 1685 BGB.

44 See also for this in §158 para. 3 No. 1 FamFG-New, 'Entwurf eines Gesetzes zur Bekämpfung sexualisierter Gewalt gegen Kinder', BT-Drucksache 19/23707, 27 October 2020, p. 13.

45 Indications for the court are, for example, opposing requests of the parents, see S. Hammer, *FamFG Gesetz über das Verfahren in Familiensachen und in den Angelegenheiten der freiwilligen Gerichtsbarkeit,* 5th ed., Otto Schmidt, Cologne 2020, §158 FamFG, No. 17.

46 BT-Drucksache 13/4899, p. 131; S. Hammer, *FamFG Gesetz über das Verfahren in Familiensachen und in den Angelegenheiten der freiwilligen Gerichtsbarkeit,* 5th ed., Otto Schmidt, Cologne 2020, §158 FamFG, No. 17.

of the child's best interest pursuant to §§1666 and 1666a BGB;[47] if there is consideration of withdrawal of care of the person of the child in whole or in part (No. 2); if separation of the child from the person currently caring for him/her will occur (No. 3); in proceedings regarding the return of the child or an order concerning the child's place of residence (No. 4); or if exclusion or significant limitation of contact is under consideration (No. 5).[48] The child has no explicit right to apply for a guardian.[49]

In proceedings that concern the person of the child[50] the court shall hear the youth welfare office (§162 para. 1 FamFG).[51] Within this scope, the youth welfare office shall inform the court about the family's current situation and thus submit the necessary basis for the decision.[52] Home visits are undertaken by employees of the youth welfare office, as well as further discussions with those involved.[53] This also includes conversations between a youth welfare officer and the child, which might be considered as a form of 'hearing of the child' by the youth welfare system, but without the child expressly having a right of participation towards the youth welfare system. At this point, the hearing of the child only serves the purpose of investigations by the youth welfare office. Expert opinions (§163 FamFG) may also play a decisive role. The court decides ex officio, exercising its best judgement, whether it is necessary to obtain an expert's opinion.[54] As assistants of the court, experts are required to follow its instructions.[55] Experts reach a scientifically backed conclusion by means of their own data collection, such as diagnostic interviews, interaction and behavioural observations.[56]

---

47 §1666 BGB: court measures in the case of endangerment of the child's best interest; §1666a BGB: principle of proportionality; priority of public support measures.

48 See for the individual numbers in the new version of §158 para. 2 and para. 3 FamFG-New 'Entwurf eines Gesetzes zur Bekämpfung sexualisierter Gewalt gegen Kinder', BT-Drucksache 19/23707, 27 October 2020, p. 13.

49 According to draft legislation, the appointment of a guardian should be required if the child requests it; however, this bill did not pass. For more details, see BT-Drucksache 16/6308, p. 40; for reasons for an application right, p. 238.

50 See above nn. 42, 43, 44 for the respective type of cases.

51 See also §50 para. 1 No. 1 of the SGB VIII, according to which the youth welfare office must participate in parent and child matters.

52 H. Hennemann, *Münchener Kommentar zum Bürgerlichen Gesetzbuch,* 8th ed., C.H. Beck, Munich 2020, §1671 BGB, No. 190.

53 OLG Cologne 6 October 1998 – 25 UF 102/98, *FamRZ* 1999, 1517; H. Hennemann, *Münchener Kommentar zum Bürgerlichen Gesetzbuch,* 8th ed., C.H. Beck, Munich 2020, §1671 BGB, No. 190.

54 S. Hammer, *FamFG Gesetz über das Verfahren in Familiensachen und in den Angelegenheiten der freiwilligen Gerichtsbarkeit,* 5th ed., Otto Schmidt, Cologne 2020, §163 FamFG, No. 4.

55 S. Hammer, *FamFG Gesetz über das Verfahren in Familiensachen und in den Angelegenheiten der freiwilligen Gerichtsbarkeit,* 5th ed., Otto Schmidt, Cologne 2020, §163 FamFG, No. 20a; M. Stötzel, 'Möglichkeiten der Interventionen der professionellen Verfahrensbeteiligten' [2010] *FPR* 425, 427.

56 R. Balloff and E. Walter, 'Anforderungen an familienrechtspsychologische Gutachten bei Kindeswohlgefährdungen nach §1666 BGB' [2015] *NZFam* 580.

These interviews and behavioural observations[57] include conversations between the expert and the child[58] and thus allow the child to be 'explored' without directly 'participating' in a legal sense.[59]

These different forms of participation exist side by side as a result of the inquiry ex officio. However, the legal decision remains a matter for the court.[60] It is the court's responsibility to weigh the respective evidence, such as the expert's opinion or the youth officer's testimony, and ultimately reach a decision.[61]

3. MODES OF CHILD PARTICIPATION

3.1. DIRECT FORMS OF PARTICIPATION

According to previous law, in parent and child matters the court is under a duty to hear children aged 14 and above.[62] If the child has not reached that age, he/she shall be heard when his/her preferences, relationships or wishes are significant to the decision or when a hearing is otherwise indicated (§159 para. 2 FamFG). After the amendment, the mandatory child hearing is now ruled in §159 para. 1 FamFG-New independent of the child's age.[63] According to confirmed Federal Constitutional Court rulings, the child must be heard from the age of three in proceedings concerning the person of the child because, from this point on, children are generally able to verbally or non-verbally express their needs, wishes, feelings and fears.[64] Nevertheless, there are still decisions in parent and

---

57 N. Dethloff, *Familienrecht*, 32nd ed., C.H. Beck, Munich 2018, §13, No. 211.

58 K. Lack and A. Hammesfahr, *Psychologische Gutachten im Familienrecht, Handbuch für die rechtliche und psychologische Praxis*, Bundesanzeiger Verlag, Cologne 2019, No. 272 et seq.; M. Stötzel, 'Möglichkeiten der Interventionen der professionellen Verfahrensbeteiligten' [2010] *FPR* 425, 427.

59 Regarding §163a FamFG; K. Lack and A. Hammesfahr *Psychologische Gutachten im Familienrecht, Handbuch für die rechtliche und psychologische Praxis*, Bundesanzeiger Verlag, Cologne 2019, No. 105.

60 N. Dethloff, *Familienrecht*, 32nd ed., C.H. Beck, Munich 2018, §1, No. 44.

61 BGH 5 October 2016 – XII ZB 280/15, *NZFam* 2016, 1179, with a note I. Plattenberg, p. 1185.

62 But the court must accept if the child does not want to say anything, see for more information S. Hammer, *FamFG Gesetz über das Verfahren in Familiensachen und in den Angelegenheiten der freiwilligen Gerichtsbarkeit*, 5th ed., Otto Schmidt, Cologne 2020, §159 FamFG, No. 21.

63 See therefore 'Entwurf eines Gesetzes zur Bekämpfung sexualisierter Gewalt an Kinder', BT-Drucksache 19/23707, 27 October 2020, p. 15.

64 BVerfG 14 July 2010 – 1 BvR 3189/09, *FamRZ* 2010, 1622; BVerfG 23 March 2007 – 1 BvR 156/07, *FamRZ* 2007, 1078; BGH 15 June 2016 – XII ZB 419/15, *FamRZ* 2016, 1439, 1444; D. Zorn, *Kommentar zum Gesetz über das Verfahren in Familiensachen und in den Angelegenheiten der freiwilligen Gerichtsbarkeit*, 3rd ed., Gieseking, Bielefeld 2018, §159 FamFG, No. 15.

child matters in which children younger than 14 are not heard.[65] In other cases, children are heard, but their wishes are not reflected in the decision.[66]

In parentage matters the court shall conduct a hearing with a child who has reached the age of 14. The court may conduct a hearing with a younger child.[67] In adoption matters the hearing situation is different, because no age limit for a mandatory child hearing exists (§192 para. 1 FamFG). The right of objection[68] is also related to the age of the child, as only children aged 14 and over can expressly object to the transfer of sole custody. Moreover, the right of minors to complain on appeal[69] also applies exclusively to those who have already turned 14.

In principle, the hearing of the child is conducted by the judge responsible for the decision.[70] A hearing by way of judicial assistance, such as by a designated alternative judge, is not excluded, for example in the case of interim legal protection in which the judge would otherwise have to abstain from a hearing altogether due to the urgency of the case.[71]

In custody and contact matters, it is necessary, according to the case law of the Federal Court of Justice, for the court taking the decision to obtain a genuine impression of the child, and his/her preferences and relationships.[72] Accordingly, in appeal proceedings, a hearing by the appointed judge is held not to be sufficient, but must rather be conducted by the entire senate.[73] In contrast, German literature argues that the hearing of the child should normally be conducted by only one judge, even in a complaint procedure, in order not to overwhelm the child.[74]

---

65 As was the case, for example, in a decision by the Karlsruhe Higher Regional Court. There, the Court ruled that with regard to the age of the children (at the time of the decision, the children were nine and 13 years old), their preferences, relationships or desires were not particularly significant to the decision, OLG Karlsruhe 26 March 2015 – 18 UF 304/14, *FamRZ* 2015, 2168, 2170.

66 A ruling by the Higher Regional Court of Brandenburg, for example, disregarded the wish of the child, stating that children under 12 are not able to form an autonomous wish, OLG Brandenburg 8 January 2018 – 10 UF 21/17, *juris*, No. 27; OLG Brandenburg 16 April 2008 – 9 UF 191/07, *FamRZ* 2008, 1474; in this direction, see also OLG Stuttgart 28 August 2006 – 17 UF 151/06, *FamRZ* 2006, 1857 et seq.

67 See §175 para. 2 s. 2 FamFG.

68 On the proposal of the parents to transfer sole custody where the parents live apart, §1671 para. 1 s. 2 BGB.

69 In all matters that affect the child, see §60 s. 3 FamFG.

70 BGH 11 July 1984 – IVb ZB 73/83, *FamRZ* 1985, 169.

71 S. Hammer, *FamFG Gesetz über das Verfahren in Familiensachen und in den Angelegenheiten der freiwilligen Gerichtsbarkeit*, 5th ed., Otto Schmidt, Cologne 2020, §159 FamFG, at No.18.

72 BGH 28 April 2010 – XII ZB 81/09, *FamRZ* 2010, 1060.

73 BGH 28 April 2010 – XII ZB 81/09, *FamRZ* 2010, 1060; BGH 11 July 1984 – IVb ZB 73/83, *FamRZ* 1985, 169.

74 E. Carl, M. Clauss and M. Karle, *Kindesanhörung im Familienrecht, Rechtliche und psychologische Grundlagen sowie praktische Durchführung*, C.H. Beck, Munich 2015, p. 160; D. Büte, *Familienrecht Scheidung, Unterhalt, Verfahren*, 6th ed., C.H. Beck, Munich 2015, §159 FamFG, No. 12.

The hearing of the child may also be conducted in the presence of other people, such as experts, psychologists or representatives from the youth welfare system.[75] The parents, however, do not take part in the hearing of the child.[76] If a guardian is appointed, the hearing shall take place in his/her presence.[77] It is at the court's discretion to determine whether he/she should actively participate in the hearing or merely observe.[78]

The court shall keep notes concerning court hearings and in-person hearings; the notes shall set forth the essential occurrences of the hearing (§28 para. 4 s. 1, s. 2 FamFG).[79] In order to protect impartial and open communication with the minor, audio/video recording is not common in family court proceedings[80] and is widely opposed.[81] If information obtained at the child's hearing is relevant to the judicial decision, the parents must be informed about it and given the opportunity to comment (§37 para. 2 FamFG).[82] Therefore, the judge has to let the child know that he/she will inform the parents about the main content of the hearing.[83] In particular, handling confidential information shared by the child is a difficult issue. While judges cannot remain silent given their duty of neutrality, they are obliged to consider the child's welfare.[84] Accordingly, the child's legitimate interest in confidentiality, the parents' right to be heard, the principle of fair trial, and, in particular, the child's welfare must be weighed

75 BVerfG 5 November 1980 – 1 BvR 349/80, *NJW* 1981, 217, 219; D. Zorn, *Kommentar zum Gesetz über das Verfahren in Familiensachen und in den Angelegenheiten der freiwilligen Gerichtsbarkeit*, 3rd ed., Gieseking, Bielefeld 2018, §159 FamFG, No. 17.

76 BVerfG 5 June 2019 – 1 BvR 675/19, *NJW* 2010, 2532; H. Hennemann, 'Die Anhörung des Kindes in Kindschaftssachen, §159 FamFG' [2014] *NZFam* 871, 872.

77 According to §159 para. 4 s. 3 FamFG.

78 BGH 28 April 2010 – XII ZB 81/09, *NJW* 2010, 2805; J. Klein, 'Die verfahrensrechtliche Stellung des Minderjährigen in Kindschaftssachen' [2019] *RdJB (Recht der Jugend und des Bildungswesens)* 16, 23.

79 See in more detail D. Zorn, *Kommentar zum Gesetz über das Verfahren in Familiensachen und in den Angelegenheiten der freiwilligen Gerichtsbarkeit*, 3rd ed., Gieseking, Bielefeld 2018, §159 FamFG, No. 21.

80 See BVerfG 5 June 2019 – 1 BvR 675/19, *NJW* 2019, 2532, where it reads: 'There is no constitutional requirement to allow parents to follow the hearing of the child by video recording'; in this way, see also E. Carl, M. Clauss and M. Karle, *Kindesanhörung im Familienrecht, Rechtliche und psychologische Grundlagen sowie praktische Durchführung*, C.H. Beck, Munich 2015, No. 150; M. Karle, E. Carl and M. Clauss 'Kindesanhörung aus psychologischer Sicht' [2014] *NZFam* 875, 880.

81 See the results of the 23. Deutscher Familiengerichtstag, Brühl 2019, Working Group 24, 'Beteiligung von Kindern im Verfahren'.

82 S. Hammer, *FamFG Gesetz über das Verfahren in Familiensachen und in den Angelegenheiten der freiwilligen Gerichtsbarkeit*, 5th ed., Otto Schmidt, Cologne 2020, §159 FamFG, No. 29.

83 E. Carl, M. Clauss and M. Karle, *Kindesanhörung im Familienrecht, Rechtliche und psychologische Grundlagen sowie praktische Durchführung*, C.H. Beck, Munich 2015, No. 128.

84 S. Hammer, *FamFG Gesetz über das Verfahren in Familiensachen und in den Angelegenheiten der freiwilligen Gerichtsbarkeit*, 5th ed., Otto Schmidt, Cologne 2020, §159 FamFG, No. 29.

against each other – with the protection of the child, where his/her welfare is threatened, taking priority over the parents' procedural rights.[85]

Minors with capacity to participate shall be summoned in person, even if they have an authorised representative such as an attorney; the authorised representative shall be informed of the summons (§33 para. 2 FamFG).[86] During the hearing, the court shall inform the child of his/her right to complain on appeal.[87] For this purpose, it is necessary that the child is provided with all relevant information, such as expert opinions.[88] In contrast, for children under 14 years of age no special rules exist. Therefore, the child's summons is directed to the legal representative – and thus usually the parents.[89] If a guardian has been appointed, he/she can inform the child as well as prepare the child for the hearing.[90] Ultimately, however, children are only indirectly informed about their participation rights – through either their parents or guardian. Nevertheless, courts may attach an additional letter to the child that informs him/her of the summons to the hearing in an age-appropriate manner. Family judges in Germany have already developed sample letters addressed to children in which they explain the purpose of the hearing and also explicitly invite them to participate.[91] Although some courts already use these sample letters, such child-friendly involvement remains at an early stage, and these methods do not appear to be comprehensively applied in practice.[92]

---

85 E. Carl and P. Eschweiler 'Kindesanhörung – Chancen und Risiken' [2005] *NJW* 1681, 1682; E. Carl, M. Clauss and M. Karle, *Kindesanhörung im Familienrecht, Rechtliche und psychologische Grundlagen sowie praktische Durchführung*, C.H. Beck, Munich 2015, No. 130 et seq.; S. Hammer, *FamFG Gesetz über das Verfahren in Familiensachen und in den Angelegenheiten der freiwilligen Gerichtsbarkeit*, 5th ed., Otto Schmidt, Cologne 2020, §159 FamFG, No. 29.

86 For more details, see S. Hammer, *FamFG Gesetz über das Verfahren in Familiensachen und in den Angelegenheiten der freiwilligen Gerichtsbarkeit*, 5th ed., Otto Schmidt, Cologne 2020, §159 FamFG, No. 16; in the event of repeated absences, the presentation of the child may ordered pursuant to §33 para. 3 s. 3 FamFG, see also E. Schumann, *Münchener Kommentar zum FamFG*, 3rd ed., C.H. Beck, Munich 2018, §159 FamFG, No. 12.

87 OLG Karlsruhe 12 November 2015 – 20 WF 162/15, *FamRB* 2016, 234 et seq.; E. Schumann, *Münchener Kommentar zum FamFG*, 3rd ed., C.H. Beck, Munich 2018, §159 FamFG, No. 13.

88 BGH 15 January 2014 – XII ZB 289/13, *FamRZ* 2014, 648; D. Zorn, *Kommentar zum Gesetz über das Verfahren in Familiensachen und in den Angelegenheiten der freiwilligen Gerichtsbarkeit*, 3rd ed., Gieseking, Bielefeld 2018, §159 FamFG, No. 16.

89 E. Schumann, *Münchener Kommentar zum FamFG*, 3rd ed., C.H. Beck, Munich 2018, §159 FamFG, No. 12.

90 S. Hammer, *FamFG Gesetz über das Verfahren in Familiensachen und in den Angelegenheiten der freiwilligen Gerichtsbarkeit*, 5th ed., Otto Schmidt, Cologne 2020, §158 FamFG, No. 43.

91 E. Carl, M. Clauß and M. Karle, *Kindesanhörung im Familienrecht, Rechtliche und psychologische Grundlagen sowie praktische Durchführung*, C.H. Beck, Munich 2015, No. 113 et seq.

92 With a similar result, E. Carl, M. Clauß and M. Karle, *Kindesanhörung im Familienrecht, Rechtliche und psychologische Grundlagen sowie praktische Durchführung*, C.H. Beck, Munich 2015, No. 113 et seq.; Y. Gottschalk, 'Wie kindgerecht ist die Justiz?' [2018] *ZRP* 249, 251.

If the parents do not bring the child to the hearing, coercive measures may be imposed against them (§35 FamFG).[93] This is due to the fact that only the court may forego hearing the child when there are substantial grounds to do so,[94] and the hearing as an element of the inquiry ex officio is not subject to the parents' disposition.[95] While parents cannot prevent the hearing of the child,[96] it is within their remit to inform the child, if aged under 14, about the hearing as well as to bring the child to it. In addition, parents can refuse out-of-court contact with the guardian[97] and object to an expert opinion.[98] Thus they play a decisive role in their child's rights of participation. Therefore, it is even more important to both inform the child about the hearing and hear the child as early as possible. In addition, this has the advantage of considering the child as an independent subject from the start.

The decision against which the child has the right to file a complaint on appeal shall be announced directly to the child if he/she has reached the age of 14 and possess the capacity to contract (§164 s. 1 FamFG). In this context, 'directly to the child' means that the decision must be addressed to the child's home address separately; notification to the legal representative is not sufficient.[99] The notification of the decision is made either by letter or formal notification following the German Civil Code of Procedure.[100] As a result, the child is authorised to receive the outcome of the proceeding.[101] If the child is not

---

93 E. Schumann, *Münchener Kommentar zum FamFG*, 3rd ed., C.H. Beck, Munich 2018, §159 FamFG, No. 12.

94 See §159 para. 3 s. 1 FamFG, §159 para 2. No. 1 FamFG-New.

95 S. Hammer, *FamFG Gesetz über das Verfahren in Familiensachen und in den Angelegenheiten der freiwilligen Gerichtsbarkeit*, 5th ed., Otto Schmidt, Cologne 2020, §159 FamFG, No. 10; D. Zorn, *Kommentar zum Gesetz über das Verfahren in Familiensachen und in den Angelegenheiten der freiwilligen Gerichtsbarkeit*, 3rd ed., Gieseking, Bielefeld 2018, §159 FamFG, No. 15.

96 BGH 16 March 2011 – XII ZB 407/10, *FamRZ* 2011, 796; OLG München 8 October 2009 – 26 UF 1569/09, *FamRZ* 2010, 486; S. Hammer, *FamFG Gesetz über das Verfahren in Familiensachen und in den Angelegenheiten der freiwilligen Gerichtsbarkeit*, 5th ed., Otto Schmidt, Cologne 2020, §159 FamFG, No. 11.

97 KG Berlin 17 May 2019 – 18 UF 32/19, *FamRZ* 2019, 1702, et seq.; R. Balloff, *Kinder vor dem Familiengericht*, 3rd ed., Nomos, Baden-Baden 2018, p. 154; A. Bauer, *Verfahrensbeistandschaft ein Handbuch für die Praxis*, 4th ed., Bundesanzeigerverlag, Cologne 2019, No. 290; J. Klein 'Die verfahrensrechtliche Stellung des Minderjährigen in Kindschaftssachen' [2019] *RdJB* 16, 22.

98 BGH 17 February 2010 – XII ZB 68/09, *FamRZ* 2010, 720.

99 D. Büte, *Familienrecht Scheidung, Unterhalt, Verfahren*, 6th ed., C.H. Beck, Munich 2015, §164 FamFG, No. 2; J.A. Rohmann, 'Anhörung des Kindes und der Eltern sowie die Bekanntmachung der Entscheidung an das Kind als kommunikativer Prozess' [2013] *FPR* 464, 470.

100 Y. Gottschalk, 'Wie kindgerecht ist die Justiz?' [2018] *ZRP* 249, 250; E. Schumann, *Münchener Kommentar zum FamFG*, 3rd ed., C.H. Beck, Munich 2018, §164 FamFG, No. 5.

101 But according to §164 s. 2 FamFG, the child shall not be informed of the grounds for the decision if it is feared that this would be detrimental to his/her development, education or health.

notified of the decision, it does not come into force.[102] No statutory provision exists that outlines how children younger than 14 are to be informed about the outcome of the proceeding. Accordingly, a decision does not necessarily have to be announced to the child.[103] The decision is usually relayed to legal representatives.[104]

3.2. REPRESENTATION FORMS OF PARTICIPATION

In general, minors cannot conclude a contract with an attorney without the legal representative's consent because minors have limited capacity to contract[105] if the contract is not merely legally beneficial for them (§§106, 107 BGB). However, when minors are capable of participating in proceedings, they must have the power to appoint an attorney[106] and apply for legal aid.[107] In order to be able to apply for legal aid, a supplementary curator[108] can be appointed for the child.[109]

In addition to the lawyer, there is also the possibility that the court appoints the child a guardian (§158 para. 1 FamFG). The appointment shall not be made or shall be rescinded when the interests of the child can be reasonably represented by an attorney (§158 para. 5 FamFG).

In any case, the statute requires the appointment of a 'suitable' guardian without giving any further specifications so far. In response, a federal working

---

[102] H. Engelhardt, *FamFG, Gesetz über das Verfahren in Familiensachen und in den Angelegenheiten der freiwilligen Gerichtsbarkeit*, 20th ed., C.H. Beck, Munich 2020, §164 FamFG, No. 8.

[103] E. Schumann, *Münchener Kommentar zum FamFG*, 3rd ed., C.H. Beck, Munich 2018, §164 FamFG, No. 4.

[104] Usually the parents: S. Hammer, *FamFG Gesetz über das Verfahren in Familiensachen und in den Angelegenheiten der freiwilligen Gerichtsbarkeit*, 5th ed., Otto Schmidt, Cologne 2020, §164 FamFG, No. 8; W. Schael, 'Minderjährige und ihre formelle Beteiligung in Verfahren über Kindschaftssachen nach dem FamFG' [2009] *FamRZ* 265, 268; E. Schumann, *Münchener Kommentar zum FamFG*, 3rd ed., C.H. Beck, Munich 2018, §164 FamFG, No. 5.

[105] A minor who has reached the age of seven has limited capacity to contract under §§107–113 BGB; majority begins at the age of 18, §2 BGB.

[106] The payment of the attorney is in turn problematic, see H.O. Burschel, *Beckscher Online Kommentar FamFG*, 32nd ed., C.H. Beck, Munich 1 October 2019, §9 FamFG, No. 9.

[107] OLG Hamburg 2 May 2017–12 WF 70/17, *FamRZ* 2018, 105: according to the meaning and purpose of §9 para. 1 No. 3 FamFG, a limited capacity for minors to contract must be assumed to the effect that children can effectively mandate an attorney in their own affairs; M. Weber, 'Die Entwicklung des Rechts der elterlichen Sorge' [2019] *NZFam* 100, 104; S. Pabst, *Münchener Kommentar zum FamFG*, 3rd ed., C.H. Beck, Munich 2018, §9 FamFG, No. 6a.

[108] §1909 para. 1 s. 1 BGB.

[109] H.O. Burschel, *Beckscher Online Kommentar FamFG*, 34th ed., C.H. Beck, Munich 1 April 2020, §9 FamFG, No. 9.

group defined standards for suitability, which foresee the guardian having basic legal, pedagogical and psychosocial qualifications.[110] Consequently, a legal education is not mandatory, but legal knowledge is recommended.[111] With the new law passed by the legislature on 25 March 2021, the suitability of the guardian is now specified in §158a FamFG-New.[112] In practice, the majority of judges indicate that they choose a guardian based on how he/she behaves during the proceedings, his/her psychological knowledge and his/her experience with children.[113]

The guardian shall inform the child about the object, course and potential result of the proceedings in a suitable manner (§158 para. 4 s. 2. FamFG, §158b para. 1 FamFG-New). In the explanatory memorandum, the German legislative body expressly pointed out that the guardian's task must include considering both the subjective (child's will) and objective interests (child's welfare).[114] To the extent that the circumstances of the given matter require, the court may assign additional duties to guardians, such as conducting interviews with the parents and other persons whom the child trusts, as well as assisting in facilitating an agreed settlement concerning the issues at hand (§158 para. 4 s. 3 FamFG, §158b para. 2 FamFG-New). Through the guardians' appointment the guardians become participants in the proceedings (§158 para. 3 s. 2 FamFG, §158b para. 3 s. 1 FamFG-New). While guardians represent the child's interests in their own name and may lodge appeals on the child's behalf (§158 para. 4 s. 5 FamFG, §158b para. 3 s. 2 FamFG-New), they are not legal representatives (§158 para. 4 s. 6 FamFG, §158b para. 3 s. 3 FamFG-New).[115]

Guardians shall be appointed as early as possible (§158 para. 3 FamFG, §158 para. 1 FamFG-New) and thus, as a rule, before the first hearing of the child.[116]

---

110 See Bundesarbeitsgemeinschaft Verfahrensbeistandschaft/Interessenvertretung für Kinder und Jugendliche e.V. (BAG), 'Standards Verfahrensbeistandschaft', 2.1.

111 See also the results of the evaluation of the FamFG, Bundesministerium der Justiz und für Verbraucherschutz (BMJV) together with S. Ekert and B. Heiderhoff, 'Die Evaluierung der FGG-Reform', Abschlussbericht zum Forschungsvorhaben, Berlin 15 January 2018, p. 111 et seq.

112 See 'Entwurf eines Gesetzes zur Bekämpfung sexualisierter Gewalt gegen Kinder', BT-Drucksache 19/23707, 27 October 2020, p. 14.

113 Bundesministerium der Justiz und für Verbraucherschutz (BMJV) together with S. Ekert and B. Heiderhoff, 'Die Evaluierung der FGG-Reform', Abschlussbericht zum Forschungsvorhaben, Berlin 15 January 2018, p. 109 et seq.

114 BT-Drucksache 16/6308, p. 239; E. Schumann, *Münchener Kommentar zum FamFG*, 3rd ed., C.H. Beck, Munich 2018, §158 FamFG, No. 27; H. Schürmann, *Rollenverteilung und Rechtsstellung von Kindern in familiengerichtlichen Verfahren*, *Göttinger Juristische Schriften*, Universitätsverlag Göttingen, Göttingen 2012, pp. 232, 236; Bundesarbeitsgemeinschaft Verfahrensbeistandschaft/Interessenvertretung für Kinder und Jugendliche e.V. (BAG), 'Standards Verfahrensbeistandschaft', 3.1.

115 See also BT-Drucksache 16/6308, p. 240.

116 Bundesministerium der Justiz und für Verbraucherschutz (BMJV) together with S. Ekert and B. Heiderhoff, 'Die Evaluierung der FGG-Reform', Abschlussbericht zum Forschungsvorhaben, Berlin 15 January 2018, p. 105.

The appointment shall expire when not previously rescinded, upon the decision concluding the proceedings becoming final and binding, or upon any other conclusion of the proceedings.[117]

Guardians can be engaged either as professionals or as non-professionals.[118] With regard to compensation (§158 para. 7 FamFG, §158c FamFG-New), a distinction between professional and non-professional guardians is necessary. The court must determine whether the guardian is a professional[119] or non-professional. If guardians conduct this activity as their professional occupation, they receive as compensation for the performance of their duties the one-time amount of €350 in each instance of the proceedings (§158 para. 7 s. 2 FamFG, §158c para. 1 FamFG-New). Non-professional guardians receive a reimbursement of their expenses (s. 1, §158c para. 2 FamFG-New). The reimbursement of expenses and the compensation are always paid from the public treasury (s. 5, §158c para. 3 FamFG-New).

3.3. CHILD LITIGATING ON OWN BEHALF

3.3.1. Child Participation in Litigation

The capacity to participate (§9 para. 1 No. 3 FamFG) does not give children the right to initiate proceedings themselves.[120] However, children who have reached the age of 14 can request a contact order with one parent on their own initiative;[121] younger children must be represented by the other parent who has custody.[122] If the child's welfare is endangered,[123] the child can only propose

---

117 See §158 para. 6 No. 1, No. 2 FamFG, §158 para. 4 FamFG-New.

118 See S. Hammer, *FamFG Gesetz über das Verfahren in Familiensachen und in den Angelegenheiten der freiwilligen Gerichtsbarkeit*, 5th ed., Otto Schmidt, Cologne 2020, §158 FamFG, No. 56 et seq.

119 In this regard, a guardian is a professional one if inter alia the scope of the activity is expected to be not less than 20 hours per week, see E. Schumann, *Münchener Kommentar zum FamFG*, 3rd ed., C.H. Beck, Munich 2018, §158 FamFG, No. 45.

120 See S. Pabst, *Münchener Kommentar zum FamFG*, 3rd ed., C.H. Beck, Munich 2018, §9 FamFG, No. 6; see also H. Sschürmann, 'Stellung der Kinder im familiengerichtlichen Verfahren' [2009] *FamFR* 153, 155.

121 N. Heiter, 'Verfahrensfähigkeit des Kindes in personenbezogenen Verfahren nach dem FamFG' [2009] *FamRZ* 85, 87; H. Hennemann, *Münchener Kommentar zum Bürgerlichen Gesetzbuch*, 8th ed., C.H. Beck, Munich 2020, §1684 BGB, No. 5; for a different view, see W. Schael, 'Minderjährige und ihre formelle Beteiligung im Verfahren über Kindschaftssachen nach dem FamFG' [2009] *FamRZ* 265, 267.

122 BGH 14 May 2008 – XII ZB 225/06, *NJW* 2008, 2586; H. Hennemann, *Münchener Kommentar zum Bürgerlichen Gesetzbuch*, 8th ed., C.H. Beck, Munich 2020, §1684 BGB, No. 5.

123 Pursuant to §1666 BGB.

the commencement of litigation (§24 FamFG), but not commence it.[124] A child takes part in the proceeding as a participant if one of his/her rights is directly affected by the proceeding (§7 para. 2 No. 1 FamFG). A minor shall not have any costs of proceedings imposed on him/her in parent and child matters (§81 para. 3 s. 3 FamFG).[125]

3.3.2. Child Participation in Alternative Dispute Resolution

In comparison to court proceedings, the child's procedural rights to participate in counselling or alternative dispute resolution are not sufficiently regulated. According to §17 para. 1 s. 1 and s. 2 No. 3 German Social Security Law (*Achtes Sozialgesetzbuch*, SGB VIII), parents have a legal right to counselling. Counselling is intended to support parents to create beneficial conditions for the child's welfare in the event of separation or divorce.[126] The support of the parents takes place with appropriate participation by the child (§17 para. 2 SGB VIII). Children should be involved in accordance with their maturity (§8 para. 1 SGB VIII). Apart from this, there is no explicit norm concerning hearing the child or appointing a guardian.

In addition, the court may also order the parents, individually or jointly, to participate in a free consultation concerning mediation[127] or other options for out-of-court conflict resolution with a person or agency named by the court.[128] In contrast to counselling,[129] participation in mediation or other options for out-of-court conflict resolution cannot be ordered.[130] It is rather the task of

124 N. Heiter, 'Verfahrensfähigkeit des Kindes in personenbezogenen Verfahren nach dem FamFG' [2009] *FamRZ* 85, 87; K. Lugani, *Münchener Kommentar zum Bürgerlichen Gesetzbuch*, 8th ed., C.H. Beck, Munich 2020, §1666 BGB, No. 223.

125 C. Feskorn, *FamFG Gesetz über das Verfahren in Familiensachen und in den Angelegenheiten der freiwilligen Gerichtsbarkeit*, 5th ed., Otto Schmidt, Cologne 2020, §81 FamFG, No. 14a.

126 See §17 para. 1 s. 2 No. 3 SGB VIII.

127 In practice this only happens rarely. 74% of local court judges never use this possibility, see Bundesministerium der Justiz und für Verbraucherschutz (BMJV) together with S. Ekert and B. Heiderhoff, 'Die Evaluierung der FGG-Reform', Abschlussbericht zum Forschungsvorhaben, Berlin 15 January 2018, p. 357.

128 §151 para. 1 s. 3 FamFG; see for more information F. Bartels and O. Elzer, *FamFG Kommentar zum Gesetz über das Verfahren in Familiensachen und in den Angelegenheiten der freiwilligen Gerichtsbarkeit*, 3rd ed., Gieseking, Bielefeld 2018, §36a FamFG, No. 13; U. Meyer-Holz, *FamFG Gesetz über das Verfahren in Familiensachen und in den Angelegenheiten der freiwilligen Gerichtsbarkeit*, 19th ed., C.H. Beck, Munich 2017, §36a FamFG, No. 7; S. Hammer, *FamFG Gesetz über das Verfahren in Familiensachen und in den Angelegenheiten der freiwilligen Gerichtsbarkeit*, 5th ed., Otto Schmidt, Cologne 2020, §156 FamFG, No. 20 et seq.

129 According to §156 para. 1 s. 4 FamFG.

130 S. Hammer, *FamFG Gesetz über das Verfahren in Familiensachen und in den Angelegenheiten der freiwilligen Gerichtsbarkeit*, 5th ed., Otto Schmidt, Cologne 2020, §156 FamFG, No. 38; D. Zorn, *Kommentar zum Gesetz über das Verfahren in Familiensachen und in den Angelegenheiten der freiwilligen Gerichtsbarkeit*, 3rd ed., Gieseking, Bielefeld 2018, §156, No. 13.

the person or agency named by the court to persuade the parents during the consultation to opt for out-of-court dispute resolution.[131] As is apparent in the applicable German Mediation Act,[132] the German legislator has refrained from including the child's procedural rights of participation – neither a hearing nor a guardian are provided for. Children can even be kept away from the mediation process entirely.[133] The number of children involved in mediation is very low.[134]

4. RESEARCH

Child participation is undoubtedly significant and has gradually achieved increasing legal recognition in the German legal system. The question of whether the FamFG's procedural rules in turn adequately guarantee this has recently been under review, especially during an overall evaluation of the FamFG. The final report of this evaluation of the reform of the Family Procedure Act (FGG-Reform) from 2018[135] reaches the conclusion that the FamFG has considerably improved the right to be heard as a whole. It has made the system of procedural participation and the concept of 'participant' more effective. The FamFG has also implemented innovative approaches by drawing on the results of interdisciplinary cooperation,[136] such as the *Cochemer Modell*.[137]

---

131 S. Hammer, *FamFG Gesetz über das Verfahren in Familiensachen und in den Angelegenheiten der freiwilligen Gerichtsbarkeit*, 5th ed., Otto Schmidt, Cologne 2020, §156 FamFG, No. 38; H. Krabbe and S. Thomsen, 'Werkstattbericht Familienmediation' [2011] *ZKM (Zeitschrift für Konfliktmanagement)* 111, 112.

132 Gesetz zur Förderung der Mediation und anderer Verfahren der außergerichtlichen Konfliktbeilegung, BGBl. I No. 35 from 25 July 2012, p. 1577.

133 See §2 para. 4 Mediation Act; see for more information B. Nietfeld, *Mediation als Verfahren der konsensualen Konfliktbeilegung bei Trennung und Scheidung*, Peter Lang, Frankfurt am Main 2015, p. 140.

134 B. Nietfeld, *Mediation als Verfahren der konsensualen Konfliktbeilegung bei Trennung und Scheidung*, Peter Lang, Frankfurt am Main 2015, pp. 132, 140; R. Bastine B. Römer-Wolf, F. Decker, A. Haid-Loh, S. Mayer and K. Normann, 'Praxis der Familienmediation in der Beratung' [2006] *Praxis der Kinderpsychologie und Kinderpsychiatrie* 584, 595; overall, however, the number of mediations carried out is at a consistently low level. In 2015, 2.3% of family court cases were referred to a mediator; see therefore Die Bundesregierung, 'Bericht der Bundesregierung über die Auswirkungen des Mediationsgesetzes auf die Entwicklung der Mediation in Deutschland und über die Situation der Aus- und Fortbildung der Mediatoren', Berlin July 2017, pp. 2, 48.

135 Bundesministerium der Justiz und für Verbraucherschutz (BMJV) together with S. Ekert and B. Heiderhoff, 'Die Evaluierung der FGG-Reform' Abschlussbericht zum Forschungsvorhaben, Berlin 15 January 2018.

136 Bundesministerium der Justiz und für Verbraucherschutz (BMJV) together with S. Ekert and B. Heiderhoff, 'Kurzfassung – Evaluierung der FGG-Reform', Berlin 15 January 2018, pp. 7, 8, 12.

137 The *Cochemer Modell* was developed in 1992 to ensure that conflicts in family proceedings did not escalate. The most important aspects are the principle of priority and expediting

Nevertheless, the evaluation also indicates that the FamFG still has room for improvement with regard to children's rights: in interim legal protection, children are rarely heard, the procedural capacity of minors is very limited, and, moreover, the possibility of ordering a free consultation concerning mediation or other options for out-of-court conflict resolution is only rarely used.[138] Above all, the child is still not provided with a guardian in all parent and child matters concerning the child.[139]

5. POLICY OR PRACTICE DEVELOPMENTS

The participation of minors in family court proceedings should be ensured through qualified hearings.[140] After each hearing of the child, a written statement should be requested by the guardian, the youth welfare office and, if necessary, the experts.[141] More specifically, it is also being considered whether to guarantee an age-appropriate hearing situation for children, to set up an ombudsperson's office to which children can turn,[142] and to specify children's participation at the youth welfare office.[143] At the same time, the continuous education of judges should be promoted, and quality assurance in family court proceedings guaranteed.[144] For this, requirements developed from an interdisciplinary perspective for expert opinions in parent and child matters, as well as improved

proceedings, the promotion of the dialogue between the parents as well as the support of children and parents by employees of the youth welfare office. See for more details about the *Cochemer Modell*, W. Flemming, 'Das Wunder von Cochem' in C. Müller-Magdeburg (ed.), *Festschrift für Jürgen Rudolph*, Nomos, Cologne 2009, p. 55 et seq.

138 Bundesministerium der Justiz und für Verbraucherschutz (BMJV) together with S. Ekert and B. Heiderhoff, 'Kurzfassung – Evaluierung der FGG-Reform', Berlin 15 January 2018, pp. 8, 9, 13.

139 In 2015, only in 27.9% of proceedings before local courts and in 40.4% of proceedings before Higher Regional Courts, Bundesministerium der Justiz und für Verbraucherschutz (BMJV) together with S. Ekert and B. Heiderhoff, 'Die Evaluierung der FGG-Reform', Abschlussbericht zum Forschungsvorhaben, Berlin 15 January 2018, p. 338.

140 This means a hearing by qualified persons; Enquete-Kommission, 'Kinderschutz und Kinderrechte weiter stärken', Drucksache 21/16000, 19 December 2018, p. 20.

141 See for these suggestions the Enquete-Kommission, 'Kinderschutz und Kinderrechte weiter stärken', Drucksache 21/16000, 19 December 2018, p. 132.

142 BT-Drucksache 19/8568, pp. 5, 6; BT-Drucksache 18/5103, p. 3, according to which the role and tasks of such office would be: independently inform about the law, individual claims and options and communicate with the Youth Welfare Office; help with the organisation of contacting a legal adviser and support the person concerned in any legal proceedings; balance out structural power hierarchies and asymmetries of power; and reach a fair agreement in disputes.

143 R. Balloff, *Kinder vor dem Familiengericht*, 3rd ed., Nomos, Baden-Baden 2018, p. 262.

144 See public hearing in the legal committee of the Bundestag from 25 September 2019, 'Qualität familiengerichtlicher Verfahren verbessern'; also 23. Deutscher Familiengerichtstag, Brühl 2019, Working Group 24, 'Beteiligung von Kindern im Verfahren', thesis 11.

further education of experts would also be necessary.[145] Last but not least, it is currently being considered whether the child's right to be heard should be expressly regulated in the German Constitution (*Grundgesetz*, GG).[146]

6. CONCLUSION

The consideration of the child's will within the meaning of Article 12 UNCRC is covered in Germany in only a few provisions in the FamFG and BGB. In particular, the fact that the capacity to participate, the mandatory hearing of the child,[147] the right of minors to complain on appeal and the right of objection are subject to minimum age requirements prevents the comprehensive participation of the child and consideration of the child's views, as provided for in Article 12 UNCRC.

Considering these weaknesses, it cannot be said that the FamFG makes the participation rights of children equal to those of adults. Children still have only limited opportunities to take procedural action without their legal representative.[148]

The consideration of including children's rights in the GG does not change this. It could be a first step towards a concrete implementation of the child's participation rights in the GG as defined by Article 12 UNCRC. However, Article 12 UNCRC provides that 'the views of the child [shall be] given due weight in accordance with the age and maturity of the child', a principle which, by contrast, is not being considered for inclusion in the GG. Rather, the GG would only indicate that 'children's constitutional right to be heard must be ensured'.[149]

---

145 See Bundesministerium für Justiz und Verbraucherschutz, Familienrechtliche Gutachten, *Mindestanforderungen an die Qualifikation von Sachverständigengutachten im Kindschaftsrecht*, 2nd ed., Berlin 2019, p. 3.

146 Bundesministerium für Justiz und Verbraucherschutz, Abschlussbericht der Bund-Länder-Arbeitsgruppe, 'Kinderrechte ins Grundgesetz' from 14 October 2019, pp. 112 et seq; draft bill Bundesministerium für Justiz und Verbraucherschutz 'Entwurf eines Gesetzes zur Änderung des Grundgesetzes zur ausdrücklichen Verankerung der Kinderrechte' from 20 January 2021, p. 4.

147 See now for the mandatory child hearing independent from the child's age, §159 para. 1 FamFG-New, 'Entwurf eines Gesetzes zur Bekämpfung sexualisierter Gewalt gegen Kinder', BT-Drucksache 19/23707, 27 October 2020, p. 15.

148 R. Balloff, *Kinder vor dem Familiengericht*, 3rd ed., Nomos, Baden-Baden 2018, p. 418.

149 See draft law Bundesministerium für Justiz und Verbraucherschutz 'Entwurf eines Gesetzes zur Änderung des Grundgesetzes zur ausdrücklichen Verankerung der Kinderrechte' from 20 January 2021, p. 4; originally draft law Bundesministerium für Justiz und Verbraucherschutz, Wissenschaftliche Dienste des Deutschen Bundestages, Ausarbeitung WD 3-3000-012/20 'Kinderrechte ins Grundgesetz: Zum Gesetzentwurf des Bundesministeriums der Justiz und für Verbraucherschutz aus November 2019 und seiner Diskussion' from 23 January 2020, p. 4; on the criticism of the inclusion of children's rights in the GG, Wissenschaftliche Dienste des Deutschen Bundestages, Ausarbeitung WD 3-3000-272/19 'Zur Aufnahme von Kinderrechten in das Grundgesetz: Gegenüberstellung verschiedener Formulierungsvorschläge zur Verankerung von Kinderrechten in Art. 6 GG' from 18 December 2019, pp. 10 et seq.

Thus, the draft falls short of Article 12 UNCRC and fails to implement a fundamental principle of the UNCRC.[150]

Consequently, it can by no means be ruled out – and indeed appears essential – that the German legislator will need to again attend to family court procedural regulations in order to strengthen and expand children's rights and, above all, their opportunities to participate. Any further reforms should be preceded by an independent in-depth evaluation of children's existing participation rights. Ultimately, comparative and interdisciplinary research is urgently needed, as it will provide the necessary basis for critical reflection on the procedural position of the child in the respective legal system and reveal the need and potential for future reforms.

150 Wissenschaftliche Dienste des Deutschen Bundestages, Ausarbeitung WD 3-3000-276/19 'Zur Aufnahme von Kinderrechten ins Grundgesetz – Gegenüberstellung eines Formulierungsvorschlages mit vier kinderrechtlichen Grundprinzipien der UN-Kinderrechtskonvention' from 16 December 2019, p. 10.

ISRAEL

Rhona Schuz and Tamar Morag

1. INTRODUCTION

In Israel, there are around nine million residents, of whom 75% are Jews and 20% Arabs, who are mainly Muslims.[1] Children form around a third of the population.[2] The rate of divorce is 26–27% of married couples. In 2018 there were 8,281 child custody and visitation cases: of them, 4,239 took place in the Courts for Family Matters (hereinafter Family Courts), 1,939 in the Rabbinical Courts, and 2,103 in Sharia and Druz courts.[3] In addition, there were 20 child abduction cases dealt with in the Family Courts.[4]

---

1 Statistical Abstract of Israel, https://www.cbs.gov.il/en/publications/Pages/2020/Population-Statistical-Abstract-of-Israel-2020-No-71.aspx.

2 National Council for the Welfare of the Child, *Statistical Yearbook of Children in Israel*, 2019, p. 7.

3 National Council for the Welfare of the Child, above n. 2, pp. 256–259.

4 National Council for the Welfare of the Child, above n. 2, p. 441.

Israel's legal system is a mixed jurisdiction, which reflects its complex history. It is primarily based on common law, while incorporating facets of civil law. In relation to most issues of family law, both Family Courts, which are part of the civil court system, and religious courts (including rabbinic courts for Jews, and other religious courts for Muslims and Christians) have parallel jurisdiction.[5] As seen above, most custody cases are litigated in the Family Courts, with appeals heard by the District Courts and, with leave, by the Supreme Court.

The Ministry of Welfare and Social Services operates Welfare Units that are adjunct to the Family Courts as well as to the religious courts. The Welfare Units are staffed by social workers and psychologists and their function is to assist the court in reaching decisions on matters involving family disputes.

In 2015, the Law Regulating Legal Proceedings in Family Conflicts Law (Temporary Provision), 5774-2014, was enacted and in 2020 it was re-enacted as a permanent law with minor amendments. This law aims to help spouses and parents and their children to resolve a family conflict among themselves. According to this law, all family law litigation is to be referred to the Welfare Units for four IFC meetings (information, familiarisation and coordination) in order to promote out-of-court settlements. Research findings on the operation of this law are considered to be encouraging[6] and indicate that in more than half of the cases following the IFC meeting, parties come to agreement or resolve their dispute without litigation.[7]

There are two ways in which a child may participate in family disputes in the Family and Rabbinical Courts:

(a) participation via the Welfare Units adjunct to these courts in accordance with the procedure set out in Chapter 2 of the Family Court Regulations 2020 (hereinafter Child Participation Regulations),[8] which will be explained in detail below; and
(b) participation via direct invitation for the child to meet with the judge in his/her chambers, initiated by the judge under his/her inherent jurisdiction.

In addition to these two options, the child's views may be presented to the court by a guardian ad litem, appointed by the court to represent the child, or in a report submitted to the court by a social worker which sets out his/her position.

---

5 However, in relation to the actual divorce itself, the religious courts have exclusive jurisdiction.

6 T. Bayer-Kapilski and Y. Sorek, *Implementation of the IFC Law – National Research*, Myer- JDC, Brookdale 2019 (Hebrew), p. i.

7 T. Bayer-Kapilski and Y. Sorek, above n. 6, p. 33.

8 These Regulations were formerly Chapter 20(2) Civil Procedure Regulations 198. As part of an overall reform of civil procedure, the Regulations dealing with family court proceedings were moved into an independent code, with effect from 1 January 2021.

2. STATUTORY PROVISIONS

The central law regulating legal relations between parents and children is the Legal Capacity and Guardianship Law of 1962 (hereinafter Guardianship Law). Whilst under this Law parents have authority to represent their minor children, section 68 provides that the court may at any time appoint a guardian ad litem for the minor in order to safeguard his/her interests.[9] Section 3(d) of the Family Matters Court Law 1995 provides that a minor may initiate legal proceedings in relation to any family law matter in which his/her interest is liable to suffer real harm.

There is no express provision in primary legislation dealing with participation of children in family law proceedings to which they are not a party,[10] but this lacuna is filled by secondary legislation. The Child Participation Regulations provide that in contested proceedings relating to a minor, the court should give the minor the opportunity to express his/her feelings, views and wishes in relation to the matter in question and that these should be given appropriate weight in the court's decision.[11]

The Regulations provide that the court should refer children over the age of six to the Welfare Unit, unless there are special reasons why, in the judge's view, realisation of the child's right to be heard will cause him/her more harm than depriving him/her of that right.[12] In the Welfare Unit, a social worker trained in child participation (PSW) will explain to the child, in a manner appropriate to his/her age and degree of maturity, that he/she has a right to be heard directly by the judge or through the social worker as the child chooses. If the child chooses to be heard by the judge, a meeting will be set up in the judge's office. Should the child choose not to be heard by the judge directly, then the child can convey his/her views to the PSW, who will provide a record of them to the court, together with his/her impression of the child's behaviour and situation during the hearing.[13]

---

9 In addition, the laws dealing with child protection proceedings and adoption contain provisions authorising the court to appoint a guardian ad litem.

10 In comparison, in child protection proceedings, the court is obligated to give a minor an opportunity to be heard, Youth (Care and Supervision) Law 1960, s 8.

11 Family Court Regulations 2020, reg. 49. The wording of the section reads: 'A court dealing with a claim in family matters as per Rules 15(a)(3), (6), (11) relating to a child, shall give the child an opportunity to express his feelings, opinions, and desires on the matter before it (hereinafter – hearing the child) and give them appropriate weight in its decision, according to the child's age and level of maturity, unless the court decides, for special reasons which shall be recorded, that the child shall not be heard, if it is persuaded that implementing the child's right to be heard would cause the child greater harm than that which would be caused by the denial of this right.'

12 Family Court Regulations 2020, regs. 49-51. Children under six with older siblings may also be heard.

13 Family Court Regulations 2020, reg. 54.

The Regulations also make provision for situations where the parents have come to an agreement concerning arrangements for their children and have submitted this to the court for its approval. In such situations, the court is supposed to send an explanation to the parents about the importance of hearing the child in relation to matters concerning the child and, before giving its approval, to check with the parents that they have indeed heard the child's views, and where necessary to refer them to the Welfare Unit.[14] However, in practice, this part of the Regulations has not been implemented.

3. MODES OF CHILD PARTICIPATION

3.1. DIRECT FORMS OF PARTICIPATION

Under the Child Participation Regulations, children may choose whether to express their views to the judge directly or to a PSW, who will pass them onto the judge.[15] In addition, meetings between the child and the judge might take place at the request of the judge or at the request of the child, as explained above. Where the child chooses to be heard by the PSW, the latter provides a record of what the child said together with his/her impression of the child's behaviour and situation during the hearing.[16]

The Regulations expressly provide that the child's parents and lawyers should not be present during the hearing of the child (whether by the PSW or the judge) and that usually children should be heard separately from their siblings.[17] Where the judge hears the child, he/she may decide to hear the child in the presence of the PSW or the child's guardian ad litem.[18] The PSW's report and court protocol are confidential and are to be kept in the court's safe, available only to the court of appeal if there is an appeal.[19] In its decision, the court will not provide details of what the child said at the hearing, but may disclose some or all of this information, so long as the child consented and, in the opinion of the court, disclosure will advance the child's best interests.[20] The Regulations provide that the judge's decision should be explained to the child by the PSW in a manner appropriate to the child's age and degree of maturity.

Specialist Child Participation Units have been established within the Welfare Units adjunct to the Family Courts and the religious courts.

14 Family Court Regulations 2020, reg. 57.
15 Family Court Regulations 2020, reg. 52.
16 Family Court Regulations 2020, reg. 54.
17 Family Court Regulations 2020, reg. 51(c), (d).
18 Family Court Regulations 2020, reg. 53.
19 Family Court Regulations 2020, reg. 55.
20 Family Court Regulations 2020, reg. 55.

Social workers working in these units undergo ongoing training in the area of child participation

As mentioned above, section 3(d) of the Family Matters Court Law 1995 provides that a minor may initiate legal proceedings in relation to any family law matter in which his/her interest is liable to suffer real harm. Within the framework of the activities of the Child Representation Unit in the Legal Aid Department, efforts have been made to reach out to youth in order to increase awareness of the possibility of initiating an independent lawsuit in court and of the right to obtain legal aid for this purpose. In 2016, the Legal Aid Department conducted a campaign on social networks in relation to the right of minors to legal aid, called 'A Lawyer of My Own'. This provided a link to a special site designed for youth, and resulted in numerous applications by youth for legal aid.[21]

Over the last few years, the Legal Aid Department has submitted around 150 independent legal claims on behalf of minors each year, most of them in the field of personal status. Thus, for example, claims have been initiated on behalf of minors in relation to the following matters: change of surname of a teenage girl; psychological treatment without the consent of the parents; cancelling a stop order which prevented the minor from exiting the country; and paternity.

3.2. REPRESENTATION FORMS OF PARTICIPATION

Separate representation of children in family proceedings is provided by the Child Representation Unit in the Legal Aid Department of the Ministry of Justice. The representation is provided by lawyers who are assisted on a needs basis by social workers and psychologists with whom they may consult. Appointment of the lawyers is made by the court and, in most cases, the lawyer is appointed as a guardian ad litem for the child.

According to the draft rules of conduct of the Child Representation Unit, a guardian ad litem for a child under the age of 15 will represent the child's best interests. If the minor is 15 or older, the guardian ad litem is to represent the child's wishes unless his/her wishes are found to present an imminent and immediate danger to the child. According to the draft rules,[22] at any age, the guardian ad litem has a duty to promote meaningful and effective participation of the child in the case, including in determining the goals and developing the strategy of the case.

---

21 Report of Activities of the Legal Aid 2015/16, https://www.gov.il/BlobFolder/reports/report20162017/he/2016_2017.pdf (Hebrew).

22 The draft rules are in the process of obtaining approval (communication from Adv. Racheli Yarden, 8 January 2020, who kindly provided the authors with a copy).

3.3. TYPES OF PROCEEDINGS AND LEADING CASE LAW

The Child Participation Regulations apply in relation to the following issues: child custody; visitation rights; education; prohibition to leave the country; child abduction;[23] age of marriage; and name change. The Regulations do not apply to adoption. The Adoption Law does not establish a specific rule as to child participation, but does state that a child over the age of nine, or under that age of sufficient understanding, should not be adopted if the child does not consent to the adoption.[24]

According to the Child Participation Regulations, children are to be invited to participate from the age of six. Yet, in special cases, such as when a child over the age of six has a younger sibling who wishes to participate, the court may hear a child who is younger than six.

While several mediators have begun to include children in custody mediation, child participation in non-adversarial proceedings is still quite rare in Israel. In some collaborative law proceedings, an expert on children is appointed, who meets with the child and presents the child's views in the proceedings.

Israeli case law has repeatedly recognised children's right to participation in custody proceedings, as expressed for example in the following quotes from the Israeli Supreme Court:

> From the conception of the child as an independent entity is derived his right to have his will and desires considered, within the bounds of that which is possible. This approach was expressed in art. 12 of the UN Convention on the Rights of the Child.[25]

> Hearing the child's views anchored in article 12 of the UN Convention on the Rights of the child expressed the recognition of the child as an autonomous person and as a rights bearer.[26]

Nevertheless, while the court declaratively recognises the significance of the right to participation, very little discussion can be found in Israeli law as to the

---

23 The chapter of the Family Court Regulations concerning child abduction cases includes express reference to child participation. Regulation 106(e) provides: 'Where a child is of sufficient age and level of maturity that it is appropriate to take into account his views, the Court shall not decide the case before it hears the child unless the Court does not see any need for this for special reasons which will be recorded.' For discussion of the implementation of this regulation, see M. Freeman, N. Taylor and R. Schuz, *The Voice of the Child in International Child Abduction Proceedings under the 1980 Hague Convention. A Project Report,* University of Westminster, London 2019, https://westminsterresearch.westminster.ac.uk/item/qx8q8/the-voice-of-the-child-in-international-child-abduction-proceedings-under-the-1980-hague-convention.

24 Adoption of Children Law 1981, s 7.

25 ACP 7015/94 *The Attorney General v Plonit* IsrSC 50 (1) 48, 65 [1995], per Justice Dorner.

26 RFamA 27/06 *Ploni v Plonit* tak-al 2006(2) 1055, para. 18 of Justice Arbel's judgment.

weight that is to be attributed to the child's views once they are heard. A review of Israeli case law points to mixed views of the courts on this issue [27]

4. RESEARCH

4.1. RESEARCH PROJECTS

Three main research projects have been published on participation of children. The first related to cases decided before the Child Participation Regulations were adopted and the second accompanied the pilot of the scheme introduced by the Regulations. The third involved follow-up research on the pilot conducted in 2013. We will discuss each of these projects in turn and then report on the available data about the number of children heard in recent years.

Rhona Schuz undertook an analysis of child participation in contested custody and visitation disputes, published in selected databases during the years 2005, 2006 and 2007, in which children over the age of six were involved.[28] This found that in 14 of the 52 cases in the sample the children were heard by the judge.[29] When cases in which all of the children who were under 12 were excluded from the sample, the child was heard in nearly half of the cases (13 out of 28).[30] The research also examined the weight given to the views of

27 See T. Morag, 'The Case Law after Israel's Ratification of the UN Convention on the Rights of the Child: Indeed a New Era?' in T. Morag (ed.), *Children's Rights and Israeli Law*, Hamishpat Law Review in Collaboration with Ramot, 2010, pp. 101–129 (Hebrew). For the approach which recognises the right to participate but considerably limits the right to influence, see for example: per Justice Arbel in RFamA 27/06, above n. 26: 'Hearing the child doesn't mean that the wishes which he expresses will tilt the scales of the determination. The wishes which the child expresses do not necessarily reflect his objective best interests and so the court has to remember that, in respecting the child's wishes on the one hand and keeping in mind its responsibility for the determination on the other, hearing the child is separate from the weight to be given to the wishes which he expresses'; and per Justice Alon in FamC 8622/05 *EA v ESh* tak-mish 2006(3) 1, para. 18: 'Whilst taking into consideration the wishes of the child and his views, is an important element of the right to participation … the wishes of the child are not all-important.' For the approach which attributes heavy, even conclusive, weight to the views of a sufficiently mature child, see for example the decision of Justice Geifman in FamC 49123/03 *Ploni v Almoni* tak-mish 2006(4) 282 to cancel an order preventing the child from leaving the country which had been made at the request of his father; majority decision in FamA 477/09 *Plonit and Almoni v Plonim* tak-mech 2009(4) 1846 to place two children (whose father had been convicted of murdering their mother) in the custody of their paternal grandparents in accordance with their strongly held views, against recommendation of the expert; the words of Judge Rosman Gillis in FamC 22809-02-16 (29 October 2017, published in Nevo): 'Art. 12 of the UNCRC … is based on recognition that not only are the views of adults of value in determining the best interests of the child, but also and perhaps mainly his view.'

28 R. Schuz, 'The Right of the Child to Participate: Theory and Practice in the Israeli Family Court' (2008) 2 *The Family in Law Review* 207 (Hebrew).

29 R. Schuz, above n. 28, p. 242.

30 R. Schuz, above n. 28, p. 242.

children in the cases. In 24 of the 52 cases, the views of the child were mentioned, but in half of these the decision was not in accordance with those views.[31] Disappointingly, in most of the cases, there was no express discussion as to the weight to be given to the child's views and the impression was that, in practice, little weight was accorded to them.[32]

The pilot of the scheme introduced by the Child Participation Regulations,[33] which ran in two Family Courts (Jerusalem and Haifa) from 2006 to 2009,[34] was accompanied by a formative evaluation research project conducted in two stages. Data in relation to the 448 children who were invited to the Welfare Unit was obtained by means of information documents filled in by the PSWs. In addition, telephone interviews were conducted with a sample of the children and parents and with a small number of PSWs and judges. According to the research findings, children were referred to the Welfare Unit by the judge in about 40% of the cases.

Significant differences in participation rates were recorded between the first and second stages of the pilot. At the end of the first stage, only 35% of the children who had been invited to participate had attended the meeting. The main reason for children's low participation rates was parental opposition. To increase child participation, PSWs adopted steps aimed at explaining to all parents whose children were invited to participate in the pilot study the programme's aims and operating methods. The wording of the judges' invitation to the participation process was changed, from a formulation stating, 'The child is invited to the Child Participation Unit' to 'I order the child to come to the Child Participation Unit'. These steps led to a significant rise in child participation rates, from 35% in the first stage to 60% in the second. In-depth interviews with the PSWs showed that changes in the children's rates of participation in general and in the rates of meetings with judges in particular followed not only from changes in the format of the pilot but also, and perhaps mainly, from ongoing changes in the attitudes of the PSWs, who became increasingly convinced of the project's benefits and were therefore more successful in persuading the parents to allow their children to participate.

Significant changes were also noted between the first and second part of the pilot as to children's requests to meet with the judge. During the first stage of the pilot, only 15% of the children who met with the PSW chose to meet with the judge. The pilot's steering committee instructed the PSWs to encourage children to take advantage of this option. The PSWs proceeded to explain to children

---

31 R. Schuz, above n. 28, p. 253.

32 R. Schuz, above n. 28, p. 254.

33 For a detailed discussion of the project and the research, see T. Morag, D. Rivkin and Y. Sorek, 'Child Participation in the Family Courts – Lessons from the Israeli Pilot Project' (2012) 26 *International Journal on Law Policy and the Family* 1.

34 T. Morag, D. Rivkin and Y. Sorek, above n. 33, p. 2.

the nature of these meetings and showed them photographs of the court in an attempt to reduce their anxiety about the setting. These efforts proved effective and, at the second stage of the pilot, the percentage of children asking to meet with the judge rose to 32%.[35] The interviews indicated high levels of satisfaction, including among the children who did participate.[36] When the participating children were asked whether they thought it was a good idea to give children in general the chance to express themselves on the subject of their parents' conflict, 93% answered in the affirmative. To the question of whether participation had helped them, 62% of the children said it had. When asked how, they mostly reported that they felt their opinions and feelings had been respected, that the conversation had helped them decide what they really wanted, and that the involvement with the PSWs had contributed to improved relationships with one of the parents. Children who said that participation had not helped them were asked why not. The most frequent response was that participation had changed nothing or that it had not swayed the judicial decision in the direction they would have liked.

Moreover, PSWs and some judges became convinced of the benefits of hearing children.[37] In-depth interviews with judges and with PSWs revealed that judges felt that the meeting had contributed by strengthening their own impressions or contributing another perspective. Only toward the end of the formative evaluation study did judges point to a few isolated cases where the meeting had led to a significant change in the judicial decision.

The research also sheds light on two claims which are often made against judicial meetings, namely that meetings with judges are intimidating for children and that children simply repeat what their parents tell them to say. According to the assessment of the PSWs, those children who met with the judge expressed themselves more easily and were more relaxed than in the meeting with the PSW,[38] and there was little evidence of incitement of children.[39] Moreover, the research revealed that in some cases child participation had positive therapeutic benefits.[40] For example, in some cases children who had not felt comfortable talking directly to their parents agreed for their views to be passed onto their parents and this resulted in an improved relationship.

The third research project was a qualitative study conducted by Tamar Morag and Yoa Sorek in 2013, after the end of the pilot project, which referred to the

---

35 T. Morag, D. Rivkin and Y. Sorek, above n. 33, p. 18.

36 For example, 92% said they would recommend to a friend to participate: T. Morag, D. Rivkin and Y. Sorek, above n. 33, p. 15.

37 T. Morag, D. Rivkin and Y. Sorek, above n. 33, pp. 15–17.

38 T. Morag, D. Rivkin and Y. Sorek, above n. 33, p. 22. One possible explanation for this is that they had already had the experience with talking to the PSW.

39 86% were assessed as expressing their own views: T. Morag, D. Rivkin and Y. Sorek, above n. 33, p. 24.

40 T. Morag, D. Rivkin and Y. Sorek, above n. 33, p. 17.

implementation of the model in the Jerusalem and Haifa courts.[41] The research included 14 in-depth interviews with judges, lawyers and PSWs working within the Haifa and Jerusalem courts, as well as a questionnaire sent to all Welfare Units working with the Israeli Family Courts. Findings pointed to growing acceptance of the model among PSWs, lawyers and parents after the end of the pilot. Thus, for example, one PSW commented: 'Before the pilot, I opposed children's hearings on professional grounds. Now it's reversed.'

Judges' attitudes proved more complex. Interviews with judges and with PSWs revealed that, together with their growing support for child participation in what they perceive to be difficult complex cases, judges at this stage had greater reservations than at the time of the formative evaluation regarding implementation of a universal right to child participation in all cases. One judge summed up this attitude as follows: 'The issue is to identify the proper case, that's the main problem, not to invite children to participate as a set ritual in all cases. Proportions, that's the key.'[42] Judges pointed mainly to considerations of workload and efficiency as grounds for this position and for the decline in their referrals of less complex cases to the Welfare Unit. However, they also pointed to the emotional strains evoked by the hearings, where they faced the children's distress without access to any tools to help them. These strains come to the fore in the following statement of a Family Court judge:

> I feel deeply frustrated because we lack genuine power to deal with these cases. … Has anyone ever thought of what the child is going through? What tools do I have for coping with this? Judicial involvement in every detail? I cannot do this and that is the frustrating part of the work as a Family Court judge. All of this has become clearer to me since the meetings with the children.[43]

PSWs added that the perception of children's participation as a therapeutic function was another possible reason for judges' reluctance to recognise participation as a universal right, since they don't see their function as a therapeutic one.[44]

A prominent finding of the follow-up study is the growing influence of children's participation on judicial decisions. In the formative evaluation, the

---

41 T. Morag and Y. Sorek, 'Child Participation in Family Courts in Israel. An Account of an Ongoing Learning Process' in T. Gal and B. Faedi-Duramy (eds.), *International perspectives and empirical findings on child participation from social exclusion to child inclusive policies*, Oxford University Press, New York 2015.

42 T. Morag and Y. Sorek, above n. 41.

43 T. Morag and Y. Sorek, above n. 41.

44 For a critical discussion of Family Court judges' perception of their role in relation to participation of children and in relation to the importance of adopting an approach which sees therapeutic aspects as part of the judicial function, see T. Morag and K. Feldman, 'My Voice will be Heard – Therapeutic Jurisprudence and Child Participation in the Israeli Family Court' (2016) 22 *Hamishpat* 49 (Hebrew).

judges had noted that children's hearings had provided additional insights and perspectives. Toward the end of the pilot, they pointed out that in isolated and relatively rare cases, participation led to changes in the judicial decision. By contrast, in the follow-up study, both the judges and the PSWs cited many examples where participation had not only contributed to the proceedings, but had also played a decisive role in the decision-making process and, at times, had even led to changes in a judicial ruling.

An interesting finding of the follow-up study is that granting children's views absolute confidentiality was accepted unquestionably in both the Jerusalem and Haifa Family Courts and judges reported no significant problem in the implementation of this regulation. This finding is particularly important in the light of the apparent assumption in other countries that views expressed by children to judges cannot be kept confidential.[45]

4.2. STATISTICS REGARDING EXTENT OF CHILD PARTICIPATION

According to data provided to us by the Department of Employment, Welfare and Social Services, between the beginning of 2015 and the middle of 2019, 2,061 cases were referred to the Welfare Unit for child participation and 3,174 children participated in meetings, out of whom 1,012 also met with judges.[46] Data provided by the Ministry of Justice show that in 2018, 1,124 guardians ad litem were appointed in custody cases. This marks an increase of 74% from the previous year and of 400% since 2015.[47] Anecdotal evidence suggests that over the years a growing number of judges have decided to refrain from referring cases to the Welfare Unit and instead directly invite children to be heard. In most of these cases a social worker will be present at the meeting, but since this procedure is not conducted in accordance with the Child Participation Regulations, it is not recorded and no data is available as to the extent of direct judicial invitations to hear children.

It should also be noted that there is no information available regarding the number of cases that relate to children under six years of age and that most

45 See, for example, article by Sir Mark Potter (formerly President of the Family Division of the High Court of England and Wales): M. Potter, 'The Voice of the Child: Children's "rights" in Family Proceedings' (2008) 2 *The Family in Law* xv, xxxi, https://mishpat.ac.il/wp-content/uploads/2019/03/Sir-Mark-Potter-The-Voice-of-the-Child-Children%E2%80%99s-%E2%80%9Crights%E2%80%9D-in-Family-Proceedings.pdf.

46 Most of these were in connection to cases in the Family Matters Court, but a few were in relation to cases in the Rabbinical and Sharia Courts.

47 Statistics provided by Adv Lydia Rabinovich, Head of the Child Representation Unit in the Legal Aid Department.

custody files are not contested.[48] Thus, a comparison between the number of custody files mentioned in the introduction to this chapter and the number of reported cases of participation does not provide an accurate picture of the percentage of cases in which children participate. Nonetheless, it is still evident that many children do not participate in court proceedings in family matters relating to them.

5. POLICY OR PRACTICE DEVELOPMENTS

A recent and very important development is the establishment of a new comprehensive training course on child participation in family law proceedings, in which all Israeli Family Court judges are to take part. The course will include extensive theoretical material on child participation and will equip participants with practical tools for hearing children. It will be operated by the Institute for Judicial Education in the Supreme Court.

6. CONCLUSION

Analysis of the extent to which Israeli law ensures that children have the right to significant and effective participation in family law proceedings, as required by the United Nations Convention on the Rights of the Child (UNCRC), reveals a complex picture. On the one hand, there have been important developments and Israeli law possesses a number of positive features. On the other hand, however, significant deficiencies, difficulties and challenges can be identified.

For convenience, the strengths of the Israeli legal system in relation to child participation can be divided into two categories: statutory and case law/practice. The adoption of comprehensive Regulations governing child participation in family proceedings gives statutory expression to the right of children to participate in these proceedings from the age of six, which is very young from an international perspective. These Regulations also provide for the establishment of dedicated units in Family Courts for child participation and a guarantee of complete confidentiality to the child. In addition, statute expressly provides that minors may initiate legal proceedings in the Family Court.

In case law, widespread declaratory recognition of the right of children to participate in these proceedings can be found in judgments of the Supreme Court and the lower courts. In addition, examination of the Israeli case law

48 D. Hacker, *Parenting in Law. Behind the Scenes of Designing Custody and Visitation Arrangements Following Divorce*, Hakkibutz Hameuchad, Tel-Aviv 2008, pp. 158–159 (Hebrew).

and practice shows a significant increase in the extent of child participation as compared with the period before the UNCRC. Moreover, research provides evidence of a significant attitudinal change among a large proportion of the professionals involved in the family justice system and increasing support for child participation among PSWs, parents and lawyers and to a limited extent among judges. Similarly, the issue of child participation has become part of the public agenda, reflected, for example, in the large number of conferences devoted to the subject in recent years in Israel. One of the important developments in promoting child participation is the recent initiative to provide comprehensive in-depth training on the subject of participation of children for all Family Court judges.

An additional important practical development is the establishment of a dedicated Child Representation Unit within the Legal Aid Department, with emphasis being placed in the guidelines for guardians ad litem on ensuring significant child participation. The efforts made by this Unit to make it known to young people, particularly those at risk, that they are entitled to legal representation and to initiate proceedings independently have led to greater access to justice for younger people.

The deficiencies and difficulties experienced by the Israeli legal system in relation to child participation can be divided into four main areas. The first is the limited extent of child participation. The picture which emerges from the information set out above, taking into account its limitations, is that in practice many children do not participate in family proceedings concerning them. A possible explanation, arising from the research of Morag and Sorek, is the lack of judicial recognition of the right of children to participate as a universal right and to the difficulties experienced by judges in hearing children.

The second deficiency relates to the variety of different ways in which courts choose to hear a child's views. It is striking that some judges refer children to be heard via the Regulations, some invite them directly to be heard and yet others appoint a guardian ad litem to put forward the child's perspective. Lack of uniformity raises concerns about inequality between children in terms of the way in which they are being heard. Moreover, whilst the steady and significant trend of increased appointment of guardians ad litem per se is an encouraging and important development, it is necessary to examine to what extent it is replacing direct hearing of the children by the court.

The third deficiency is that the lack of clear guidelines in case law and statute in relation to the weight to be given to the views and wishes of children leads to lack of consistency between different judges. There is no up-to-date comprehensive research on this subject. A troubling picture emerged from Schuz's research, which suggested that in practice in most cases little weight is given to the child's views. On the other hand, Morag and Sorek's more recent research documented an increase in the weight given to children's views in difficult and complex cases.

The final deficiency is that Israel has not developed any significant practice in relation to participation of children in non-adversarial proceedings.[49] Given the large number of cases which are resolved via non-adversarial proceedings, especially as the Law Regulating Legal Proceedings in Family Conflicts Law 5774-2014, has led to an increase in the number of cases referred to alternative dispute resolution, there is an urgent need to increase awareness of child participation procedures which might be used in these proceedings[50] and to encourage their use.

In summary, it can be seen that the Israeli legal system has undergone a process of significant development in relation to children's participation in family law disputes. This process has included the express recognition in case law and Regulations of children's right to participate in family law proceedings and, even more importantly, a very considerable change in the professional discourse relating to child participation. Nevertheless, the process has not yet been completed. As we have sought to show in this chapter, there are still many challenges to be faced in order to ensure fully children's right to significant and effective participation. Perhaps the most prominent challenges are the need to increase the number of children who participate in family law proceedings and to ensure recognition of children's right to participate in decisions concerning parenting arrangements after parental separation as a universal right.

---

49 As noted above, the Regulations provide that courts should check that parents who came to an agreement concerning arrangements for their children did hear their children's views, but this part of the Regulations has not been implemented in practice.

50 See e.g. J.D. McIntosh, Y.D. Wells, B.M. Smyth and C.M. Long, 'Child-Focused and Child Inclusive Mediation: Comparative Outcomes from a Prospective Study of Post-separation Adjustment' (2008) 46 *Family Court Review* 105; and F. Bell, J. Cashmore, P. Parkinson and J. Single, 'Outcomes of Child-Inclusive Mediation' (2013) 27 *International Journal of Law, Policy and the Family* 116.

ITALY

Ester di Napoli and Francesca Maoli*

1. INTRODUCTION

Child participation is experiencing considerable development in Italian family law at the legislative and judicial levels, and is also progressively taking hold in the policy-making field, where some authorities have cautiously started introducing child participation as a form of consultation.

The fragmentation that historically and culturally underlies the Italian system in family law proceedings, and which traditionally divides competence between ordinary and juvenile courts,[1] also concerns the child's right to be heard, enshrined in Article 12 of the UN Convention on the Rights of the Child (UNCRC). The right to be heard, in fact, is not uniformly applied in Italy, as it does not exist as a national (neither procedural nor substantive) rule, which

* This chapter is the result of a collaboration between both authors. Sections 3.1, 3.2, 3.5 and 4 are attributed to Ester di Napoli and sections 2, 3.3 and 3.4 are attributed to Francesca Maoli. The introduction and the conclusion are attributed to both authors.

1 According to Art. 38 of the preliminary provisions to the Italian Civil Code (c.c.), as modified in 2013 by Art. 96, para. 1, let. c) of Legislative Decree No. 154 of 28 December 2013, which also added Art. 38*bis*.

would ordinarily safeguard its effective implementation throughout all types of family law proceedings.[2]

In general, ordinary courts (*tribunali ordinari*)[3] deal with parental responsibility issues, mainly in the context of separation and divorce proceedings (custody, placement, maintenance), while juvenile courts (*tribunali per i minorenni*)[4] deal with requests for limitation and loss of parental responsibility (so-called *de potestate* proceedings). In some circumstances, ordinary courts may 'attract' juvenile courts' competence (*vis attractiva*).[5]

Juvenile judges, ordinary judges and public prosecutors work closely with all key actors involved in the proceedings, such as social and health services, communities, attorneys, and local authorities. They mainly rely on social services and local authorities during proceedings and to have their decisions enforced.

The Italian population, on 1 January 2020 comprised 60,317,000 residents, of whom 9,433,159 were children. In the year ending 31 December 2019, there were 184,088 marriages, 85,349 divorces and 94,474 separations (absolute values); per 1,000 marriages, 53.6% of separations and 40.5% of divorces involved children.[6]

---

2 Regarding the field of family law proceedings as 'child-friendly' ones, see E. D'Alessandro, 'Verso una giustizia "a misura di minore" nella giustizia civile: garanzie e giusto processo', in Autorità garante per l'infanzia e l'adolescenza (ed.), *La Convenzione delle Nazioni Unite sui diritti dell'infanzia e dell'adolescenza. Conquiste e prospettive a trent'anni dall'adozione*, 2019, p. 334, available (with English abstracts) at: https://www.garanteinfanzia.org/sites/default/files/agia_30_anni_convenzione.pdf and https://www.garanteinfanzia.org/sites/default/files/agia-30-anni-crc-abstracts.pdf.

3 There are currently 145 ordinary courts; after 2022, according to Legislative Decree No. 162/2019, there will be 135.

4 Juvenile courts are specialised courts established by Royal Law-Decree No. 1404 of 20 July 1934, converted into Law No. 835 of 27 May 1935. Each juvenile court (one in each district court of appeal – 29 in total) is a collegiate body made up of four judges: two professional judges (the president and a side judge) and two 'honorary magistrates' (a man and a woman), who are professionals with jurisdictional functions (among others, psychologists, attorneys, pedagogues, anthropologists). Each juvenile court has its own public prosecutor, who has a leading controlling function in civil proceedings. Juvenile courts were created before the adoption of the Italian Constitution in 1948 and of the UNCRC in 1989. However, the principles underlying the creation of this special jurisdiction, as well as their unique specialisation and commitment to children's rights, anticipated and fully responded to the principle of the best interests of the child enshrined therein (Art. 3). The list of Italian juvenile courts is available at: http://www.tribmin.milano.giustizia.it/it/Content/Index/28721.

5 According to the modifications introduced to Art. 38 in 2013, the competence of juvenile courts is excluded pending – between the same parties and before an ordinary court – separation or divorce proceedings, or proceedings concerning parental responsibility of children born out of wedlock. In such cases, the ordinary court shall also have jurisdiction in proceedings concerning the limitation or revocation of parental responsibility. See G. Buffone, 'Riparto di competenza tra T.O. e T.M in materia di provvedimenti ablativi: *iudicium finium regundorum* della Cassazione' (2015) *Famiglia e Diritto* 653.

6 ISTAT, available at: https://www.istat.it/it/archivio/253756 (published on 18 February 2021).

2. STATUTORY PROVISIONS

Children's participation in family law proceedings has been transformed in the Italian legal system. The hearing of the child was first introduced in 2006,[7] within parental responsibility proceedings, where the new Article 155*sexies* of the Italian Civil Code (c.c.) established a new obligation for the judge to hear children aged 12 years or over, or younger if capable of discernment (i.e. of forming their own views).[8] However, the current legal framework is mainly attributable to the reform of 2012–2013 when significant changes to substantive and procedural family law were made.[9]

Addressing child participation in judicial proceedings before Italian courts starts with distinguishing the nature of civil proceedings carried out before juvenile courts (limitation or revocation of parental responsibility, as a child protection measure)[10] and before ordinary courts (regulation of parental responsibility within separation and divorce proceedings).[11]

With respect to the second category, with Law No. 219/2012 the Italian lawmaker introduced Article 315*bis* c.c., which expressly states that the child has the right to be heard in all matters and proceedings affecting him/her, and not only in divorce or separation proceedings. However, the right to be heard is still limited to children of 12 years of age or over, or younger if they are capable of discernment.[12]

Subsequently, Legislative Decree No. 154/2013[13] introduced a new and more specific framework regarding the admissibility and the requirements for the

---

7 Law No. 54 of 8 February 2006 on separation and shared custody. On the topic G. Campese, 'L'ascolto del minore nei giudizi di separazione e divorzio' (2011) *Famiglia e Diritto* 958 ff.; G. De Marzo, 'L'affidamento condiviso. I. Profili sostanziali' (2006) *Foro Italiano V* 92; M. Dogliotti, 'I procedimenti: la separazione personale' in G. Ferrando (ed.), *Il nuovo diritto di famiglia* I, Zanichelli, Bologna 2007, p. 1052; F. Tommaseo, 'Le nuove norme sull'affidamento condiviso: b) profili processuali' (2006) *Famiglia e Diritto* 397; L. Salvaneschi, 'I procedimenti di separazione e divorzio' (2006) *Famiglia e Diritto* 371; F. Danovi, 'L'affidamento condiviso: le tutele processuali' (2007) *Diritto di Famiglia e delle Persone* 1921.

8 Before Art. 155*sexies* c.c., the hearing of the child was considered a mere faculty of the judge, as stated by Arts. 4(8) and 6(9) of Law No. 74/1987.

9 Law No. 219 of 10 December 2012 is well known in the Italian legal system because it inaugurated a season of reforms, inspired by the fundamental scope to eliminate (or at least significantly reduce) the differing status of children born in or out of wedlock, or adopted.

10 According to Arts. 330 and 336 c.c.

11 According to Arts. 336*bis* et seq. c.c.

12 The assessment of the capacity of discernment is discussed in section 3 of this chapter.

13 Above n. 2. On the reform L. Querzola, 'La revisione delle norme in materia di filiazione: profili processuali' (2014) *Rivista Trimestrale di Diritto e Procedura Civile* 185; F. Tommaseo, 'I profili processuali della riforma della filiazione' (2014) *Famiglia e Diritto* 530; F. Danovi, 'Il d.lgs. n. 154/2013 e l'attuazione della delega sul versante processuale: l'ascolto del minore e il diritto dei nonni alla relazione affettiva' (2014) *Famiglia e Diritto* 535; G. Buffone, *Le novità del decreto filiazione*, Giuffrè, Milan 2014; V. Carbone, 'Il D. Lgs. n. 154/2013

hearing of the child, contained in Articles 336(2), 336*bis* and 337*octies*(1) c.c. These provisions confirm the age threshold of 12 years, with children under this age only being heard if their capacity of discernment is assessed. They also contain further indications on the modalities of the hearing, as well as on the cases in which the judge may refuse to hear the child. The direct participation of the child at a hearing is the main method envisaged by the legal system.

Alongside these, a further initiative is occurring to develop institutionalised forms of 'advocacy' for the child. A professional, external to the court and independent from the child's family, has the duty of helping children to express their opinion to adults who have to take a decision concerning the child's future.[14] This is not a substitute for representation of the child, but a mechanism to allow the child to benefit from practical help and support in expressing their opinion. The appointed professional does not speak on behalf of the child, but helps the child in giving voice to his/her position when they experience difficulties in expressing their views to adults. Currently, advocacy is not operating on a regular basis in the entire Italian judicial system, but experimental models of advocacy are running in several courts, with advocacy professionals appointed by the social services.

In addition, participation may occur indirectly through the expression of the child's views when an expert witness is appointed. A technical consultancy (*consulenza tecnica d'ufficio*, CTU) in parental responsibility, separation, divorce or adoption proceedings (as well as in other proceedings where a child is involved) may request the preliminary hearing of the child by the appointed expert.

The hearing of the child is also foreseen in proceedings for the appointment of a guardian when both parents are deceased or, in general, when no one is exercising parental responsibility over the child (Art. 348(3) c.c.).[15] The same age threshold of 12 years applies. A child is also heard in proceedings when the judge has to take certain important decisions concerning the child's future. In particular, according to Article 371 c.c., the judge shall hear a child of 10 years of age or over, or younger depending on his/her capacity of discernment, before

---

sulla revisione delle disposizioni vigenti in materia di filiazione' (2014) *Famiglia e Diritto* 447; P. Schlesinger, 'Il D.Lgs. n. 154 del 2013 completa la riforma della filiazione' (2014) *Famiglia e Diritto* 443.

14 See V. Calcaterra, 'L'*advocacy* nella tutela minorile. Prime esperienze italiane del lavoro del portavoce professionale' (2016) *Minorigiustizia* 155; J. Boylan et al., *Cos'è l'*advocacy *nella tutela minorile. Guida per educatori e assistenti sociali*, Erickson, Trento 2011. The first Italian pilot projects on the institution of independent advocacy professionals were carried out in 2013 in the area of Varese, through a project that saw the implementation of case advocacy interventions at the request of child protection services. Case advocacy interventions were carried out at the request of the Juvenile Court of Milan, the Ordinary Court of Varese and, to date, a request for the activation of advocacy services has also been received from the Juvenile Court of Turin.

15 Introduced by Legislative Decree No. 154/2013.

taking a decision on the place where the child will be raised, on their education or their professional future.[16]

3. MODES OF CHILD PARTICIPATION

3.1. DIRECT FORMS OF PARTICIPATION

Doctrine[17] and case law[18] (the law is not clear on this point) agree that the child is a party – like his/her parent(s) – only in proceedings that take place before juvenile courts. In such proceedings, the child is therefore also the direct recipient of the decision's effects and, as such, has the right to be informed of any pending proceedings and to participate in them.

In proceedings concerning parental responsibility, the conditions and forms of the hearing are contained in Article 336*bis* c.c. The judge may decide not to hear the child if such hearing is against the child's best interests, provided that this assessment is supported by adequate reasoning.[19] The hearing must take place with particular caution and with the help of experts. The parents, the representatives of the parties and the public prosecutor may participate in the hearing if authorised by the judge.[20]

Finally, the child must always receive information 'on the nature of the proceeding and on the effects of the hearing'.[21] Despite the positive obligation stated in Article 336*bis* c.c., the law does not provide further indications as to how, and by whom, the information is to be provided to the child. The courts' practice in this regard is highly inconsistent, since there are no common guidelines and the omission of this duty to provide information has not been addressed by the case law.

Further provisions on the hearing of the child are contained in Article 337*octies* c.c., which specifically refers to the exercise of parental responsibility following separation, divorce or marriage annulment, or concerning children born out of wedlock. Apart from reiterating the specific obligation to

16 Note that this age threshold is lower than the usual limit of 12 years of age

17 B. Poliseno, *Profili di tutela del minore nel processo civile*, Edizioni Scientifiche Italiane, Napoli 2017, p. 99.

18 Constitutional Court, decision of 14 July 1986, No. 185, in Giur. it. 1988, 1112; Constitutional Court, decision of 30 January 2002, in *Foro italiano* 2003, 423.

19 Art. 336*bis*(1) c.c.

20 Art. 336*bis*(2) c.c. Surprisingly, a slightly different approach is affirmed in Art. 38 of the Implementing Provisions of the Civil Code, where it is stated that, when the protection of the child is ensured by appropriate means (e.g. with the use of a mirror glass and an intercom system), the parents, the representatives, the special curator of the child and the public prosecutor may follow the hearing without requesting any authorisation from the judge.

21 Art. 336*bis*(3) c.c.

hear the child (with the same age threshold contained in Arts. 315*bis*, 336(2) and 336*bis* c.c.), the provision provides for an exception to the general rule. If the proceedings concern the mere judicial homologation of an agreement made by the parents regarding the exercise of parental responsibility, the hearing of the child does not take place if it conflicts with his/her best interests or is manifestly unnecessary.[22]

3.2. REPRESENTATION FORMS OF PARTICIPATION

While hearing the child constitutes a general obligation for the judge (even with limits and exceptions), the separate representation of the child is not foreseen in proceedings concerning the exercise of parental responsibility over a child.[23] A child cannot initiate legal proceedings or be brought to court alone (Art. 75 of the Italian Code of Civil Procedure (c.c.p.)). In order to do so, the child needs a legal representative (i.e. a person holding parental responsibility as a parent or guardian).

Whenever there is a conflict of interest between the child and the holder of parental responsibility, whether before the ordinary or juvenile courts, the judge appoints a special representative for the child (*curatore speciale*) whose aim is to safeguard the child's interests, according to Article 78 c.c.p. The same provision does not specify in which proceedings the child's special representative shall be appointed, as it only requires certain conditions (e.g. urgency). Article 79 c.c.p. further specifies that the appointment of the special representative can be requested 'in any case' by the public prosecutor, by the child or by any interested party to the proceedings. The Italian legal system does not provide any rules regarding the *curatore speciale* (e.g. conditions for the appointment, record-keeping, training). This has led to the proliferation of regional practices (mainly protocols between courts and key actors, including professional bodies), the establishment of registers and their governance, as well as training activities required for registration.[24]

---

22 This means that the obligation to hear the child is 'softened', since there is an implicit presumption that an amicable solution already reached by the parents would be consistent with the child's best interests, in particular where the right of the child to maintain regular contact with both parents is respected. On this *amplius* M.A. Inannicelli, 'La crisi della coppia genitoriale e il "diritto" del figlio minore di essere ascoltato' (2016) *Familia* 87, 98.

23 The appointment of a representative is obligatory only in proceedings concerning the limitation or withdrawal of parental responsibility (Art. 336(4) c.c.) and the declaration of adoptability (Art. 17 of Law No. 184 of 4 May 1983 on adoption and foster care), for which the juvenile court is competent and where there is a concrete conflict of interests between the child and the parents. Outside of these cases – which are categorised within the child protection measures – Italian law does not foresee the appointment of a separate representative of the child.

24 This is the case, for example, of the protocol agreed on the 7 February 2018 between the Court of Milan and the Milan Bar Association.

Nor are there any rules specifying the ways in which the hearing of the child or the preliminary assessment of the child's best interests should be undertaken. This lack of rules has paved the way for a number of decisions and practices establishing modes of direct or indirect hearing. The practices have been mainly formalised through the creation of protocols between courts, public prosecutors, social services, professional bodies and associations active in the field of protecting and promoting children's rights.

3.3. TYPES OF PROCEEDINGS AND AGE/MATURITY/CAPACITY REQUIREMENTS

The right of the child to be heard in every matter and proceeding affecting him/her, including in family law proceedings, established by Article 315*bis* c.c., represents a positive step forward in Italian legislation. Indeed, the provision represents the acknowledgment, in the Italian legal system, of the fundamental right of the child consecrated in the UNCRC and in the 1996 Strasbourg Convention.[25]

However, a specific age threshold establishes a difference in treatment. For children older than 12, the hearing represents an essential procedural step, the omission of which may lead to the invalidity of the judgment, if not based on adequate grounds. The judge may omit the hearing only if it would be against the child's best interests,[26] or if the hearing is considered to be superfluous (for instance, because the factual circumstances of the case are clear and uncontested, or because the child has already been heard in connected proceedings). However, for children aged up to 12, the judge can only order a hearing if the child is capable of discernment. This means that the child should be able to form his/her own views and to understand the circumstances of the meeting with the judge, being mature enough to communicate in a conscious way. These circumstances are the object of a free and discretionary evaluation by the judge.[27] Since this

---

25 As already invocated by the Italian case law before the reform of 2012–2013: see Corte di Cassazione, Sezioni Unite, 21 October 2009, No. 22238; Corte di Cassazione, 16 June 2011, No. 13241; Corte di Cassazione, 11 August 2011, No. 17201; Corte di Cassazione, 15 May 2013, No. 11687. The same reasoning can be found, *a fortiori*, in the case law subsequent to the introduction of Art. 315*bis*: see Corte di Cassazione, 26 March 2015, No. 6129.

26 Even before the introduction of the new discipline, the omission of the hearing was justified on the basis of the child's best interests: see Corte di Cassazione, Sezioni Unite, 21 October 2009, No. 22238/2009. On this topic A. Graziosi, 'Ebbene sì, il minore ha diritto di essere ascoltato nel processo' (2010) *Famiglia e Diritto* 364. See also Corte di Cassazione, 8 March 2013, No. 5847; Corte di Cassazione, 15 May 2013, No. 22687.

27 Corte di Cassazione, 29 September 2015, No. 19327; Corte di Cassazione, 19 January 2015, No. 752.

constitutes a specialised assessment, the judge can appoint a psychologist or a social assistant for this purpose. This practice happens very frequently with children younger than eight years of age, but is generally also used for children between eight and 12 years old. There are no specific legal provisions governing this, as these are practices developed in the civil courts that are sometimes incorporated in official soft-law guidelines.

The case law provides further clarification on the different modes of the right to be heard as applied to 12-year-old children compared to younger ones. The *Corte di Cassazione* has stated that the judge has a margin of discretion regarding the hearing of children up to 12 years of age and that the omission of the hearing does not require a specific reasoning if the parties have not submitted a request indicating the topics on which the child's opinion was considered necessary.[28] This is different for children aged 12 or older, who it is mandatory to hear, unless this is superfluous or contrary to their best interests; in the latter case, the failure to provide reasons renders the decision null and void.[29]

3.4. INTERNATIONAL CHILD ABDUCTION

There is a specific provision on children's participation in international child abduction proceedings, where the relevant legal framework is represented by the 1980 Hague Convention on the Civil Aspects of International Child Abduction[30] and, as regards abductions occurring within the European Union, Regulation No. 2201/2003.[31] With Law No. 64/1994,[32] Italy ratified the 1980 Hague Convention and introduced the necessary implementing rules governing the procedure for return of the child. According to Article 7(3) Law No. 64/1994, the juvenile court shall hear the child 'if appropriate'. While the provision does not explicitly state that the hearing is mandatory (nor qualifies it as a right of the child), the latter has been given a flexible interpretation by

---

28 Corte di Cassazione, 7 March 2017, No. 5676, on which A. Nascosi, 'Nuove direttive sull'ascolto del minore infradodicenne' (2018) *Famiglia e Diritto* 354; Corte di Cassazione, 6 December 2018, No. 31671; Corte di Cassazione, 14 December 2018, No. 32520.

29 See all the decisions above n. 28.

30 Hague Convention of 25 October 1980 on Civil Aspects of International Child Abduction (http://www.hcch.net).

31 Council Regulation No. 2201/2003 of 27 November 2003 concerning jurisdiction and the recognition and enforcement of judgments in matrimonial matters and the matters of parental responsibility, *OJ L* 338, 23 December 2003, 1. The Regulation has been applicable since 1 March 2005 (Art. 72). Recently, the Regulation has been subject to a recast with Council Regulation 2019/1111 of 25 June 2019 on jurisdiction, the recognition and enforcement of decisions in matrimonial matters and the matters of parental responsibility, and on international child abduction, *OJ L* 178, 2 July 2019, 1, which will apply as from 1 August 2022.

32 Law No. 64 of 15 January 1994.

Italian courts over the years on the basis of the evolving understanding of the fundamental right of the child to be heard.[33] Most recently, the *Corte di Cassazione* has confirmed that the judge must hear the child, according to Article 315*bis* c.c., unless there are particular reasons (to be specifically indicated) that would prevent the hearing, such as when it could be harmful to the child.[34] The obligation to provide for an adequate statement of reasons has been taken very seriously by the court of final instance in the aforementioned decision, which annulled the decision on the merits when the motivation was generically based on the child's immaturity or insufficient evidence was provided on the harmful effects of the hearing.

3.5. ADOPTION

The principles set out by Article 315*bis* c.c. apply to all proceedings concerning the child. Therefore, the judge must also hear the child in adoption proceedings that are governed by Law No. 184/1983.[35] The child shall be heard in proceedings for the determination of the state of adoptability,[36] before the declaration of adoption,[37] and in proceedings concerning foster care,[38] in line with the same age and maturity requirements established by Article 315*bis* c.c The modes of the hearing are the same stated in Articles 336(2) and 336*bis* c.c.

4. RESEARCH

In April 2020, the Italian Independent Authority for Children and Adolescents[39] carried out a survey on the implementation of the child's right to be heard in

---

33 See also the chapter by T. Kruger and F. Maoli in this Handbook.

34 Most recently, Corte di Cassazione, 4 April 2019, No. 10874. On the same terms, Corte di Cassazione, 4 June 2019, No. 15254.

35 Above n. 23. See also B. Poliseno, 'La tutela del minore nel procedimento per la dichiarazione dello stato di adottabilità' (2018) *Rivista di Diritto processuale* 1026.

36 Law No. 184/1983, Arts. 10 and 15.

37 Law No. 184/1983, Arts. 7 and 25.

38 Law No. 184/1983, Arts. 22 and 23.

39 The Italian Independent Authority for Children and Adolescents (*Autorità garante per l'infanzia e l'adolescenza*), established by Law No. 112/2011, is the independent body aimed at verifying the correct application of the UNCRC in Italy. All information is available at: https://www.garanteinfanzia.org/. Within the Italian Authority for Children and Adolescents operates the *Consulta dei ragazzi*, it is an advisory board established in 2018, which comprises boys and girls aged under 18 who meet on a weekly basis and is involved anytime the Authority is asked to give its opinion to the competent institutions or adopts recommendations related to children's rights. The *Consulta dei ragazzi* was heard, inter alia, in the adoption of the Charter of Children's Rights within their Parents' Separation, available at: https://www.garanteinfanzia.org/landing2EN/children-s-rights-within-their-parents-separation.html.

all juvenile courts and in a selection of 22 ordinary courts.[40] With reference to the ordinary courts, the child's capacity of discernment was particularly taken into account, despite the frequent absence of ad hoc spaces in these courts. In general, this illustrates the lack of uniform operating procedures, which creates uncertainty and leaves room for discretion in such a sensitive area.

5. CONCLUSION

Despite the developments that have occurred over the last decade in Italy, at both the legislative and jurisdictional level, much still needs to be done to fully implement Article 12 of the UNCRC. In particular, the Italian legislator should adopt rules recognising the child's right to be heard at the national level, and provide further practical guidelines to judges and other professionals involved in family proceedings. While the legislative provisions introduced in the Civil Code have been able to set more precise standards, and have received concrete implementation in the subsequent case law, the practice of the ordinary and juvenile courts reveals that a further step forward is needed. Moreover, the fact that a growing number of couples are choosing to conclude out-of-court divorce agreements should be considered:[41] in this context, there could be important limitations concerning the possibility for the child to express their views. The current legal system still seems quite fragmentary with respect to the implementation of the child's right to participation in different subject matters and procedures. Legal professionals and other practitioners working in the field cannot rely on common standards and/or common best practices at the national level. More needs to be done to create practical methods and guarantees on the hearing of children and, more generally, clear-cut proceedings, along with clarification at the national level of general aspects regarding all actors involved (e.g. the *curatore speciale*). In this context, the Italian legislation still provides an age limit regarding the hearing of the child (which creates an obligation for the judge to hear the child only if the child is 12 years of age or older). This contrasts with the latest developments and trends in human rights law, and studies concerning the wellbeing of children, which require a genuine case-by-case assessment of the opportunity for child participation.[42]

---

40 Autorità garante per l'infanzia e l'adolescenza, 'Il diritto all'ascolto delle persone di minore età in sede giurisdizionale. Indagine relativa alle modalità messe in atto sul territorio nazionale dai tribunali per i minorenni, tribunali ordinari e relative procure della Repubblica', 2020, https://www.garanteinfanzia.org/sites/default/files/ascolto-minorenni-procedimenti-giurisdizionali.pdf.

41 ISTAT, available at https://www.istat.it/it/files//2021/02/Report-matrimoni-unioni-civili-separazioni-divorzi_anno-2019.pdf.

42 See the study carried out by K. Van Hoorde et al., *Bouncing Back. The Wellbeing of Children in International Child Abduction Cases*, 2017, http://missingchildreneurope.eu/.

In February 2019, the UN Committee on the Rights of the Child adopted its Concluding Observations on the combined fifth and sixth periodic reports of Italy,[43] and recommended that the State

> [i]ntroduce a comprehensive legal provision establishing the right of the child to be heard without any discrimination due to age, disability or any other circumstance, both in the family environment and in any administrative, judicial or mediation procedure in which the child is affected, and ensure that the child's opinion is taken into account in accordance with the child's age and maturity, and adopt national uniform standards implementing regulations and guidelines accordingly, in particular in relation to all decisions concerning unaccompanied or separated children having arrived in the State party.[44]

These Concluding Observations encourage an approach that addresses the issue from a broader perspective, rather than just focusing on judicial proceedings. In this regard, the implementation of children's participation measures should sit alongside the empowerment of out-of-court decision-making processes. A new frontier of child participation would be the effective implementation (starting with its dissemination) of the 2011 Optional Protocol to the UNCRC,[45] which allows children (on their own behalf or represented by adults) to submit communications concerning the infringement of rights contained in the UNCRC and its Optional Protocols to the Committee. This entered into force in Italy in 2016,[46] but it is still almost unknown, not just to children and families, but also amongst family justice professionals.

---

43 UN Committee on the Rights of the Child, *Concluding observations on the combined fifth and sixth periodic reports of Italy*, adopted at its 80th session (14 January–1 February 2019), https://tbinternet.ohchr.org/_layouts/15/treatybodyexternal/SessionDetails1.aspx?SessionID=1226&Lang=en.

44 UN Committee on the Rights of the Child, *Concluding Observations*, above n. 43, point 17(a).

45 Optional Protocol to the Convention on the Rights of the Child on a communications procedure, adopted and opened for signature, ratification and accession by General Assembly resolution A/RES/66/138 of 19 December 2011 and entered into force on 14 April 2014.

46 Law No. 199 of 16 November 2015.

THE NETHERLANDS

Mariëlle BRUNING and Wendy SCHRAMA

1. INTRODUCTION

The focus on the child's right to participate in the legal domain is relatively recent in Dutch family law. Even so, the actual right for children aged 12 years and over to be heard by a court was first introduced in 1982 in the Dutch Civil Code. The aim was to improve the legal protection of minors.[1] In 1990 the right of children to informally approach a family court was added to the package of children's right to participate; it is not a right to initiate proceedings, but an informal access to court (see section 2.2).[2] Participation rights are therefore not new, but the focus has shifted, partially as a result of the growing importance of children's

[1] *Kamerstukken II* 1979/80, 16 127, no. 1–3, p. 1. See: C. MOL, S. BOU-SFIA and J. HUIJER, 'Mijn wil is wet! De autonomie van minderjarigen in het Nederlandse personen- en familierecht' in W.M. SCHRAMA and S. BURRI (eds.), De rol van de staat, de familie en het individu in het personen- en familierecht, Boom juridische uitgevers the Hague, 2020, para. 3.2.1.

[2] In Art. 1:162a (old) Dutch Civil Code, which was later changed to Art. 1 377g Dutch Civil Code. See C. MOL, S. BOU-SFIA and J. HUIJER, above n. 1, para. 3.1.2.

rights in general. In legal proceedings related to divorce and separation, children now have the right to be informed and to give their opinion about the parenting plans of their parents. In the last decade there has been a tendency to better implement the child's right to participate in legal proceedings. This has led to policy improvements for the judiciary and to further use and professionalisation of guardians ad litem, who can be appointed to represent and support children in family law proceedings when there is a conflict of interests between parent(s) and child.

In 2018 the Dutch population of 17 million inhabitants consisted of 3.4 million children aged 0–18 years.[3] Of particular interest for children's participation rights are divorce and separation proceedings (see below). In 2018, 93,500 children were born to married parents, and 55,800 to unmarried parents. It is not exactly known how many of these unmarried parents cohabit.[4] Each year, a substantial number of children face their parents' divorce or separation. The most recent data indicate that, in 2016, 50,000 couples with minor children split up. Of these, 27,000 were married couples with children and another 23,000 of these parents were informal cohabitants. In total, these separations involved 86,000 minor children.[5]

In this chapter, Dutch statutory provisions and current policy relevant to child participation in family law proceedings are discussed. The various modes of child participation in family law proceedings are also explained, with a focus on legal practice. Furthermore, relevant research is presented and consideration is given to how the Dutch system of child participation could be improved.

2. STATUTORY PROVISIONS

2.1. CHILDREN'S LEGAL STATUS IN FAMILY LAW PROCEEDINGS

Child participation is not regulated coherently in one Act or code, but consists of different rights of children in regard to various family law proceedings, in both substantive family law in the Civil Code, as well in the Code of Civil Procedure. It depends on the matter at hand what right(s) a child has but, in all family law proceedings, children aged 12 or older have the right to be heard in person by a court. There is no overarching definition of the term 'family law proceedings'.

---

3 Central Statistics The Netherlands, open data files: https://opendata.cbs.nl/ ('bevolking, kerncijfers').

4 Central Statistics The Netherlands, https://opendata.cbs.nl/#/CBS/nl/dataset/37975/table?ts=1613630996628.

5 M. ter Voert, *Factsheet 2019-1, Scheidingen 2018, Gerechtelijke procedures en gesubsidieerde rechtsbijstand.*

In general, these include parental responsibilities, care and access, relocation issues and child abduction (although this has its own framework due to international law), adoption and parentage issues. Three aspects of participation rights may be discerned. Firstly, there are issues related to legal standing (section 2.2). In some cases children have the right to initiate legal proceedings and thus to be a party to legal proceedings. In addition, children have a veto in respect of some family law issues, such as adoption. Also related to legal standing is the child's right to informally approach the court in specific family law matters. The second aspect is the right to be represented by a parent or third person in legal proceedings (section 2.3); and the third the right to be heard by the court (section 2.4). Children's participation rights in out-of-court proceedings – or rather the lack of them – are also discussed (section 2.5).

2.2. LEGAL STANDING

In general, children have no legal standing in civil law proceedings, including family law proceedings. Children are in principle incapable of autonomously participating in legal proceedings and lack *locus standi*. They are represented by their parents (or guardian). Thus, children have no independent rights in family law proceedings, such as the right to information and to receive case files,[6] the right to receive judgments of the court, or the right to appeal a decision of a family court. Children are interested parties (*belanghebbende*) in all family law proceedings. Children are normally represented by their parents (or guardian), which implies that their parents are supposed to share information and to make use of the right to appeal. In 2014, the Dutch Supreme Court ruled that a child is an interested party in family court proceedings which regard them, but not a legal party to the proceedings with an independent right to access all files.[7] An 11-year-old girl had requested access to all documents in the proceedings in order to decide about the possibility to be heard, but this was declined by the District Court and the Court of Appeal. The girl's mother lodged an appeal complaining that her child was denied the right to access all case files as an element of the child's right to be effectively heard in light of, for example, Article 12 of the UN Convention on the Rights of the Child (UNCRC). The Supreme Court upheld the judgment of the lower courts and ruled that the child's right to access to justice, as laid down in Article 6(1) of the European Convention on Human Rights (ECHR) and Article 12 UNCRC, had

6 Children aged 12 and older do have the right to access all case files in family law proceedings (Art. 811 Dutch Civil Code of Procedure) unless they are deemed incapable to oversee their best interests.

7 Dutch Supreme Court 05.12.2014, ECLI:NL:HR:2014:3535, available (in Dutch) at: https://uitspraken.rechtspraak.nl/.

been sufficiently safeguarded and the lack of independent access to all relevant documents was not in violation with these standards. According to the Supreme Court, neither Article 6(1) ECHR nor Article 12 UNCRC nor any other legally binding provision of international law proclaim that a child can only effectively make use of their right to access to justice and be heard if the child has such an independent right, which can be exercised autonomously from their legal representative(s).[8]

Several exceptions have been introduced in recent decades to allow the child to litigate independently. Children sometimes have veto rights (adoption)[9] or the right to initiate proceedings regarding a limited number of topics. For example, children aged 16 and older can initiate proceedings with regard to changing the registration of gender on their birth certificate. They may request the Registrar of Civil Status to do this when they are convinced they are of another gender.[10] Another example concerns underage mothers aged 16 or older who want to care for and raise the child: they can request to be emancipated before the Family Court.[11] These and other exceptions are fragmented in the Dutch Civil Code and have 12 years, and sometimes 16 years, as the lower age limit. Various reasons for these differences can be found in parliamentary history, but they are inconsistent as there is no clear objective, policy or uniform view with regard to the civil procedural position of children.[12]

In some family law matters, Dutch law provides children aged 12 or older with the possibility of approaching the court informally and asking for a specific decision. Informal access to court is available in matters related to parental responsibilities after divorce and separation (including relocation matters) and care and contact arrangements between a child and a parent.[13]

---

8 T. Liefaard and M. Bruning, 'Hoge Raad 5 December 2014: Judgment and Commentary' in H. Stalford, K. Hollingsworth and S. Gilmore (eds.), *Rewriting Children's Judgments: From Academic Vision to New Practice*, Hart Publishing, Oxford 2017, pp. 173–192; according to the authors the Supreme Court has completely disregarded the recognition of the child as a rights holder under the UNCRC and the ECHR and a less restrictive approach can be defended.

9 Art. 1:228 section 1 under a Dutch Civil Code; age limit of 12 years plus the younger ones who are sufficiently mature.

10 This was introduced in Art. 1:28 Dutch Civil Code in 2014; *Stb.* 2014, 1. In adoption cases, children from the age of 12 and older have the right to veto an adoption (one of the requirements for the adoption of a child of 12 or older is that the child did not object to the granting of an adoption request at its hearing in court, Art. 1:228 section 1 sub a Dutch Civil Code). A recognition of paternity is null and void if it is done without the prior consent of the child of 12 or older (Art. 1:204 section 1 sub d Dutch Civil Code); children who have reached the age of 16 years can recognise paternity (Art. 1:204 section 1 sub b Dutch Civil Code).

11 Art. 1:253ha Dutch Civil Code.

12 M.R. Bruning et al., *Kind in proces: van communicatie naar effectieve participatie*, Meijers-reeks no. 335, Wolf Legal Publishers, Nijmegen 2020, p. 63; C. Mol, S. Bou-Sfia and J. Huijer, above n. 1, paras. 1 and 5.

13 Art. 1:251a section 4, Art. 1:253a section 4 and Art. 1:377g Dutch Civil Code; see M.R. Bruning and J. Peper, 'Giving Children a Voice in Court?' [2020] *Erasmus Law Review*, http://www.erasmuslawreview.nl/tijdschrift/ELR/2020/1%20(incomplete)/ELR-D-19-00030.pdf.

This option can also be used when the child has not yet reached the age of 12 years, but may be regarded as capable of making a reasonable evaluation of their interests in the matter. Children can request that joint parental responsibilities be changed to sole parental responsibilities or to bring a case with respect to access rights or care plans subsequent to divorce or separation. Children can informally contact the court (e.g. by writing a letter or sending an email) without (legal) representation.[14] Children can thus approach the court informally in these matters, but they do not have a right to court proceedings. Judges have discretionary powers to decide if a child will be heard on such request and if this will lead to a judgment ex officio.

2.3. GUARDIAN AD LITEM

The general idea is that parents with parental responsibilities represent their children in the legal domain. However, there are situations where the interests of parents and child might not align. The Dutch Civil Code allows for the appointment of a guardian ad litem by the family court in the event of a potential conflict of interests regarding who can act on the child's behalf as a (formal) litigant. However, courts are only allowed to appoint a guardian ad litem in two types of cases: (i) matters relating to the care and upbringing of the child or the child's property[15] and (ii) proceedings regarding issues of legal parentage. A guardian ad litem cannot be appointed for any other family law proceedings.

The first scenario concerns concrete conflicts of interest between the parents and child. When there is no fundamental, specific conflict of interest, the Dutch Supreme Court has ruled that the criteria to appoint a guardian ad litem are not met.[16] Among the issues covered are, for example, those related to parental responsibilities, care and access, relocation, and the main residence of the child. Often guardians ad litem are appointed in complex divorce cases, where the parents' and child's interests might easily conflict.

The guardian ad litem is responsible for instigating proceedings when this – according to the guardian – is necessary in the child's best interests.[17] The aim of introducing a guardian ad litem in 1995 in these matters, and thereby enlarging the possibilities for children to be represented by others than their parents, was to strengthen their legal position in family law cases.[18]

---

14 Arts. 1:251a section 4, 1:377g and 1:253a section 4 Dutch Civil Code. Children younger than 12 who are considered competent can also use this opportunity.

15 Art. 1:250 Dutch Civil Code.

16 Dutch Supreme Court 04.02.2005, ECLI:NL:HR:2005:AR4850, *NJ* 2005/422.

17 Art. 1:250 Dutch Civil Code. Since 1995 a guardian ad litem can be appointed in matters relating to the care and upbringing of the child.

18 *Kamerstukken II* 1991/92, 33487, 3, p. 7.

Secondly, the guardian ad litem also plays an important role in proceedings on legal parentage, such as recognition of the child by the father where the mother does not consent, paternity requests and challenges to existing legal parentage. Family courts are obliged to always appoint a guardian ad litem (ex officio) to represent the child.[19] The court has no discretionary power in such proceedings to decide whether it will appoint a guardian.[20] In these matters, the guardian ad litem can act as a representative of the child and can initiate proceedings on behalf of the child, including when the child is very young.[21] The statutory provision does not make clear whether the child himself can approach the court for the appointment of a guardian ad litem, if the parents do not commence legal proceedings. In legal doctrine it has been argued that it is possible.[22]

Guardians ad litem are usually trained as (family or children's) lawyers or educationalists (behavioural experts).[23] In a recent pilot where a psychologist, but not a lawyer, was appointed, the outcomes were generally quite positive.[24] The court can appoint a guardian ad litem ex officio. Children can also request the appointment of a guardian ad litem. Judges have wide discretionary powers to decide about appointing a guardian ad litem, except in legal parentage cases, where the appointment is mandatory.

2.4. THE RIGHT TO BE HEARD IN FAMILY LAW PROCEEDINGS

Children aged 12 and older have the right to be heard by the court. The Dutch Civil Code of Procedure provides that the judge will give these children the opportunity to present their views/opinion in family law proceedings that regard them.[25] Only for child maintenance proceedings is the higher age of 16 years applicable. The right to be heard is not a duty but an option for the child. In Dutch law, participation forms and methods of communication are not regulated.

---

19 Art. 1:212 Dutch Civil Code; this was introduced in 1998 to give children a voice in parentage proceedings; Wet van 24.12.1997, *Stb.* 772.

20 Dutch Supreme Court 23.11.2012, ECLI:NL:HR:2012:BY3968.

21 Dutch Supreme Court 31.10.2003, ECLI:NL:HR:2003:AJ3261, *NJ* 2004/315, annotated by J. de Boer.

22 W.M. Schrama, commentary on Art. 1:212 BW, aant. 7 in S.F.M. Wortmann (ed.), *Groene Serie Personen- en familierecht*, Wolters Kluwer, Deventer 2018.

23 See also the professional standards on appointing a guardian ad litem ('*Werkproces benoeming bijzondere curator op grond van art. 1:250 BW, 14 October 2014*'; '*Werkproces benoeming bijzondere curator in afstammingszaken op grond van 1:212 BW*') that were established by the judiciary. In December 2017 a Foundation of Dutch Guardians ad Litem was launched aimed at safeguarding professional standards; see C. van Leuven and I. Pieters, 'Stichting bijzondere curator Nederland', *Relatierecht en Praktijk* 2018/201.

24 M. Valenkamp, E. Sondorp and A. van Montfoort, 'Pilot bijzondere curator/ gedragsdeskundige in de rechtbank Zeeland-West-Brabant, locatie Breda. Het belang van het kind in complexe scheidingen', Research Memoranda 2017, no. 1.

25 Art. 809 Dutch Civil Code of Procedure.

Children younger than 12 may also be given the opportunity to be heard on the basis of the statutory provision in the Dutch Civil Code of Procedure. They are not invited by default by the judge for a child hearing, but if they request to be heard in family law proceedings, the judge has a discretionary power to decide on hearing the child when the child is sufficiently mature.

The purpose of the child's right to be heard has not been explicitly mentioned in any statutory provision. It can be inferred from the parliamentary history that the child's right to be heard was introduced to offer legal protection to children.[26] Nowadays, the child's right to be heard is more perceived as giving substance to the right of every child to be heard in proceedings as laid down in Article 12 UNCRC.

There are a few exceptions to the rule to hear every child aged 12 and older – for example, when the case is of minimal relevance to the child.[27] The Dutch legislator has underlined that when it is plausible that the minor does not want to be heard, the judge is not obliged to hear them.[28] The same applies for minors who are unable to be heard due to physical or mental health problems.[29] A final exception concerns the situation in which the judge fears that hearing the child will negatively influence the child's health and development.[30]

2.5. OUT-OF-COURT SETTLEMENT

What are children's participation rights in out-of-court proceedings? The Dutch Civil Code and Civil Procedural Code promote mediation in family law disputes and this has become more common than before.[31] However, little attention is given to the position of children.[32] Their participation rights in mediation are not regulated by statutory law, which focuses solely on court proceedings. If there are no court proceedings, it is a matter for the parents and the mediator

---

26 *Kamerstukken II* 1979/80, 16 127, 3, p. 1.

27 Art. 809 section 1 Dutch Civil Code of Procedure.

28 *Kamerstukken II* 1992/93, 22 487, 6, p. 16; see also Dutch Supreme Court 19.03.1982, *NJ* 1982, 559.

29 *Kamerstukken II* 1991/92, 22 487, 3, p. 10 (MvT).

30 This exception is not mentioned in legislation, but is introduced by the Dutch Supreme Court with reference to a similar exception in France, the UK and Germany. In her annotation Wortmann explains that this comparison is rather weak; she suggests to define this exception with a higher threshold ('significant harm for the child's health and development') in order to promote children being heard in court: Dutch Supreme Court 01.11.2013, ECLI:NL:HR:2013:1084, *NJ* 2014/24 (annotated by S.F.M. Wortmann).

31 Art. 1:253a section 5 Dutch Civil Code; Art. 818 section 2 Dutch Civil Code of Procedure. In 2018, 1,911 family and youth law cases were referred by the court to a mediator: Jaarverslag Raad voor de rechtspraak, 2018, p. 28.

32 B.E.S. Chin-A-Fat and M.J. Steketee, *Evaluatie Experimenten Scheidings- en Omgangsbemiddeling*, Verwey-Jonker Instituut, Utrecht 2001; and B.E.S. Chin-A-Fat, *Scheiden:(ter)echter zonder rechter? Een onderzoek naar de meerwaarde van scheidingsbemiddeling*, Sdu, The Hague 2004.

what the child's role will be. There is one exception in the law: while making a parenting plan, which is mandatory, the parents have to involve the child. The parenting plan concerns agreements on care and upbringing of the child, the right to information and child maintenance.[33] It applies to all parents, married or not, and regardless of whether they use mediation or not. All parents with custody have to make a parenting plan.

3. MODES OF PARTICIPATION

3.1. PRACTICE AND EXPERIENCES WITH THE LEGAL STANDING OF CHILDREN

Children do not often start proceedings in legal practice; the small number of cases where this occurs usually involve parental responsibilities and access rights.[34] Dutch Children and Youth Law Centres that are run by law students can support children in proceedings and can inform them about their rights. Judges indicate that the opportunity for children to litigate independently is rarely used and that informal access to justice (namely informal requests with regard to custody, care and access, with discretionary power of the judge to decide whether to proceed or reject the request) is rarely used.[35]

3.2. HEARING CHILDREN BY THE COURT IN FAMILY LAW PROCEEDINGS IN PRACTICE

Bearing in mind that there is no guidance from statutory provisions on the modalities and methods on the hearing of the child, the four Courts of Appeal have developed a professional standard on 'child conversations'. However, lower district courts, which deal with most cases, do not have such guidelines. Children aged 12 or older are invited for a child hearing by the court with an invitation letter. These letters vary from court to court, since there is no default letter. Children are invited to either accept the invitation to be heard or to express their views in writing by returning a form enclosed with the invitation which leaves space for them to write their views down. Children often do not respond to the invitation letter.[36] In family law cases about 15 minutes are available for

---

33 Art. 815 section 2 Dutch Civil Code of Procedure.

34 M.R. Bruning et al., above n. 12, pp. 39–40.

35 M.R. Bruning et al., above n. 12, pp. 214–215.

36 Almost half of the judges who participated in the research of M.R. Bruning et al., above n. 12 (pp. 179–180) indicated that most children do not respond to the invitation; of the youngsters who participated and had experienced family or child law proceedings, about 40% expressed that they had not responded to the invitation letter.

the child hearing.[37] Its location varies; it might take place in a child-friendly room, in the courtroom or in the council chamber. Often only one judge and a clerk are present during the child interview, but sometimes three judges (the full chamber) take part. It is not common practice to take a support person (e.g. a family member or friend) to the child hearing. Children are informed by the court that the child will be heard alone. When the child asks to bring a support person, judges appear to be lenient. After the hearing, the judge discusses with the child what information is to be shared with the parents. The child's views are not confidential and, at the hearing with the parents, it appears that judges regularly summarise the most important aspects of the child's view. This is particularly relevant when the court takes a decision which is consistent with the child's view, but not with the parents' view. The clerk prepares notes that are included in the court's file, but these notes are not made available to the parties.

Children in family law proceedings regularly talk with a social worker from the Child Protection Agency before the hearing. This Agency participates as an expert for the court in family law proceedings.[38] This cannot be considered as a way of indirectly hearing the child in family law proceedings, since the Agency's aim is to prepare advice for the court and not to represent the child or express their views to the court.

There is no regulation addressing how the child will learn of the court's decision and how their views were taken into account. As mentioned, children are not supported by a guardian ad litem or another support person during a family law hearing and a child conversation. The legal system presumes that parents will inform their child about the outcome of the case. Therefore, it is rare for there to be feedback on the decision by a state authority (court, child protection services) in relation to the child (explaining how the child's views are given due weight) and an explanation of the decision. More recently, some 'child-friendly' judgments have been issued using clear, plain language to explain a decision to the child and parents.[39] However, judges emphasise that they have insufficient time to prepare these special judgments. Sometimes, during the hearing, judges ask the parents to explain the decision to their child. Since family law judgments are not given directly after the hearing, but weeks later, there is no opportunity for the judge to explain the decision to the child in the

---

37 In child protection cases it appears that much less time is available for a child hearing and these conversations usually last five minutes; M.R. Bruning et al., above n. 12, pp. 186–187.

38 Art. 810 Dutch Civil Code of Procedure; the court can request the advice of the Child Protection Agency or the Agency can independently express its views to the court in family law proceedings (with the exception of alimony proceedings).

39 There are different modes: a child-friendly judgment without any complicated legal language (e.g. District Court Midden-Nederland 22.03.2017, ECLI:NL:RBMNE:2017:1541), a special paragraph with explanation for children in the judgment (e.g. Court of Appeal Arnhem-Leeuwarden 21.03.2017, ECLI:NL:GHARL:2017:257) or a separate letter that explains the judgment to the child (e.g. District Court Limburg 29.01.2019, ECLI:NL:RBLIM:2019:1253); see M.R. Bruning et al., above n. 12, pp. 75–76.

courtroom – it is common practice for the judgment to be sent to the parents and their lawyers rather than being given during a court session.

Hearing children younger than 12 years of age practically never happens, although statutory provisions provide for this possibility.[40] Nevertheless, some initiatives have occurred in recent years, including for younger children. In 2016 the Amsterdam District Court initiated a pilot to reduce the age limit. This was a success and it has now become common practice in Amsterdam to invite all children from the age of eight to be heard in the most common family law proceedings (access, relocation and parental responsibilities).[41] The District Court of The Hague started a pilot in international child abduction cases that has also become common practice since 2018.[42] All children from the age of three are heard (in two meetings) by a guardian ad litem, who subsequently informs the court about the child's views before the hearing. Children aged six and older are invited to be heard directly in court after the interview with the guardian ad litem.[43] The guardian ad litem will support children who wish to be heard in court, and will explain the court's judgment to the child. In 2018 the District Court of Overijssel commenced a pilot to actively have children participate in parenting plans by way of a 'bridge conversation', in which parents talk with their children about the parenting plan, followed by a court hearing. During the court hearing, the judge asks the parents and their lawyers about the results of the parenting plan and the conversation with their children. Research shows that in about 75% of all cases in the pilot the parents did discuss the parenting plan with their children.[44]

4. RESEARCH

In recent decades, there have been repeated calls for strengthening the procedural position of children. These proposals have always been rejected by Parliament because of a desire to protect children and to involve them as little as possible in legal proceedings.

Recently, child participation has been a more frequent research topic. The Ministry of Justice commissioned large-scale multidisciplinary research on

---

40 M.R. Bruning et al., above n. 12, pp. 78–80.

41 M.R. Bruning et al., above n. 12, pp. 162–163.

42 De Rechtspraak Blik, *Annual Report 1 January 2014–1 January 2015.*

43 A.C. Olland, 'De procedure bij de Nederlandse rechter' in F. Ibili and A.C. Olland, *Internationale Kinderontvoering*, Kluwer, Deventer 2019, pp. 81–82.

44 T. van den Berg and H. Schröder, 'Participatie van het kind bij het ouderschapsplan' in M. Jonker and F. de Kievit (eds.), *Actuele ontwikkelingen in het familierecht: Dertiende UCERF symposium*, Ars Aequi Libri, Nijmegen 2019; and https://www.rechtspraak.nl/Organisatie-en-contact/Organisatie/Rechtbanken/Rechtbank-Overijssel/Nieuws/Paginas/Proef-kinderen-betrekken-ouderschapsplan-succesvol-afgerond-.aspx.

child participation in family and child protection proceedings.[45] The findings were presented in 2020 (and are referred to below as 'the 2020 research') and shed light on the experiences, needs and opinions of professionals in legal practice.[46]

Regarding the legal standing and the initiating of family law proceedings, the research found that children rarely start proceedings and in the small number of cases where this does occur – on the basis of the above-mentioned informal access to court – it is usually in parental responsibilities and access cases. These findings confirm earlier research that pointed to unfamiliarity and scarce use of the informal legal entry by children to initiate family law proceedings.[47] Furthermore, it has become clear that requests from children through informal access to justice do not always lead to a judicial decision; judges do indeed make use of their discretionary powers to reject a child's request.[48] Judges mention that many children are probably unaware of this option.[49] Furthermore, a majority of the professionals participating in the research believed that children currently receive insufficient support during legal proceedings and that parents should not be the ones representing the child in family and child protection proceedings.[50]

In the last decade, there has been an increase in court appointments of guardians ad litem in matters relating to the care and upbringing of the child.[51] In 2017, 320 requests for guardians ad litem for state support were submitted, compared to 94 in 2014. This is also evident in legal parentage cases, where appointments rose from 306 in 2014 to 898 in 2017.[52] Whether this is a result of a change in policy favouring children's participation rights or the fact that legal parentage is more contested than before is unclear. Still, a guardian ad litem is not always appointed by the court upon request.[53] In the 2020 research, many experts wanted the criteria for appointing a guardian ad litem to represent

---

45 *Kamerstukken II* 2017/18, 33836, 24.

46 The empirical part of this research involved questionnaires and interviews; 272 participants from legal practice completed the questionnaire (judges, lawyers, guardians ad litem, social workers, Children and Youth Law Centres). Furthermore, 136 adolescents aged 16–24 years participated (43 had experienced family or child protection proceedings as a child) and 131 parents.

47 M.H.L. van den Hoogen and P.J. Montanus, 'Hoe staat het anno 2017 met de informele rechtsingang?', *Tijdschrift voor Familie- en Jeugdrecht* 2017/62, 286–289.

48 M.R. Bruning et al., above n. 12, p. 216.

49 M.R. Bruning et al., above n. 12 p. 332. This aligns with other research outcomes that found absence of knowledge about the child's procedural rights, unfamiliarity and scarce use of the informal access to court by children; e.g. Dutch Children's Ombudsman, *De bijzondere curator: een lot uit de loterij*, Den Haag 2012; M.H.L. van den Hoogen and P.J. Montanus, above n. 47; M.J. Steketee, A.M. Overgaag and K.D. Lünneman, *Minderjarigen als procespartij?*, Verwey-Jonker Instituut, Utrecht 2003; H. Bouma et al., 'Meaningful participation for children in the Dutch child protection system: A critical analysis of relevant provisions in policy documents' (2018) 79 *Child Abuse & Neglect* 279–335.

50 M.R. Bruning et al., above n. 12, p. 332.

51 M.R. Bruning et al., above n. 12, pp. 45 and 49.

52 M.R. Bruning et al., above n. 12, pp. 51–52.

53 M.R. Bruning et al., above n. 12, pp. 48–49. See also Dutch Children's Ombudsman, above n. 49.

children to be broadened. It should not be limited to the requirements of Article 1:250 of the Dutch Civil Code and should be used to support children.[54]

The 2020 research did, for the first time, ask children themselves how they felt about being heard by the court. Adolescents emphasised the importance of speaking with the judge in person (and not via an indirect hearing with an expert). Children often found the child hearing stressful; however, they felt this was not a reason not to use their right to be heard. On the contrary, almost all the adolescents indicated that they thought it was important to give their opinion. Some of the reported reasons for stress were the possibility of bumping into a parent in the court and raising problems when the situation has just become stable. Most adolescents strongly felt they were taken seriously during their conversation with the judge. They were less satisfied with the information provided to them about the procedure and the child hearing.[55] Moreover, they need support to understand the invitation letter.[56]

The duration of the child hearing in family proceedings and in child protection proceedings, the location of the child hearing and the way of hearing the child (with one or three judges) differ.[57] The empirical research also shows that the degree to which the child's opinion is taken into account varies between judges. Feedback to the child about the decision is often absent. In some exceptional cases, a 'child-friendly' judgment is prepared by the judge. In addition, children under the age of 12 are rarely heard in family law cases; the judges' discretionary power with regard to hearing children younger than 12 is sometimes applied to a limited extent in practice with regard to hearing children.[58] This is also one of the conclusions of another empirical research project, which found that the participation of children in making parenting plans is rather limited.[59] Furthermore, it is unclear to what extent judges take the views of the child into account in arriving at their decision.[60]

---

[54] M.R. Bruning et al., above n. 12, p. 332.

[55] M.R. Bruning et al., above n. 12, p. 330.

[56] M.R. Bruning et al., above n. 12, p. 182; only 16% of the parents (N=61) indicated that their child understood the invitation letter without support. Only four out of 18 youngsters who had experienced a child hearing mentioned that the invitation letter was clear and they did not need any support.

[57] M.R. Bruning et al., above n. 12, p. 330. See also M.H.L. van den Hoogen and P.J. Montanus, above n. 47, 286–289.

[58] M.R. Bruning et al., above n. 12, pp. 176–177; see also H.C.M. Aalders, 'De rechtspraktijk inzake gezagsbeëindiging vanuit kinderrechtelijk perspectief', *Tijdschrift voor Familie- en Jeugdrecht* 2018/63, 61–66; K.A.M. van der Zon and M.P. de Jong-de Kruijf, 'Hoger beroep tegen een uithuisplaatsingsbeslissing en de rol van de minderjarige', *TREMA* 2015, no. 3, 298–307; A. van Triest, 'Het kinderverhoor in het ressort Den Bosch onder de loep', *Tijdschrift voor Familie- en Jeugdrecht* 2004/26, 16–26.

[59] V.M. Smits, *Participatie van het kind bij het ouderschapsplan*, Maklu Uitgevers, Apeldoorn/Antwerp 2015, p. 286.

[60] V.M. Smits, above n. 59, p. 288.

5. CONCLUSION

The main issue is probably not whether Dutch law meets the requirements of Article 12 UNCRC, but rather how children's participation rights can be improved. There is significant political understanding that this would be a good idea. The debate on child participation should be seen in the context of the general status of children in the law. Child participation rights in Dutch family law proceedings are fragmented and vary depending on the types of proceedings (such as international child abduction, parentage, custody and care, and access). In family law legislation a patchwork construction of instruments and participation tools, which are not aligned, can be observed. In practice, many initiatives to improve child participation in family law proceedings can be seen over the last decade. Judges are more open to hearing children in court and are better trained.

Child participation can be promoted in different ways. It calls for joint efforts by the judiciary, solicitors and academics to rethink current policy, legislation and practice. Research shows that children do have positive experiences in court, but indicates that further improvements are needed. For example, judges could more often hear children younger than 12. Even though there is child-friendly information available on the Internet on the hearing by the court, it is often not easy to find information on children's informal access to court and the possibility of appointing a guardian ad litem. Therefore, work is needed to better inform children about their procedural rights and about what to expect when being heard in court. An issue to be considered is how courts can communicate effectively with children. Invitation letters are one way, but digital and online means could be explored as alternatives, and help avoid children being dependent on their parents handing the letter over to them. The invitation letter (or other mode of communication) should be made more child-friendly in, for example, its use of language. Once that is achieved, ways of improving communication of the outcome of the case to the child should be considered. This is not necessarily a task that rests solely with courts; solicitors could play a role since they are also the ones explaining the decision to the parents. Another issue needing attention is how children are involved in out-of-court proceedings.

There should be greater coherency about the relevance of the age of children in civil law, criminal law and youth law and their right to participate. What can minors be presumed to be accountable for and what rights and duties come with that? This perspective would enable a broader discussion on the role of minors and adults, seen in the context of rising number of divorces, and societal expectations about the increasing influence of children's rights and individualisation. We should critically reflect on the main principle that parents represent children in the legal world. This is probably a good starting point in balancing all the interests involved, which are manifold: individual rights of children and parents, but also costs and efforts balanced against outcomes. Starting from the principle that parents are usually good representatives of children's interests, a number of scenarios could be identified in which the interests of parents and children are more likely not to align, including in complex separations and divorces. The question then is: what type of participation is preferable? Direct hearing by the court is one of the options that must be available to children, but it is necessary to rethink the other options: the guardian ad litem, giving legal standing to children, informal access to the court, and mediation. The outcome should be less complicated and less of a patchwork, but rather a consistent and effective way of promoting children's participation rights.

NEW ZEALAND

Nicola TAYLOR

1. INTRODUCTION

New Zealand is a small South Pacific nation with a population of 5 million people.[1] The majority of the population is of European descent (70%), with indigenous Māori being the largest minority (16%), followed by Asians (15%) and Pacific Islanders (9%). There are 1,124,000 children aged 0–17 years, comprising 23% of the population.[2]

New Zealand was settled from islands in the tropical Pacific around 750 years ago and later mapped by the British explorer James Cook in 1769–1770, leading

---

1 Stats NZ, *National Population Estimates: At 31 March 2020*, https://www.stats.govt.nz/information-releases/national-population-estimates-at-31-march-2020-infoshare-tables.

2 Office of the Children's Commissioner, *Population, Ages and Ethnicities of Children*, Wellington 2018.

to colonisation by Britain from the 18th century.[3] Constitutionally, New Zealand began as an extension of the Australian colony of New South Wales, but became a separate colony in 1841 after the Treaty of Waitangi 1840 was signed between the British Crown and Māori Chiefs. Indigenous rights stemming from this Treaty, which value Māori *tamariki* (children) as *taonga* (treasures), are central to New Zealand's contemporary social, cultural and economic development and have significantly influenced legal developments over the past half-century.[4] The New Zealand Parliament (the House of Representatives) has jurisdiction over all aspects of law nationally. The jurisdiction of the Family Court, introduced in 1981 as a specialist court, also extends across the entire country.[5] A range of dispute resolution processes is available within the Family Court and, since extensive reforms in 2014, out of court as well (primarily through Family Dispute Resolution (FDR) mediation).

Almost half of all divorces in New Zealand involve children.[6] In 2018, the Family Court granted divorces to 7,455 couples, affecting 5,598 children under 17 years of age.[7] This was 7.7 divorces for every 1,000 estimated existing marriages and civil unions. The number of children affected by the separation of parents in de facto relationships is unknown, but the separation rate for de facto relationships is thought to be higher than the divorce rate.[8]

Guardianship is the legal concept setting out the duties, powers, rights and responsibilities that a parent of the child has in relation to the upbringing of the child.[9] Guardians must act jointly, by consulting wherever practicable with the aim of securing agreement, regarding important matters affecting the child.[10] When parents separate, then day-to-day care (who the child will live with) and contact (when the child will see, stay or talk with their non-resident parent) needs to be determined. Shared care is gradually increasing in New Zealand, but most children continue to live with one parent (usually their mother) and have contact with their other parent (usually their father).[11] If the parents/guardians

---

3 P. Mein Smith, *Australia and New Zealand – Shared Colonial History*, Te Ara – The Encyclopedia of New Zealand, Wellington 2012.

4 A current challenge is how best to enable culturally appropriate child participation practices in the context of collectively oriented cultures like those of Māori and Pacific peoples.

5 N.J. Taylor, 'Establishment of the New Zealand Family Court' (2006) 5(7) *New Zealand Family Law Journal* 169–80.

6 Law Commission, *Relationships and Families in Contemporary New Zealand: He hononga tangata, he hononga whānau i Aotearoa o nāianei – Study Paper*, Wellington 2017.

7 Stats NZ *Marriages, Civil Unions, and Divorces: Year Ended December 2018*, 2019, http://www.stats.govt.nz/information-releases/marriages-civil-unions-and-divorces-year-ended-december-2018.

8 Law Commission, above n. 6, p. 26.

9 Care of Children Act 2004, ss 15–20.

10 Care of Children Act 2004, s 16(5) – these important matters include the child's name, place of residence, medical treatment, education, culture, language and religion.

11 Law Commission, above n. 6, p. 58.

are unable to agree on their children's post-separation care arrangements, then dispute resolution processes can be utilised out of court (e.g. counselling, mediation) or by application to the Family Court, where parenting orders can be made by consent or imposed by the judge at a defended hearing.[12] When family law disputes arise between separated parents over the care of their children, the welfare and best interests of the child, in their particular circumstances, is the first and paramount consideration.[13] Decisions must be made in a timeframe appropriate to the child's sense of time.[14] The current emphasis in family transitions is on maintaining, where possible, a child's enduring and meaningful relationships with both parents.

New Zealand has a long history of child participation in family law proceedings via liberal statutory provisions governing the ascertainment of children's views and the appointment of a lawyer to represent the child.[15] In addition, judicial meetings with children are common within the Family Court. The Family Court can order a psychological report to help inform the judge's decision,[16] but this specialist report cannot solely, or primarily, seek to ascertain the child's wishes.[17] Opportunities for children to engage in out-of-court dispute resolution processes are much more recent, having only been introduced into FDR mediation services since 2016.[18]

2. STATUTORY PROVISIONS

2.1. PRIVATE LAW DISPUTES

New Zealand's commitment to ascertaining children's views in private law disputes predates the UN Convention on the Rights of the Child 1989 (UNCRC). Previously, the Guardianship Act 1968 required the Family Court to ascertain the child's wishes if the child was able to express them and to take them into account to such extent as the court thought fit, having regard to the age and maturity of the child.[19] In practice, this meant that children could have their

---

12 Care of Children Act 2004, ss 47–52.

13 Care of Children Act 2004, s 4. Section 5 sets out the six principles relevant to determining what is in a child's welfare and best interests.

14 Care of Children Act 2004, s 4(2)(a)(i).

15 N.J. Taylor, *Care of Children: Families, Dispute Resolution and the Family Court*, PhD thesis, University of Otago, Dunedin 2005.

16 Care of Children Act 2004, s 133 – medical, psychiatric and cultural reports can also be sought; and social work reports under s 132.

17 Care of Children Act 2004, s 133(6)(e).

18 N.J. Taylor, 'Child Participation: Overcoming Disparity Between New Zealand's Family Court and Out-of-court Dispute Resolution Processes' (2017) 25 *The International Journal of Children's Rights* 658–671.

19 Guardianship Act 1968, s 23(2).

wishes ignored purely on the basis they were not of sufficient age and maturity.[20] However, New Zealand's ratification of the UNCRC in 1993, and the growing body of research and theory on children's participation, subsequently led to a more expansive statutory provision being introduced when the Care of Children Act 2004 replaced the Guardianship Act 1968 in 2005.[21] The new world-leading provision dispensed with the traditional 'age and maturity' criteria, changed 'wishes' to the broader concept of 'views', and required the Family Court to take any of the child's expressed views into account regardless of the child's age:

> In proceedings involving the guardianship of, or the role of providing day-to-day care for, or contact with, a child; … a child must be given reasonable opportunities to express views on matters affecting the child; and any views the child expresses (either directly or through a representative) must be taken into account.[22]

The child's views are not, however, determinative, but rather contribute to the weight of evidence considered by the judge. This approach to the ascertainment of children's views also applies in relocation disputes where one parent wants to move, with the children, a significant distance away from the other parent, either within New Zealand or overseas. The child's place of residence is an important matter[23] on which guardians must agree, so, when agreement is not possible, the courts scrutinise applications to relocate very carefully because the move, if allowed, will significantly impact on the child's relationship and contact with the left-behind parent.[24] The child's views about the proposed move will be taken into careful consideration by the judge, who then decides whether to allow or decline the application depending on what is in the child's welfare and best interests.[25]

2.2. INTERNATIONAL CHILD ABDUCTION

The Family Court deals with international child abduction cases quite differently from guardianship, day-to-day care, contact and relocation disputes,

---

20 N.J. Taylor, above n. 15.

21 N.J. Taylor, 'What Do We Know About Involving Children and Young People in Family Law Decision making? A Research Update' (2006) 20(2) *Australian Journal of Family Law* 154–178.

22 Care of Children Act 2004, s 6(1) and (2).

23 Care of Children Act 2004, s 16(5).

24 N.J. Taylor, M. Gollop and R.M. Henaghan, *Relocation Following Parental Separation: The Welfare and Best Interests of Children*, Research Report for New Zealand Law Foundation, Children's Issues Centre and Faculty of Law, University of Otago, Dunedin 2010.

25 R.M. Henaghan, 'Relocation Cases – The Rhetoric and the Reality of a Child's Best Interests – A View From the Bottom of the World' (2011) 23(2) *Child and Family Law Quarterly* 226–250.

as New Zealand acceded to the 1980 Hague Convention on the Civil Aspects of International Child Abduction in 1991.[26] As these Hague cases involve summary proceedings, a lawyer is not always appointed to represent the child, the court will not request a specialist psychological report, and the paramount principle governing the court's decision-making is not the child's welfare and best interests. Rather, the focus is on returning the abducted child as quickly as possible to their country of habitual residence so that issues of parental responsibility can be resolved by the courts there. Children who object to being returned[27] always have a lawyer appointed to represent them. This Lawyer for the Child ascertains the child's views and, if the child wishes, can also arrange for them to meet with the judge. The court will take the views into account provided the child is considered to be of sufficient age and maturity for their views to be given weight. However, even if the child's objection is made out, exercise of the judicial discretion can result in the child being returned anyway.

2.3. ADOPTION

Historically, a child over the age of 12 years had to consent to their adoption,[28] but this right later became discretionary,[29] and was subsequently removed entirely by the Adoption Act 1955. Instead, the welfare and interests of the child have to be promoted by the adoption, with due consideration being given to the wishes of the child, having regard to their age and understanding.[30] This provision, which was the first time the ascertainment of children's wishes was prescribed in New Zealand family law, remains current today. Children's wishes are usually elicited via the social worker's report prepared for the Family Court.[31] Under the court's inherent jurisdiction, Counsel to Assist can also be appointed to meet the child and obtain their wishes, or there may be a judicial interview with the child. These steps are usually only taken when the adoption application is defended, complex or opposed by the social worker, for example on cultural grounds. Few adoptions, other than step-parent and intercountry adoptions and those by commissioning parents in surrogacy contexts, currently occur in New Zealand. There is, therefore, very little engagement by children in adoption proceedings.

---

26 Guardianship Amendment Act 1991. This was subsequently replaced by subpart 4 of the Care of Children Act 2004.

27 Care of Children Act 2004, s 106(1)(d) – this provision is used sparingly.

28 Adoption Act 1895, s 5(4).

29 Statutes Amendment Act 1942, s 15.

30 Adoption Act 1955, s 11(b).

31 Adoption Act 1955, s 10.

3. MODES OF CHILD PARTICIPATION

3.1. REPRESENTATION FORMS OF PARTICIPATION

3.1.1. Lawyer for the Child

In the family justice system, children's views are most commonly ascertained by a Lawyer for the Child – an experienced family lawyer who is appointed by the Family Court to represent the child or sibling group in proceedings under the Care of Children Act 2004.[32] They are appointed in every case that is likely to reach court when there are concerns for the safety or wellbeing of the child and the court considers the appointment necessary.[33] No age thresholds apply as Lawyers for the Child must meet with every child they are appointed to represent (including a baby or toddler) unless, because of exceptional circumstances, a judge directs that this is inappropriate.[34] The child can choose not to express any view to their lawyer, but any view they do express that is relevant to the proceedings is communicated by the lawyer to the court.[35]

The lawyer will usually meet the child more than once, for example at each parent's home or by asking each parent to bring the child to the lawyer's office. Sometimes the meeting occurs at the child's school. No-one other than the lawyer and child(ren) is present at these meetings. With sibling groups, the Lawyer for the Child often initially meets with the children together, for example to explain their role and to get a sense of the sibling dynamics, and then spends time with each child individually to give them the opportunity to express their views privately. The notes the lawyer makes of what the child tells them, and of their observations and enquiries, help form the basis of the report they prepare for the Family Court.

Best Practice Guidelines further elaborate on the role of the Lawyer for the Child so as to promote quality and consistency in practice across the country.[36] The lawyer is to provide independent representation and advice to the child in a manner that the lawyer considers promotes the child's welfare and best interests. The lawyer also has a duty to ensure that any views expressed by the child to the lawyer (and not expressed to another person, such as a psychologist, social worker or teacher), on matters affecting the child and relevant to the proceedings, are communicated to the Family Court. The Lawyer for the Child

---

32 Family Court Practice Note, *Lawyer for the Child: Selection, Appointment and Other Matters*, Principal Family Court Judge, Wellington 2020.

33 Care of Children Act 2004, s 7(a) and (b).

34 Family Courts Act 1980, s 9B(2) and (3).

35 Family Courts Act 1980, s 9B(1)(b).

36 *Lawyer for the Child Best Practice Guidelines*, Family Law Section Executive Committee, Wellington 2018.

has a duty to ensure that all factors relevant to the child's welfare and best interests are before the court. Should there be a conflict between the child's views and what the lawyer considers to be the child's best interests, the lawyer must attempt to resolve this with the child. If it is not possible to reconcile these, then it is sometimes possible for a second lawyer to be appointed to represent the child's welfare and best interests.

Prior to the hearing, the Lawyer for the Child advises the court whether it is appropriate for the child to meet the judge and advises the parties and the court of the child's views about such a meeting.[37] If a judicial meeting is held, then the lawyer will be present with the judge and the child(ren).

The Lawyer for the Child prepares a written report for the court and can call and cross-examine the parties and any witnesses. At the conclusion of the case, the lawyer meets with the child again to explain the outcome and the effect of any Parenting Order to the child in a manner, and in language, that the child understands and to inform them of their right of appeal against the court's decision.[38] The Lawyer for the Child's appointment then concludes. The cost is usually met by the government. However, judges are required to consider whether the parties should contribute to the cost of the appointment and can make a Costs Contribution Order whereby the parties pay two thirds and the government pays the other third.[39]

3.1.2. FDR Mediation

Children's participation in out-of-court dispute resolution processes has only recently emerged in New Zealand as a result of 2014 reforms to the family justice system that shifted the focus away from the Family Court and introduced a new FDR mediation service for resolving parenting and guardianship matters.[40] An approved FDR provider (a mediator) assists separated parents to identify the issues in dispute, facilitates discussion, and helps them to reach an agreement that focuses on the needs of their children. FDR is mandatory for most parties prior to commencing Family Court proceedings. However, in cases where it is inappropriate (such as where there are safety risks or a significant power imbalance), then the parties can bypass mediation and go directly to court on the urgent track. The cost of FDR is NZ$897, but this is fully subsidised for parties who meet the eligibility test for out-of-court support.

The 2014 reforms were disappointingly silent on children's participation, but when the Ministry of Justice introduced a new FDR 12-hour service model

37 *Lawyer for the Child Best Practice Guidelines*, above n. 36, para. 10.

38 Care of Children Act 2004, s 55(4); *Lawyer for the Child Best Practice Guidelines*, above n. 36, para. 6.7.

39 The Costs Contribution Order can also require the parties to pay toward the cost of specialist reports or the appointment of lawyer to assist the court.

40 Family Dispute Resolution Act and Regulations 2013.

in 2016, which increased the hours and flexibility of the FDR process, child participation was identified (along with cultural competency) as one of the new areas of practice critical for FDR mediators to implement.[41] As a result, the national FDR suppliers (agencies who are responsible for FDR intake, screening and mediation) each developed their own models of child participation. The process starts during the FDR assessment phase when the parents and mediator discuss options for how the children's voices can be incorporated into the mediation – including the children having no involvement, the parents or a trusted family friend speaking on their behalf, use of a child specialist, or the children attending part of the mediation (which is rare). If it is agreed that a child-inclusive approach is appropriate, each service then implements its specific model. At the FDR Centre, a Child Inclusion Specialist, who is specifically trained and experienced in child-inclusive practice, meets with both parents and with the child separately, provides feedback to the parents, attends the FDR mediation to speak on behalf of the child, and later provides feedback to the child on the outcomes agreed by the parents to ensure the child understands the agreements reached and to offer support.[42] At Fairway Resolution, a Voice of Child Specialist (VOCS) meets with the child and then attends the mediation for a short period to share what the children want their parents to hear when considering decisions which affect them.[43] At the Family Works Resolution Service, a Child Consultant undertakes a one-off, 45-minute meeting to ascertain a child's thoughts and feelings in relation to care arrangements and key relationships.[44] They then prepare a brief, legally privileged report for the family mediator, which is summarised to the parents at the first mediation meeting. None of these child participation processes incur any additional cost for parties eligible for public FDR funding.

3.2. DIRECT FORMS OF PARTICIPATION

3.2.1. *Judicial Meetings*

Over the past 15 years, judicial meetings with children have become increasingly common when separated parents are involved in contested proceedings within the Family Court.[45] The child is asked by their lawyer whether they would like to meet with the judge and, if they do, the lawyer makes the arrangements with

41 N.J. Taylor, above n. 18.

42 www.fdrc.co.nz/parenting-and-guardianship-fdr-mediation/voice-of-the-child/.

43 www.fairwayresolution.com/got-a-dispute/family-disputes/giving-children-a-say.

44 www.resolution.org.nz/family-mediation/child-consultation.

45 N.J. Taylor and J. Caldwell, 'Judicial Meetings with Children: Documenting Practice within the New Zealand Family Court (2013) 3 *New Zealand Law Review* 445–463.

the court and is also present at the meeting. Since the Lawyer for the Child already has a relationship with the child, and has ascertained their views, they can be very helpful in facilitating the discussion with the judge. Some judges engage in a 'meet and greet' role with the child, while others use the opportunity to directly hear the child's views and to better understand the child as a person.[46] Most judges meet the child in their chambers, but some use a vacant courtroom if they wish to use court facilities to audio-record the meeting. Recording was initially recommended, but now occurs much less frequently as judges find it can unduly formalise the discussion and create delays awaiting receipt of the typed transcript.[47] Judges instead provide the parents with oral feedback when the hearing next resumes and some prepare a formal written 'minute' for the record. Judges report that it is rare for a child to request confidentiality.[48] They tell the child at the start of the meeting that any information that is disclosed will need to be shared with the parents, but they reassure the child they will do this in a sensitive way. Some judges also check with the child at the end of the meeting whether there is anything they would prefer not to be passed onto the parents or they discuss with the child an acceptable way of conveying the information. Judges have received skills-based training in child interviewing techniques, follow written guidelines[49] and report very positively about their experiences of meeting with children.[50] Children are informed of the outcome of the case by the Lawyer for the Child and one, or both, of their parents. Very occasionally, a judge will ask to meet with the child to explain the decision to them personally.

3.2.2. *Child Litigating on Own Behalf*

It is uncommon for a child to be a party to family law proceedings in New Zealand as it is usually the child's parents/caregivers/guardians who are the parties in a litigated parenting dispute. However, this is possible if the child comes within the category of 'any other person' granted leave by the court to apply for a Parenting Order (for example, for contact)[51] or to have a person appointed as their guardian.[52]

---

46 J. Caldwell and N.J. Taylor, 'Natural Justice and Judicial Meetings with Children: Documenting Practice within the New Zealand Family Court' (2013) 7(11) *New Zealand Family Law Journal* 264–271.

47 J. Caldwell and N.J. Taylor, above n. 46, p. 267.

48 J. Caldwell and N.J. Taylor, above n. 46, p. 265.

49 P.F. Boshier, *Judges Guidelines: Decisions with Children*, Chambers of the Principal Family Court Judge, Wellington 2007; N.J. Taylor, *Judicial Meetings with Children. Research Update*, Family Court Judges' Benchbook, Wellington 2020.

50 J. Caldwell and N.J. Taylor, above n. 46, p. 270.

51 Care of Children Act 2004, s 47(1)(e).

52 Care of Children Act 2004, s 27(1)(a).

A child does have an independent right of appeal to the High Court, against a decision of the Family Court, because they are a child to whom the court proceedings related.[53] The Lawyer for the Child informs the child of this right at the conclusion of the case and also provides them with advice on the merits of pursuing an appeal, via a litigation guardian.[54] If leave is granted, the child then becomes a party for the purposes of the appeal. However, such appeals are rare, partly because their funding is problematic. Sometimes one parent might pay if, for example, they consider their child's appeal may advance their desired outcome. Other times, counsel may successfully argue for limited state funding to meet their costs or simply act on a pro bono basis.

4. RESEARCH

A range of empirical and socio-legal research on child participation has been undertaken in New Zealand over the past 20 years. The Children's Issues Centre ascertained the perspectives of 154 children and young people aged 5–18 years on their level of inclusion in parental and/or court decision-making processes regarding their post-separation living arrangements.[55] The children wanted to be consulted on matters that affected them, to be listened to, and to have their views respected by their parents and family justice professionals. Another study examined children's perspectives on their legal representation in post-separation parenting disputes.[56] Case law analyses on cases involving day-to-day care, contact, relocation, family violence and alienation have investigated the expression of children's views, appointment of the Lawyer for the Child and use of judicial meetings.[57] Despite the removal of age and maturity criteria in New Zealand's key statutory provision, children's views were most likely to be followed when the children were aged 11 or older and their views were strongly and consistently held. Usually these views revolved around wanting to spend more time with their non-resident parent. Young children aged under seven years tended to have their views ignored, as did those whose views were considered to be influenced, coached or aligned. Interviews with the entire

---

53 Care of Children Act 2004, s143(3).

54 *Lawyer for the Child Best Practice Guidelines*, above n. 36, para. 6.7.

55 M. Gollop, A.B. Smith and N.J. Taylor, 'Children's Involvement in Custody and Access Arrangements after Parental Separation' (2000) 12(4) *Child and Family Law Quarterly* 383–399.

56 N.J. Taylor, M. Gollop and A.B. Smith, 'Children and Young People's Perspectives on Their Legal Representation' in A.B. Smith, N.J. Taylor and M. Gollop (eds.), *Children's Voices: Research, Policy and Practice*, Pearson Education, Auckland 2000, pp. 110–133.

57 A. Robinson and R.M. Henaghan, 'Children: Heard But Not Listened To? An Analysis of Children's Views Under s 6 of the Care of Children Act 2004' (2011) 7(2) *New Zealand Family Law Journal* 39–52.

Family Court bench to document their practice of meeting with children found positive judicial attitudes to these meetings and a general sense of ease that the dictates of natural justice were being met.[58] Just one child-inclusive model, predicated on family collaboration principles, has been empirically piloted, but this predated the introduction of FDR.[59] More recently, doctoral research has explored the history and scope of child participation provisions and proposed a new seven-step model to better ensure Article 12 compliance in mediation and Family Court settings.[60] A study evaluating New Zealand's 2014 reforms from the perspective of 364 family justice professionals found that children's participatory rights were being breached and greater opportunities for children to have a voice in out-of-court processes were required.[61]

5. POLICY OR PRACTICE DEVELOPMENTS

The 2014 reforms have recently been reviewed by an Independent Panel appointed by the Minister of Justice in 2018.[62] Despite these reforms being intended to be more responsive to the needs and interests of children caught up in parental disputes over their care or contact, the Panel found there was no legislative requirement regarding children's participation in decision-making and no certainty that children's voices are heard.[63]

> Child inclusive practice is developing in an ad hoc way, and there has been no resolution of critical issues relating to children's participation, such as how they might be involved, models for child-inclusive mediation and appropriate professional development and experience requirements for practitioners working with children.[64]

The Panel recommended that legislation be amended to include children's participation in decision-making as a guiding principle, with explicit reference to the UNCRC.[65] In addition, they suggested the Care of Children Act 2004 be amended to require parents and guardians to consult children on important

---

58 N.J. Taylor and J. Caldwell, above n. 45; J. Caldwell and N.J. Taylor, above n. 46.

59 J. Goldson, *'Hello, I'm a voice, let me talk' – Child-inclusive Mediation in Family Separation*, Families Commission Innovative Practice Report No. 1/06, Wellington 2006.

60 D. Inder, *Children's Participation in the Context of Private Law Disputes in the New Zealand Family Justice System*, PhD thesis, University of Otago, Dunedin 2020.

61 N.J. Taylor, M. Gollop and N. Liebergreen, *Parenting Arrangements after Separation Study: Evaluating the 2014 Family Law Reforms – Family Justice Professionals' Perspectives*, Research Report for New Zealand Law Foundation, Children's Issues Centre, University of Otago, Dunedin 2019.

62 Independent Panel, *Te Korowai Ture ā-Whānau: The Final Report of the Independent Panel Examining the 2014 Family Justice Reforms*, Ministry of Justice, Wellington 2019.

63 Independent Panel Report, above n. 62, p. 34, para. 25.

64 Independent Panel Report, above n. 62, p. 34, para. 28.

65 Independent Panel Report, above n. 62, p. 35, Recommendation 2.

matters affecting them, taking account of the children's age and maturity.[66] The Panel also directed the Ministry of Justice, in conjunction with relevant experts and key stakeholders, to undertake a stocktake of appropriate models of child participation, including at FDR, as a priority.[67] This stocktake should include consideration of key principles for children's participation, including requiring professionals to promote children's participation, consideration of how children's views should be taken into account in cases where there is family violence, and development of a best-practice toolkit co-designed with children and young people.

The Minister of Justice responded to these recommendations in August 2020 with the Family Court (Supporting Children in Court) Legislation Bill.[68] While this Bill does not address many of the Panel's excellent recommendations, it does propose amending the Care of Children Act 2004 to insert a new principle relating to the child's welfare and best interests – a child should have reasonable opportunities to participate in decisions affecting their care and welfare and their views should be taken into account commensurate with their age and maturity.[69] The Bill, when passed by Parliament, will also insert three new sections in the Care of Children Act 2004 to:

- state that the purpose of section 6 is to implement Article 12 of the UNCRC;[70]
- require that, when appointing a lawyer to represent a child, a lawyer's personality, cultural background, training and experience must be taken into account;[71] and
- require that, so far as is reasonably practicable, a lawyer appointed to represent a child must explain the nature of the proceedings to the child in a manner that the child is most likely to understand.[72]

In addition, the Bill proposes amending the Family Dispute Resolution Act 2013 to require a FDR provider to make every endeavour to facilitate participation by children who are the subject of a family dispute in the discussions between the parties during a FDR process.[73]

---

66 Independent Panel Report, above n. 62, p. 35, Recommendation 3.

67 Independent Panel Report, above n. 62, p. 35, Recommendation 4.

68 Hon. A. Little, Minister of Justice, *Bill introduced to fix National's Family Court reform failures*, Parliamentary media release, 6 August 2020, https://www.beehive.govt.nz/release/bill-introduced-fix-national%E2%80%99s-family-court-reform-failures. See also: *$62 million package to support families through the Family Court*, Parliamentary media release, 15 May 2020, https://www.beehive.govt.nz/release/62-million-package-support-families-through-family-court.

69 Clause 4, which will amend s 5 of the Care of Children Act 2004.

70 Clause 6, which will insert s 6(1AAA).

71 Clause 7, which will insert s 7(2).

72 Clause 8, which will insert s 7AA.

73 Clause 11 amends s 11.

6. CONCLUSION

New Zealand has had a longstanding commitment to child participation in Family Court proceedings involving separated parents, primarily via the appointment of the Lawyer for the Child and judicial meetings. The key statutory provision governing the ascertainment of children's views[74] adopts the language of the UNCRC and gives effect to Article 12.[75] Engaging children in out-of-court dispute resolution processes has been a more recent development in New Zealand, made possible by the introduction of FDR mediation in the 2014 reforms and its subsequent expansion in 2016. While this was undoubtedly a step forward in addressing the previous imbalance between child-participatory in-court and out-of-court processes, it has occurred in a legislative and policy vacuum that has allowed different models of practice to emerge across each of the FDR suppliers depending on their resources and philosophy regarding child engagement. It is therefore unsurprising that, in 2019, the Independent Panel described the situation as 'ad hoc' and called for a stocktake of appropriate models of child participation across the family justice sector. There is, as yet, no momentum to incorporate the UNCRC into New Zealand's domestic law, but the Panel's report does provide a sound blueprint for the future development of child participatory best practice in a consistent and rigorous fashion across the country. Once enacted by Parliament, the 2020 Bill will elevate children's participation as a guiding principle of our key private law and dispute resolution statutes.[76] However, its other clauses primarily give effect to existing practice. Disappointingly, the Bill represents a missed opportunity to implement the Panel's more extensive recommendations, which we can now only hope may nevertheless still influence child participation policy and practice in coming years.

74 Care of Children Act 2004, s 6.

75 Independent Panel, above n. 62, p. 35, para. 30. This will be made even more explicit when clause 6 of the Family Court (Supporting Children in Court) Legislation Bill inserts s 6(1AAA) into the Care of Children Act 2004 to state that the purpose of s 6 is to implement Article 12 of the UNCRC.

76 Care of Children Act 2004 and Family Dispute Resolution Act 2013.

NORWAY

Anna Nylund

1. INTRODUCTION

Norway has a population of 5.3 million people, of whom 1.1 million are children, i.e. under the age of 18. Almost half of marriages in the country end in divorce; the rest end by the death of one of the partners. In 2018, the number of new marriages was 20,949, and there were 10,630 separations and 9,545 divorces. The number of minor children experiencing their parents' divorce was 8,900.[1] To file for divorce, spouses must either first file for separation and then wait 12 months or have been separated for at least two years.[2] The prevalence of cohabitation is also high: 29% of children living with both parents have unmarried parents.[3] The divorce statistics do not therefore reflect the number of children whose parents cease to cohabit.

1 Statistisk sentralbyrå, *Barn som opplevde skilsmisse*, https://www.ssb.no/statbank/table/05703/tableViewLayout1/.

2 Statistisk sentralbyrå, *Ekteskap og skilsmisser*, https://www.ssb.no/befolkning/statistikker/ekteskap/aar-hovudtal.

3 Statistisk sentralbyrå, *Barn 0-17 år med antall foreldre i familien*, https://www.ssb.no/statbank/table/06239/tableViewLayout1/. A registered partnership is equivalent to marriage.

In 2017, 12,647 families participated in mandatory post-separation mediation; almost half (47%) of the parents in these cases were cohabitants.[4] Cohabiting parents tend to be younger and to have younger children at the time of separation than married parents, but otherwise there are no significant demographic differences between the two groups. Parents who have cohabited need a higher number of mediation sessions than parents who have been married, which is likely to result from their shorter experience with co-parenting.[5] Researchers estimate that 20–25% of separated families have high levels of conflict, including negative emotions as well as disruptive and destructive conflict and communication patterns.[6]

In 2019, 75 children from 47 families were registered as abducted from Norway. Additionally, 11 children from 11 families were registered as abducted to Norway.[7]

In Norway, both parents are usually employed outside the home, and two thirds of employed women work full time.[8] Children aged one to nine years have a right to high-quality, affordable day care and after-school care. Health services are free of charge for children under 16, and schooling, including higher education, is also free. Social benefits and services are universal and individual.[9] After separation, both spouses are expected to provide for themselves and for their children. Spousal maintenance is practically non-existent. Hence, economic issues are seldom subject to overt litigation. Most divorces do not require any involvement of a lawyer; rather, one or both spouses file for separation and divorce, and afterwards the spouses agree on the division of the matrimonial property.[10]

Out-of-court mediation is mandatory for separating families with children under the age of 16. Participation in mediation is a prerequisite both for

---

4 Statistisk sentralbyrå, *Avsluttede mekling og deltakere, etter meklingsinstans*, https://www.ssb.no/statbank/table/10936/tableViewLayout1/.

5 M. Ådnanes, G.M.D. Haugen, H. Jensberg, T.L. Husum and M. Rantalaiho, 'Hva karakteriserer vanskelige saker i foreldremekling, og er meklingsordningen godt nok tilpasset?' [2011] *Fokus på familien* 86, 109.

6 M.S. Helland and I. Borren, *Foreldrekonflikt; identifisering av konfliktnivåer, sentrale kjennetegn og risikofaktorer hos høykonfliktpar*, Rapport 2015:3, Folkehelseinstituttet, Oslo 2015.

7 Regjeringen, *Statistikk for internasjonal barnebortføring*, https://www.regjeringen.no/no/sub/barnebortforing/nettsider-og-litteratur/statistikk-for-internasjonal-barnebortforing/statistikk-for-barnebortforingar-20052019/tal-pa-barnebortforingssaker-20052019/id2690841/.

8 Statistisk sentralbyrå, *Flere heltidsarbeidende*, https://www.ssb.no/arbeid-og-lonn/artikler-og-publikasjoner/flere-heltidsarbeidende.

9 For more detailed information see, for example, J.H. Petersen, 'Nordic Model of Welfare States' in P. Letto-Vanamo, D. Tamm and B.O.G. Mortensen (eds.), *Nordic Law in European Context*, Springer, Cham 2019, pp. 21–39.

10 For more information see, for example, I. Lund-Andersen and A. Kronborg, 'Marriage and Family Relations' in P. Letto-Vanamo, D. Tamm and B.O.G. Mortensen (eds.), *Nordic Law in European Context*, Springer, Cham 2019, pp. 97–113.

registration as a single parent and for court proceedings on custody, residence, contact and relocation. Mandatory out-of-court and pre-filing mediation lasts one to seven hours depending on the needs and wishes of the family; the average duration is approximately two hours.[11] After the first hour, the parents receive a certificate of attendance regardless of the outcome and progress. The certificate enables the parents to file child custody proceedings in court.[12] The mediator has discretion to exempt families from mediation, for instance when the mediator suspects that mediation would be inappropriate due to the presence of violence, child neglect and so forth, or it would be unsuccessful for other reasons. If one parent does not attend mediation, the mediator has the discretion to issue a certificate of attendance.[13]

Mediation takes place at one of the state-funded Family Counselling Offices or with a registered mediator.[14] Registered mediators include psychologists, social workers, lawyers and members of the clergy. Most families (80%) choose the Family Counselling Offices, which offer mediation free of charge in child-friendly premises.[15]

A parent can file a case at court within six months of the first mediation session. After this time limit has passed, the parents must return for further mediation before filing for litigation (pre-filing mediation). The same mediation process as that used in post-separation mediation is applicable for pre-filing mediation.

Less than 20% of separating families start court proceedings.[16] Courts use court-connected mediation as the main method of dispute resolution, unless the case involves child abuse or neglect. The court appoints an expert to mediate, provide advice to the parents and assess the family's situation. Sometimes the expert and the judge co-mediate.[17] If mediation is unsuccessful, or is considered inappropriate due to child abuse or neglect, the case proceeds to regular court proceedings. The expert continues to be involved in the case, now providing an evaluation of the family and the best interests of the child.

---

11 Barne-, ungdoms- og familiedirektoratet, *Årsrapport 2018*, https://www.bufdir.no/globalassets/documents/arsrapport-2018.pdf, p. 31.

12 For more details, see A. Nylund, 'A Dispute Systems Design Perspective on Norwegian Child Custody Mediation' in A. Nylund, K. Ervasti and L. Adrian (eds.), *Nordic Mediation Research*, Springer, Cham 2018, pp. 9–26.

13 Decree on mediation in accordance with the Marriage Act and the Children Act (Forskrift om mekling etter ekteskapsloven og barneloven) FOR-2006-12-18-1478, ss 7 and 8.

14 Lawyers, social workers, psychologists and priests provide family mediation services. Mediators at Family Service Offices are psychologists and social workers.

15 Statistisk sentralbyrå, above n. 4.

16 Annually, about 12,500 mandatory out-of-court mediations are held, and the number of court cases is approximately 2,600. However, some are repeat cases.

17 For more details, see C. Bernt, 'Custody Mediation in Norwegian Courts: A Conglomeration of Roles and Processes' in A. Nylund, K. Ervasti and L. Adrian (eds.), *Nordic Mediation Research*, Springer, Cham 2018, pp. 105–32.

2. STATUTORY PROVISIONS

The Norwegian Constitution,[18] section 104, protects the right to be heard for all children. The provision is a shorthand for Article 12 of the UN Convention of the Rights of the Child (UNCRC). However, participation is narrowly construed and uses the term 'right to be heard' instead of the broader term 'right to participate'.[19]

The Children Act,[20] section 31, regulates child participation in family law in more detail. Children have a right to express their views in matters concerning themselves when they have become mature enough to form their own opinion or, at the latest, when they turn seven years old. Weight is given to the views of children according to their age and maturity. Particular weight must be given to the views of children aged 12 years or older. As a rule, the parents represent children in decision-making processes, and the obligation to hear children rests on the parents. However, authorities do not control whether and how parents fulfil their obligations.

The Children Act, section 51, mandates separating parents with children under the age of 16 to attend mediation. However, the Act does not explicitly direct mediators and courts to enable children to participate in decision-making, nor does it give any indication as to the forms of participation to be used.

There is no direct obligation to let children under the age of seven participate in mediation; consequently, participation rates are significantly lower for young children. However, some mediators invite children to participate from the age of four, especially if the children have older siblings, and invite siblings above the age of 16 and up to around 20 to participate in mediation.[21] While the usual minimum age of seven suggests that children are expected to have sufficient verbal and cognitive skills to communicate, some mediators have developed models to cater to younger children and children with disabilities. Nonetheless, there are currently no official guidelines on how to involve younger children and children with cognitive or language-related disabilities. Furthermore, mediation

---

18 Constitution of the Kingdom of Norway, Kongeriget Norges Grundlov (Grunnloven), 17 May 1814.

19 For a more detailed analysis of the constitutional protection of children's participatory rights in Norway, see A. Nylund, 'Children's Right to Participate in Decision-Making in Norway: Paternalism and Autonomy' in T. Haugli, A. Nylund, R. Sigurdsen and L.R.L. Bendiksen (eds.), *Children's Constitutional Rights in the Nordic Countries*, Brill, Leiden 2019, pp. 201–224.

20 Act on Children and Parents (Children Act), Lov om barn og foreldre (barnelova), 8 April 1981 no. 7, in force since 1 January 1982.

21 R. Thørnblad and A. Strandbu, 'The Involvment of Children in the Process of Mandatory Family Mediation' in A. Nylund, K. Ervasti and L. Adrian (eds.), *Nordic Mediation Research*, Springer, Cham 2018, pp. 183, 191.

is mandatory only for families with children under the age of 16. Thus, children who are 16 or 17 years old do not participate in mediation unless they have younger siblings and are invited to participate.

According to the Children Act, section 61 no. 4, children who have expressed their opinion on custody, residence or contact during litigation have a right to be informed of the outcome and of how their views have been taken into account. According to the Norwegian Supreme Court, this rule must be interpreted in conjunction with the Children Act, section 31, and the Constitution, and thus it involves an obligation for the court to invite children from the age of seven to be heard.[22] This entails a shift towards a recognition of the inherent value of child participation; previously, child participation was often considered harmful for the child. Nonetheless, the obligation to hear the child in court-connected mediation is unclear, and participation in mandatory out-of-court mediation is not regulated at all in statutory law. Mediation processes are not considered to be decision-making processes and thus are not considered processes in which the child should be allowed to participate. Even when the court hears the child, the child has limited influence on contact and residence arrangements.[23]

According to Norwegian law, the parents represent the child in family law court proceedings, and the child does not have legal standing. Hence, children cannot initiate mediation or litigation, nor can they make claims independently of their parents or appeal cases. Children have a right to receive information about their case, but they do not have the right to be present at court hearings or to access case documents. However, they have a right to be informed of the content of documents in an age-appropriate manner. Parentage cases are the only exception: the child has legal standing in them.

The rules regarding participation in international child abduction cases in the Child Abduction Act[24] and participation of children in adoption proceedings in the Adoption Act[25] are general and tacitly refer to the Children Act. Thus, in court proceedings the rules and practices in child custody, residence, contact and relocation apply *mutatis mutandis*.

---

22 E.g. HR-2017-18-U.

23 G.M.D. Haugen, K. Dyrstad and M. Ådnanes, *Barns innflytelse på samværsordninger og bosted*, Rapport, SINTEF, NTNU Samfunnsforskning, Trondheim 2015.

24 Act Relating to the Recognition and Enforcement of Foreign Decisions Concerning Custody of Children etc. and on the Return of Children (Child Abduction Act), Lov om anerkjennelse og fullbyrdelse av utenlandske avgjørelser om foreldreansvar m.v. og om tilbakelevering av barn (barnebortføringsloven), 8 July 1988.

25 Act Relating to Adoption (Adoption Act), Lov om adopsjon (adopsjonsloven), 16 June 2017 no. 48, in force since 1 July 2018. Participation in child protection cases is regulated in the Act Relating to Child Welfare (Child Welfare Act), Lov om barneverntjenester (barnevernloven), 17 July 1992 no. 100, in force since 1 January 1993.

3. MODES OF CHILD PARTICIPATION

3.1. DIRECT FORMS OF PARTICIPATION

Guidelines, recommendations and other official documents contain unequivocal support for direct child participation in both court-connected and out-of-court mediation. The Ministry of Children and Families has obliged the Family Counselling Offices to include children in mediation more often.[26] This reflects a shift in the beliefs regarding child participation over the last few decades. Participation is important not only because it encourages a child-centric shift in the parents' attitudes and behaviour and in their eliciting of information regarding the best interests of their child, but also because it empowers the child and honours the child's human dignity.[27] Child participation brings the child's needs and wishes to centre stage and gives the child the opportunity to gain a better understanding of the situation.[28]

3.1.1. Out-of-Court Mediation

Despite shifts in attitudes, child participation in out-of-court mediation is still uncommon and is subject to parental consent. The parents have a duty to inform children of their right to participate in mediation and their right to be heard. However, the parents' duty to hear the child is not enforced. Moreover, for low-conflict families, the mandatory mediation session is treated as a formality rather than a true forum for decision-making. In 2018, children's participation in out-of-court mediation was still the exception, with only 26% of children participating after they turned seven. Nonetheless, this does represent a significant increase from the early 2010s, when children participated in only 4% of mediations.[29]

There is significant variation among the Family Counselling Offices regarding child participation. This variation can be attributed to several factors, such as how comfortable the employees are in allowing children to participate, whether high-conflict families are given priority, and the local mediation culture.[30] When parents are told, and gain the impression from other parents, that children are routinely invited to participate, they are more likely to consent to child

---

26 Barne- og familiedepartementet, *Tildelingsbrev til Barne-, ungdoms- og familiedirektoratet 2021*. https://www.regjeringen.no/contentassets/e3c03f39789d433a9ade95467740b6ab/tildelingsbrev-til-bufdir-2021-sendt-ut-181220.pdf, pp. 4–5.

27 A. Nylund, above n. 19.

28 Domstoladministrasjonen, *Den gode barnesamtalen i foreldretvistar*, https://www.domstol.no/domstoladministrasjonen/publikasjoner/veiledere/den-gode-barnesamtalen-i-foreldretvistar/.

29 Barne-, ungdoms- og familiedirektoratet, above n. 11, p. 28.

30 Barne-, ungdoms- og familiedirektoratet, above n. 11, p. 28.

participation. Likewise, children expect to participate in mediation when they learn that their peers have done so.

Several Family Counselling Offices have implemented the child-inclusive BIM model (*Barn i mekling*, Children in Mediation) of mediation.[31] Mediation commences with a short introductory session. After the introduction, the parents exit the room and the mediator has a conversation with the child. Three questions guide the conversation: (1) What is happening/has happened? (2) How are you feeling? (3) Is there anything you would like to say to your parents? Based on these questions, the mediator encourages the child to convey a message to the parents. The role of the mediator is to document the message as literally as possible to retain authenticity. Thereafter, the mediator begins mediation by conveying the child's message to the parents. Often, the child's message regards issues beyond residence and contact, such as maintaining or establishing relationships and traditions. However, the mediator asks the parents to discuss the issues the child has raised regardless of their legal relevance. The mediation session concludes with the child entering the room. The settlement, or lack thereof, is then explained to the child. The child also receives feedback on how his/her input has influenced the outcome.

The BIM model reflects an understanding of children's participation as a way to bring the child's perspective to the mediation table. The open questions allow children to select freely which issues they wish to discuss and what message they wish to convey. It thus reorients the parents towards the children and shapes the agenda, as well as potentially providing new information. Children are not specifically asked to indicate their preferences regarding residence and care arrangements, although the open questions allow children to express such preferences if they wish to do so. While not asking children to state their views on care arrangements relieves children of the pressure to side with one parent, it could, in some cases, amount to depriving children of the opportunity to express their views, since some children may not perceive open questions as an invitation to do so.

Other models for child participation are also applied. All models include an introduction in which the children receive information about the mediation process and their role in it and a conclusion in which the children receive information and feedback on their participation. Some mediators utilise a one-way mirror to enable the children to see how the parents react to their messages.[32]

In the last few years, a programme designed for high-conflict families has been launched. It is called process mediation (*prosessmekling*), and consists of a mini-course, individual sessions with each parent, conversations with children

31 R. Thørnblad and A. Strandbu, above n. 21, pp. 186–187.

32 *Barn i familievernet*, Familievernets skriftserie no. 1/2011, https://www.bufdir.no/globalassets/global/Barn_i_familievernet_1_2011_Skriftserie.pdf, pp. 22–23 and 28–29.

and mediation. Currently, standardised methods for the conversations with children are being developed. The new model enables children to participate in decision-making through a conversation with the mediator and through a more child-centred subsequent mediation session.[33] Usually, two mediators are assigned to each case. One or both of them hear the children at the Family Counselling Office. After the mediation, children are given feedback on why a specific outcome was chosen.

Registered private mediators apply the mediation method they find most suitable. In 2018, 15% of children aged seven or above participated in mediation with private mediators, which is significantly less than at the Family Counselling Offices.[34]

3.1.2. Participation in Court Proceedings in Family Law Cases

In most cases, the court proceedings start with the judge having an audio-conference with counsel. The aim is to ensure the case is suitable for mediation, to plan the first court hearing and to discuss who should be appointed as an expert.[35] The court-appointed expert has multiple roles: to assist the court in mediating the case, to provide advice to the parents and, if the parents do not settle, to make an evaluation of the best interests of the child. Alternatively, the court can oblige the parents to attend out-of-court mediation. However, only 1–2% of cases are returned to the Family Counselling Offices each year.[36]

At a preparatory hearing, the parents, the expert and the judge discuss the proceedings and the role of the expert in them. Usually, the expert holds individual meetings with each parent, discusses the situation with the child or children and finally mediates with the parents. The role of the judge varies: some judges are involved in both hearing the child and mediation sessions, while others only co-mediate or are not involved at all.[37] Experts are often appointed from a list of registered experts and include psychologists and psychiatrists with specific training and experience.[38] However, the use of non-registered experts is widespread.

---

33 Barne-, ungdoms- og familiedirektoratet, above n. 11, p. 26.

34 Barne-, ungdoms- og familiedirektoratet, above n. 11, p. 33.

35 The Norwegian Courts Administration has issued guidelines for handling the cases; see Domstoladministrasjonen, *Nasjonal veileder for behandling av foreldretvister*, Versjon 2.0, https://www.domstol.no/contentassets/2af0ab33bb6146ffa161a41154de85f7/nasjonal-veileder-for-foreldretvister-2019-1.pdf.

36 Statistisk sentralbyrå, above n. 4.

37 Oxford Research, *Kartlegging av foreldretvister etter barneloven*, 2016, https://evalueringsportalen.no/evaluering/domstolsbehandlingen-av-foreldretvister-kartlegging-av-foreldretvister-etter-barneloven, pp. 23 ff.

38 Norsk psykologforbund, *Studieplan for barnefaglig sakkyndigutdanning*, https://www.psykologforeningen.no/medlem/kurs-og-utdanning/andre-utdanningsprogram/utdanning-av-barnefaglig-sakkyndige.

According to the current recommendation issued in February 2019,[39] the judge shall ensure as early as possible that children are informed of their right to be heard and the methods of involving children. Children who wish to speak directly with the judge should be given an opportunity to do so, unless the best interests of the child require otherwise. In the latter case, the expert will hear the child. In 2015, an expert conducted the conversations in 70% of the cases surveyed, the judge and the expert in 32% and only the judge in 16% of the cases involving children aged seven and above.[40] Judges seldom participated in conversations with younger children.[41] The judge must evaluate the time and place for hearing the child and whether information should be obtained prior to this occurring. Sometimes children should be given several opportunities to be heard, such as when the family trials care arrangements for a certain period of time. The timing of the appointment should respect children's needs (e.g. not conflicting with schoolwork, hobbies, etc.).[42]

However, if the parents resist the expert, judge or both having a conversation with the child, the judge must consider how to proceed. The judge must attempt to convince the parents of the benefits of child participation and, if necessary, give the parents time to reconsider. If one or both parents still resist the conversation, the judge can decide to proceed anyway, since pursuing a conversation against the outspoken wishes of a parent could be detrimental to the child.[43] The decision to give parents a de facto right to veto participation is likely to result from unclear rules on child participation and the tendency to treat mediation as a private process.

Conversations with children are scheduled at court in the judge's chambers, in a meeting room or in a special room for hearing children. When the judge is not involved, the expert has discretion to choose a suitable place for hearing the child. The parents are not present at the hearing, and siblings have the opportunity to talk with the judge or expert without their other siblings being present. At the beginning of the conversation, the expert or the judge informs the child about the court case, the child's right to participate, and the right to refrain from speaking with the judge and/or answering questions. The child is also told they do not decide the outcome, although their views will inform the outcome. In addition, the child is informed about how the judge or expert will document the hearing and how the account from the discussion will be used.

---

39 Domstoladministrasjonen, *Praktiske anbefalinger for domstolsbehandling til barnet beste i foreldretvistsaker, og saker om tvangsfullbyrdelse jf. barneloven §65*, 1 February 2019, https://www.domstol.no/contentassets/2af0ab33bb6146ffa161a41154de85f7/praktiske-anbefalinger-foreldretvister.pdf.

40 Oxford Research, above n. 37, p. 78. The respondents could select more than one option, thus the total exceeds 100%.

41 Oxford Research, above n. 37, p. 78.

42 Domstoladministrasjonen, above n. 35.

43 Domstoladministrasjonen, above n. 28.

Since the parents will have access to this account, it is imperative that children are given appropriate information and the opportunity to review the account and to correct any misunderstandings or provide additional information.[44] A recent study revealed that written accounts are not drafted in all cases,[45] in which case neither the child nor the parents can access information from the conversation. There are no statistics available regarding whether and when children are heard in court-connected mediation and litigation proceedings.

According to the national guidelines for hearing children in cases on parental responsibility, the aim is to discuss the child's views in a broad sense by asking the child how they feel about, and perceive, the current situation to elicit information on their needs and wishes. Direct questions on residence and contact should not be used, since these could cause the child to perceive a conflict of loyalty vis-à-vis the parents.[46]

When the child is at risk of abuse or neglect, court-connected mediation is not attempted. Instead, the expert is assigned the role of an evaluator and, as part of the evaluation, the expert, the judge or both hear the child. The expert can also observe the child. As a rule, the child is not invited to participate in the main hearing. The child's views are presented by way of the expert evaluation report or as a written account from a conversation with the child. The same applies when the parents do not settle in a preparatory hearing or in court-connected mediation. In these cases, the judge has discretion to decide whether a new conversation with the child should be scheduled.

Depending on the outcome of mediation and the level of conflict between the parents, either the parents, the expert or the judge informs the child of the outcome. During the court proceedings, the parents often make interim arrangements, through either agreement or court order. The child must be informed of the interim arrangement, its duration and the process that will be followed after the interim period. For permanent outcomes, whether based on a settlement or on a judgment, the child has a right to feedback on whether, and how, their views have been taken into account. The information must be tailored to the age and development of each child. The court has a duty to document when, how and by whom the feedback was given to the child.[47] Usually, the expert or the parents inform the child.[48]

Framing participation as a conversation with the child presupposes fairly developed verbal skills on the part of the child. Thus, other methods of

---

44 Domstoladministrasjonen, above n. 35, and Domstoladministrasjonen, above n. 39.
45 Oxford Research, above n. 37, p. 79.
46 Domstoladministrasjonen, above n. 28.
47 Domstoladministrasjonen, above n. 35 and Domstoladministrasjonen, above n. 39.
48 Oxford Research, above n. 37, p. 80.

communication, such as play, are often overlooked, and many young children or children with cognitive disorders are consequently deprived of the right to participate even when their participation could be beneficial.

Court-connected mediation has been criticised due to the mediator having multiple roles that in some cases may be incompatible.[49] Hence, children may not wish to disclose information to the expert and the judge. The expert has no right to confidentiality vis-à-vis the judge; thus, any information the child shares with the expert could be used either indirectly or directly in the expert evaluation or in the judgment or interim order.

According to the Child Abduction Act, section 17, the court has a duty to hear children aged seven or above and younger children who are capable of forming their own opinion. Moreover, the child has a right to receive relevant information, and the child's opinion is given weight according to the age and maturity of the child. The court proceeds in the same manner as in cases involving parental responsibility; that is, the court, an expert or both hear the child.[50]

3.2. REPRESENTATION FORMS OF PARTICIPATION

During litigation, the court has the power to appoint a (legal) representative for the child if there is a particular need to do so, such as when there is reason to suspect child abuse or neglect.[51] The role of the representative is to ensure that the court process is conducted in a manner that is compatible with the best interests of the child, that all necessary steps are taken, that the child is given sufficient opportunity to state their views, that their views are taken into account and that the proceedings are not overly burdensome for the child. The representative is not the legal counsel of the child and only advocates for the procedural rights of the child. The government pays for these representatives.

Legal representatives are appointed in less than 1% of all cases, with most courts never having appointed a representative.[52] The role of the representative is unclear and limited. Therefore, most judges believe that appointing a representative provides little or no added value and may only serve to make the process more complicated.

---

49 See C. Bernt, above n. 17.

50 Rundskriv om internasjonal barnebortføring G-2015-6, part 6.4.3.

51 Children Act, s 62 no. 5.

52 B. Sundsdal, 'Barnets representant i foreldretvister – en innholdsløs styrking av barns rettssikkerhet?' [2015] *Tidsskrift for familierett, arverett og barnevernrettslige spørsmål* 177.

3.3. CHILD LITIGATING ON OWN BEHALF

Children have legal standing in parentage cases. The child has the right to initiate proceedings to establish and revoke parentage. If the child is under 15 years of age, the child must first receive a guardian ad litem who acts on the behalf of the child. Children who are 15 years or older can commence litigation on their own behalf, and a guardian can only commence litigation with the permission of the child.

The rules of procedure are flexible in parentage cases and are tailored to the specific case. Hence, the forms of child participation vary. The government pays for the proceedings. Legal aid is awarded to the child.

4. RESEARCH

In recent years, models for child participation in mediation have been developed. Research on the BIM model indicates that children appreciate the opportunity to participate in mediation.[53] A survey of children in 217 mediations found that around 90% of the children felt they were able to say what they wanted to the mediator, that the mediator understood them and that they enjoyed talking to the mediator. The vast majority, 88%, agreed that children in general should be able to take part in mediation. A higher level of conflict slightly reduced children's level of satisfaction; however, the effect was small.

The researchers also analysed the messages children wished to convey to their parents based on the notes of the mediator.[54] These messages fell into four analytical categories. 'Breakdown' messages included statements related to the process of changing from one family constellation to another. 'Preservation and improvement' messages related to the child wanting the parents to reunite or expressing a desire to preserve family relations and traditions or improve communication within the family. 'Reorientation' messages referred to establishing new relationships with the parents' new partners. Finally, 'security' messages related to the child's care situation. These were not directly related to the marital breakdown, although the breakdown could intensify security issues. Only the final category, 'security', had direct implications for residence and contact; however, information related to all four categories was relevant for improving the level of co-parenting.

Interviews with 12 mediators at Family Counselling Offices that use the BIM model found that including children changes the function and focus of mediation from an adult-centred information session dominated by details

---

53 R. Thørnblad and A. Strandbu, above n. 21, pp. 199–204.
54 R. Thørnblad and A. Strandbu, above n. 21, pp. 194–199.

related to parental responsibility to a child-centred discussion on co-parenting.[55] Discussions on economic aspects and other 'adult' issues yielded to issues pertaining to daily life, such as toys, activities and holidays. Children's messages could also make mediation more complex, since these shaped the agenda and the information available, and parents could not define the agenda alone. Moreover, the mediation addressed issues and perspectives that were important to the specific child or children concerned, not just children in general.

5. POLICY OR PRACTICE DEVELOPMENTS

In December 2020, the government-appointed Children Act Commission recommended that the Children Act should explicitly state that children have a right to participate in out-of-court mediation and that children should have a right to initiate out-of-court mediation. Moreover, the Commission proposed that the threshold for appointing a representative for the child should be lowered.[56]

6. CONCLUSION

The requirements of Article 12 of the UNCRC are being met formally in Norway: the Children Act, Child Abduction Act and Adoption Act give children above the age of seven the right to participate and to receive information on the issues to be decided and the final decision. Since the specific sections regulating decision-making processes do not explicitly set out the right to participate, nor state what participation entails, the obligations under Article 12 are not always met in practice.

Flexible rules enable mediators and judges to tailor the proceedings to each case. However, flexibility also results in considerable differences in practice. The level of knowledge and training in using child-inclusive practices varies among judges and court-appointed experts: at larger courts, only some judges hear cases concerning children (i.e. custody, contact, parentage and welfare cases); in most small courts, all judges hear these cases, which in turn might reduce the level of child participation.[57] A government report has recommended limiting cases concerning children to selected courts to ensure that the judges and experts

---

[55] R. Thørnblad, A. Strandbu and A. Salamonsen, 'Hvordan påvirker barns deltakelse foreldremekling? Barns deltakelse som mål og middel' [2019] *Barn* 67.

[56] NOU 20209: 140, *Ny barnelov. Til barnets beste*, Departementenes sikkerhets- og serviceorganisasjon, Oslo 2020, pp. 289–290 and 300–301.

[57] Oxford Research, above n. 37, pp. 24–26 and 85–88.

have the necessary training and experience.[58] Similar problems apply to Family Counselling Offices. However, the development and spread of new models for child participation have resulted in increased child participation.

Although Norway has made significant progress in recognising the intrinsic value of child participation, the lack of specific rules and procedures still reduces the level and quality of participation.

58 NOU 2017: 8, *Særdomstoler på nye områder? – Vurdering av nye domstolsordninger for foreldretvister, barnevernsaker og utlendingssaker*, Departementenes sikkerhets- og serviceorganisasjon, Oslo 2017, https://www.regjeringen.no/contentassets/57139c34d05943b4829ad0839a4f5116/no/pdfs/nou201720170008000dddpdfs.pdf.

ROMANIA

Simona FLORESCU

1. INTRODUCTION

Romania emerged as a democracy in the early 1990s after the fall of the Communist dictatorship which lasted for more than half a century and which has been considered of a more ruthless type than elsewhere in Eastern Europe, with the exception of the Soviet Union.[1] The ensuing democratisation process included the rapid accession to most international (human rights) conventions and the enactment of new laws so as to reflect the new neoliberal ambitions.[2]

---

1 V. PERJU, 'The Romanian double executive and the 2012 constitutional crisis' (2015) 13(1) *International Journal of Constitutional Law* 246–278, p. 246, citing V. TISMANEANU, *Stalinism for all Seasons: A Political History of Romanian Communism*, University of California Press, Berkley/Los Angeles 2003.

2 D.J. BEERS, 'Understanding Corruption in the Post-Communist Courts: Attitudinal Data from Romania and the Czech Republic', 11th Annual International Young Researchers Conference, 'Post-communist Corruption: Causes, Manifestations, Consequences', 29–31 March 2012, Miami University, Oxford, OH. The ratification of the Convention on the Rights of the Child (UNCRC) occurred in 1990, shortly followed by the accession to the Council of

The modernisation of the laws was not followed by a similarly fast-paced change in mentalities. Allegations of corruption of public officials continue to be rampant, leaving Romanian institutions to function in an unhealthy judicial culture, plagued by attitudes of distrust both from within the judiciary and from the population in general.[3]

The family law system, albeit seemingly detached from the political scene, operates against a background of conservative and patriarchal attitudes. For example, the concept of family is narrowly linked to the marriage between a man and a woman, with no meaningful discussion on changing laws so as to allow same-sex unions.[4] Women remain the main caretakers of children and Romania has been recently condemned for not providing appropriate protection to victims of domestic violence.[5] At the same time, family judges are increasingly exposed to cross-border disputes due to massive emigration.[6]

The Romanian legal system follows a civil law tradition inspired by its French counterpart.[7] The 1991 Constitution is the supreme law of the land.[8] The Constitution establishes the High Court of Cassation and Justice (*Inalta Curte de Casatie si Justitie*) (the Supreme Court) as the highest court of the land, which among other things is responsible for overseeing the unitary application of law by other courts of justice.[9] Few family disputes would be in practice decided by the Supreme Court; jurisdiction for private family cases has been allocated to the courts of first instance (*judecători*) whose judgments are subject to appeal to the district courts.[10] In 2017 there were 177 courts of first instance and 42 district courts across the country, leaving a lot of room for diverging practices in approaches to child participation.[11]

Europe in 1993 and the ratification of the European Convention of Fundamental Rights and Freedoms in 1994. Romania has also been a European Union Member State since 2007.

3 D.J. Beers, above n. 2.

4 Under the influence of religious groups, a referendum was organised in 2018 to amend the Constitution so as to redefine marriage as the union between a man and a woman. This referendum did not succeed as the quorum was not met. In any event Art. 259(1) of the Civil Code does define marriage as the union between a man and a women, leaving any changes possible only subject to the (unlikely) amendment of the Civil Code.

5 Among others, ECtHR *Buturugă v Romania* (Appl. No. 56867/15), 11 February 2020; ECtHR *MGC v Romania* (Appl. No. 61495/11), 15 March 2016.

6 N. Mateoc-Sîrb, T. Mateoc, C. Mănescu and I. Grad, 'Analysis on the phenomenon of population's migration in Romania' [2014] *14 (1) Scientific Papers Series Management, Economic Engineering in Agriculture and Rural Development* 212.

7 V. Perju, above n. 1, p. 250.

8 The Romanian Constitution entered into force on 8 December 2001 and was published in the Official Journal, Part I, no. 233 of 8 December 1991.

9 Law 304/2004 regarding the judiciary.

10 Art. 265 of the Civil Code.

11 Art. 94 taken together with Art. 114 of the Code of Civil Procedure adopted through Law 134/2010, republished in the Official Journal, Part I, no. 247 of 10 April 2015. The figures are based on information provided by the Superior Council of Magistrates: https://www.csm1909.ro/271/Prezentarea-sistemului-judiciar.

The Constitutional Court was also established under the Constitution.[12] This Court reviews the conformity of legislation with the Constitution, both prior to and post-enactment, through the possibility for citizens to bring constitutional challenges against laws in the context of pending litigation.[13] As discussed later in this chapter, the issue of child participation in family law proceedings has already been brought before the Constitutional Court.

The latest census data shows that as of 1 January 2019, there were 19.5 million people resident in Romania.[14] In 2018, children represented 18.8% of the total population.[15] The official (provisional) figures for 2018 indicate that the marriage rate was 6.4 marriages for 1,000 inhabitants,[16] and that there were 1.4 divorces per 1,000 inhabitants.[17] During the same year, the ratio of marriages and divorces settled through final court judgments or administrative proceedings was 4.6 marriages to one divorce.[18]

Children in Romania are primarily born to married parents, with a ratio of 68.8% of children born to married parents to 31.2% children born to unmarried parents (either single or in a de facto partnership). Currently marriage is the only form of union recognised in Romania.[19]

2. STATUTORY PROVISIONS

Article 29 of the Child Protection Act (CPA)[20] and Article 264 of the Civil Code (CC)[21] lay down the general obligation for courts and administrative authorities to hear children over the age of 10 in all proceedings concerning them. Children younger than 10 years of age may also be heard if the competent

---

12 Art. 142 of the Constitution.

13 Art. 146 of the Constitution.

14 According to the National Institute for Statistics, http://www.insse.ro/cms/sites/default/files/com_presa/com_pdf/poprez_ian2019r.pdf (the numbers refer to residents, meaning all individuals, regardless of their citizenship, who have been habitually resident in Romania for a period of at least 12 months).

15 https://www.economica.net/numarul-copiilor-cu-varsta-cuprinsa-intre-0-18-ani-a-fost-de-4-17-milioane-la-1-ianuarie-2018_154388.html. This data was recorded on 1 January 2018.

16 According to the National Institute for Statistics, https://insse.ro/cms/sites/default/files/field/publicatii/evenimente_demografice_in_anul_2018.pdf; Eurostat, https://ec.europa.eu/eurostat/en/web/products-eurostat-news/-/EDN-20190214-1.

17 According to the National Institute for Statistics, https://insse.ro/cms/sites/default/files/field/publicatii/evenimente_demografice_in_anul_2018.pdf.

18 According to the National Institute for Statistics, https://insse.ro/cms/sites/default/files/field/publicatii/evenimente_demografice_in_anul_2018.pdf, p. 25.

19 Art. 48 of the Constitution lays down the principle that marriage between consenting adults is the foundation of families.

20 Law 272 of 21 June 2004 *privind protecția și promovarea drepturilor copilului*, republished in the Official Journal, no. 159 of 5 March 2014.

21 Law 287/2009, republished in the Official Journal, no. 505 of 15 July 2011.

authorities deem this is necessary for the resolution of the case.[22] These authorities have full discretion to assess the necessity of hearing younger children. On the basis of discussions with professionals (judges and attorneys) that the author undertook for the purposes of this contribution,[23] it appears that in the context of parental separation judges consider it is necessary to hear children from the age of six years.

The purpose of hearing children is to give them a platform for expressing their views before courts or other administrative authorities, and ultimately to assess their best interests.[24] The best interests of the child is laid down as a matter of principle in all relevant laws, including the Romanian Constitution, the Civil Code and the Child Protection Law.

Children in family disputes are not heard in open court, but in chambers, and their declarations are recorded in a protocol which is attached to the case file.[25] According to the professionals interviewed for the purposes of the present contribution, children may request judges to not include certain aspects of their discussion. The protocol itself will be used as evidence for the case file; however, it will usually consist of a short description of the conversation with the child, rather than a verbatim transcription.

Other than in specifically designated cases, children are not parties to family law proceedings. The Civil Code distinguishes between two age limits for children: 10 years old where courts have the obligation to hear children, and 14 years old when children may become parties in their own name to certain proceeding. For example, Article 498 CC provides that a child aged at least 14 years may request in court approval to change his/her educational course if the parents disagree. In addition, children older than 14 years are entitled to choose their own religion or enter into certain contracts in their own name but with the authorisation of the parents or the legal guardian, as the case may be. Prior to that age, they will not be litigants in their own name.

In addition to laying down the general obligation to hear children over the age of 10, the Civil Code is replete with specific provisions mandating the direct hearing of children over the age of 10. This obligation is laid down in the context of various family proceedings, such as divorce, adoption, or parental responsibilities. The same age limits apply to children subject to

---

22 Art. 264(1) Civil Code and Art. 29 of the Code of Civil Procedure.

23 Considering the lack of empirical data on court practice (see also section 4 below), the author has interviewed six professionals (four practicing attorneys and two judges) to assess how children participate in practice in family proceedings. Where reference is made to 'professionals' or 'practitioners', such reference is to be understood to refer to the opinions of the practitioners consulted on this occasion.

24 Decision no. 15/2019 on rejecting the challenge to the constitutionality of Art. 264 para. (1) of the Civil Code (Decizia nr. 15/2019 referitoare la respingerea excepției de neconstituționalitate a dispozițiilor art. 264 alin. (1) din Codul civil), para. 26.

25 Art. 226 of the Code of Civil Procedure.

international child abduction proceedings as provided under Article 11(4) of Law 369/2004.[26]

Thus, in the case of divorce, even if the parties agree to the terms of the separation, courts must hear children from 10 years of age (Art. 506). Further, as per Article 497 CC, taken together with Article 254 CC, children must be heard if the parents do not agree on changing the child's residence, provided the envisaged change influences the exercise of parental responsibilities. *Per a contrario*, if the parents agree with the child's place of residence and such a change does not arise in the context of divorce or another court dispute, the child will not be involved in the decision-making. Further, the child may participate in proceedings concerning the exercise of parental responsibilities after divorce (Art. 396 CC), as well as in proceedings concerning any disagreements between parents on the exercise of parental responsibilities (Art. 496 CC).

The Civil Code also envisages situations where the child and his/her parents or guardian may disagree over the child's personal relationship with other persons. The legal provision in the Civil Code is meant to address primarily situations where a child would like to maintain contact with grandparents or other persons against the wish of the parents. The principle under Article 494 CC is that a child under 14 years of age is free to choose his/her personal relations and correspondence. Parents or guardians may only restrict this right in exceptional circumstances and, should there be disagreements, courts will decide after having heard the child.

Article 463(3) of the Civil Code provides that the adoption of a child over the age of 10 cannot be carried out without the consent of such a child. More detailed provisions for hearing children in the context of adoption are laid down in Law 273/2004 on adoption (specifically in Article 92). For example, under Article 92(3) of this law, judges are to provide reasoning on each case where they take a decision which is contrary to the expressed wish of the child.

For all of the provisions above, the Civil Code and the other relevant laws lay down the obligation for courts and administrative authorities to hear children *directly*. This does not entail that children are given party status in the proceedings, nor that a guardian or another representative is appointed for the child. As explained in more detail in section 3, the obligation to hear children means that judges will invite children to a discussion, which will take place without the parents or guardians being present.

Further, of all the disputes mentioned above, court statistics published in 2013 indicate that the most prevalent family disputes are divorces and maintenance obligations.[27] Children over 10 years old will be heard in all

---

26 Law 369/2004, published in the Official Journal, no. 888 of 29 September 2004.

27 According to the *Activity report of Romanian courts for the first semester of 2013* (*Raport privind activitatea instanțelor de judecată în primul semestru al anului 2013*), published by the Superior Council of Magistrates.

divorce cases. There is some divergence among judges as to whether the law requires that children should be heard in maintenance proceedings as well; for some judges this obligation is derived from Article 264 CC, whereas others see it as discretionary – in that maintenance is not an issue that requires the participation of the child unless the facts of the case so indicate.[28]

3. MODES OF CHILD PARTICIPATION

Romanian legislation and practice favour the direct participation of children in family disputes. It is also possible to involve psychologists or other social workers; however, for children over the age of 10, such professional involvement will take place *in addition to* the direct hearing of the child by a judge.

3.1. DIRECT FORMS OF PARTICIPATION

Three different fora are available for settlement of family disputes: (i) mediation; (ii) public notaries; and (iii) courts.

3.1.1. Mediation

Mediation has existed as an option in Romania since 2006, when the Mediation Law entered into force.[29] As of 2012, prior to going to court, parties to private family law disputes have the duty to participate in one session where they are informed of the benefits of mediation.[30] By establishing this new obligation it was hoped to reinforce the visibility of mediation, which to date does not appear to be frequently used.[31] If parties reach an agreement in mediation, that agreement is submitted to the court for approval.

There are no specific provisions or norms on children's participation in mediation. The text of Article 262 CC is in principle applicable to mediation as well; thus, mediators should involve children on this basis.[32] Nevertheless, it

---

28 This information was provided during the interviews with practitioners.

29 Law 192 of 16 May 2006 regarding mediation, published in the Official Journal, no. 441/2006 of 22 May 2006.

30 Arts. 60 and 65 of the Mediation Law.

31 D. Sandru, D. Radulescu and D. Calin, *Medierea in Romania. Legislatie si jurisprudenta*, 3rd ed., Universitara, Bucharest 2014, pp. 12–20.

32 It is sometimes suggested that the judge who will validate the mediation agreement shall hear the children before approving such an agreement. See for example C.M. Crăciunescu and T. Bădin, *Acordul de mediere în acţiunea de divorţ prin acordul soţilor*, available at: http://inm-lex.ro/fisiere/d_175/Consideratii%20privind%20actiunea%20de%20divort%20prin%20acord%20cu%20acord%20de%20mediere.pdf.

is unclear to what extent mediators do involve children in practice and, if they do, how they proceed. One of the few online sources discussing the position of children during mediation presents this process as advantageous precisely because children are not being heard, and thus they are spared the trauma inherent in a hearing.[33] Some of the professionals interviewed by the author for the purposes of the present contribution indicated, however, that children are being heard directly by mediators as well.

3.1.2. *Public Notaries*

Another legal possibility is to have divorces concluded before public notaries if both spouses agree to all the terms thereof, including those on the exercise of parental responsibilities and visiting rights.[34] Public notaries also have the duty to hear children prior to authenticating the parenting agreements.[35] No further details are included in the law on the procedure for hearing children. A sample protocol available online suggests that a public notary will only hear the child in the presence of both parents.[36]

3.1.3. *Court Proceedings*

The most important venue for children to express their views remains, however, the courts of law. Judges will always hear children directly. Under Article 226 CC, it is up to the judge to decide who will be present with the child during the hearing. In some cases, if the judge deems it necessary, a psychologist will also be present. This is not however a routine process, with the judge having wide discretion to decide on the necessity of a psychologist's presence. There are some voices suggesting that legislation should change so as to make the presence of a psychologist mandatory; however, there is no indication of any (imminent) legislative initiative in this sense.[37] Currently, having a psychologist available

33 For example this appears on the website of a mediator's office: https://academiademediere.ro/audiere-a-copilului-in-procesul-de-divort/; F Lisman, *Minutes of a mediators' meeting on the best interests of the child and the interests of the parents. The impartiality of the mediator in cases concerning children*, available at: https://www.juridice.ro/298932/armonizarea-intereselor-parintilor-prin-prisma-interesului-superior-al-copilului-impartialitatea-mediatorului-in-cauzele-cu-minori-raport-atelier-2.html – the author notes that mediators involve children solely if parents jointly request this.

34 Art. 375 of the Civil Code.

35 Art. 102 of Law 36/1995 concerning public notaries, republished in the Official Journal, no. 237 of 19 March 2018.

36 *Model de proces-verbal de audiere minor cu vârsta de peste10 ani*, available at: https://legeaz.net/modele/model-de-proces-verbal-de-audiere-minor-cu-varsta-peste-10-ani.

37 D.I. Olac, 'Instanța de judecată vs. ascultarea copiilor: este atitudinea copiilor în mod corect percepută de judecător? Partea I – problema juridică', https://www.juridice.ro/414281/instanta-de-judecata-vs-ascultarea-copiilor-este-atitudinea-copiilor-in-mod-corect-perceputa-de-judecator-partea-a-ii-a-problema-practica.html.

for all hearings of children is only mandatory for cases of international child abduction.[38]

Courts summon children to participate through their parents, and in the event that the parents do not live together, through the parent with whom the child lives. There is no designated authority in charge of providing information to children on their rights or on the hearing itself. Lawyers mention that they instruct parents to adequately prepare their children. The public perception is that children *have to* attend the meeting with the judge(s).[39] Once present, a child may choose not to answer the judge's questions; however, there is no right to be absent from this meeting. All the professionals approached reported that they have never experienced cases where parents refused to bring the children or where the children themselves refused to come for the scheduled meeting. Should there be a refusal from a parent, that parent is liable to civil sanctions.

Judges never hear children in open court, but rather in a specially designated space.[40] In practice this will mostly be the judge's office, which is not necessarily decorated in a child-friendly manner.[41] Judges, however, do not wear their official gowns and it is generally agreed that the atmosphere should be as friendly as possible so as to minimise the negative impact on the child.[42]

The Code of Civil Procedure also envisages the possibility for judges to hear children outside courts (for example in their homes). However, there is no indication that this happens in practice.

According to the discussions with the professionals interviewed for the purposes of the present contribution, the hearing of the child consists of an informal discussion between the child and the judge. The judge will start by asking general questions and try to direct the discussion in such a way that he/she identifies the child's opinion on the subject matter of the dispute. Some of the professionals indicated that children are asked to express preferences as to one or the other parent, whereas others pointed out that in their experience a judge will never ask a child to choose between the parents. Rather, the aim of judges is to identify the parent who is most involved in the child's life. Questions that would help uncover this would for example be 'who takes you to school?' or 'who do you go to [that extracurricular activity] with?'.

---

38 Art. 11(5) of Law 369/2004 on the implementation of the Child Abduction Convention, published in the Official Journal, no. 888 of 29 September 2004.

39 This appeared from the discussions with professionals. It is also the author's interpretation of the Constitutional Court decision no. 15/2019.

40 Art. 226 of the Code of Civil Procedure.

41 A. Teacă, 'Ascultarea minorului în sistemul de drept românesc şi alte sisteme de drept' [2018] 4 *Revista Universul Juridic* 63.

42 This was mentioned by all practitioners interviewed by the author; see also A. Teacă, above n. 41; M.M. Pivniceru and C. Luca, *Ghid de audiere a copilului în proceduri judiciare*, Hamangiu, Bucharest 2009.

The length of the discussion between the child and the judge varies. On average, according to the discussions with professionals, it lasts about 15 minutes. It was however indicated that, for more difficult situations, judges will meet with children for longer. The child will be heard alone by the judge, with a court clerk present to record the minutes of the conversation.[43]

It has been noted that, in practice, children will be heard at the beginning of litigation, before having submitted any other evidence in the file.[44]

Furthermore, all professionals emphasised that the child will only be heard once. While it is possible to hear the child more than once, this is considered detrimental and only occurs in very rare cases.

The hearing is not recorded via audio-visual or other means, but a protocol of the hearing is drafted. This protocol is not automatically submitted to the parties; it is however attached to the file, with both parties having the option to access it.[45]

Judges are the ones who decide on the weight to be given to the child's voice, on a case-by-case basis. There is no official guide on how to conduct the hearings or criteria for determining the weight to be given, but several NGOs, together with the National Institute for Magistrates, have developed a (general) guide for hearing children applicable to all proceedings.[46] Judges, however, routinely follow courses and conferences in the context of their continuing education obligations regarding children's rights; therefore, such training courses may be of use in assessing the weight to be given to the child's voice.[47]

From the discussions with professionals, it appears that in practice the voice of the child has significant weight in the outcome of the litigation. The reasons put forth varied from the fact judges consider it to be in the best interests of children to have a strong say in proceedings concerning them. On the other hand, it was also mentioned that it is very difficult to enforce judgments that go against the voice of the child. All professionals indicated, however, that the

---

43 A. Teacă, above n. 41, p. 17.

44 T. Becheanu, 'Instanța de judecată vs. ascultarea copiilor: este atitudinea copiilor în mod corect percepută de judecător?', 16 December 2015, https://www.juridice.ro/414281/instanta-de-judecata-vs-ascultarea-copiilor-este-atitudinea-copiilor-in-mod-corect-perceputa-de-judecator-partea-a-ii-a-problema-practica.html.

45 A. Teacă, above n. 41, p. 18.

46 M.M. Pivniceru and C. Luca, above n. 42.

47 This information was provided by the judges interviewed. The author has also participated in one such training course and was involved in giving a course herself. The courses are given by both national and international experts and are generally offered through the Superior Council of Magistrates, which acts as the training institute for judges. All the training courses available for 2019 (for all fields of law, including children and family law) may be accessed on the website of the Superior Council of Magistrates: http://inm-lex.ro/programul-de-formare-continua-2021-1/. In addition, judges have the obligation under the law to attend training courses (Regulation on the professional evaluation of judges and prosecutors, Official Journal, no. 304 of 4 April 2018).

child's voice is not the only factor taken into account in the decision-making process. It will be given significant weight only if it is corroborated by other evidence added to the case file. Attorneys sometimes criticise the court's choice to give decisive weight to the voice of the child, arguing that this ultimately gives too much room for one parent to influence the child and is not consistent with the child's best interests.[48]

Other than this one meeting with the judge, there is no follow-up with the child after the hearing. It is for the parent(s) to inform the child of the outcome and there is no process or procedure laid down in this regard.

3.2. REPRESENTATION FORMS OF PARTICIPATION

In addition to these possibilities for hearing children *directly* in court, judges may, if they deem it necessary, order the parties (and the child) to undergo psychological counselling. In such cases, authorised psychologists will set out a schedule with the children and the parties and they will present a report on the outcome to the judge. That specific report is to be considered as evidence in court, and will follow the general rules (on administration) of evidence. Having a psychologist's report does *not* relieve judges of the requirement to hear children directly.

Further, none of the three proceedings above (mediation, divorce before a public notary, and private family law disputes in court) may be completed without having obtained a prior psychosocial report. This report is drafted by a social worker employed by the City Hall and it provides information on the living conditions of the parent with whom the child is residing, the way the child is being taken care of, the child's education, and the parents' finances and professional background.[49] The social worker has no background in psychology, and therefore even though termed a 'psychosocial report', the evaluation lacks any elements of child psychology.[50] It is however unclear to what extent children are heard for the purposes of drafting this report. Several of the professionals interviewed mentioned that children will not be heard by social workers.

Article 262(3) of the Civil Code also envisages the possibility of appointing a guardian ad litem for children in cases of conflicts of interests. The law does not further clarify the meaning of 'conflicts of interests'. Disputes over the exercise of parental authority, visitation or the child's place of residence are in practice not considered to fall under the category of disputes revealing a conflict of interests between the parties. In practice, guardians are appointed in cases concerning

48 T. Becheanu, above n. 44.

49 I. Nicolae, 'Ancheta psihosocială – un mijloc de probă neadaptat cerințelor codului civil' [2017] 3(1) *Revista Universul Juridic* 36–45.

50 I. Nicolae, above n. 49.

patrimonial conflicts, where for example a parent intends to sell an asset that is part of the child's property, inheritance, etc. Guardians usually have legal training and are registered on special lists within City Halls. It may also be – but this does not happen frequently in practice – that members of the child's extended family are appointed as guardians.

Further, under Article 92 CC, the prosecutor is entitled to bring any claim on behalf of the child, and may intervene in any litigation should it be necessary for the rights of vulnerable individuals. The Civil Code envisages some instances where the prosecutor has to participate on behalf of the child (such as paternity cases).

3.3. CHILD LITIGATING ON OWN BEHALF

Children are not usually parties to family disputes. The Civil Code provides for some limited exceptions for children over 14 years old, who may initiate litigation in their own name in cases concerning a change in their religion, the course of their education or in relation to administration of assets. In these situations, children over the age of 14 are parties to the litigation; however, they need to be represented by one of the parents or a guardian. In other words, a court petition filed by a 14-year-old child without a representative (a parent or guardian) will be dismissed as void. Should there be a conflict of interests between the child and the parents, only courts are competent to appoint a guardian ad litem for the children (Art. 58 Code of Civil Procedure).

Litigation regarding maintenance obligations is one common situation where children (over 14 years old) litigate in their own name.[51] In practice, however, this seems to only mean that the child is the signatory of the court petition, and in most cases the parent with whom the child resides is the child's representative.

Other than the child being a party to the litigation in his/her own name, there are no legislative provisions or measures taken to ensure that such right can be exercised effectively in practice. The child's access to documents, right to appeal or information are discharged through the child's legal representative, in the same way as for adults.

3.4. LEADING CASE LAW ON CHILD PARTICIPATION

The constitutionality of Article 264 CC, which sets out the child's right to be heard, has been recently challenged on account of non-compliance with

[51] Decision no. 5254/2015, Judecatoria Bistrita, Decision no. 8/2016, Tribunalul Buzau, 06 Ianuarie 2016.

Article 12 of the UN Convention on the Rights of the Child (UNCRC).[52] The challenge was brought by a parent who claimed that the *right* of the child to be heard has been transformed into an *obligation* for the child. The child in that particular case had been repeatedly summoned to be heard in various separate and interrelated family disputes, including for interim proceedings. The parent bringing the challenge claimed that this had been traumatising for the child. The Constitutional Court dismissed the allegations on several grounds. First, the Constitutional Court highlighted that the provisions of Article 264 CC are the consequence of Article 8 of the European Convention of Human Rights, which imposes a positive obligation for states to enact legislation. Further, the Constitutional Court considered that even though authorities have the obligation to hear the child, the child does not have to answer their questions, and there is no sanction for the child's refusal to answer.

From the judgment of the Constitutional Court it can be inferred that the child will always have to appear for the hearing, yet the *right* to be heard is manifested in that there is no sanction for the child's refusal to answer questions.

4. RESEARCH

To date, there has been no empirical research conducted on any aspect of child participation in family disputes. The available public documents on child participation usually discuss the existing international standards and in some cases the practice of other countries.[53] Some of the practitioners interviewed for the purposes of the present chapter highlighted the need for more empirical research and good practice examples. This was considered particularly necessary since many judges are competent to hear children in practice, leading to a heightened risk of divergent practices.

5. POLICY OR PRACTICE DEVELOPMENTS

There are no major practice developments at the moment.

6. CONCLUSION

This chapter has analysed the current Romanian practice on participation of children in family disputes. It has been shown that children over the age of 10

---

52 Decision no. 15/2019 on rejecting the challenge to the constitutionality of Art. 264 para. (1) of the Civil Code (Decizia nr. 15/2019 referitoare la respingerea excepției de neconstituționalitate a dispozițiilor art. 264 alin. (1) din Codul civil).

53 M.M. Pivniceru and C. Luca, above n. 42; A. Teacă, above n. 41.

are always heard directly by judges in family proceedings. In addition, there are indications that younger children are also being routinely heard directly in court.

Despite this positive note, several aspects of Romanian laws and their practical application need more attention so as to fully comply with the child's right to participate. One such aspect is the lack of specialised services assisting children involved in family disputes. Children do not have access to a guardian, a lawyer or any other specially trained individual to guide them through the process. Further, other than the hearing itself, there is no information provided to the child before or after the (court) process. In addition, it does seem that there is a fine line between the right of the child to be heard and the obligation to be present in court. The right to be heard is translated in Romanian practice into the obligation for children to come for a meeting with the judge with the option to remain silent during the conversation. It is doubtful that this practice meets the substance of the child's right to be heard as laid down under Article 12 UNCRC.

In this chapter it has also been shown that in certain circumstances, children over the age of 14 have standing to litigate cases in their own name. Yet, other than having been granted this right, there is no legal provision or practice direction for adjusting the process for children. Thus, it is unlikely that children will actually participate in these cases. The proceedings follow the same legal rules as they do for adult litigants, with the consequence that one parent will be the 'actual' litigant in the name of the child.

Last but not least, it is recommended that professional standards for hearing children are adopted so as to ensure more uniformity. Such professional standards, if preceded by much-needed (and currently non-existent) empirical research, may provide the necessary link between law and practice and would ensure that the requirements for child-friendly justice are adapted to the Romanian context.

SCOTLAND

E. Kay M. TISDALL*

1. INTRODUCTION

With the UK having ratified the United Nations Convention on the Rights of the Child (UNCRC) in 1991, policy-makers in Scotland have sought to ensure that domestic family law meets the UNCRC requirements. The UNCRC was much referenced when forming the primary legislation for family law, the Children (Scotland) Act 1995 (1995 Act). The UNCRC has become even more important in current family law reforms, as the First Minister of Scotland committed to incorporating the UNCRC into domestic law by the end of the 2021 Parliamentary session.[1] Children's participation rights in family law

* The author would like to acknowledge the collaborative learning that has informed this chapter, with children, young people and adults. This includes partnership research, such as Child Contact Proceedings for Children Affected by Domestic Abuse (funded by the then Scottish Commissioner for Children and Young People), Children's Participation in Family Actions: Probing Compliance with Children's Human Rights (funded by the Scottish Government), and Improving Justice in Child Contact (funded by the European Union's Rights, Equality and Citizenship Programme (2014–2020)).

1 As of February 2021, the UNCRC Incorporation (Scotland) Bill is at its last stage in the Scottish Parliament.

in Scotland have been continuously influenced by the UNCRC for several decades.

Beyond the UNCRC, Scottish law must be compatible with the European Convention on Human Rights (ECHR).[2] Its provisions and subsequent legal judgments by the European Court on Human Rights therefore are relevant to Scottish law on children's participation and parental responsibilities.

Human rights treaties thus strongly frame children's participation rights in family law in Scotland. However, existing research and recent consultations suggest that implementation is poor, with a lack of consistency across courts and children often reporting dissatisfaction. These issues are subject to current family law reform, in the Children (Scotland) Act 2020 passed during the writing of this chapter. Both the evidence and the proposed changes are discussed below.

Scotland has a small population of 5,438,000, which is 8.2% of the UK population.[3] Its population is ageing, with only 17% of children aged 0–15 in 2018.[4] It is estimated that at least one third of children currently will experience parental separation at some point during their childhood.[5] Official court statistics show that there were 2,416 parental responsibilities and rights cases initiated in civil courts in 2017–2018, which was a small rise of 2% from over a decade earlier.[6] More generally, the Scottish Civil Justice Survey found that 1% of adults reported a civil law problem related to child contact, residence or maintenance in 2017–2018.[7] Police recorded 230 cases of child abduction in 2016–2017.[8]

This chapter reviews the current legal context for children's participation rights when there are disputes about parental responsibilities and rights, under section 11 of the 1995 Act. It then considers contested court cases, usually concerning child contact and involving allegations of domestic abuse. The chapter then outlines what is known about children's participation rights when cases do not come to court. The chapter concludes by considering how well the Scottish system is meeting children's participation rights under Article 12 of the UNCRC.

---

2 Scotland Act 1998, ss 29(2) and 57(2); see also Human Rights Act 1998.

3 Mid-2018 estimate, based on https://www.ons.gov.uk/peoplepopulationandcommunity/populationandmigration/populationestimates/datasets/populationestimatesforukenglandandwalesscotlandandnorthernireland.

4 https://www.nrscotland.gov.uk/files//statistics/population-estimates/mid-18/mid-year-pop-est-18-pub.pdf.

5 https://childreninscotland.org.uk/is-the-future-5050/.

6 https://www.gov.scot/publications/civil-justice-statistics-scotland-2017-18/pages/3/.

7 https://www.gov.scot/publications/civil-justice-statistics-scotland-2017-18/pages/3/.

8 Scottish Government, *Review of Part 1 of the Children (Scotland) Act 1995 and creation of a Family Justice Modernisation Strategy*, 2018, https://www.gov.scot/publications/review-part-1-children-scotland-act-1995-creation-family-justice/pages/24/, p. 150.

2. STATUTORY PROVISIONS

Scotland has long been a separate jurisdiction for family law in the United Kingdom. The 1995 Act's family law provisions were implemented in 1996. Important amendments were made by the Family Law (Scotland) Act 2006 and more will be implemented due to the Children (Scotland) Act 2020, which are discussed below. The Scottish Government has announced a Family Justice Modernisation Strategy (FJMS),[9] which details current and proposed changes beyond legislation to improve family justice.

The 1995 Act sets out the responsibilities parents have to their children in section 1, followed by parents' consequential rights in section 2. Amongst these are parents' responsibility and right to maintain personal relations and direct contact with their child, on a regular basis until a child is aged 16.[10] The right is qualified, so that the responsibilities only apply so far as is practicable and in the child's interests. Under section 6, a parent must have regard to their child's views as far as is practicable, when the parent is making any major decision in relation to a parental responsibility or right under sections 1 and 2.[11] The parent needs to take account of the child's age and maturity and the views of any other people with parental responsibilities or rights in regard to the child. A child aged 12 or above is presumed to be of sufficient age and maturity to form a view.[12] Thus the 1995 Act intentionally sets out a framework that focuses on the child, including the child's right to participate and to have their interests considered, in relation to parental responsibilities and rights.[13]

When parental responsibilities and rights are disputed and court proceedings initiated, courts are charged with giving due regard to children's views. Under section 11 of the 1995 Act, when a court is making a decision about parental responsibilities and rights, it shall so far as practicable and taking account of the child's age and maturity:

> i) give him [the child] the opportunity to indicate whether he wishes to express his views;
> ii) if he does so wish, give him an opportunity to express them; and
> iii) have regard to such views as he may express.[14]

---

9 https://www.gov.scot/publications/family-justice-modernisation-strategy/.

10 Sections 1(1)(c) and 2(1)(c).

11 Similarly, a person with 'care or control' of the child but who does not have parental responsibilities nor rights, when doing 'what is reasonable in all the circumstances to safeguard the child's health, development and welfare' (s 5), are also under these duties in s 6.

12 Section 6(1).

13 E.K.M. Tisdall, *The Children (Scotland) Act 1995*, The Stationery Office, Edinburgh 1997.

14 Section 11(7)(b).

Again, a child aged 12 or above is presumed to have sufficient age and maturity to form views.[15]

The court's paramount consideration is the child's welfare and the court must not make an order unless it would be better for the child that the order be made than none being made.[16] No legal presumption currently exists in favour of contact between parent and child. There is a general principle that maintaining contact with a parent is conducive to the child's welfare.[17] The court must have regard to protecting the child from any 'abuse', the risk and/or effect of any abuse on the child.[18] The court must also consider whether relevant persons (those with parental responsibilities or a parent of the child without parental responsibilities or rights) will cooperate with each other in regard to matters affecting the child.[19]

Child abduction cases[20] are subject to the Hague Convention on the Civil Aspects of International Child Abduction, which was incorporated into domestic law by the Child Abduction and Custody Act 1985.[21] They also have been subject to European Union regulation, for cross-border cases in the European Union, which have increasingly strong rights for children to have their wishes considered.[22] However, with the UK leaving the European Union, these provisions would need to be re-instituted.[23]

3. MODES OF CHILD PARTICIPATION

In order to realise children's participation rights, a range of mechanisms were put in place subsequent to the 1995 Act for section 11 proceedings.

---

15 Section 11(10).

16 Section 11(7)(a).

17 Lord Rodger stated: 'it is conducive to the welfare of children if their absent parents maintain personal relations and direct contact with them on a regular basis' (*White v White* 2001 SC 689, 17).

18 Section 11(7A)–(7C).

19 Section 11(7D)–(7E).

20 The Central Authority for Scotland team, which handles such cases, did so with 13 incoming cases and 20 outgoing cases in 2016. Scottish Government, *Review of Part 1 of the Children (Scotland) Act 1995 and creation of a Family Justice Modernisation Strategy*, 2018, https://www.gov.scot/publications/review-part-1-children-scotland-act-1995-creation-family-justice/pages/24/, para. 8.02.

21 In Scotland, there is also a common law offence of 'plagium', which is a crime of child stealing committed against a child below the age of puberty.

22 Regulation (EC) No. 2201/2003 Celex No. 32003R2201 and now Regulation (EU) No. 2019/1111 Celex No. 32019R1111.

23 For further elaboration, see R. Kelsey and J. West, *International relocation of children in the UK (Scotland)*, 2018, https://uk.practicallaw.thomsonreuters.com/6-622-5707?transitionType=Default&contextData=(sc.Default)&firstPage=true#co_pageContainer.

3.1. DIRECT FORMS OF PARTICIPATION

If children are officially contacted once the case enters the court process (called 'intimation'), they receive a Form F9 requesting their views. The form goes back to the sheriff.[24] The sheriff may express the wish to hear directly from the child and ask for the child to be brought to the court. The child may give evidence as a witness, at a proof.[25] The child can use 'special measures'[26] to help them give evidence, as a 'vulnerable witness' under section 11 of the Vulnerable Witnesses (Scotland) Act 2004.

3.2. REPRESENTATION FORMS OF PARTICIPATION

The court may appoint a child welfare reporter or a curator ad litem to report on the child's views. A child welfare reporter will likely be instructed to ascertain a child's views by the court. A curator ad litem is appointed to protect the child's interests and can be requested by the court to ascertain a child's views. Neither a child welfare reporter nor a curator ad litem has a responsibility to advocate for the child nor to support the child to state their views directly to the court.

3.3. CHILD LITIGATING ON OWN BEHALF

A child may take independent legal advice. If this were done, the child's views can be expressed in several ways. The lawyer may help the child to fill in the Form F9, the lawyer may write to the court on the child's behalf, or the lawyer may seek to have the child involved as a party to the action. Alternatively, if the case were in the Sheriff Court, the lawyer may appear on the child's behalf at the Child Welfare Hearing to represent the child and assist in having the child's views communicated to the court. The Child Welfare Hearing provides an early hearing to resolve any disputed issues in family actions, particularly in relation to children.

---

24 A sheriff's main role is to sit as a trial judge. At the time of writing, there are 142 permanent or resident sheriffs sitting in 39 courts across Scotland, as well as floating sheriffs moving between courts. Sheriffs hear almost all family actions, including adoptions, child welfare and divorce. See https://www.judiciary.scot/home/judiciary/judicial-office-holders/sheriffs/sheriffs-1 for more information about sheriffs in Scotland.

25 A 'proof' is where a sheriff will hear evidence in the case and then issue a written judgement. There are often various procedural steps and hearings before a proof is held. See https://www.scotcourts.gov.uk/coming-to-court/attending-a-court/attending-a-civil-court.

26 'Special measures' is a statutory term for protective measures for vulnerable witnesses. Measures are set out in the Act, which include giving evidence by a live television link or behind a screen, and with a supporter. For more information see https://www.mygov.scot/being-a-witness/help-and-support/.

A child under the age of 16 has the legal capacity to ask a solicitor to represent them in any civil matter, where the child has a general understanding of what it means to do so.[27] There is a presumption that a child aged 12 or above will have such an understanding. However, restrictions in legal aid introduced in 2011[28] curtail this possibility for most children, for section 11 proceedings.

Disputes about contact and parental responsibilities can find their ways into other court proceedings. Children's hearings, for example, deal with children both in need of care and protection and who offend. The hearings can issue compulsory supervision orders, which can affect child contact and parental responsibilities: for example, the order could limit or specify contact between a child and their parent, and decide on with whom a child should live. The children's hearing system has an array of legal responsibilities intended to ensure a child's views are considered; equally, there have been longstanding concerns that children's right to participate is inadequately considered.[29] Those working in the system are committed to improving this, such as creating more appropriate children's hearing venues. The Scottish Government has announced that advocacy will become available for children in the children's hearing system. Parental responsibilities can also be modified in international child abduction cases and domestic orders for permanency or adoption. In all these proceedings, children's views should be considered. These multiple proceedings can create a confusing array, as they do not always articulate with each other and can lead to a parent using the system to gain their preferred result or to prolong abuse.[30]

For disputed parental responsibilities, there are alternatives to the courts for settling these disputes. For example, judges in family actions can refer the issue to a mediator accredited to a specified mediation organisation. As yet, these are not mandatory referrals, although there have been high-level recommendations that they become so, and the Scottish Government perceives mediation as underused for resolving disputes.[31] Further advice is

---

27 Age of Legal Capacity (Scotland) Act 1991, s 2(4A).

28 Due to the Advice and Assistance (Scotland) Amendment Regulations 2010 and the Civil Legal Aid (Scotland) Amendment Regulations 2010. Previously a child or young person would be assessed financially in the same way as an adult, on the basis of the child or young person's own disposable income and capital. Since changes in January 2011, a solicitor assessing a child or young person who applies for civil legal assistance must take account of the financial circumstances of anyone who owes a duty of ailment to that child or young person. There is an exemption – if it would be unjust or inequitable to do so, in the particular circumstances of the case.

29 Scottish Parliament Education and Skills Committee, *The Children's Hearing System – Taking stock of recent reforms*, 2017, http://www.parliament.scot/S5_Education/Reports/ESS052017R05.pdf.

30 H. Douglas 'Legal systems abuse and coercive control' (2018) 18(1) *Criminology & Criminal Justice* 84.

31 Scottish Government, *Family Justice Modernisation Strategy*, 2019, https://www.gov.scot/publications/family-justice-modernisation-strategy/.

available for individuals considering seeking a court order under section 11, about other options than going to court. This includes an informal agreement, called a Parenting Plan, which is aimed at supporting parents to discuss what is best for their child. A formal agreement – called a minute of agreement – is another option; this is registered and legally binding. The Scottish Government proposes to suggest templates to the professional legal bodies, so parents can record what steps they have taken to obtain the child's views. No monitoring is being proposed of mediation, parenting plans or minutes of agreement. For most children, their right to participate will be very reliant on what their parents choose to do.

3.4. LEADING CASE LAW

Children's views are now more regularly mentioned in reported case law on section 11 cases. Previously, children's views were rarely mentioned in decisions and even less likely to be discussed as influential on the court's decision.[32] Now, children's views are often mentioned and particularly after the case of *Shields v Shields*.[33]

Shields v Shields was a relocation case, with the mother requesting a residence and specific issue order, in regard to her son who was seven and a half years old. On appeal to the Inner House of the Court of Session, it was established that sheriffs must exercise their discretion as to whether and, if so, how an opportunity should be given to a child to express their views in the particular circumstances, under section 11(7). Courts could not necessarily rely on an early decision but had to consider whether there was a 'material change of circumstances' between that early decision and the order being made. The case goes on to clarify the participation provisions of the 1995 Act. 'Practicability' is the first test under section 11(7), with a low threshold: 'But, if, by one method or another, it is "practicable" to give a child the opportunity of expressing his views, then, in our view, the only safe course is to employ that method'.[34] In a subsequent case, concerns about a child's welfare were added:

> It would … be most unsatisfactory if considerations of physical practicability obliged this court to follow a course which risked causing further distress, and perhaps lasting harm, to a young child.[35]

---

32 K. Tisdall, A. Cleland, K. Marshall and A. Plumtree, 'Listening to the Views of Children? Principles and Mechanisms within the Children (Scotland) Act 1995' (2002) 24(4) *Journal of Social Welfare and Family Law* 385.

33 2002 SC 246.

34 2002 SC 246, para. 11.

35 *S v S* 2012 Fam LR 32, para. 36.

Thus, the issue should be largely *how* rather than *whether* a child's views should be ascertained, while ensuring a child is protected from further distress or potential lasting harm.

In child abduction cases across national borders, reported case law underlines that a child's views may be taken account by the courts. If the child were of sufficient age and maturity, and did not want to be returned, the child's views may be taken into account, but the views are neither determinative nor setting a presumption.[36]

Other case law is integrated into the discussion below, on the evidence showing advancements and problems for children's participation in section 11 proceedings.

4. RESEARCH

Should a case reach the courts, because parents or others cannot resolve their dispute about parental responsibilities, then the mechanisms listed above should support children's right to participate. This section addresses how these are working in practice.

4.1. CHILDREN'S OPPORTUNITIES TO GIVE THEIR VIEWS TO THE COURT

A recent review of reported cases found that cases regularly mention whether or not a child's views are sought.[37] If they were not sought, a simple statement is generally made in the case law that the children are too young to be able to express their views. Often the courts rely on the submissions of parties' solicitors, rather than an assessment of the child's ability to express views independent from their parents and their parents' agents. There is no apparent pattern by age regarding whether a child's views will be considered by the courts: there are examples of children as young as three and four years of age having their views considered by the court, while research by Mackay in two Sheriff Courts found children over the age of 12 being excluded from participating.[38]

---

36 *YG v EEP* [2017] CSOH 75, 11. See also *M Petitioner* 2005 SCLR 396, and *MM v VM* [2008] 1 AC 1288.

37 F. Morrison, E.K.M. Tisdall, J. Warburton, A. Reid and F. Jones, *Children's Participation in Family Actions – Probing Compliance With Children's Rights Research Report*, 2020, http://hdl.handle.net/1893/31100.

38 K. Mackay, *Hearing children in contact disputes*, 2013, https://www.era.lib.ed.ac.uk/bitstream/handle/1842/6557/briefing%2065.pdf;jsessionid=34DC22EC1503E28F8E5ACAC8F0DEF332?sequence=1.

Mackay's study found that only 42% (125 of 299) of children had their views taken into account by one or more of the mechanisms listed above.[39] The presumption that a child aged 12 or above would have sufficient age and maturity, either for sufficient understanding to instruct a solicitor or to form views under section 11, has not delivered on its expectations. Too often it has dissuaded courts from ensuring children under the age of 12 are supported to provide their views and has not guaranteed those 12 or over do have their views duly considered.[40]

All mechanisms have been subjected to considerable criticism. In response to criticisms of the Form F9, it has been revised to be more child and young person friendly. It has been clarified that a child can receive the Form F9 without having the official writ, which contains the details of their parents' dispute. Further, children under the 12 years should receive the forms, unless it is considered inappropriate to do so.[41] However, courts and parties can doubt the 'independence' of the child's views expressed on the Form, as there is no check that a child has not been unduly influenced when completing it.[42] The Form F9 is issued early in the proceedings, which can be before the sheriff knows the child's personal circumstances and the child's views may have changed by the time the sheriff makes a decision.[43] The Form F9 may be increasingly used in Scotland but it is widely regarded as unsatisfactory.

If a child's views were heard, they are most often heard by a court-instructed professional. In Mackay's study, 68 of 299 children (23%) saw a court reporter (now called a child welfare reporter) and a further 15 children (5%) saw a curator ad litem.[44] Research has uncovered poor practice by such professionals, such as spending insufficient time with children to establish rapport and trust, asking children inappropriate questions, and children reporting that their views have been inaccurately relayed.[45] Yet the courts highly rely on these reports, which can be treated by the court as the recorded views of the child.[46]

---

39 For similar findings, see K. Laing and G. Wilson, *Understanding Child Contact Cases in Scottish Sheriff Courts*, 2010, https://www.webarchive.org.uk/wayback/archive/20180514221659/http://www.gov.scot/Publications/2010/12/08145916/0.

40 Scottish Government, *Policy Memorandum Children (Scotland) Bill*, 2019, https://www.parliament.scot/S5_Bills/Children%20(Scotland)%20Bill/SPBILL52PMS052019.pdf, para. 17.

41 Under r 33.7A(2) of the Ordinary Cause Rules, inserted by Act of Sederunt (Rules of the Court of Session 1994 and Ordinary Court Rules 1993 Amendment) (Views of Child) 2019.

42 *X v Y* 2018 SLT (SH Ct) 215.

43 *X v Y* 2018 SLT (SH Ct) 215.

44 K. Mackay, Hearing children in contact disputes, 2013, https://www.era.lib.ed.ac.uk/bitstream/handle/1842/6557/briefing%2065.pdf;jsessionid=34DC22EC1503E28F8E5ACAC8F0DEF332?sequence=1.

45 F. Morrison, E.K.M. Tisdall and J.E.M. Callaghan, 'Manipulation and Domestic Abuse in Contested Contact – Threats to Children's Participation Rights' (2020) 58(2) *Family Court Review* 403.

46 *L v L* 2013 GWD 25-496, para. 22.

However, these professionals are not necessarily transmitting children's views but rather interpreting or translating them in light of the court's paramount consideration – the child's welfare.[47]

Children's direct involvement in court proceedings has often been discouraged by courts.[48] The courts decide on the mode of children's participation.[49] Appeal cases show a strong reluctance to interfere in the initial judge's discretion, and consider the judge in the first instance as best placed to make the case-by-case decision.[50] More judicial interviewing may be happening, which is reported ad hoc,[51] but the extent of this is not captured by statistics. Concerns are whether judges are suitably skilled and trained to do this and how they will deal with any confidential information they hear privately from the child.[52] Reported case law ebbs and flows about children gaining legal representation and becoming a party to the case.[53] Of late, it has been particularly difficult due to the constraints in legal aid funding and the concern about children becoming overly involved.

Instead of promoting meaningful engagement directly with courts on section 11 cases, concerns are often expressed in reported case law of children being overly involved, with detrimental consequences for their welfare as a result. The Supreme Court was sharply critical in *B v G* about the unnecessarily lengthy contact proceedings, which were 'inimical to the best interests of the child'.[54] This led to changes in the procedural rules and encouragement of active judicial case management[55] and a proposed duty on courts to have regard to 'any risk of prejudice to the child's welfare that delay in proceedings would pose'.[56] The rise of self-represented litigants may have also discouraged courts from hearing directly from children, with reported case law expressing criticism of parents'

---

47 Research in England drew this distinction between transmitting and translating. The Office of Children's Commissioner in England drew this distinction between transmitting and translating, in their 2011 response to the Family Justice Review Interim Report.

48 K.M. Mackay, 'The approach in Scotland to child contact disputes involving allegations of domestic abuse' (2018) 40(4) *Journal of Social Welfare and Family Law* 477.

49 E.g. *S v A* 2015 GWD 13-222.

50 E.g. *Stewart v Stewart 2007* SC 451, para. 12.

51 G. Hassan and A. Masson, 'Court to Child: A different approach' (2017) 62(9) *The Journal of the Law Society of Scotland*.

52 L. Barnes, '"Moral actors in their own right": consideration of the views of children in family proceedings' (2008) 21 *Scots Law Times* 139.

53 E.g. *B v B* 2011 SLT (Sh Ct) 225.

54 [2012] UKSC 21, para. 21.

55 The Family Law Committee of the Scottish Civil Justice Council has consulted on new case management in family actions. See http://www.scottishciviljusticecouncil.gov.uk/consultations/scjc-consultations/consultation-on-the-case-management-of-family-and-civil-partnership-actions-in-the-sheriff-court.

56 Children (Scotland) Bill, s 11ZA(2A).

inappropriately involving their children.[57] The case law suggests a tendency to see courts as not only inappropriate for children but actively detrimental to their welfare, with a preference for children to be kept separate from the parental dispute.[58]

In short, the promise of the 1995 Act and its lengthy list of mechanisms for children's participation have not been realised. Few children appear to have their views considered at all, with easy assumptions made about 'age and maturity' with no independent assessment. The mechanisms are not used consistently, nor always well, with concerns about children's welfare often disenfranchising children and their right to participate.

4.2. THE WEIGHT GIVEN TO CHILDREN'S VIEWS IN COURT DECISIONS

From reported case law, it is often difficult to ascertain what weight has been given to a child's views in the court decisions. Often a child's view is *described*, but how it was *weighed* in the decision is not stated. This may be a protective approach by the courts, so as not to place responsibility unduly on the child in contested cases. However, it makes it difficult for others to know to what extent this element of a child's right to participate is met.

Reported case law shows that children are more likely to have their views described approvingly by the courts if the views were considered rational, consistent and autonomous.[59] If a child is reported as changing their mind, or unduly emotional or anxious, their views are less likely to weigh into the decisions.[60] Age can be mentioned as relevant: for example, a court can be reluctant to issue an order against a child's views if the child were nearly 16.[61]

Of ever-increasing debate is the concern about children being 'unduly influenced' in high-conflict contact cases. If a court considers that children might be unduly influenced, the court can be even more reluctant to involve the child and give weight to their views. Further, children's views may be ignored

---

57 E.g. *Hall v Hall* 2014 GWD 26-521.

58 E.K.M. Tisdall, F. Morrison and J. Warburton, 'Challenging undue influence? Rethinking children's participation in contested child contact' (forthcoming) *Journal of Social Welfare and Family Law.*

59 E.K.M. Tisdall, 'Subjects with Agency: Children's participation in family law proceedings' (2016) 38(4) *Journal of Social Welfare and Family Law* 362.

60 E.K.M. Tisdall, 'Subjects with Agency: Children's participation in family law proceedings' (2016) 38(4) *Journal of Social Welfare and Family Law* 362.

61 Most parental responsibilities and rights end when a young person becomes 16. See L. Barnes Macfarlane, *The Children (Scotland) Bill 2019. Balancing the Rights of Parents and Children*, 2019, https://www.parliament.scot/S5_JusticeCommittee/Inquiries/Balancing_the_Rights_of_Parents_and_Children_Reportv2.pdf.

or used to opposite effect, as evidence of the children's alienation from one parent.[62]

Such high-conflict cases often involve allegations of domestic abuse.[63] Because of continued difficulties in ensuring criminal proceedings adequately deal with domestic abuse, many allegations are unproven. The connections between criminal and civil proceedings are not always made. Abuse is not consistently defined across legislation.[64] Rather than recognising domestic abuse as the 'norm' by the courts, and organising the courts and mechanisms around this, evidence suggests that parties, solicitors and courts have often avoided addressing allegations of domestic abuse[65] and attempt to create boundaries so children do not become enmeshed in parental disputes.[66] Children repeatedly report that this is not working: they are directly affected by the domestic abuse between their parents, and the attempts to protect them from it are failing.[67]

In summary, provisions in the Children (Scotland) Act 1995 were promising in terms of supporting children's right to participation in contested parental responsibilities cases. However, their implementation has not realised this promise, with recognition now that more needs to be done to ensure this right is met.

5. POLICY OR PRACTICE DEVELOPMENTS

Scottish family law is in a period of reform, with poor implementation of children's participation rights now well recognised. Certain changes have been made through the Children (Scotland) Act 2020 to address this, significantly amended after campaigning by young people and other members of civic society.

---

62 E.K.M. Tisdall, F. Morrison and J. Warburton, 'Challenging undue influence? Rethinking children's participation in contested child contact' (forthcoming) *Journal of Social Welfare and Family Law.*

63 Cafcass and Women's Aid, *Allegations of domestic abuse in child contact cases*, 2017, https://www.cafcass.gov.uk/wp-content/uploads/2017/12/Allegations-of-domestic-abuse-in-child-contact-cases-2017.pdf. This research refers to England but is considered likely applicable to Scotland (e.g. K. Mackay, *Hearing children in contact disputes*, 2013, https://www.era.lib.ed.ac.uk/bitstream/handle/1842/6557/briefing%2065.pdf;jsessionid=34DC22EC1503E28F8E5ACAC8F0DEF332?sequence=1, had similar findings).

64 F. Morrison, E.K.M. Tisdall, F. Jones and A. Reid, *Child contact proceedings for children affected by domestic abuse*, 2013, http://www.sccyp.org.uk/.

65 R. Whitecross, 'Section 11 Orders and the "Abuse" Provision' (2017) 21(2) *The Edinburgh Law Review* 269.

66 F. Morrison, E.K.M. Tisdall and J.E.M. Callaghan, 'Manipulation and Domestic Abuse in Contested Contact – Threats to Children's Participation Rights' (2020) 58(2) *Family Court Review* 403.

67 Commissioner for Children and Young People in Scotland and Scottish Women's Aid, *Power Up/Power Down*, 2017, https://womensaid.scot/project/power-up-power-down/.

For example, the presumption of age 12 is largely repealed from the provisions (although it would still apply for a child's legal representation). Feedback must be provided to the child, with the court ensuring that a decision is explained to the child concerned in a way that the child can understand (with some exceptions).[68] The Scottish Government reworded sections 6 and 11 with the intention of expanding the instances of children's views being heard, with a presumption that the child is 'capable of forming a view unless the contrary is shown'.[69] A child will be able to express their views in the manner preferred by the child (with some exceptions).[70] However, it is possible that the court will not give a child the opportunity to express their views, or for those views not to be given due regard, if the child is not capable of forming a view or the child's location is not known.[71] These exceptions and 'get out' clauses will benefit from monitoring and review, to see how they are being implemented.

The Government will tighten the regulation regarding child welfare reporters to require them to be registered and to receive regular training.[72] This may well improve practice, if suitably resourced. After considerable pressure, the legislation was amended to include future provision of child advocacy services.[73] The latter has been consistently asked for by children and young people through research and advocacy, so attention will be needed to ensure the successful implementation of these provisions.

The policy development does not result in wholescale reform but seeks – substantially – to improve the present system. These advancements are welcomed, but there remains considerable concern about inconsistency across courts and as experienced by children. This is not addressed by the primary legislation and faces opposition about interfering with judicial independence. To help ensure attention to this, a review of children's ability to participate is required by the Act, which is to be completed in five years.[74]

6. CONCLUSION

With the Scottish Government's commitment to incorporating the UNCRC into Scottish domestic law, issues of compliance are to the fore for all policy decision-makers. This is evident in the Children (Scotland) Act 2020 in amending the

68 Section 20.
69 As amended by the Children (Scotland) Act 2020, s 1.
70 For the Children (Scotland) Act 1995, ss 6 and 11, as amended by the Children (Scotland) Act 2020, s 1.
71 As amended by the Children (Scotland) Act 2020, s 1.
72 Children (Scotland) Act 2020, s 9.
73 Children (Scotland) Act 2020, s 21.
74 Children (Scotland) Act 2020, s 31.

Children (Scotland) Act 1995, which draws welcome attention to children's participation rights.

Given that Article 12 in itself is a weak participation right,[75] the 1995 Act was already largely congruent with the article. In practice, research and analysis suggest that children's Article 12 rights are often not being met: children are often not given their opportunity to give their views and, with concerns of undue influence or manipulation, these views may not be given due weight. When one considers the obligations set out in the UN Committee on the Rights of the Child's General Comment on Article 12, the evaluation is even poorer. For example, the General Comment underlines that:

- all children should be presumed to have the capacity to form their own view;[76]
- there is no age limit on the right of the child to express their views;[77] and
- children need not have comprehensive knowledge to be considered capable.[78]

Yet children are too often excluded from having their views considered in section 11 proceedings, with unsubstantiated statements about 'age and maturity', with no independent assessment. The General Comment on Article 12 states that the rights of the child to express their views and the best interests of the child (Article 3) are complementary, not in conflict, concluding that 'there can be no correct application of article 3 if the components of article 12 are not respected'.[79] While cross-national comparison may look on Scottish practice favourably in contrast to their own, there is a growing consensus in Scotland that the current experiences of children in relation to their participation rights is unacceptable and must be improved.[80]

The General Comment on Article 12 directs that, wherever possible, children should be heard directly in proceedings if the children wish to do so.[81] In Scotland, children's views are largely mediated by adults, primarily by child welfare reporters, and children are rarely heard directly by the courts. To change this requires support and preparation both for the child and for the judiciary, as well as the court staff who would facilitate this taking place. Virtual connections

75 E.K.M. Tisdall, 'Children and Young People's Participation' in W. Vandenhole, E. Desmet, D. Reynaert and S. Lembrechts (eds.), *Routledge International Handbook of Children's Rights Studies*, Routledge, Abingdon 2015.

76 General Comment No. 12, para. 20.

77 General Comment No. 12, para. 21.

78 General Comment No. 12, para. 21.

79 General Comment No. 12, para. 74.

80 The Justice Committee of the Scottish Parliament underlines this growing consensus in Scotland, in its Stage 1 Report on the Children (Scotland) Bill, 2020, SP Paper 721, https://sp-bpr-en-prod-cdnep.azureedge.net/published/J/2020/5/1/Stage-1-Report-on-the-Children--Scotland--Bill/JS0520R07.pdf. For cross-national comparisons, see other country chapters in this Handbook.

81 General Comment No. 12, para. 35.

(video or through secure social media channels) could provide other channels for children to be heard directly by courts.

The UN Committee on the Rights of the Child states in General Comment No. 5 that there must be access to effective remedy for rights to be meaningful.[82] Provisions need to be in place for child-friendly opportunities for remedy and redress when children's rights have been breached. For example, children have pointed out that they have no recourse if a child welfare report is submitted that does not represent or misrepresents their views.[83] A key precondition for children's access to remedy is that they have sufficient child-friendly information. The Family Justice Modernisation Strategy proposes that child-friendly guidance be prepared for children who attend court to take part in a case about them or to give views to a sheriff or judge.[84] This needs to be wider, to cover a child's right to participate in a manner suitable to them and options if they were unhappy with how this right is being provided for.

Effective monitoring is needed, with sufficient and robust data gathered and published so that all can evaluate (and hold duty-bearers accountable) whether children's rights are being met. No published statistics, for example, are currently available on how often children's views are considered in contested section 11 proceedings. Even less data, evaluation and research are available on children's participation rights outwith court proceedings. Given most disputes are settled outwith courts, this is a serious concern for realising children's rights.

While Scotland's primary and secondary legislation can no doubt be improved, the current changes may merely make it somewhat better, rather than revolutionising the realisation of children's participation rights. More fundamental options would include: considering whether a non-adversarial system would better deal with contested cases and identify how that might work; investing seriously in accessible legal education and information for children to know their rights; and ensuring there is accountability to children, which requires monitoring, evidence and child-friendly complaints. These may need to come sooner rather than later, once Scotland incorporates the UNCRC in domestic law and greater prominence is given to children's rights implementation as a result.

---

[82] United Nations Committee on the Rights of the Child, *General Comment No. 5: General Measures of Implementation of the Convention on the Rights of the Child*, CRC/GC/2003/5, 27 November 2003, https://tbinternet.ohchr.org/_layouts/15/treatybodyexternal/Download.aspx?symbolno=CRC%2fGC%2f2003%2f5&Lang=en, para. 24.

[83] YELLO!, *Response to Call for Views on the Children (Scotland) Bill*, 2020, https://womensaid.scot/wp-content/uploads/2019/12/Yello-Response-to-Children-Scotland-Bill-call-for-views.pdf.

[84] Scottish Government, *Family Justice Modernisation Strategy*, 2019, https://www.gov.scot/publications/family-justice-modernisation-strategy/, para. 6.21.

SOUTH AFRICA

Julia SLOTH-NIELSEN

1. INTRODUCTION

South Africa was characterised by formal apartheid (separation of races), which was enforced until 1994. This has deeply affected various aspects still associated with the family law system, including the court system, laws regulating marriage and divorce, and the societal organisation of family life. The fault lines of the past are in many respects reproduced today, 25 years after the formal ending of institutionalised racial segregation.

With a population touching 58 million people (and an unknown number of undocumented migrants), detailed information about family make-up and the incidence of divorce in South Africa has only recently become available. Data on registered marriages is held by the Department of Home Affairs. Registered marriages include civil marriages,[1] customary marriages,[2] and

[1] Concluded in accordance with the Marriage Act 1961. Registration is compulsory.

[2] Concluded in accordance with the requirements of the Recognition of Customary Marriages Act 1998. Registration is not compulsory and non-registration does not affect the validity of the customary marriage. Very few customary marriages are in fact registered.

civil unions.[3] In a report released in February 2019, a total of 135,458 civil marriages, 2,588 customary marriages and 1,357 civil unions were registered in 2017.[4] In comparison with 2016 data, registration of civil marriages and customary marriages dropped by 2.9% and 34.9% respectively, whereas that of civil unions increased by 0.3%.

Information on divorces is derived from data held by the Department of Justice. In 2017, 25,390 completed divorce forms were processed, indicating an increase of 0.3% from the 25,326 processed in 2016. More plaintiffs were female (12,938, 51.0%) than male (8,878, 35.0%). The median ages at divorce in 2017 were 44 years for men and 40 years for women. Four in 10 divorces, 11,330 (44.6%) of the 25,390 in 2017, occurred in marriages that did not reach their tenth wedding anniversary. In 2017, there were 14,121 (55.6%) divorces with children aged less than 18 years affected – 44.5% of divorces were from the African population group, 23.6% from the white population, 17.5% from the coloured (mixed-race) population group, and 5.51% from the Asian group. In up to 80% of all family law disputes, one or more of the parties is unrepresented, and approximately only 6% of cases go to trial.[5] The majority of divorces (55.6%) involve children younger than 18 years.[6]

Part of the legacy of apartheid includes the extremely high number of children born out of wedlock, approximating 58% of all births in the country. In addition, partly reflective of the legacy of the migrant labour system of apartheid, only 34.9% of children lived with both biological parents in 2017 (with 21% living with neither biological parent, but often growing up in what are called skip-generation families, where the grandparents raise children either as a consequence of HIV/Aids or due to labour migration of working adults).[7]

The Constitution of South Africa of 1996 explicitly provides for the assignment of legal representation for children in civil matters if substantial injustice would otherwise result.[8] Few commentators – if any – have provided any insight into the provenance of this provision, which was not included in the interim constitution of 1994. It can be speculated that it was added in an attempt to give constitutional expression to Article 12 of the UN Convention on the Rights of the Child (UNCRC). It has been noted that section 28(1)(h) has

---

3 Concluded in terms of the Civil Union Act 2006, between same-sex or heterosexual partners, and subject to compulsory registration.

4 Statistics South Africa, *Marriages and Divorces*, P0307 28, February 2019.

5 South African Law Reform Commission, *Discussion Paper 148 (Alternative Dispute Resolution in Family Matters*, 2019, (hereafter SALRC Discussion Paper), para. 2.1.2.

6 SALRC Discussion Paper, above n. 5, para. 2.1.2.

7 SALRC Discussion Paper, above n. 5, para. 2.1.2.

8 Section 28(1)(h). Legal representation for children facing criminal charges is found under the constitutional section dealing with the fair trial rights of all criminal defendants.

broad application and includes family law proceedings. It matters not whether the child is a party to proceedings, or directly before the court.[9]

The circumstances in which 'substantial injustice' might result that would give rise to the need for a legal representative for the child to be appointed has been debated by several authors.[10] Whilst some of the criteria adduced pertain to public law matters, some are indicative of the need for separate legal representation in family law matters, such as the fact that a drastic order of relief might sever all contact with the non-custodian parent; that the litigation is, or is going to be, lengthy and acrimonious; that there are reasons to believe one of the parents is emotionally unstable, or sexually or physically abusing the child; where there is reason to believe one party is withholding information from the court; or where the impact on the child's daily life will be significant. This is not a finite list.

South Africa has a tiered and fairly complicated court system, with jurisdiction for various family law matters split between different courts. The three tiers of courts are District or Magistrates Courts, Regional Courts, and High Courts, which have the largest geographical area of coverage and jurisdiction to try the most serious criminal cases and civil cases with the largest monetary claims at stake. Until 2008, High Courts had exclusive jurisdiction to hear divorce matters, including where children's interests might be at stake through the need to allocate parental responsibilities and rights in the post-divorce period. Now, Regional Courts enjoy divorce jurisdiction too.[11] However, High Courts have exclusive jurisdiction over any matter involving guardianship of a child, for instance termination of guardianship or consenting to encumbering a child's immovable property. The definition of guardianship and the specificities of what it entails are now provided in section 18(3) of the Children's Act 38 of 2007.[12]

---

9 South African Law Reform Commission, *Family Dispute Resolution: Care of and Contact with Children*, Project 100D Issue Paper 31, December 2015 (hereafter SALRC Issue Paper), para. 2.2.45.

10 D. Kassan, 'Children's Right to Legal Representation in Divorce Proceedings' in J. Sloth-Nielsen and Z. Du Toit (eds.), *Trials and Tribulations, Trends and Triumphs*, Juta, Cape Town 2008, pp. 237–238; J. Sloth-Nielsen, 'Children' in H. Cheadle, D. Davis and N. Haysom (eds.), *South African Constitutional Law: The Bill of Rights*, Butterworths, Durban 2002.

11 The existing separate justice systems for different population groups could not survive a constitutional democracy based on freedom and equality. Hence, in 2008, the Jurisdiction of the Regional Courts Act 31 of 2008 awarded civil jurisdiction to courts which had hitherto enjoyed only criminal jurisdiction, collapsing the previous 'black divorce courts' into the existing Regional Court structure. They now have jurisdiction over all forms of divorce, and have become a less expensive and more accessible option for ordinary citizens than the High Court process; hence they do deal with vast numbers of divorces and, as such, are implicated in any overview of child participation in family law proceedings. No studies have yet been conducted on the operation of the Regional Courts' approach to family law proceedings.

12 Amending legislation that would alter this situation and confer the power to deal with guardianship issues to lower courts as well was gazetted in late 2019, and is currently being debated in Parliament.

Divorce is regulated by the Divorce Act 70 of 1979. This law introduced 'no fault' divorce and paved the way for the possibility of divorces being completed just on the court papers submitted, without the need for evidence to be presented. How child participation manifests in the context of divorce litigation is discussed in the ensuing sections.

Following a commission of inquiry into the functioning of the courts in the 1980s, the legislature introduced the Mediation in Certain Divorce Matters Act 24 of 1987. Contrary to its stated title, the Act did not introduce mediation. Instead, it set up an Office of the Family Advocate (with decentralised branches) staffed by Advocates and Counsellors (with a social work background). Their purpose was to furnish a Divorce Court with a report confirming that the party-led arrangements for the post-divorce period for the child or children were in the best interests of the child.[13] The Family Advocate, as an officer of the court, could also present expert reports to the court on the best interests of the child and, to that end, would have completed an investigation into the child's and family's circumstances which would routinely involve interviewing the child. However, the Mediation in Certain Divorce Matters Act does not specifically require the Family Advocate to listen to the views of the child.[14]

The mandate of the Family Advocate is said to be a 'best interests' mandate, rather than that official acting as a representative of the child.[15] This, too, is elaborated on below.

The High Court also has exclusive jurisdiction over matters emanating from the Hague Convention on the Civil Aspects of International Child Abduction (Hague Convention), ratified by South Africa in 1996. The Act which initially domesticated this treaty designated the Chief Family Advocate as the Central Authority for the Convention. Hague Convention matters are now comprehensively regulated under Chapter 17 of the Children's Act 38 of 2007.

At District Court level, the lowest-level jurisdiction, certain courts established in terms of dedicated legislation may be regarded as performing family law type functions. These are: Maintenance Courts,[16] which can review and amend child support awards, even if these initially emanated in a divorce order granted by a High Court; Domestic Violence Courts;[17] and Children's Courts, established now in Chapter 4 of the Children's Act 38 of 2005. Children's Courts have wide

13 Section 4 of the Mediation in Certain Divorce Matters Act.

14 SALRC Issue Paper, above n. 9, para. 2.2.32. The prescribed questionnaire used by the Family Advocate 'includes no questions to probe or record the wishes of the child and his or her views with regards to the proposed arrangements' (para. 2.2.33).

15 *Soller v G* 2003 (5) SA 430 (W).

16 Established by the Maintenance Act 1999 of 1998.

17 Established by the Domestic Violence Act 116 of 1998. Their function is to grant interim and final protection orders in order to deter a perpetrator from behaviour which constitutes domestic violence.

powers to intervene in family life, including for child protection reasons (which falls outside the scope of this chapter), but more pertinently in the allocation, amendment or termination of all aspects of parental responsibilities and rights (such as care and contact) which do not constitute guardianship.[18] Hence, in many areas of family law, Children's Courts, Regional Divorce Courts and High Courts enjoy concurrent jurisdiction.

2. STATUTORY PROVISIONS

The role of the Family Advocate is to ensure the best interests of the child have been catered for, which does not necessarily require or mandate child participation in any pre-trial processes overseen by this body. Although there is a provision in the Divorce Act permitting a legal representative to be appointed for a child, this is extremely rare. In *Legal Aid Board v R*,[19] the court confirmed that the child's right to legal representation was independent of parental wishes or consent – in this case a high-conflict divorce involving care and contact of a child that had been waged for more than seven years. With the appointment of her own counsel, the case settled almost immediately.[20] The case is unusual, though, insofar as it concerned independent legal representation of a child in a divorce matter.

The Children's Act itself is unusually sensitive to the need to hear children's voices in matters that affect them.[21] Examples in point are section 10 of the Children's Act, which states as a general principle that '[e]very child that is of such an age, maturity and stage of development as to be able to participate in any matter concerning that child has the right to participate in an appropriate way and views expressed by the child must be given due consideration.' Section 14 provides that every child has the right to bring, and be assisted in bringing, a matter to a court, provided that matter falls within the jurisdiction of that court. That children enjoy the legal standing to bring cases independently on

---

18 Until the amendment referred to in n. 12 above is enacted.

19 2009 (2) SA 262 (D).

20 The girl had contacted a child helpline and requested assistance in getting her views presented to the court. A legal representative was then appointed by the Legal Aid Board, despite the mother's objections.

21 Thus far there has been no elaboration of the meaning of 'matters that affect children'. However, using *B v B* [2012] ZASCA 151 as a precedent, it is likely that matters beyond those dealt with in the Children's Act itself would be implicated. *B v B* was a case where the applicable legislation (the Maintenance Act of 1998) did not provide for children's interests to be independently articulated, but the court allowed a legal representative for the child to be appointed. The rationale for this was s 10 of the Children's Act. See C.J. Davel and A.M. Skelton (eds.), *Commentary on the Children's Act*, 2nd revision, Juta, Cape Town 2018, pp. 2–20.

matters falling within the jurisdiction of the Children's Court is evident.[22] Hereafter, section 60(1)(c)(i) provides that a presiding officer in a matter before the Children's Court controls the conduct of the proceedings, rather than the parties, and may, 'to the extent necessary to resolve any factual dispute which is directly relevant in the matter, allow that person to be questioned or cross examined by (i) *the child* involved in the matter' (emphasis added).

In section 61, relating to Children's Court matters, entitled 'Participation of Children', the presiding officer of the Children's Court[23] is required to allow the child in the matter to express a view and preference, if the court finds that the child, given his/her age, maturity and stage of development and any special needs that the child may have, is able to participate in the proceedings and the child chooses to do so. There is no age limit specified for the child to be able to participate. Importantly, if the presiding officer finds that the child is unable to participate in the proceedings or is unwilling to express a view or preference in the matter, he/she must record the reasons for this finding. However, the bulk of Children's Court matters concern child protection, rather than family law matters. Furthermore, as yet no jurisprudence exists to enable a more elaborate understanding of how this provision is, or should be, applied in practice.

3. MODES OF CHILD PARTICIPATION

3.1. REPRESENTATION FORMS OF PARTICIPATION

3.1.1. *Separate Legal Representation of Children and Expert Reports*

As mentioned, the Divorce Act permits the appointment of a legal representative for the child, although this is very rare. Other than those provisions, the general provision of the Children's Act in section 10 does not prescribe or regulate how a child's view should be placed before a presiding officer. Nor does it limit the accessing of a child's view to any particular age group, as the twin criteria of age and maturity are determinant, as is the case with Article 12 of the UNCRC.[24] If it is not clear whether the child is of an age and maturity to express views (or brief a legal representative), it is open to a court to consider an expert report specifically on the child's age and maturity.[25] More usually, though, the court makes its own finding based on factors such as the reasons for the child's view, the degree to

22 As above. Children's legal standing is discussed more fully below.

23 This is usually a magistrate, never a judge, as judges only preside in High Court cases.

24 C.J. Davel and A.M. Skelton, above n. 21; C. Du Toit, 'Legal Representation of Children' in T. Boezaart (ed.), *Child Law in South Africa*, 2nd ed., Juta, Cape Town 2017, p. 130.

25 T. Boezaart, above n. 24, p. 131.

which the child may have been influenced by one or another parent, and so forth. Capacity to express views (or give instructions to a legal representative) is therefore assessed on a case-by-case basis.[26]

As noted, the Family Advocate is accorded the role of confirming that the best interests of the child have been satisfied, if needs be through providing an expert report to the court. The Family Advocate's report will reflect the views and wishes of the child obtained through interviews, although the recommendation might differ from, or even be in conflict with, the child's perspective.[27]

Rarely will judicial officers interview or speak to a child directly.[28] Parties (either parent) can also employ their own experts (social workers, psychologists), for which they must pay.[29] The expert provides an independent report which fairly consistently includes reflecting on the wishes or views of the child. It is not uncommon in high-conflict cases for several expert reports to be commissioned, and tales of reports prepared by what are, in effect, 'hired guns' surface not irregularly. The upshot of this, too, is multiple interviews and observations of the child by different experts, often at the behest of 'warring' parents.[30] There are presently no firm guidelines or procedures governing the presentation of expert reports, other than general evidentiary rules that apply to expert reports in any sphere of litigation.

As mentioned, section 28(1)(h) of the South African Constitution elevates the possibility of separate legal representation of children at state expense (if substantial injustice would otherwise result) to a justiciable constitutional principle. Section 55 of the Children's Act provides that where a child in Children's Court proceedings is not represented, and the court is of the opinion that it would be in the best interests of the child to have legal representation, the court must refer the matter to the Legal Aid Board for consideration to be given to appointing a legal representative.[31]

Due to the anticipated increase in demand for children's legal representation following implementation of the Children's Act, Legal Aid South Africa[32] established dedicated Children's Units to service children in conflict with the

26 T. Boezaart, above n. 24, p. 132.

27 See T. Boezaart, above n. 24; C.J. Davel and A.M. Skelton, above n. 21.

28 Z. Du Toit, 'Child Exceptions/Representing the Child in South Africa', *The Judges Newsletter*, The Hague Permanent Bureau, 2018, https://assets.hcch.net/docs/a8621431-c92c-4d01-a73c-acdb38a7fde5.pdf, pp. 9–62.

29 See, for instance, *F v F* 2006 (3) SA 42 (SCA).

30 See *J v J* 2008 (6) SA 30 (C) where the child objected to the many assessments he was subject to as a 'lab rat'.

31 Section 54 provides for the possibility of appointment of a legal representative of own choice at own expense. Criteria spelling out when such decision might be indicated in children's best interests have not yet been developed. The ultimate decision will therefore be an administrative one taken by officials at Legal Aid South Africa.

32 Previously named the Legal Aid Board.

law, as well as children who might require legal representation in civil matters,[33] including family law proceedings.[34] Although initial uptake was much lower than expected in civil matters affecting children, the latest Annual Report of Legal Aid South Africa indicates that children's civil matters now form 38% of the total number of cases in which children were represented, numbering 6,200 in that financial year.[35]

In *Soller NO v G*, the court examined the role of a child's legal practitioner and, in particular, how this role differed from that of the Family Advocate:

> [I]t would seem that the Family Advocate and the section 28 legal representative occupy dissimilar positions. The Family Advocate provides a professional and neutral channel of communication between the conflicting parents (and perhaps the child) and the judicial officer. The legal practitioner stands squarely in the corner of the child and has the task of presenting and arguing the wishes and desires of the child. This task is not without certain inbuilt limitation. The legal practitioner does not only represent the perspective of the child concerned. The legal practitioner should also provide adult insight into those wishes and desires which have been confided and entrusted to him or her as well as apply legal knowledge and expertise to the child's perspective. The legal practitioner may provide the child with a voice but is not merely a mouthpiece.[36]

The court went further to say that the desired attribute of the child's legal representative is that he/she will use his/her particular skills and expertise to represent the child. 'Neutrality is not the virtue desired but rather the ability to take the side of the child and act as his or her agent or ambassador.'[37]

3.1.2. Relocation Proceedings

There is no specific statute regulating or guiding the resolution of relocation disputes, be they internal relocations (in-country) or international. However, section 7

33 J. Sloth-Nielsen, 'Realising Children's Rights to Legal Representation and To Be Heard in Judicial Proceedings: An Update' (2008) 24(3) *SA Journal on Human Rights* 495.

34 Section 29(6) of the Children's Act provides that: '[t]he court may, subject to section 55 – (a) appoint a legal representative to represent the child at the court proceedings [care, contact and guardianship proceedings]; and (b) order the parties to the proceedings or any one of them, or the state if substantial injustice would otherwise result, to pay the costs of such representation'.

35 Legal Aid South Africa, *Annual Report 2019–2020*, https://legal-aid.co.za/annual-reports/, p. 27. 62% of cases involving children were criminal matters.

36 2003 (5) SA 430 (W), para. 27.

37 2003 (5) SA 430 (W), para. 26. See, in general, J. Sloth-Nielsen and B. Van Heerden, 'Access to Justice for Children in Africa', paper presented at the conference 'Gender, Inclusivity and Protecting the 21st Century Family', July 2019, London, and C. Du Toit, above n. 24.

of the Children's Act, which elaborates in non-exhaustive fashion the criteria underpinning the 'best interests of the child',[38] contains some factors specially relevant to relocation.[39] However, there is no explicit requirement that the voice of the child is to be heard. Nonetheless, it is routine for this to occur, usually through the medium of an expert report. An example in point is *HG v CG*,[40] involving the intended relocation by a custodian mother to Dubai for three years with her two children aged 11 and 14 years. Despite the children's clearly expressed views that they did not wish to relocate to Dubai, and had a close bond with their father, the experts favoured relocation with their mother. However, the judge stated that ignoring their wishes would be in direct contrast to sections 10 and 31 of the Children's Act and that the Act obliged him to give effect to the views and wishes of the children, who were mature enough to make an informed decision.

3.1.3. *Hague Child Abduction Proceedings*

Section 279 of the Act makes legal representation of the child obligatory in all applications in terms of the Hague Convention. This changes the former position, where children's interests would be furthered by the Office of the Family Advocate. The role of the Family Advocate now in relation to children is a 'best interests' one, rather than being client-focused. The Act does not stipulate a minimum age for the consideration of children's views in Hague abduction cases, and gives no real guidance for assessing a child's maturity.[41] Although there is limited case law on hearing child's views, and more particularly on the child's objections to return under Article 13 of the Hague Convention, there are notable instances of a child's view being decisive. Judgments have held that the court will give greater or lesser weight to the child's views in accordance with the child's age, and degree and level of maturity. According to Du Toit, feedback is given to the child on the finding of the judge either by the Office of the Family Advocate, or by an expert witness or the child's representative.[42]

3.1.4. *Appointment of a Curator Ad Litem*

A curator ad litem[43] conducts litigation in the name and in the interests of the child. Usually, an advocate of the High Court would be appointed to serve this

38 Which is also enshrined in the Constitution, s 28(2).
39 See those listed in s 7 of the Children's Act (those relevant to relocation).
40 2010 (3) SA 352 (ECP).
41 Z. Du Toit, above n. 28.
42 As above p. 60.
43 In the High Court. The same function would be served by a legal representative in the Children's Court (C. Du Toit, above n. 24, p. 131).

role (often acting pro bono).[44] One established ground for such an appointment is that the interests of the minor are in conflict with those of the parent or guardian, or there is a possibility of such a conflict.[45] Boezaart[46] refers to *Ex parte Van Niekerk: In re Van Niekerk v Van Niekerk*,[47] where De Villiers J was of the view that the case was not an appropriate one in which to appoint a curator ad litem because the children's mother was available and willing to assist them. He was not persuaded by arguments regarding a potential conflict of interests. The case concerned a dispute over access by a father, whose daughters were refusing to visit him. The appointment of a curator ad litem serves to fulfil the constitutional obligation in section 28(1)(h)[48] and fulfils a 'best interests' function in its advice to a court, rather than representing the views or wishes of a child directly.

3.2. DIRECT FORMS OF PARTICIPATION

The Children's Act makes it possible for children to litigate in their own name, independent of parental or other consent. The Act has its own provisions for children's *locus standi*, which mirror to a large extent those in the Constitution.[49] These have actually been described as amongst the most liberal in the world.[50] It is implicit (but not explicit) in the Children's Act that independent legal standing would require the child to have the assistance of a legal representative.[51]

---

44 *Legal Aid Board: in re four children* [2011] ZASCA 39.

45 T. Boezaart, 'The Role of a Curator ad Litem and Children's Access to Courts' (2013) 46(3) *De Jure* 708. See too C. Mol, 'Children's Representation in Family Law Proceedings: A Comparative Evaluation in the light of Article 12 of the United Nations Convention on the Rights of the Child' (2019) 27(1) *International Journal on Children's Rights* 66.

46 T. Boezaart, above n. 45.

47 [2005] JOL 14218 (T).

48 T. Boezaart, above n. 45, p. 712.

49 Section 38 of the Constitution provides for the following persons, bodies or institutions to approach a court for the enforcement of rights contained in the Bill of Rights: anyone acting in their own interest; anyone acting on behalf of another person who cannot act in their own name; anyone acting as a member of, or in the interests of, a group or class of persons; anyone acting in the public interest; and an association acting in the interest of its members. See, too, ss 53 and 15 of the Children's Act, which refer to a child who is affected by or involved in the matter to be adjudicated as having legal standing to bring a case.

50 J. Sloth-Nielsen, 'Legal Empowerment of Children' (paper presented at the conference 'From a Protected to an empowered childhood', 2 and 22 November 2019, Leuven), citing the only four examples of child initiated litigation that could be traced to date. Z. Du Toit, above n. 28, however, notes that there are many cases in which children have litigated independently of their parent's or guardian's assistance where the interests of the parent or guardian are adversarial to or out of kilter with that of the children, without providing any examples.

51 Z. Du Toit, above n. 28.

3.3. MEDIATION

The Children's Act already provides direct opportunities for mediation. Where an unmarried father does not qualify automatically for parental responsibilities and rights, or where there is a dispute as to whether he qualifies or not, the possibility of mediation is provided for;[52] further, a parental responsibilities and rights agreement might be negotiated by the holder of parental responsibilities and rights to confer parental responsibilities and rights on the unmarried father.[53] It is expressly provided that a child who is the subject of this agreement must be informed and allowed to express an opinion.[54] Presumably, those drafting the agreement bear the responsibility to inform the child and hear the opinion. Finally, in the event of a dispute about the contents of a parenting plan (which is the agreement intended to lay the basis for post-divorce exercise of parental responsibilities and rights), mediation must be attempted before resorting to litigation.[55]

There is also a discretion granted in the Children's Court to refer a matter to a lay forum for mediation provided for in section 49. Family group conferences are also a possibility.[56] Courts have begun to be disparaging of expensive and time-consuming litigation where the parties were not first advised to attempt resolution via mediation. In one notable case, a punitive costs order was awarded affecting the amount that the attorneys could claim from their clients, as they had not advised the route of mediation.[57] Mediation in South Africa has been largely unregulated until now. Current developments are described in the next section.

Questions arise as to the voice of the child in mediation. Marici Corneli,[58] a practising mediator who has also been accredited in a court-annexed mediation project,[59] describes how the 'collaborative child focused mediation' process and the 'voice of the child' works in her jurisdiction (a large urban centre in South Africa).[60] Step 1(a) includes a team of two co-mediators who mediate with the parents and they involve a 'voice of the child' professional. Step 1(b) involves an introductory session with the mediator and parents. Step 2 comprises individual sessions with the child and the 'voice of the child' practitioner (one to three sessions). In Step 3, the 'voice of the child' professional gives feedback to the

52 Children's Act, s 21(3).

53 Or any other party seeking to exercise these – such as a grandparent.

54 Regulation 8(3)(a) of the Regulations promulgated under the Children's Act.

55 Children's Act, s 33(5).

56 Children's Act, s 70.

57 *MB v NB* 2010 (3) SA 220 (GSJ).

58 *De Rebus*, July 2019, pp. 29–30.

59 These were implemented on a pilot project basis in 2014, initially in two courts nationally, now in approximately 17 courts.

60 Since no research on the topic (or on child participation generally) exists, it is not possible to establish whether the practices she describes are used in other mediation projects as well.

parents in the mediation, during which the mediators, together as a team, consider the elements on the table and custom-make a parenting plan. In Step 4, the 'voice of the child' practitioner writes the report attached to the parenting plan. Step 5 involves the facilitation-mediator informing the child of the decisions that affect them and explaining the parenting plan when the parents and 'voice of the child' professional are present. Finally, Step 6 results in a signed parenting plan and this, together with the 'voice of the child' practitioner's report, are handed in at the Office of the Family Advocate for approval.

4. POLICY OR PRACTICE DEVELOPMENTS

The South African Law Reform Commission has been seized with an investigation into alternative dispute resolution in family matters for more than five years. The Issue Paper released for public comment in 2015 was superseded by a Discussion Paper in late 2019. Covering various issues pertaining to family mediation, collaborative dispute resolution, family arbitration[61] and parenting coordination (or post-divorce case management), this Discussion Paper concludes with a proposed draft Family Dispute Resolution Bill. Once enacted, this Bill will regulate alternative dispute resolution processes.[62] The voice of the child seems destined to play a prominent role, since clause 7 provides, as a general principle, that during all dispute resolution processes child participation in family disputes involving children should be actively facilitated in accordance with the provisions of the Children's Act. Insofar as arbitration will be extended to family law disputes, the child's voice must also be heard and legal representation made available for the child if required. Given the lengthy time that consultation and law reform processes take, as well as the preparatory work needed before the envisaged alternative dispute resolution system can operate, it is like to be some years before these plans come to fruition.

5. CONCLUSION

At best, it can be deduced that South Africa's scorecard on child participation is rather patchy. There is evidence some good practice has developed in the last two decades, and whilst there is a cohort of committed and child-rights-oriented professionals, as well as some attempt by the state to lay the basis for

61 At present family law matters are excluded from arbitration by operation of law.

62 Alongside a Mediation Act, which is being developed in a separate investigation of the SALRC for alternatives to justice processes more generally (SALRC Discussion Paper, above n. 5, para. 1.2.3).

an infrastructure able to ensure that children's voices are heard (Legal Aid South Africa, the Office of the Family Advocate), in reality children's voices are mostly obscured and their interests neglected in family law disputes. Of particular concern is the recent devolution of jurisdiction to lower courts, in which the majority of adults are themselves unrepresented; it is unlikely, therefore, that children's voices will play a particularly prominent role.

In addition, the law itself, whilst reasonably commendable insofar as the Children's Act is concerned, currently lacks detailed guidance on when soliciting children's views, or appointing a legal representative, would be in children's best interests.

Therefore, while the requirements of Article 12 UNCRC exist on the statute book, it is nigh on impossible to conclude that, in practice, Article 12 is being fully implemented at all levels and in all disputes where children's voices might have a material bearing.

UNITED STATES OF AMERICA

Linda D. Elrod

1. INTRODUCTION

A child's perspective in a private custody case may differ from that of parents or other professionals. Most nations recognise the importance of a judge seeking the views of the child who is most impacted by the decision. The United States, however, lacks a uniform approach to when, how or if a child can participate. As private custody cases are heard in state, not federal, courts, the laws and policies vary widely in the 50 states, the District of Columbia, and the territories.[1] Whether, and how, a child's voice is heard depends upon if the custody case arises in the context of an initial action, such as a divorce, paternity or adoption case, or in the context of a modification of an existing order, such as a relocation case.

Historically, judges did not include the child's voice in private custody cases. Presumptions for one of the parents and fitness played major roles. The 1973 Uniform Marriage and Divorce Act listed the child's voice as one of five factors

1 L.D. Elrod, *Child Custody Practice and Procedure*, Thomson Reuters, Eagan, Minn. 2020, ch. 4.

to consider. It has only been since the mid-1990s, however, with the push for appointing a lawyer for a child by child advocacy groups that legislatures and courts have begun a serious dialogue about including the child's views in custody decisions. Concerns still exist about the capacity of a child to express a view, the need to insulate the child from parental conflict, and the underlying assumption, not always valid, that parents will act in their child's best interest. There is, however, a growing recognition of children's rights both in the United States and around the world.[2]

Three international treaties provide opportunities to hear the child's perspective: the United Nations Convention on the Rights of the Child (UNCRC),[3] the Hague Convention on the Civil Aspects of International Child Abduction (the Hague Abduction Convention)[4] and the Hague Convention on Jurisdiction, Applicable Law, Recognition, Enforcement and Co-operation in Respect of Parental Responsibility and Measures for the Protection of Children (1996 Hague Child Protection Convention).[5] Of these three, the United States has ratified only the Hague Abduction Convention.

The United States census documents around 380 million people; 72 million of them are children. The actual number of cases involving the custody of children, however, is more difficult to ascertain. In child welfare cases, the federal government collects data. Whether children are involved in the state civil divorce case filings is not reported separately. One estimate is that nearly half of marriages end in divorce[6] and 40% of children are born out of wedlock.[7] Estimates based on the number of domestic divorce and paternity filings indicate that over a million children annually may be involved in some type of legal proceeding affecting their custody.[8]

The United States Supreme Court has found that parents have a constitutionally protected right to the care, custody and control of their children; parental

2 M. Ventrell, 'The Practice of Law for Children' (2006) 28 *Hamline Journal of Public Law and Policy* 75, 77.

3 United Nations Convention on the Rights of the Child, 28 ILM 1448 (20 November 1989), Art. 12.

4 Hague Convention on the Civil Aspects of International Child Abduction, 25 October 1980, TIAS No. 11,670, 1343 UNTS 89.

5 Hague Convention of 19 October 1996 on Jurisdiction, Applicable Law, Recognition, Enforcement and Co-operation in Respect of Parental Responsibility and Measures for the Protection of Children, https://www.hcch.net/en/instruments/conventions/fulltext/?cid=70.

6 A. Abrams, 'Divorce Rate in U.S. Drops to Nearly 40-Year Low', *Time*, 4 December 2016 (the 2015 divorce rate was 16.9 divorces per 1,000 married women; the marriage rate was 32.2 per 1,000). The divorce rate, however, is probably less than 50% because the people divorcing in a single year were married in many different years.

7 Centers for Disease Control and Prevention, *Births: Final Data for 2017*, 67:8 National Vital Statistics Report 1, 5–6, 7 November 2018).

8 The National Center for State Courts, Domestic Relations Caseloads Chart of Trial Court Filings 2018 (filings in New York –537,155; California –361,230; Texas –351,825; Virginia –306,190; Florida –230,848; Ohio –204,565.

decisions regarding custody and access are entitled to great weight.[9] In 80% of cases, the parents, often with help from lawyers or a mediator, create a parenting plan which details the custody and residency arrangements for their child. Most state statutes presume that the parents' agreement is in the best interests of the child. The judge routinely approves parental agreements without inquiring if the child had any input or expressed any opposition. If the parents cannot agree, a trial judge, under the doctrine of *parens patriae*, determines custody and parenting time according to the 'best interests' of the child.[10] Almost all state statutes include the child's preference as to custodian as a factor if a child is of sufficient age and maturity. Few states, however, require the judge to hear from the child directly. Even fewer have enacted any rules or procedures to ensure the judge hears or knows the child's perspective.

2. STATUTORY PROVISIONS

No federal law requires a child to be heard in private family law custody cases. The United States Supreme Court has never addressed the right of a child to be heard in matters concerning his/her familial relations. Most states do have a statutory list of factors that a judge must consider in awarding custody of a child. Most statutes, but not all, include as a factor the preference of a child of sufficient age and maturity.[11] In a few states, a judge must ascertain a child's preference if the child has reached a certain chronological age, usually 12 or 14 years.[12] Most states, however, reject an arbitrary age standard as inappropriate. For example,

---

9 *Troxel v Granville*, 530 U.S. 57 (2000).

10 L.D. Elrod and M.D. Dale, 'Paradigm Shifts and Pendulum Swings in Child Custody: The Interests of Children in the Balance' (2008) 42(3) *Family Law Quarterly* 381.

11 Alaska Stat. §25.24.150(c)(3); Ariz. Rev. Stat. Ann. §25-403(a)(4); Ark. Code Ann. §9-13-101(a)(1)(A)(ii); Cal. Fam. Code §3042; Colo. Rev. Stat. §14-10-124(1.5)(a)(II); Conn. Gen. Stat. §46b-56(c)(3); Del. Code Ann. tit. 13, §722(a)(2); D.C. Code §16-914(a)(3)(A); Fla. Stat. Ann. §61.13(3)(i); Ga. Code Ann. §19-9-3(a)(5), (6) Haw. Rev. Stat. §571-46(a)(3); Idaho Code §32-717(1)(b); 750 Ill. Comp. Stat. 5/602(a)(2); Ind. Code §31-17-2-8(3); Iowa Code Ann. §598.41(3)(f); Kan. Stat. Ann. §23-3203(a)(3); Ky. Rev. Stat. Ann. §403.270(2)(b); Me. Rev. Stat. Ann. tit. 19-A, §1653(3)(c); Mich. Comp. Laws Ann. §722.23(i); Minn. Stat. §518.17, subd. 1(a)(2); Miss. Code Ann. §93-11-65; Mo. Rev. Stat. §452.375(2)(8); Mont. Code Ann. §40-4-212(1)(b); Neb. Rev. Stat. §43-2923(6)(b); Nev. Rev. Stat. §125C.0035 4(a); N.H. Rev. Stat. Ann. §461-A:6(II); N.J. Stat. Ann. 9:2-4; N.M. Stat. Ann. §40-4-9(A)(2); N.D. Cent. Code §14-09-06.2(1)(i); Ohio Rev. Code Ann. §3109.04(B)(1); Okla. Stat. tit. 43, §113; 23 Pa. Cons. Stat. §5328(a)(7); S.C. Code Ann. §63-15-30; Tenn. Code Ann. §36-6-106(a)(7); Tex. Fam. Code Ann. §153.009; Utah Code Ann. §30-3-10(1)(e); Va. Code Ann. §20-124.3(8); Wash. Rev. Code §26.09.187(3)(a)(vi); W. Va. Code §44-10-4; Wis. Stat. §767.41(5)(am)(2); Wyo. Stat. Ann. §20-2-201.

12 See e.g. Cal. Fam. Code §3042(c) (a 14-year-old addressed the court); Miss. Code Ann. §93-11-65(1)(a) (court may consider the preference of a child older than 12 and shall explain in detail why the child's wishes were or were not honoured). Georgia, Indiana, Maryland, New Mexico, Ohio, Oklahoma, Tennessee, and Texas also hear children over a certain age.

the Michigan statute includes the child's preference if the child is of 'sufficient' age, but does not state an age. As a general rule, the older the child, the more likely the court will try to ascertain the child's preference. Adolescents, in particular, benefit from having direct input into their future living arrangements.[13] Failure to at least listen to an older teenager's preference for custody may be a reversible error and invites rebellion.[14]

Age and maturity are not the same. If the judge feels the child is too immature, the judge may decline to interview the child. Even a young child, however, may have sound reasons for the preference of one parent. For example, a nine-year-old may prefer to live with the parent who listens and helps him/her with homework, rather than the parent who is constantly on social media. On the other hand, a teenager may express a preference to live with the parent who has few rules and allows him/her to play video games rather than go to school.[15] If there is a question about whether the child is mature enough, the judge may inquire as to the child's preference, but then give the preference little weight in the decision-making process.[16] In some states, the judge is required to make a finding on each custody factor. In these states there must be some evidence of whether the child was of sufficient age and maturity to have a preference and what that preference is.[17]

In the adoption context, 47 states and the District of Columbia require that older children consent to their adoption. Twenty-three states set the age of consent at 14 years of age; 18 states set the age at 12; and seven states set the age at 10.[18] In some states, this consent is not necessary if the child lacks mental capacity or it is in the child's best interest to dispense with consent. In other states, an adoption cannot be granted over the child's objection.

The International Child Abduction Remedies Act, the federal law that implements the Hague Abduction Convention, allows cases to be filed in

---

13 *Schlieve v Schlieve*, 846 N.W.2d 733 (N.D. 2014) (trial court gave weight to preference of 14- and 17-year-old children to live with their mother).

14 *D.A. v R.C.*, 105 A.3d 1103 (N.J. Super. App. Div. 2014) (court was required to consider the preference of a 14-year-old); *Duguma v Ayalew*, 145 A.3d 511 (D.C. App. 2016) (judge should have interviewed children aged 14, nine and seven); *Mackowski v Mackowski*, 721 A.2d 12 (N.J. Super. App. Div. 1998) (a 16-year-old had a right to be heard); *Kubicki v Sharpe*, 858 N.W.2d 57 (Mich. App. 2014) (10-year-old); *Beran v Beran*, 450 N.W.2d 688 (Neb. 1990) (15-year-old).

15 *Frueh v Frueh*, 771 N.W.2d 593 (N.D. 2009) (lack of interest in his own education and in the wider world indicated lack of maturity).

16 Compare *Bak v Bak*, 511 N.E.2d 625 (Mass. App. 1987) (10-year-old's preference not given much weight) with *Passero v Giordano*, 861 N.Y.S.2d 479 (App. Div. 2008) (11-year-old's preference should have been given some consideration).

17 *David v LoPresti*, 111 N.Y.S.3d 356 (App. Div. 2019) (remanding for *de novo* hearing where judge denied relocation and changed custody without evidence of the 10-year-old child's preference).

18 J. Fairfax, *The Adoption Law Handbook: Practice, Resources, and Forms for Family Law Professionals*, 2nd ed., ABA, Chicago, Ill. 2019.

federal or state court.[19] Article 13 of the Abduction Convention provides an exception to return if it is found that the child objects and has attained an age and degree of maturity at which it is appropriate to take account of its views.[20] The Hague Convention does not define the age at which a child has sufficient age and maturity. The cases in the United States also have no definitive age.[21] As to maturity, one court gave little weight where the 10-year-old child's testimony indicated no particular objection to return to her mother in Canada, the habitual residence, but rather just a generalised desire to stay in Pittsburgh where the father had kept her for three years.[22] The trial court has discretion as to the weight to give the objection.[23] It is possible that the child's wishes can be the sole reason why a court declines to return the child.[24]

The United States Supreme Court's recent Hague case on defining habitual residence opens the door for viewing the facts from the child's perspective. The court noted that if a child is too young to be acclimatised to the location, the parents' shared intent could be used to determine habitual residence.[25]

The Indian Child Welfare Act (ICWA), also federal law, protects Indian families from disruption and mentions the possibility of hearing the child's voice. ICWA lists placement preferences in adoption and child welfare cases. ICWA states that, where appropriate, the preference of the Indian child or parents can be considered in determining whether there is good cause to depart from those ICWA preferences.[26] There is no age given.

3. MODES OF CHILD PARTICIPATION

The judge can ascertain a child's perspective through the child's testimony in court, through an interview with the child in chambers, from testimony of the parents, or from evidence presented by the child's attorney or guardian

---

19 The International Child Abduction Remedies Act, 42 USC §11603 et seq., recodified as 22 USC §§9001 et seq.

20 See *Ochoa v Suarez*, No. 1:15-CV-1104, 2016 WL 6956609, at 2 (W.D. Mich. 29 November 2016) (children aged 11 and 13 mature enough to express preference not to return to Mexico). See also L.D. Elrod, 'Please Let me Stay: Hearing the Voice of the Child in Hague Abduction Cases' (2011) 63(4) *Oklahoma Law Review* 663.

21 Compare *England v England*, 234 F.3d 268, 271 (5th Cir. 2000) (finding a 14-year-old not mature enough) with *Eghaghe v Haro*, 131 F. Supp. 2d 953, 957–958 (E.D. Mich. 2001) (ordering examination of an eight-year-old to determine degree of maturity). But see *Kufner v Kufner*, 519 F.3d 33 (1st Cir. 2008) (not allowing an eight-year-old to testify).

22 *Yang v Tsui*, 499 F.3d 259 (3d Cir. 2007).

23 Compare *Custodio v Samillan*, 842 F.3d 1084, 1089 (8th Cir. 2016) (mature child defence precluded returning a 15-year-old to Peru) with *Trudrung v Trudrung*, 686 F. Supp. 2d 570 (M.D. N.C. 2010) (returning a 15-year-old to Germany despite his objection).

24 *Blondin v Dubois*, 189 F.3d 240, 247 (2d Cir. 1999).

25 *Monasky v Taglieri*, 140 S. Ct. 719 (2020).

26 25 USC §1915(c).

ad litem. The court may also obtain the preference indirectly from reports of psychiatrists, court services officers, or testimony of other witnesses. For example, the Oregon statute allows a judge to elicit the child's views in three ways: by appointing counsel for the child; by retaining an expert to interview the child; or by hearing directly from the child through testimony or conference.[27] The method used depends upon the state and judicial discretion.[28]

3.1. DIRECT FORMS OF PARTICIPATION

3.1.1. Child's Testimony

The Federal Rules of Evidence, which most states have adopted in whole or in part, allow a child to testify under oath in any matter. The test is whether the child is 'competent' to testify. Theoretically, then, either party may call the child as a witness. Some states have specific statutes. For example, Virginia law allows the court to call a child as a witness in a custody proceeding if it finds after a hearing that the child's testimony is necessary, the probative value outweighs the potential detriment, and the evidence is not otherwise available. An attorney must be appointed for the child witness.[29] A California statute allows a 14-year-old to address the court.

Most judges, however, disapprove of calling a child to the witness stand in his/her parents' divorce for any reason.[30] A New York court summed up the reasons, noting that 'a child, already suffering from the trauma of a broken home, should not be placed in the position of having [his/her] relationship with either parent further jeopardized by having to publicly relate [his/her] difficulties with them or be required to openly choose between them'. While the 14-year-old's preferences were entitled to great weight, the court felt that an interview *in camera* would have limited the harm and would have been 'far more informative and worthwhile than the traditional procedures of the adversary system – an examination of the child under oath in open court.'[31]

---

27 Or. Rev. Stat. Ann. §107.425(2). See also *Holiday v Holiday*, 247 P.3d 29, 33 (Wyo. 2011) (listing ways to get child's voice heard and remanding to hear views of 11-year-old).

28 J. Clarke, 'Do I Have A Voice? An Empirical Analysis of Children's Voices in Michigan Custody Litigation' (2013) 47(3) *Family Law Quarterly* 457.

29 Va. Stat. Ann. Ch. 15 § 594(b).

30 See *American Academy of Matrimonial Lawyers Bounds of Advocacy – Goals for Family Lawyers.* Rule 6.4 states that an attorney should not bring a child to court or call a child as a witness without full discussion with the client and a reasonable belief that it is in the best interests of the child.

31 *McGovern v McGovern*, 870 N.Y.S.2d 618 (App. Div. 2009). See also J. Clarke, above n. 28 (one study showed 90% of judges felt a child should not be called to the stand).

The Uniform Child Witness Testimony by Alternative Methods Act, only enacted in four states, excludes a child from testifying in person in an open forum in the presence of the judge or parties. The judge may decline to allow the child to testify if the child might be harmed by testifying or if there is evidence the child has been coached.[32] If the judge decides to allow the child to testify, the judge may permit testimony by alternate methods using special accommodations to make the child more comfortable, such as rearranging the courtroom or using more informal dress or procedures to make the child more at ease. A judge may choose to have only the attorneys for the parents, not the parents themselves, in the courtroom when the child testifies. Others may choose to have the child testify via a live video feed or to record the child's testimony before the trial and play it at the trial.

When older children want to testify, most judges will allow them to do so. A father was not entitled to prevent the oldest child from testifying about his alleged sexual abuse at the custody hearing for younger children.[33] A 15-year-old sought to testify as to why she wanted to reduce the time spent with her father after her attempts to talk to him, and her written letter, were unsuccessful in making him understand her concerns.[34]

3.1.2. *Judicial Interview with Child*

The most widely used means of discovering a child's preference is for the trial judge to conduct an *in camera* interview with a child. Several states enacted statutes patterned after the 1973 Uniform Marriage and Divorce Act §404(a) allowing a judge to interview the child in chambers to ascertain the child's wishes as to his/her custodian and as to visitation. There is an implied right to interview the child because of the statutory requirement to consider the child's wishes as a factor in a custody dispute.[35] Judges often have broad discretion regarding whether to interview the child, who may be present during the interview whether a recording is made, and to whom to disclose the recording.[36] A judge may decline to interview a child if the child's wishes have been clearly presented

---

32 *In re Allen*, 97 P.3d 1060 (Kan. App. 2004) (refusing mother's request to call child to stand where court found it would harm the child); *Sheridan v Cassidy*, 273 So. 3d 783 (Miss. App. 2019) (declining where there was evidence of mother's coaching).

33 *Chess v Lichtman*, 105 N.Y.S.3d 475 (App. Div. 2019).

34 *Wright v Kemp*, 207 A.3d 1021 (Vt. 2019).

35 *Karanikas v Cartwright*, 61 A.3d 69 (Md. Spec. App. 2013) (finding no error in interviewing a nine-year-old in chambers); *Donscheski v Donscheski*, 771 N.W.2d 213 (Nev. App. 2009) (trial court was required to conduct in camera interview with a 12-year-old).

36 *deSilva v Pitts*, 481 F. 3d 1279 (10th Cir. 2007) (Hague case judge heard child's objection in camera with a court reporter and law clerk present).

by others such as the parents, a child's attorney or guardian ad litem, or mental health professional.[37]

Until recently, many judges have not wanted to interview a child. This judicial reluctance stems from three major sources: the desire to keep the child out of the middle of the dispute, a lack of training on how to appropriately interview a child,[38] and concern for protecting the due process rights of parents. Judges generally know enough to not directly ask a child for a preference unless the child clearly wants to express one. Heightened focus on the child's desires to be heard and calls for increased child participation are leading to more judicial interest and have led to more resources for judges to interview children.[39]

The judge may interview a child privately if the parties consent; sometimes even if they do not.[40] An Oklahoma case found that if one or both parents object to being excluded from the interview, the trial court has discretion to allow parents' counsel to be present, allow counsel to question the child, or allow counsel to submit questions to be asked. Failure to make a timely objection to a private interview may waive any objections for an appeal on that ground.[41]

There is no universal requirement that the parents' counsel be present or permitted to participate in *in camera* proceedings. Typically, a trial judge will state on the record his/her preliminary determinations that it is in the child's best interest to conduct an *in camera* interview and that the child is of a sufficient age to form an intelligent preference. Some states require counsel for the parents to be present during the interview.[42] Others give the trial judge

---

37 *In re Bunita B. v Mark P.*, 89 N.Y.S.3d 55 (App. Div. 2018) (where the child's attorney stipulated the child was neutral on residence, the judge was not required to interview the child); *Addison v Addison*, 463 S.W.3d 755 (Ky. 2015) (court had multiple reports addressing the young children's wishes and best interests so court declined to interview them).

38 B.A. Atwood, 'The Child's Voice in Custody Litigation: An Empirical Survey and Suggestions for Reform' (2003) 45 *Arizona Law Review* 629 (although the study found that the few judges who did interview children felt confident in their interviewing skills).

39 See *ABA Child Custody and Adoption Pro Bono Project, A Judge's Guide: Making Child-Centered Decisions in Custody Cases*, 2nd ed., ABA, Chicago, Ill. 2008; N. Bala, R. Birnbaum, F. Cyr and D. McColley, 'Children's Voices in Family Court: Guidelines for Judges Meeting Children' (2013) 47(3) *Family Law Quarterly* 379.

40 *Cox v Cox*, 515 S.E.2d 61 (N.C. App. 1999) (no error in conducting a private examination with children in chambers with both parties' counsel present over the mother's objection); *Helen S.K. v Samuel M.K.*, 288 P.3d 463 (Alaska 2012) (in camera interview did not violate mother's rights); *T.E.G. v G.T.G.*, 986 N.Y.S.2d 313 (Misc. 2014) (in camera interview did not warrant recusal nor did it violate mother's rights).

41 *Ynclan v Woodward*, 237 P.3d 145 (Okla. 2010), as corrected (25 March 2010). See also *Holiday v Holiday*, 247 P.3d 29, 32 (Wyo. 2011) (where parent objects to private interview with child, the judge or the parties must fashion suitable alternative procedure for obtaining the child's preference). See also *Frueh v Frueh*, 771 N.W.2d 593, 600 (N.D. 2009); *Wilson v Wilson*, 170 So. 3d 340 (La. App. 2015).

42 See e.g. Conn. Gen. Stat. §46-45; 750 Ill. Comp. Stat. 5/604(a); Minn. Stat. §518.166; Mo. Rev. Stat. §452.385.

the discretion to permit counsel.[43] If the lawyers are present, in most states they are observers who do not participate or question the child.[44] In some states, the lawyers can submit questions they would like the judge to ask.[45]

Many states require a record, such as a transcript, videotape or other reliable means of recording, of the judicial interview, either automatically or upon a request of the parties.[46] If the parties did not consent to the interview, the judge should make a record. Failure to record may be prejudicial if a statute requires recording even if the parties do not object.[47]

States also differ as to what to do with the record. In some jurisdictions, the record can be viewed by the parties and becomes part of the record on appeal. Some states give the judge discretion whether to make a record and to seal it unless there is an appeal.[48] If the court's findings are made solely on the basis of other evidence received in open court, an appellate court may find no prejudice in not recording.[49] The child's testimony must be disclosed to the extent necessary for the judge to make a decision based on written findings. In some states, the judge must state the preference of the child and the weight the judge gave it.[50]

3.1.3. *Child Litigating on Own Behalf*

A child is not considered a party in a custody case between the parents. As a general rule, a child does not have the right to initiate a divorce or a custody

---

43 *Baxendale v Raich*, 878 N.E.2d 1252, 1255 (Ind. 2008) (judge may interview child with or without counsel present).

44 *Woods v Woods*, 987 So. 2d 339, 348 (La. App. 2008), writ denied, 996 So. 2d 1110 (La. 2008) (attorney's questioning is limited to the determination of child's competency); *Ottolini v Barrett*, 954 A.2d 610, 613 (Pa. Super. 2008) (counsel must be present and allowed to interrogate the child).

45 American Law Institute, *Principles of the Law of Family Dissolution*, §2.14 (judges have 'discretion to interview the child, or direct another person to interview the child. … Counsel for a parent or for a child should be permitted to propose questions to the court that may be asked of the child.')

46 See e.g. Del. Code Ann. tit. 13, §724(a); Kan. Stat. Ann. §23-3209; Tex Fam. Code Ann. §153.009(f). See e.g. *Abbott v Virusso*, 862 N.E.2d 52. 60-61 (Mass. App. 2007) (summarising literature); *McN. v R.J.H., Sr.*, 979 A.2d 1195 (D.C. 2009) (no reversal where judge failed to record in camera interview with children ages 10 and 14 but provided a detailed description of the children's conversation).

47 *Couch v Couch*, 146 S.W.3d 923, 925 (Ky. 2004) ('… unless waived … [I]f a trial court accepts and acts upon statements made by the child during the in camera interview, it is manifestly unfair not to record and disclose the contents of the interview in order to provide an opportunity for rebuttal').

48 See Mont. Code Ann. §40-4-216(5). See also *Dickison v Dickison*, 874 P.2d 695 (Kan. App. 1994); *Myers v Myers*, 867 N.E.2d 848 (Ohio App. 2007).

49 *Schneider v Schneider*, 258 P.3d 350 (Idaho 2011).

50 *Holiday v Holiday*, 247 P.3d 29 (Wyo. 2011). But see *Rivera v LaSalle*, 923 N.Y.S.2d 254 (App. Div. 2011) (finding judge breached children's right to confidentiality by revealing their *custodial* preference and erred in not considering the older child's preference).

case, nor is the child able to change contact arrangements. Even when a child has tried to hire his/her own attorney to represent him/her in the parents' custody case, courts have denied the request.[51] Maryland, however, does allow a 16-year-old to seek modification of a custody order.[52] The parents may ask for, and in some jurisdictions the court *sua sponte* may appoint, a child's attorney or a guardian ad litem because of the circumstances. The child's attorney does have the authority to pursue an appeal on the child's behalf where the child is aggrieved by the order even where a parent did not file an appeal.[53]

3.2. REPRESENTATION FORMS OF PARTICIPATION: CHILD'S ATTORNEY OR GUARDIAN AD LITEM

A judge may appoint a guardian ad litem or a child's attorney to elicit the child's perspective. While the Supreme Court requires a lawyer to be appointed for a juvenile proceeding,[54] no federal law requires appointment of a guardian ad litem in a private custody case,[55] and most states do not require appointment unless there are allegations of abuse and neglect. All courts, however, do have the inherent equitable discretionary power to appoint a guardian ad litem in an appropriate case.[56] Some statutes and court rules authorise appointment of a guardian ad litem or a child's attorney in a high-conflict case involving relocation, risk of abduction, substance abuse, past or present family violence, or parental alienation.

If a guardian ad litem is appointed, states vary substantially on the title and the role, including how to give the child a voice. Confusion arises because the guardian ad litem may be a lawyer or a layperson and a fact investigator, an advocate for the child's best interests, an advocate for the child's views or wishes, or a combination.[57] In most states, the guardian ad litem has a duty

---

51 *In re Marriage of Osborn*, 135 P.3d 199 (Kan. App. 2006); *Miller v Miller*, 677 A.2d 64 (Me. 1996); *Auclair v Auclair*, 730 A.2d 1260 (Md. Spec. App. 1999); *In re Stapleford*, 931 A.2d 1199 (N.H. 2007); *Ihinger v Ihinger*, 824 A.2d 601 (Vt. 2003).

52 Md. Code Ann. §9-103(b).

53 *Newton v McFarlane*, 103 N.Y.S.3d 445 (App. Div. 2019) (child was aggrieved by transfer of custody from father to mother where child expressed strong preference for staying with father).

54 *In re Gault*, 387 U.S. 1 (1967).

55 The Child Abuse Prevention and Treatment Act (CAPTA), 42 USC §5016(a)(2)(B)(ii) requires the dependency or child welfare court to appoint a guardian ad litem, who may be an attorney or a CASA (Court Appointed Special Advocate).

56 L.D. Elrod, above n. 1, ch. 12; see *In re Marriage of Strauss*, 539 N.E.2d 808 (Ill. App. 1989).

57 See *Auclair v Auclair*, 730 A.2d 1260 (Md. Spec. App. 1999) (guardian ad litem communicates child's views, but also presents his/her view of child's best interests); *Patel v Patel*, 555 S.E.2d

only to present evidence or recommendations as to the best interests of the child. A judge, however, cannot delegate the ultimate power to determine best interests to the guardian ad litem.[58] Another issue can arise if the guardian ad litem is a lawyer, because ethical requirements require a lawyer to keep client confidences. Many states find that a guardian ad litem is an 'officer of the court' and the relationship with the child is not confidential. A major issue arises if the guardian ad litem submits a written report on best interests that contains hearsay and the parents do not have a chance to cross-examine the guardian ad litem or the persons interviewed.[59] For example, the guardian ad litem does an independent investigation and includes in the report statements and information from a next-door neighbour, a teacher, or others who are not called into court and allowed to be examined under oath. A few states do give parents the right to cross-examine the guardian ad litem.[60] This, however, conflicts with the Model Rule of Professional Conduct 3.7, which states that a lawyer should not act as an advocate at a trial in which the lawyer is likely to be a necessary witness.

Confusion and concern about the guardian ad litem's proper role has led to a wide variety of professional guidelines, statutes, court rules and opinions.[61] While judges appear to favour the best interest model, most child advocates favour appointment of a child's attorney who uses the traditional client-based representation model.[62] The child's lawyer focuses the judge and parents on the child's perspective by presenting evidence through witnesses and documents, as any other attorney in the case.[63] Nine states specifically allow appointment

---

386, 389 (S.C. 2001) (guardian ad litem is representative of the court, advocating for child's best interests and providing court with an objective view).

58 See *Carr v Buenger*, 330 P.3d 390 (Haw. App. 2014).

59 L.D. Elrod, 'Hearsay and Custody: The Twice Told Story' (1987) 21 *Family Law Quarterly* 169.

60 See *In re Marriage of Bates*, 819 N.E.2d 714 (Ill. 2004).

61 See 'American Bar Association Standards for Practice for Lawyers Representing Children in Custody Cases' (2003) 37 *Family Law Quarterly* 131 (lawyer appointed as either child's attorney or best interest attorney); L.D. Elrod, 'Raising the Bar for Lawyers Who Represent Children: ABA Standards of Practice for Custody Cases' (2003) 37(2) *Family Law Quarterly* 105.

62 L.D. Elrod, 'Client Directed Lawyers for Children: It is the "Right" Thing to Do' (2007) 27(4) *Pace Law Review* 869 (discussing the debate over lawyers for children). See 'American Academy of Matrimonial Lawyers Representing Children: Standards for Attorneys for Children in Custody or Visitation Proceedings with Commentary' (2009) 22 *Journal of the American Academy of Matrimonial Lawyers* 227 (courts should appoint a lawyer to advocate for the outcome desired by the child); 'Recommendations of the UNLV Conference on Representing Children in Families' (2006) 6(3) *Nevada Law Journal* 592.

63 M. Guggenheim, *What's Wrong with Children's Rights*, Harvard University Press, Cambridge, Mass. 2005, p. 95 (courts often adopt attorney's views of best interest believing it is child's position). See also R.M. Henaghan, 'What Does a Child's Right to Be Heard in Legal Proceedings Really Mean? ABA Custody Standards Do Not Go Far Enough' (2008) 42(1) *Family Law Quarterly* 117.

of a child's lawyer.[64] Several states also allow the court to appoint a best interest representative.[65]

Many states now distinguish between the guardian ad litem, who is a Best Interest Attorney (BIA) who advocates for the child's best interest but performs the role as a lawyer, and a best interest representative who is a lay person, often a Court Appointed Special Advocate (CASA). The BIA advocates for the child's 'best interests' regardless of the child's wishes.[66] In a few hybrid states, the BIA must also present evidence as to the child's views and preferences. If there is a conflict, an attorney for the child can be appointed.[67] If the child is old enough to direct the representation, the child's lawyer model is preferred. There is still a debate over the role of the lawyer for the child who is too young to direct representation.[68] Two recent books on lawyer representation for children attempt to clarify roles.[69]

3.3. WEIGHT TO BE GIVEN TO PREFERENCE: 'A VOICE NOT A CHOICE'

While the express wishes of a child are not determinative, many courts have carefully considered and given weight to them in determining the child's best interests.[70] Courts will balance the child's preference against other factors, such as the maturity and age of the child, educational level, intellectual and emotional make-up of the child, relationship with parents and siblings, and physical and mental health of the parents, as well as the strength and reasons for the preference.[71]

---

64 Or. Rev. Stat. §107.425(6).

65 Alaska, Arizona, Connecticut, Georgia, Louisiana, Maryland, Massachusetts Minnesota (over age 10), Mississippi, Montana, New Jersey, New Mexico (over age 14), New York, North Dakota, Oklahoma, Pennsylvania, Puerto Rico, Tennessee, Texas, West Virginia, Wisconsin (over age 12), and the Virgin Islands.

66 Delaware, Florida, Guam, Hawaii, Iowa, Kansas, Kentucky, Maine, Maryland, Mississippi, Nevada, New Mexico (under 14), South Carolina, Vermont, Virginia, and Wisconsin (under age 12).

67 Kan. Sup. Ct. Adm. Order #110A. Other states with hybrid duty are Arizona, California, Missouri, North Carolina, Utah, and Wyoming.

68 See B.A. Atwood, 'Representing Children Who Can't or Won't Direct Counsel: Best Interests Lawyering or No Lawyering at All?' (2011) 53 *Arizona Law Review* 381; L. Kelly and A. LeVezu, 'Until the Client Speaks: Reviving the Legal Interest Model for Preverbal Children' (2016) 50(3) *Family Law Quarterly* 383, 395.

69 M.A. Kucinski, *A Practical Handbook for the Child's Attorney: Effectively Representing Children in Custody Cases*, ABA, Chicago, Ill. 2018; R.M. Stahl and P.M. Stahl, *Representing Children in Dependency and Family Court: Beyond the Law*, ABA, Chicago, Ill. 2018.

70 *Dahlke v Dahlke*, 351 P.3d 937 (Wyo. 2015) (modifying joint custody to primary in mother partly on preference of 16-year-old); *E.B. v D.B.*, 209 A.3d 451 (Pa. Super. 2019).

71 *Lao v Gonzales*, 13 N.Y.S.3d 211 (App. Div. 2015) (giving little weight to preference of eight-year-old to change custody); *Andrews v Mouzon*, 915 N.Y.S.2d 604 (App. Div. 2011) (considering opinion of child and attorney).

The preference of an older, mature child may be given considerable weight, partly because it is harder to enforce a court order against the child's wishes. A teenager's choice may have a significant effect on the outcome.[72] In a few jurisdictions, statutes provide that if the child is of a certain age, the child's preference is binding on the court absent a finding that the preferred parent is unfit.[73] While some courts seem to give much weight to a school-age (five- to 10-year-old) child's preference, other courts give little weight.[74] A few courts have put some weight on the preference of a preschool child.[75]

The preference to live with one parent over the other will not be totally disregarded, especially if there is evidence supporting the child's choice.[76] This is because the attitudes accompanying the child's choice may spread into other areas, such as the hostility the child feels for the non-preferred parent and the ability of the non-preferred parent to cope with the parenting responsibility. Sometimes the preference is for the location with friends and school or because the child does not like a parent's new partner. A child's preference does not have to be accompanied by detailed thought or critical analysis in order to be 'reasonable'.[77]

Despite a child's preference, the court may find it in the child's best interest to continue living in the current situation.[78] If the judge awards custody contrary

72 *McGovern v McGovern*, 870 N.Y.S.2d 618 (App. Div. 2009) (almost 14-year-old); *Myers v DiDomenico*, 657 A.2d 956 (Pa. Super. 1995) (honouring wishes of mature, intelligent, and articulate teenage children); *Roth v Haag*, 834 N.W.2d 337 (S.D. 2013) (considerable weight given to 14-year-old boy's preference); *In re Marriage of Moe*, 676 P.2d 336 (Or. App. 1984) (great weight to a 12-year-old with a list of reasons for preference).

73 *Klos v Klos*, 934 A.2d 724 (Pa. Super. 2007).

74 *Gianvito v Gianvito*, 975 A.2d 1164 (Pa. 2009) (no significant weight to six-year-old's preference); *Payne v Payne*, 674 S.E.2d 515 (S.C. App. 2009) (no controlling weight to eight-year-old's preference); *Simmons v Simmons*, 554 So. 2d 238 (La. App. 1989) (reversible error to give controlling weight to a nine-year-old's desire to live with a parent); *Buffalo v Buffalo*, 211 P.3d 923 (Okla. 2009) (10-year-old child's expressed preference insufficient to support modification); *DeMers v Nicks*, 366 P.3d 977 (Wyo. 2016) (10-year-old child was not of sufficient age or maturity to make a well-reasoned decision).

75 See e.g. *In re Custody of Pearce*, 456 A.2d 597 (Pa. Super. 1983) (wishes of intelligent four-year-old considered very important); *In re Marriage of G.B.S.*, 641 S.W.2d 776 (Mo. Ct. App. E.D. 1982) (six-year-old). Georgia, Ohio, Texas, and West Virginia find that the preference of a young child may be an important factor to weigh, even if not controlling.

76 See e.g. *Phillips v Phillips*, 45 So. 3d 684 (Miss. App. 2010) (considering 14-year-old child's preference to live with father because his home was 'safer' with adequate heat, her own bedroom and bathroom).

77 *Pierron v Pierron*, 765 N.W.2d 345 (Mich. App. 2009), aff'd, 782 N.W.2d 480 (2010) (13-year-old boy and eight-year-old girl had defensible reasons for preferring the new school district).

78 *Michele M. v Richard R.*, 177 P.3d 830 (Alaska 2008) (discounting preference of teenage boy to live with his mother who allowed him to miss school and sports obligations); *Halford v Halford*, 292 S.W.3d 536 (Mo. App. 2009) (15-year-old child's preference to live with mother was due to her more liberal parental rules and discipline); *Sheridan v Sheridan*, 12 N.Y.S.3d 434 (App. Div. 2015), appeal withdrawn, 59 N.E.3d 1212 (2016).

to the child's wishes, the judge may state in the findings the reason the child's wishes were not followed.[79] The usual reasons are that the child is too young to articulate a reasoned preference, the reasons for the preference are not sound, the preferred parent is unfit to be custodian or there is evidence of parental coaching or alienation.[80] A child's preference may be given less weight if the judge feels that the views expressed are the result of parental coercion or alienation. An alienated child expresses, freely and persistently, unreasonable negative feelings and beliefs (such as anger, hatred, rejection, and/or fear) toward a parent that are significantly disproportionate to the child's actual experience with that parent.[81] The judge must determine how much of the perceived negatives are real and may discount the child's preference.[82] The issue of children who resist contact has become the subject of intense debate.[83]

4. RESEARCH

There has been relatively little empirical research on child participation in private custody cases in the United States generally. From 2001 to 2009, the American Bar Association Child Custody and Adoption Pro Bono Project awarded grants for pilot projects and some research, but they were local and unpublished. Most empirical research consists of 10-year-old state-specific studies based on judicial interviews. The research has shown a wide disparity in practices among judges even within a particular state.[84] There is little national data on judicial practices about child participation. Interestingly, a couple of

---

79 *Bennett v Bennett*, 242 So. 3d 210 (Miss. App. 2018); *Rivera v LaSalle*, 923 N.Y.S.2d 254 (App. Div. 2011) (court erred in placing too little weight on child's preference where all other factors were equal).

80 *Maier v Maier*, 874 N.W.2d 725 (Mich. App. 2015).

81 *Palazzolo v Mire*, 10 So. 3d 748 (La. App. 2009); *In re Marriage of Cobb*, 988 P.2d 272 (Kan. App. 1999). See J.R. Johnston, 'Children of Divorce Who Reject a Parent and Refuse Visitation: Recent Research and Social Policy Implications for the Alienated Child' (2005) 38(4) *Family Law Quarterly* 757.

82 *Martin v Martin*, 878 N.Y.S.2d 475 (App. Div. 2009) (discounting preference where child had a list of complaints and was under pressure to make sure that entire list was disgorged to court).

83 See L.D. Elrod, 'The Best Interests of the Child When There is Conflict About Contact' in E.E. Sutherland and L.-A. Barnes Macfarlane (eds.), *Implementing Article 3 of the United Nations Convention on the Rights of the Child: Best Interests, Welfare and Well-being*, Cambridge University Press, Cambridge 2016, pp. 265–279. See also Special Issue: Parent-Child Contact Problems: Concepts, Controversies and Conundrums (2020) 58(2) *Family Court Review* 259–634.

84 J. Clarke, above n. 28, p. 458, n. 6 (discussing Michigan study and citing earlier studies); B.A. Atwood, above n. 38.

studies found that the average length of an *in camera* interview was less than 20 minutes.[85]

5. CONCLUSION

The United States lags behind other countries in hearing children's voices in family law proceedings. The United States has not ratified either the UNCRC or the 1996 Hague Child Protection Convention. While the United States Supreme Court has cited the UNCRC in the case removing the death penalty for crimes committed by a minor,[86] it has not yet determined if a child has a constitutionally protected right to be heard in private custody cases. Adopting the UNCRC would be a major step toward ensuring participation by children. Like the majority of states, the UNCRC sets no minimum age for a child to be able to express his/her views and recognises the child's evolving capacity for decision-making. The UNCRC would clarify across the country that a child has a right to be heard in a variety of contexts, including private custody cases.[87]

Ratification of the 1996 Hague Child Protection Convention would help ensure the enforcement of United States custody orders by other treaty partners. Many countries are currently using the 1996 Convention. A foreign country may refuse to recognise a private custody order if that order was made 'without the child having been provided the opportunity to be heard, in violation of the fundamental principles of procedure of the requested state.'[88] Even if the United States does not ratify the 1996 Convention, lawyers will want to ensure that the record reflects how the child's voice is heard in any state custody proceeding to ensure enforcement in a country which has it. The Hague Conference on Private International Law, at its Seventh Special Commission meeting in October 2017, concluded that a court 'should incorporate into the order for measures a record of the way the child was heard, or if a decision is made not to hear the child, an indication that consideration was given to doing so and the reasons for the decision not to hear the child.'[89]

---

85 L. Wright, 'Interviewing Children in Custody Cases' (2002) 18 *Journal of the American Academy of Matrimonial Lawyers* 295; E.S. Scott, N. Dickon Reppucci and M. Aber, 'Children's Preference in Adjudicated Custody Decisions' (1988) 22 *Georgia Law Review* 1035, 1047 (less than 15 minutes in Virginia study); F.K. Lombard, 'Judicial Interviewing of Children in Custody Cases: An Empirical and Analytical Study' (1985) *U.C. Davis Law Review* 17 807 (less than 18 minutes in Michigan study).

86 *Roper v Simmons*, 543 U.S. 551, 575–576 (2005) (citing Art. 37).

87 H.A. Davidson, 'Children's Rights and American Law: A Response to What's Wrong with Children's Rights' (2006) 20 *Emory International Law Review* 69.

88 Section 23(2)(b) of the 1996 Hague Child Protection Convention.

89 See Conclusions and Recommendations of the 7th Special Commission.

While the best interests of the child are theoretically at the centre of any decision-making, the child should also have a right to participate. A child's perspective provides valuable information that can help the judge assess how competing proposals will impact a given child and may assist in resolving the dispute. Even if the child is too young or unable to articulate a view, a child's attorney could offer a child-focused assessment of the child's needs. Listening to the child means adding the child's voice to the other voices in the room. The United States lags behind other countries which have not only enacted the UNCRC, but also created policies and procedures to effectively get the child's voice heard in custody cases. Recent debates, discussions and articles urging more inclusion of the child's perspective hold promise.

PART IV

COMPARATIVE ANALYSIS

CHILD PARTICIPATION IN FAMILY LAW PROCEEDINGS COMPARED

Charlotte Mol

1. INTRODUCTION

Ammar, a 14-year-old living in Germany, just found out his parents are going to divorce. On the other side of the world, Hannah is going through the same. They meet online and start messaging. One of their shared worries is whether they will get to have a say in the whole ordeal. If so, does Hannah in Australia have the same options as Ammar in Germany? In this chapter, not only Hannah and Ammar's participation rights are compared, but also those of children in 15 other countries.

The present Handbook is a rich comparative resource. The chapters for each of the jurisdictions grant an insight into the different manners in which children, such as Ammar and Hannah, can participate in family law proceedings. The current chapter provides a comparative analysis of the jurisdictions covered in this Handbook and serves as a springboard for further comparative research.

The similarities and differences between the various modes of participation available to children in the 17 jurisdictions will be discussed.[1]

This comparative analysis focuses on a number of key themes regarding child participation. First, the types of proceedings addressed in this comparison are introduced. Then the core focus of the comparison shifts to the modes of participation. Can Hannah speak directly to the judge? Is it possible for Ammar to have a lawyer appointed to represent him? The different domestic opportunities available to children per mode of participation will be compared. Thereafter, two specific proceedings are discussed separately: international child abduction proceedings and alternative dispute resolution processes like mediation. Do children have the same participation opportunities in these proceedings compared to general family law proceedings, or are different opportunities provided? Subsequently, from a more overarching perspective, the requirements for participation will be discussed, as well as the methods of informing the child prior to and after the proceedings. The chapter ends with concluding remarks on the similarities and differences evident from the comparative analysis.

2. TYPES OF PROCEEDINGS

Whether Ammar and Hannah are dealing with their parents divorcing, or with any other disputes concerning them, it is their right to be able to express their views in all family law proceedings affecting them. As this Handbook is focused on family law proceedings, one may therefore wonder why it is necessary to further discuss the type of proceedings. However, under the heading of family law proceedings there are many specific types of proceedings, such as divorce proceedings, custody proceedings, contact or access proceedings, parentage proceedings, etc. The delineation between these types of family law proceedings differs between jurisdictions. Some Handbook authors commented on the fragmented regulation of child participation opportunities between types of proceedings within their jurisdiction.[2] One can draw a similar conclusion for the comparative overview: in most jurisdictions, the modes of participation available to the child will depend on the type of proceeding concerned. In some jurisdictions there are modes of participation available in most proceedings;[3]

---

1 The question of the extent to which the opportunities for child participation per jurisdiction meet the international and regional human rights norms will be answered in M. Bruning, W. Schrama, M. Freeman and N. Taylor, Conclusion.

2 See E. di Napoli and F. Maoli, Italy, s 1; M. Bruning and W. Schrama, The Netherlands, s 5.

3 See for example the direct mode of participation available in the Netherlands or the separate legal representative in South Africa: M. Bruning and W. Schrama, The Netherlands, s 2.4; J. Sloth-Nielsen, South Africa, s 3.1.1.

in others the modes may only be available for a very specific type of proceeding.[4] It is therefore difficult to compare the modes of participation available per type of proceedings.[5]

Thus, in this chapter, the modes of participation are compared independently of the type of proceedings. Instead, they are discussed with the understanding that they are available at least for children in proceedings concerning the separation of parents and (subsequent) custody, parental authority, contact or access proceedings in all jurisdictions. Specific mention is made if the mode of participation in a certain jurisdiction is not available in these proceedings, but instead in another specific type of proceeding, or is limited to certain proceedings. Following the discussion on the modes of participation more generally, two specific types of proceedings are dealt with separately: those concerning international child abduction and alternative dispute resolution.

3. MODES OF PARTICIPATION

It is generally accepted, and also mandated by international human rights law, that children should be able to express their views in family law proceedings. The ways in which children participate can, however, differ. Throughout the chapters in this Handbook a wide variety of modes of participation are described. Each jurisdiction has at least one or more modes of participation available to children in family law proceedings. It is striking to see the diversity of vocabulary used to specify these modes. This alone may complicate the comparison of modes of participation, for example for Ammar and Hannah, who may not understand that they have similar opportunities to participate, albeit named differently. In this section a comparison is made of four modes of participation: (1) direct modes; (2) representation modes; (3) indirect modes; and (4) party status and litigation by children. These four categories are introduced in each of the subsections, followed by a comparison of the specific modes in the jurisdictions surveyed.

3.1. DIRECT MODES OF PARTICIPATION

Direct modes of participation are those where children are granted the opportunity to directly address the decision-making authority to express their views. There are a number of different direct modes of participation.

---

4 See for example the option of a lawyer in parentage proceedings in Denmark or the possibility to initiate proceedings only to request a contact order in Germany: C.G. Jeppesen de Boer and A. Kronborg, Denmark, s 3.3; N. Dethloff and D. Schröder, Germany, s 3.3.1.

5 Even more so because, although the chapters provide a wealth of information, it is not always clear precisely which mode of participation is available in each type of proceedings.

Most common is the hearing of a child by the court, also known as judicial meetings. Remarkably, this option is available in all 17 jurisdictions surveyed.[6] The child is heard by the judge, often alone, but in many countries it is also possible for others to be present, such as a clerk, child professional, expert, social worker, or the child's lawyer. Common to all jurisdictions is the fact that the child's parents are not present. Generally, the child is given the opportunity to express their views to the court; this is not an obligation. Remarkably, in Romania children are required to attend the judicial meeting, but they do not have to answer any of the judge's questions.[7]

In many jurisdictions the opportunity for a child to directly express views to the court is dependent on age or maturity conditions. Only in China is there a strict age limit: children are heard by courts from the age of eight years and older.[8] In three jurisdictions an open maturity condition is used. In South Africa the twin criteria 'age and maturity' are used, for which the 'capacity to express views' is assessed on a case-by-case basis, often by the court itself relying on various factors, such as the degree of potential influence.[9] In Scotland the 'age and maturity' criteria are also used, but are supplemented with the presumption that a child aged 12 years and over has sufficient age and maturity to form views.[10] In Denmark the child must have sufficient maturity for direct involvement, which has to be individually assessed, but in practice means children from the (school-) age of six or seven years and older.[11] Finally, in eight jurisdictions age limits are used with the possibility of younger children being heard directly on the basis of open or other criteria. These eight jurisdictions are discussed from the lowest age limit upwards. In Israel children from the age of six ought to be invited to participate, but younger children may also participate if they wish to and have an older sibling who is participating.[12] In Norway children may express their views when they are 'mature enough to form their own opinion or, at the latest when they turn seven years old'.[13] Romania requires courts to hear the child when they

6 See F. Bell, J. Cashmore and J. Harman, Australia, s 3.4.1; I. Boone, C. Declerck and E. Vertommen, Belgium, s 2; R. Birnbaum and N. Bala, Canada, s 3.2.1; N. Zhao, China, s 3.1; B. Rešetar and N. Lucić, Croatia, s 3.2.1; C.G. Jeppesen de Boer and A. Kronborg, Denmark, s 3; M. Freeman and N. Lowe, England and Wales, s 3.2.1; N. Dethloff and D. Schröder, Germany, s 3.1; R. Schuz and T. Morag, Israel, s 3.1; E. di Napoli and F. Maoli, Italy, s 2; M. Bruning and W. Schrama, The Netherlands, s 2.4; N. Taylor, New Zealand, s 3.2.1; A. Nylund, Norway, s 3.1.2; S. Florescu, Romania, s 3.1.3; E.K.M. Tisdall, Scotland, s 3.1; J. Sloth-Nielsen, South Africa, s 2; L.D. Elrod, United States of America, s 3.1.2.

7 S. Florescu, Romania, s 3.1.3.

8 N. Zhao, China, s 2.

9 J. Sloth-Nielsen, South Africa, s 3.1.1.

10 E.K.M. Tisdall, Scotland, s 2.

11 C.G. Jeppesen de Boer and A. Kronborg, Denmark, s 3.

12 R. Schuz and T. Morag, Israel, s 3.3.

13 A. Nylund, Norway, s 2.

have reached the age of 10 years, but it is also possible to hear younger children if the court considers it necessary.[14] In practice, therefore, for cases concerning parental separation children are often heard from the age of six years. There are three jurisdictions where the age limit is placed at 12 years of age. In Belgium children from the age of 12 are informed of their right to be heard and may make use of this right, while younger children must either request to be heard themselves, or the parties (e.g. parents) or the public prosecutor can do so (with the option for the court to decline the request when it is made by a party).[15] In Italy children under the age of 12 years may be heard if they are 'capable of discernment'.[16] The judge will evaluate whether a child can form their own views, can understand the circumstance of the hearing and is mature enough to communicate their views, but may also appoint a psychologist or other expert to assist in this assessment.[17] Children over the age of 12 in the Netherlands are by default invited to speak to the judge; younger children are not, but they can be heard if they are 'sufficiently mature', which is up to the discretion of the judge.[18] Finally, there are two jurisdictions where an age limit of 14 years exists, albeit with possibilities for younger children. In Croatia children older than 14 can directly express their opinion, while younger children can also do so, but can also be heard indirectly (as will be discussed in section 3.3).[19] In Germany the court has the duty to hear a child aged 14 or older, but a younger child may also be heard if 'their preferences, relationships or wishes are significant to the decision' or when it is otherwise indicated.[20] More specifically, case law requires children from the age of three years and older to be heard in proceedings concerning the person of the child.[21] This makes the final jurisdiction discussed the one in which perhaps the youngest children are heard. It is interesting to note that the German legislature has, in March 2021, passed a new Act by which the age limit of 14 for a mandatory child hearing included in the law will be dispensed with.[22]

Some jurisdictions have (additional) other conditions, such as Norway, where the consent of parents is required (but lack thereof may be overridden by the court), or the United States, where it is at the discretion of the court whether or not to directly hear the child.[23] Although, legally, the existence of direct hearing opportunities by courts are widespread, in practice it is not always common. This can be because other forms of participation are more

---

14 S. Florescu, Romania, s 2.
15 I. Boone, C. Declerck and E. Vertommen, Belgium, s 3.1.3.
16 E. di Napoli and F. Maoli, Italy, s 2.
17 E. di Napoli and F. Maoli, Italy, s 3.3.
18 M. Bruning and W. Schrama, The Netherlands, s 2.4.
19 B. Rešetar and N. Lucić, Croatia, s 3.2.1.
20 N. Dethloff and D. Schröder, Germany, s 3.1.
21 N. Dethloff and D. Schröder, Germany, s 3.1.
22 N. Dethloff and D. Schröder, Germany, s 3.1.
23 A. Nylund, Norway, s 3.1.1; L.D. Elrod, United States of America, s 3.1.2.

common (e.g. England and Wales, Scotland and South Africa)[24] or because most proceedings are resolved through mediation instead of court proceedings (e.g. Denmark and Norway).[25] In some jurisdictions it is even rare to directly hear the child, for example in Australia, where judges are reluctant to do so.[26] To conclude, there is no uniformity with regard to the requirements applied, neither in the type of requirement nor within the commonly applied maturity requirements.

As mentioned above, parents are not present at judicial meetings, but in most countries the parties to the proceedings – usually the parents – are informed about what their child said. This occurs to different extents. In many jurisdictions a written report, record or protocol is drafted which may, or may not, be shared with the parents depending on its confidentiality. However, it is also possible for the judge to orally report back to the parties. There is no confidentiality of the views shared by the child in Australia, Belgium, Croatia, England and Wales, New Zealand, Norway, and Romania.[27] On the other end of the spectrum is China, where the views are kept confidential.[28] In the middle we find jurisdictions in which views are only shared with the consent of the child involved (e.g. Israel),[29] or where only a summary of the views is shared as the report or notes remain confidential (e.g. Israel and the Netherlands),[30] or in which the judge has the discretion to decide how much information must be shared with the parties (e.g. Germany and the United States).[31] When there is no, or partial, confidentiality this is commonly explained to the child in advance of, or during, the judicial meeting.[32] In summary, while absolute confidentiality is the exception, the prevalence of no confidentiality and partial confidentiality is roughly even in the remaining jurisdictions.

It is also possible for children to directly participate in hearings with other decision-making authorities. In Denmark the Family Law House, an administrative authority, is the starting point for all family law proceedings. When there are disputes between parents, children have the opportunity to be heard by a child professional from the Child Unit of the Family

---

24 M. Freeman and N. Lowe, England and Wales, s 3.2; E.K.M. Tisdall, Scotland, s 4.1; J. Sloth-Nielsen, South Africa, s 3.1.1.

25 C.G. Jeppesen de Boer and A. Kronborg, Denmark, s 4; A. Nylund, Norway, s 2.

26 F. Bell, J. Cashmore and J. Harman, Australia, s 3.4.1.

27 F. Bell, J. Cashmore and J. Harman, Australia, s 3.4.1; I. Boone, C. Declerck and E. Vertommen, Belgium, s 3.1.3; B. Rešetar and N. Lucić, Croatia, s 3.2.1; M. Freeman and N. Lowe, England and Wales, s 3.2.1.1; N. Taylor, New Zealand, s 3.2.1; A. Nylund, Norway, s 3.1.2; S. Florescu, Romania, s 3.1.3.

28 N. Zhao, China, s 3.1.

29 R. Schuz and T. Morag, Israel, s 3.1.

30 R. Schuz and T. Morag, Israel, s 3.1; M. Bruning and W. Schrama, The Netherlands, s 3.2.

31 N. Dethloff and D. Schröder, Germany, s 3.1; L.D. Elrod, United States of America, s 3.1.2.

32 See for example M. Freeman and N. Lowe, England and Wales, s 3.2.1.1; M. Bruning and W. Schrama, The Netherlands, s 3.2; A. Nylund, Norway, s 3.1.2.

Law House.[33] This opportunity is conditional upon the child having sufficient maturity and the classification of the parents' dispute in a certain estimated risk category.[34] It is possible for the child's support person (offered by an NGO) to be present at this hearing and the hearing is not confidential.[35] In Romania the public notary is another authority which may hear the child directly when parents come to authenticate their parenting agreements.[36] In both these jurisdictions, these decision-making authorities do not take decisions as a court would, but instead assist parents in coming to, or authenticating, an agreement.

Another mode of direct participation is in written form instead of oral. In China children can file written views with the court.[37] Since it can be questioned whether the written views are the genuine views of the child, it is common for the child to subsequently be heard directly by the judge as discussed above. In Scotland children receive a 'Form F9' which they can fill in and return to the court.[38] Here again it is possible for the child to subsequently be called to speak to the sheriff. Similarly, in the Netherlands children receive an invitation to speak to the judge together with a form, which they may return to the court with their written views.[39]

A final mode of direct participation is the hearing of a child by a court as a witness to give evidence in family law proceedings. This is possible in Canada, Scotland and the United States.[40] However, it is generally disapproved of in both Canada and the United States as there are concerns about the effects it has on the child.[41] One may also question whether hearing a child as a witness should qualify as participation when the sole aim is to collect evidence, instead of the aim of allowing the child to express their views. The relationship between child participation and evidence is one which will further be discussed in the conclusion to this chapter.

3.2. REPRESENTATION MODES OF PARTICIPATION

Representation as participation means the action of having someone speak or act on behalf of the child. For the purposes of this comparative analysis such representatives are understood to be third parties (for example, a lawyer appointed to represent the child), not the child's parents. There are many different modes of

33 C.G. Jeppesen de Boer and A. Kronborg, Denmark, s 3.1.
34 C.G. Jeppesen de Boer and A. Kronborg, Denmark, s 3.2.
35 C.G. Jeppesen de Boer and A. Kronborg, Denmark, s 3 and 3.1.
36 S. Florescu, Romania, s 3.1.2.
37 N. Zhao, China, 3.1.
38 E.K.M. Tisdall, Scotland, s 3.1.
39 M. Bruning and W. Schrama, The Netherlands, s 3.2.
40 R. Birnbaum and N. Bala, Canada, s 3.2.1; E.K.M. Tisdall, Scotland, s 3.1; L.D. Elrod, United States of America, s 3.1.1.
41 R. Birnbaum and N. Bala, Canada, s 3.2.1; L.D. Elrod, United States of America, s 3.1.1.

representation found in the jurisdictions surveyed. Differences exist with regard to the aim of the representation, the person acting as the representative, and the requirements for and appointment of a representative.

There are generally two options regarding the aim of representation: representing the child's wishes/views or representing the child's best interests/welfare. An example of the first option is the separate legal representative available in South Africa, who must present and argue the child's wishes, through use of their legal knowledge and expertise.[42] Another example is the Israeli guardian ad litem, who, when the child is 15 years or older, ought to represent their wishes unless doing so would endanger the child.[43] In the second option the representative will hear the child's views, but represent their best interests and therefore does not act on the child's instructions. Examples can be found in Australia with the independent children's lawyer, China's agent ad litem, Germany's guardian ad litem, Italy's child special representative, the guardian ad litem in the Netherlands, and both Scotland's as well as South Africa's curator ad litem.[44] The guardian ad litem in Israel also fits in this category, though only when the child is younger than 15 years old; otherwise the aim is representation of the child's wishes.[45] Finally, some representatives represent both the child's wishes/views and their best interests/welfare. If these clash then priority must be given to one of the two. For example, in Canada the legal representative should ensure that the child's views are presented to the court, but must also tell the court how these views have affected their own assessment on the position to take regarding the child's best interests.[46] In New Zealand, the lawyer for the child represents the welfare of the child as well as ascertaining and communicating the child's views, but when these clash it is possible for a second lawyer to be appointed so that both perspectives are represented.[47] Finally, it is not clear which of the potential aims the Belgian ad hoc guardian or the Danish lawyer focus upon, and in the United States all options are possible, although the second option of representing the child's interests is most popular.[48] In any case, a different aim is that of the Norwegian (legal) representative of the child, who must only advocate the procedural rights of the child and ensure these are upheld.[49]

---

42 J. Sloth-Nielsen, South Africa, s 3.1.1.

43 R. Schuz and T. Morag, Israel, s 3.2.

44 F. Bell, J. Cashmore and J. Harman, Australia, s 3.3; N. Zhao, China, s 3.3; N. Dethloff and D. Schröder, Germany, s 3.2; E. di Napoli and F. Maoli, Italy, s 3.2; M. Bruning and W. Schrama, The Netherlands, s 2.3; E.K.M. Tisdall, Scotland, s 3.2; J. Sloth-Nielsen, South Africa, s 3.1.4.

45 R. Schuz and T. Morag, Israel, s 3.2.

46 R. Birnbaum and N. Bala, Canada, s 3.1.3.

47 N. Taylor, New Zealand, s 3.1.1.

48 I. Boone, C. Declerck and E. Vertommen, Belgium, s 3.2.1; C.G. Jeppesen de Boer and A. Kronborg, Denmark, s 3.3; L.D. Elrod, United States of America, s 3.2.

49 A. Nylund, Norway, s 3.2.

With the varying aims of the representatives in mind, the next issue is who these representatives are and which function requirements apply. Often the representative is a lawyer (with considerable family law experience).[50] In some jurisdictions it is also possible to have non-legal representatives, for example in China with relatives or recommended citizens, the United States with laypersons, or Croatia and the Netherlands where psychologists or pedagogical experts can be representatives.[51] In Germany there is no specific function requirement, but the guardian ad litem must be 'suitable' and often has legal, pedagogical or psychological qualifications.[52] Finally, in Italy, there are no centralised national conditions; therefore, it depends on the region as to which function requirements are applied.[53]

The next issue is when and how the child's representative can be appointed. In five jurisdictions courts have the discretion to appoint a representative without any specific requirements as to when to do so (although in both Australia and Canada it is also dependent on legal aid).[54] In seven jurisdictions, it is also the court who appoints a representative, but a conflict of interests between the child and their parents is required.[55] In Belgium it must be a real (potential) conflict of interests and in South Africa a potential conflict of interests also suffices, while in the Netherlands the conflict of interests has to be concrete.[56] One may question whether, and if so to what extent, these three conflict of interests requirements differ in practice. In some jurisdictions the requirement of a conflict of interests is combined with other requirements. In Denmark the option of a lawyer is only possible in parentage proceedings, while in the Netherlands a guardian ad litem is always required in parentage proceedings and the conflict of interests requirement only applies in family law proceedings

---

50 F. Bell, J. Cashmore and J. Harman, Australia, s 3.3; R. Birnbaum and N. Bala, Canada, s 3.1.3; N. Zhao, China, s 3.3; B. Rešetar and N. Lucić, Croatia, s 3.2.2; C.G. Jeppesen de Boer and A. Kronborg, Denmark, s 3 and 3.3; N. Dethloff and D. Schröder, Germany, s 3.2 (the child's attorney); R. Schuz and T. Morag, Israel, s 3.2; M. Bruning and W. Schrama, The Netherlands, s 2.3; N. Taylor, New Zealand, s 3.1.1; A. Nylund, Norway, s 3.2; J. Sloth-Nielsen, South Africa, s 3.1.1 and 3.1.4 (separate legal representative and curator ad litem); L.D. Elrod, United States of America, s 3.2.

51 N. Zhao, China, s 3.3; B. Rešetar and N. Lucić, Croatia, 3.2.2; M. Bruning and W. Schrama, The Netherlands, s 2.3; L.D. Elrod, United States of America, s 3.2.

52 N. Dethloff and D. Schröder, Germany, s 3.2.

53 E. di Napoli and F. Maoli, Italy, s 3.2.

54 F. Bell, J. Cashmore and J. Harman, Australia, s 3.3; R. Birnbaum and N. Bala, Canada, s 3.1.3; R. Schuz and T. Morag, Israel, s 3.2; E.K.M. Tisdall, Scotland, s 3,2; L.D. Elrod, United States of America, s 3.2.

55 I. Boone, C. Declerck and E. Vertommen, Belgium, s 3.2.1; B. Rešetar and N. Lucić, Croatia, s 3.2.2 (it is also possible for the social welfare centre to appoint the special guardian); C.G. Jeppesen de Boer and A. Kronborg, Denmark, s 3.3; N. Dethloff and D. Schröder, Germany, s 2 (guardian ad litem); E. di Napoli and F. Maoli, Italy, s 3.2; M. Bruning and W. Schrama, The Netherlands, s 2.3; J. Sloth-Nielsen, South Africa, s 3.1.4 (curator ad litem).

56 I. Boone, C. Declerck and E. Vertommen, Belgium, s 3.2.1; M. Bruning and W. Schrama, The Netherlands, s 2.3; J. Sloth-Nielsen, South Africa, s 3.1.4 (curator ad litem).

concerning the care and upbringing of the child.[57] In Germany the guardian ad litem can be appointed for a conflict of interests or when the child's interests are at risk of being endangered and the appointment of an attorney is not possible. In three jurisdictions the court appoints the representative and requirements other than a conflict of interests apply. In New Zealand the lawyer for the child is appointed by the Family Court in cases where there are concerns for the safety and wellbeing of the child.[58] In Norway there must be the particular need for a legal representative, for example suspected child abuse or neglect.[59] Finally, in South Africa the court can appoint a separate legal representative if it considers the child to have the capacity to instruct the representative – this is determined on a case-by-case basis.[60] It is also possible that the representative is not appointed by the court, for example in China, where the agent ad litem is appointed by the legal representatives of the child, or in Germany, where the child can appoint an attorney for themselves.[61] In the jurisdictions surveyed, the appointment of a representative is either wholly dependent on the discretion of the judge or is dependent on specific requirements. These requirements differ, sometimes concerning the child and at other times dependent on the level of conflict of interests or potential wellbeing or safety issues.

Before concluding this section on representation modes of participation it is important to make two final remarks. First, it is very common for the state to bear the costs of the representative by means of legal aid or otherwise,[62] although in some jurisdictions parties must also at times contribute to the costs.[63] Only in China, where the agent ad litem is also appointed by the child's parents, must they pay the whole cost.[64] Lastly, Croatia has detailed law on how the special guardian ought to complete its task and this may provide guidance for other states.

3.3. INDIRECT MODES OF PARTICIPATION

Indirect modes are participation opportunities in which the child does not communicate their views to the decision-maker either directly or through a

57 C.G. Jeppesen de Boer and A. Kronborg, Denmark, s 3.3; M. Bruning and W. Schrama, The Netherlands, s 2.3.

58 N. Taylor, New Zealand, s 3.1.1.

59 A. Nylund, Norway, s 3.2.

60 J. Sloth-Nielsen, South Africa, 3.1.1 (separate legal representative).

61 N. Zhao, China, s 3.3; N. Dethloff and D. Schröder, Germany, s 3.2 (the child's attorney).

62 R. Birnbaum and N. Bala, Canada, s 3.1.3; N. Dethloff and D. Schröder, Germany, s 3.2 (child's attorney and guardian ad litem); A. Nylund, Norway, s 3.2; J. Sloth-Nielsen, South Africa, ss 3.1.1 and 3.1.4 (separate legal representative and curator ad litem).

63 F. Bell, J. Cashmore and J. Harman, Australia, s 3.3; B. Rešetar and N. Lucić, Croatia, s 3.2.2; N. Taylor, New Zealand, s 3.1.1.

64 N. Zhao, China, s 3.3.

representative, but instead indirectly through a report. In some country chapters this has been qualified as an indirect mode,[65] but it is also seen as a direct mode[66] or a form of representation in others.[67] In comparison, in Germany and the Netherlands the preparation of expert reports, even where the child is questioned as to their views, is not seen as a mode of participation at all.[68] This is notable as it is considered the main mode of participation in other jurisdictions.[69]

There are nine jurisdictions in which children's views may be expressed by means of a report.[70] What all these jurisdictions have in common is that the report is drafted by a third party, not by a parent or decision-maker. Who this third party is varies. The options include social workers (Canada, Israel and Romania),[71] social science experts such as psychologists, either based within the court system or independent thereof (Australia, China, Croatia, England and Wales, Scotland and South Africa),[72] lawyers or special guardians (Canada and Croatia),[73] or any other independent third party (see e.g. China).[74] In six jurisdictions there are no child-related requirements, such as age limits, attached to having such a report drafted; in Romania it is even required in all proceedings.[75] In China and Israel, a minimum age requirement applies of, respectively, eight years and older and six years and older.[76] In Croatia a maximum maturity condition is applicable: a child younger than 14 years old can be heard indirectly when they cannot express their opinion directly, presumably due to their skills

65 F. Bell, J. Cashmore and J. Harman, Australia, s 3.2; B. Rešetar and N. Lucić, Croatia, s 3.2.1.
66 R. Birnbaum and N. Bala, Canada, s 3.2.2; R. Schuz and T. Morag, Israel, s 3.1.
67 M. Freeman and N. Lowe, England and Wales, s 3.1; S. Florescu, Romania, s 3.2; E.K.M. Tisdall, Scotland, s 3.2; J. Sloth-Nielsen, South Africa, s 3.1.1.
68 N. Dethloff and D. Schröder, Germany, s 2; M. Bruning and W. Schrama, The Netherlands, s 3.2.
69 See for example E.K.M. Tisdall, Scotland.
70 F. Bell, J. Cashmore and J. Harman, Australia, s 3.2 (family reports); R. Birnbaum and N. Bala, Canada, s 3.2.2 (voice of the child reports); N. Zhao, China, s 3.2 (social care investigation reports); B. Rešetar and N. Lucić, Croatia, s 3.2.1 (indirect hearing); M. Freeman and N. Lowe, England and Wales, s 3.1.1 (court welfare reports); R. Schuz and T. Morag, Israel, s 3.1 (welfare unit reports); S. Florescu, Romania, s 3.2 (psychosocial reports); E.K.M. Tisdall, Scotland, s 3.2 (child welfare reports); J. Sloth-Nielsen, South Africa, s 3.1.1 (expert reports and family advocate reports).
71 R. Birnbaum and N. Bala, Canada, s 3.2.2; R. Schuz and T. Morag, Israel, s 2; S. Florescu, Romania, s 3.2.
72 F. Bell, J. Cashmore and J. Harman, Australia, s 3.2; N. Zhao, China, s 3.2; B. Rešetar and N. Lucić, Croatia, s 3.2.1; M. Freeman and N. Lowe, England and Wales, s 3.1.1; E.K.M. Tisdall, Scotland, s 3.2; J. Sloth-Nielsen, South Africa, s 3.1.1.
73 R. Birnbaum and N. Bala, Canada, s 3.2.2; B. Rešetar and N. Lucić, Croatia, s 3.2.1.
74 N. Zhao, China, s 3.2.
75 F. Bell, J. Cashmore and J. Harman, Australia, s 3.2; R. Birnbaum and N. Bala, Canada, s 3.2.2; M. Freeman and N. Lowe, England and Wales, s 3.1.1; S. Florescu, Romania, s 3.2; E.K.M. Tisdall, Scotland, s 3.2; J. Sloth-Nielsen, South Africa, s 3.1.1.
76 N. Zhao, China, s 3.2; R. Schuz and T. Morag, Israel, s 2.

and maturity (which has to be assessed).[77] In any case, a report is drafted in which the views of the child are expressed – the extent thereof, in light of the aim of the report, differs between jurisdictions. In some jurisdictions the report solely reflects the views of the child, for example in Canada and Croatia.[78] In most jurisdictions the aim of reporting on the views of the child is combined with observations or recommendations regarding the welfare of the child.[79] In Romania it is even unclear whether children are heard at all, with the report focusing on the situation and welfare of the child.[80]

3.4. PARTY STATUS AND LITIGATION

It is possible for a child to be afforded party status or the procedural right to commence litigation. However, in most of the 17 jurisdictions, a child generally has no party status in family law proceedings.[81] Instead, the child has legal representatives, often their parents, who ought to represent their interests.[82] However, exceptions do exist. Most notably in Croatia the child has party status in all proceedings concerning their rights and interests.[83] In Italy children have party status only in proceedings at the juvenile courts, such as those concerning the limitation and loss of parental responsibility, not at the ordinary courts, which deal with most family law cases with regard to separation and divorce.[84] Finally, in Australia and New Zealand children can be joined as a party to family law proceedings, although this is rare in practice.[85] Similarly, in England and Wales a child may be joined as a party if the court considers it to be in the child's best interests, but this only occurs in a minority of cases.[86] If a child has been joined as a party in England and Wales, then they will be represented by either a guardian or a solicitor.[87] Representation by a solicitor only occurs if the child

77 B. Rešetar and N. Lucić, Croatia, 3.2.1.

78 R. Birnbaum and N. Bala, Canada, s 3.2.2; B. Rešetar and N. Lucić, Croatia, s 3.2.1.

79 F. Bell, J. Cashmore and J. Harman, Australia, s 3.2; N. Zhao, China, s 3.2; M. Freeman and N. Lowe, England and Wales, s 3.1.1; R. Schuz and T. Morag, Israel, s 2; E.K.M. Tisdall, Scotland, s 4.1; J. Sloth-Nielsen, South Africa, s 3.1.1.

80 S. Florescu, Romania, s 3.2.

81 See specifically F. Bell, J. Cashmore and J. Harman, Australia, s 3.4.2; M. Bruning and W. Schrama, The Netherlands, s 2.2; N. Taylor, New Zealand, s 3.2.2; S. Florescu, Romania, s 3.3.

82 See for example I. Boone, C. Declerck and E. Vertommen, Belgium, s 3.2.2; N. Zhao, China, s 3.3 and 3.4; M. Bruning and W. Schrama, The Netherlands, s 2.2; A. Nylund, Norway, s 2.

83 B. Rešetar and N. Lucić, Croatia, s 2.

84 E. di Napoli and F. Maoli, Italy, s 3.2.

85 F. Bell, J. Cashmore and J. Harman, Australia, s 3.4.2; M. Freeman and N. Lowe, England and Wales, s 3.2.2.1; N. Taylor, New Zealand, s 3.2.2.

86 M. Freeman and N. Lowe, England and Wales, s 3.2.2.1.

87 M. Freeman and N. Lowe, England and Wales, s. 3.2.2.1.

is considered able to give instructions in relation to the proceedings and the solicitor will subsequently act on these instructions. The child's guardian, on the other hand, must advocate for the welfare of the child and has representing the child's wishes as a second priority.[88]

Aside from party status, the potential for children to initiate litigation on their own behalf is either non-existent or limited to specific types of cases or through maturity requirements. Only two countries have broader provisions for initiation. South Africa has a general provision providing children legal standing to initiate proceedings when the matter affects them,[89] while in Israel a child may initiate proceedings when their 'interest is liable to suffer real harm'.[90] More commonly, rights of initiation are provided for specific proceedings. Sometimes these types of proceedings are quite broad, such as in Norway, where children may initiate parentage proceedings, or in Australia, where children can initiate parenting proceedings (although subsequently only used in extraordinary circumstance).[91] More often, specific proceedings are mentioned, such as in Germany, where a child over the age of 14 years can request a contact order with a parent,[92] or in Belgium, the Netherlands and Romania.[93] In combination with the type of proceedings, maturity requirements often also limit opportunities for child litigation, for example in Croatia, where children can independently initiate proceedings concerning their rights and interests when they have reached the age of 14 years and are 'capable of understanding the meaning and legal consequences' of the acts they undertake.[94] In England and Wales children with 'sufficient understanding' may be granted leave to seek an order concerning residence and contact,[95] and similarly in Scotland children under the age of 16 with 'general understanding' (presumed from 12 years and older) can request a solicitor to represent them in proceedings on parental responsibilities and rights.[96]

Party status or the opportunity to initiate proceedings includes the right to appeal in some countries, for example Australia and Croatia.[97] In two countries

88 M. Freeman and N. Lowe, England and Wales, s 3.2.2.1.

89 J. Sloth-Nielsen, South Africa, s 3.2.1.

90 R. Schuz and T. Morag, Israel, s 3.1.1.

91 F. Bell, J. Cashmore and J. Harman, Australia, s 3.4.2; A. Nylund, Norway, s 3.3.

92 N. Dethloff and D. Schröder, Germany, s 3.3.1.

93 I. Boone, C. Declerck and E. Vertommen, Belgium, s 3.2.2 (proceedings concerning the person of the child, e.g. status as parent or spouse, and protective measures, e.g. sealing of goods); M. Bruning and W. Schrama, The Netherlands, s 2.2 (registration of gender, emancipation, etc.); S. Florescu, Romania, s 3.3 (proceedings concerning change in religion, course of education or administration of assets).

94 B. Rešetar and N. Lucić, Croatia, s 3.2.3.

95 M. Freeman and N. Lowe, England and Wales, s 3.2.3.

96 E.K.M. Tisdall, Scotland, s 3.3.

97 F. Bell, J. Cashmore and J. Harman, Australia, s 3.4.2; B. Rešetar and N. Lucić, Croatia, s 3.2.3.

children have a right to appeal independent from party status or litigation options. In Germany children who have reached the age of 14 years can personally appeal in all matters concerning them.[98] In New Zealand children have the right to appeal against decisions of the Family Court.[99]

In addition to the above-mentioned initiation opportunities available to children, there are two countries where children can approach authorities without formal rights or a legal position. In the Netherlands children aged 12 or older (or those younger who are 'capable') can contact the court to informally ask for a decision in matters concerning parental responsibilities after divorce or separation and contact and care arrangements.[100] The court then has the discretion to hear the child and to provide a judgement ex officio. In Denmark children aged 10 or older may initiate a meeting concerning matters of parental responsibility with their parents and professionals at the Family Law House (a government authority).[101] Unlike the Dutch informal request, this meeting cannot lead to a decision ex officio by the Family Law House or by the court – instead parents must come to a new agreement or one parent can opt to initiate proceedings.

4. PARTICIPATION IN SPECIFIC PROCEEDINGS

In addition to the modes of participation within the framework of domestic family law proceedings, two other specific types of proceedings are now considered in relation to the opportunities they present for child participation: international child abduction proceedings, and methods of alternative dispute resolution.

4.1. PARTICIPATION IN INTERNATIONAL CHILD ABDUCTION PROCEEDINGS

International child abduction proceedings are considered separately due to their international nature and the existence and application of private international law conventions and regulations in these proceedings, as was also examined in Kruger and Maoli's chapter on child participation in private international law.

In comparison to the above-discussed modes of participation and requirements attached thereto, there are three ways in which jurisdictions deal with proceedings concerning international child abduction proceedings.

98 N. Dethloff and D. Schröder, Germany, s 2.

99 N. Taylor, New Zealand, s 3.2.2.

100 M. Bruning and W. Schrama, The Netherlands, s 2.2.

101 C.G. Jeppesen de Boer and A. Kronborg, Denmark, s 3.2.

The first is to consider these proceedings as equal to domestic family law proceedings. In Belgium, Croatia, Germany, Israel, Norway, Romania, Scotland and the United States, the domestic courts will provide the same or highly similar participation opportunities to children involved in an international child abduction as to those involved in other custody or parental authority disputes.[102] Two jurisdictions explicitly have more limited child participation in return proceedings compared to domestic family law proceedings. In Australia the opportunity for the child to be heard is more circumscribed: when a parent claims the child has a strong objection to return then the views will be sought; representation through an independent child's lawyer occurs only in exceptional circumstances in these cases.[103] In New Zealand the summary nature of international child abduction proceedings is also emphasised, which means that a lawyer is not always appointed.[104] However, children who object to return do always have a lawyer appointed to them who ascertains their views and can arrange a meeting with the judge.[105] In contrast, there are the five jurisdictions where the opportunity for children to participate in international child abduction proceedings is greater than in their domestic family law proceedings. In both England and Wales and the Netherlands, it has become common practice to obtain the views of younger children than in other types of proceedings. In England and Wales children as young as six years old have their views investigated primarily indirectly by Cafcass officers, but the judge may also interview the child in private directly.[106] In the Netherlands children from the age of three are appointed a guardian ad litem as a representative to communicate their views to the court, while children from the age of six are also invited to be heard directly by the court.[107] In Italy there is a specific provision for children's participation in return proceedings, which the Supreme Court of Cassation has confirmed as requiring the judge to hear the child unless there are particular reasons not to, for which adequate and specific grounds must be given.[108] In South Africa legal representation of the child is obligatory in international child abduction proceedings, with the representative having a best-interests role.[109] Finally, in Denmark requests in international child abduction proceedings must be made to the Family Court, which will hear a child with sufficient maturity

---

102 I. Boone, C. Declerck and E. Vertommen, Belgium, s 3.1.1; B. Rešetar and N. Lucić, Croatia, s 2; N. Dethloff and D. Schröder, Germany, s 1; R. Schuz and T. Morag, Israel, s 3.3; A. Nylund, Norway, s 3.1.2; S. Florescu, Romania, s 2; E.K.M. Tisdall, Scotland, s 2; L.D. Elrod, United States of America, s 2.

103 F. Bell, J. Cashmore and J. Harman, Australia, s 2.

104 N. Taylor, New Zealand, s 2.2.

105 N. Taylor, New Zealand, s 2.2.

106 M. Freeman and N. Lowe, England and Wales, s 2.3.

107 M. Bruning and W. Schrama, The Netherlands, s 3.2.

108 E. di Napoli and F. Maoli, Italy, s 3.4.

109 J. Sloth-Nielsen, South Africa, s 3.1.3.

directly, in the presence of a child professional and/or a representative for the child.[110]

To conclude, most jurisdictions offer similar participation opportunities for children in international child abduction proceedings as they do for children in domestic family law proceedings. Only in a few jurisdictions do specific provisions ensure either limited or extended participation opportunities to children in international child abduction proceedings.

4.2. PARTICIPATION IN ALTERNATIVE DISPUTE RESOLUTION

We have discussed how children such as Hannah and Ammar may participate in family law proceedings, but what happens if Hannah's parents decide – or are obliged – to try mediation first? The use of alternative dispute resolution (ADR), such as mediation, for family law disputes is steadily increasing throughout the jurisdictions studied. In several jurisdictions, such as Australia, Croatia, New Zealand, Norway and Romania, parents are required to make use of ADR prior to commencing family law proceedings, or specifically those concerning separation of parents with minor children.[111] In most jurisdictions, ADR is available as an option and parents are encouraged to reach their own parenting agreements jointly. Are children therefore offered an opportunity to express their views in ADR and, if so, how?

In only a few jurisdictions is the right for children to participate in ADR regulated by law. This is done most extensively in Croatia. The child may express their views, with their parents' consent, in the mandatory counselling prior to divorce proceedings, as well as in mediation.[112] The parenting plan drawn up by parents in counselling or through mediation needs to mention whether and how the child expressed their views and will need to be approved by the court, which can subsequently hear the child if they were not granted the opportunity.[113] In Israel, the Netherlands and South Africa there is an obligation for parents to hear their children when agreements are drafted, although doubts can be raised about its implementation in practice, for example in Israel.[114]

---

110 C.G. Jeppesen de Boer and A. Kronborg, Denmark, s 3.2.

111 F. Bell, J. Cashmore and J. Harman, Australia, s 3.1 (parents are required to consider participating in ADR prior to commencing private family law proceedings); B. Rešetar and N. Lucić, Croatia, s 3.1 (required prior to commencing divorce, parental responsibilities and contact proceedings); N. Taylor, New Zealand, s 3.1.2 (required for most parties prior to commencing family court proceedings); A. Nylund, Norway, s 2 (required prior to separation proceedings); S. Florescu, Romania, s 3.1.1 (required prior to commencing private family law proceedings).

112 B. Rešetar and N. Lucić, Croatia, s 3.1.

113 B. Rešetar and N. Lucić, Croatia, s 3.1.

114 R. Schuz and T. Morag, Israel, s 2; M. Bruning and W. Schrama, The Netherlands, s 2.5; J. Sloth-Nielsen, South Africa, s 3.3.

In most jurisdictions there are no specific laws as to how children should be able to express their views in ADR. At times this leads to low involvement by children in ADR, for example in Denmark, Germany and Romania.[115] In some countries it is slowly becoming more common, albeit without any specifics as to how, such as Canada and the Netherlands.[116] However, in other jurisdictions models and modes of participation have been developed through soft law or by other means. For example, in Australia it is possible to use 'child-inclusive' processes in ADR, in which the child is represented by a child consultant.[117] In Belgium it is generally accepted for the mediator to meet with the child so the child can express their views.[118] In England and Wales the Code of Practice requires children who are aged 10 years or older to be heard directly if they so wish, but the matter in which it occurs will depend on the mediator.[119] Several models of participation have been developed by mediation providers in New Zealand, whereby different types of specialists or consultants will speak with the child and provide relevant information to the mediator and parents.[120] Similarly in Norway, although child participation in out-of-court mediation remains uncommon, several authorities have implemented different models of child-inclusive mediation, and in South Africa there have also been models developed, such as the collaborative child-focused mediation process.[121]

To conclude, while formal regulations regarding child participation in ADR are still uncommon, there are models for child participation in mediation in multiple jurisdictions. Child participation in ADR is an evolving area of practice.

5. REQUIREMENTS FOR PARTICIPATION

Various requirements for child participation are evident in the modes of participation discussed above. The most common are age and maturity requirements, but there are also requirements like the existence of a conflict of interests or the consent of parents. In this section these requirements will not be revisited, but some general comments are made regarding the existence and use of these requirements.

The most common child-related conditions for participation are age and maturity requirements. Throughout this Handbook and in this chapter a

115 C.G. Jeppesen de Boer and A. Kronborg, Denmark, s 3; N. Dethloff and D. Schröder, Germany, s 3.3.2; S. Florescu, Romania, s 3.1.1.

116 R. Birnbaum and N. Bala, Canada, s 3.2.3; M. Bruning and W. Schrama, The Netherlands, s 2.5.

117 F. Bell, J. Cashmore and J. Harman, Australia, s 3.1.

118 I. Boone, C. Declerck and E. Vertommen, Belgium, s 2.

119 M. Freeman and N. Lowe, England and Wales, s 2.1.

120 N. Taylor, New Zealand, s 3.1.2.

121 A. Nylund, Norway, s 3.1.1; J. Sloth-Nielsen, South Africa, s 3.3.

variety of age and maturity requirements have been discussed. Taking a broad look, one can conclude that, in relation to the various modes of participation, age and maturity requirements are especially popular with regard to direct modes of participation and for litigation by the child. They are of more limited relevance for the indirect and representation modes of participation, where only a few jurisdictions apply such criteria. Turning to the specifics of these requirements, there are two main methods: the use of open norms or the use of age limits. First, the open norms. These are phrased in different ways, from simply 'sufficient age and maturity',[122] to the 'capacity to express views',[123] the 'capacity to instruct' a representative,[124] being 'capable of understanding the meaning and legal consequences' of litigation,[125] or having 'sufficient understanding'.[126] How these open norms are assessed in practice depends. In some jurisdictions, such as South Africa, the court will on a case-by-case basis assess whether the child meets the required norm by taking into account various factors.[127] In other jurisdictions the open norm is complemented by a presumption that children at a certain age satisfy the norm.[128] The latter comes close to the very common use of age limits combined with open norms for younger children. In both situations children from a certain age are automatically granted the opportunity to express views, while younger children will have to satisfy certain maturity requirements. With regard to those jurisdictions using age limits, it is noteworthy that most of those surveyed use the combination of an age limit with an open norm for younger children for the direct hearing of children by a court. In contrast, strict age limits are more common when age and maturity requirements are applied for indirect modes of participation or procedural rights to litigate.[129] With regard to age limits, it is noteworthy that there are many different ages used, from six to 15 years, with some jurisdictions hearing even younger children in practice, such as Germany, where children from the age of three years are granted the opportunity.[130] The age and maturity requirement was dispensed with in New Zealand in 2005 and any child must now be given reasonable opportunities to express their

122 C.G. Jeppesen de Boer and A. Kronborg, Denmark, s 3.2; E.K.M. Tisdall, Scotland, s 2; J. Sloth-Nielsen, South Africa, s 3.1.1.
123 J. Sloth-Nielsen, South Africa, s 3.1.1.
124 J. Sloth-Nielsen, South Africa, s 3.1.1.
125 B. Rešetar and N. Lucić, Croatia, s 3.2.3.
126 M. Freeman and N. Lowe, England and Wales, s 3.2; E.K.M. Tisdall, Scotland, s 4.1.
127 J. Sloth-Nielsen, South Africa, s 3.1.1.
128 C.G. Jeppesen de Boer and A. Kronborg, Denmark, s 3; E.K.M. Tisdall, Scotland, s 2.
129 See for example regarding indirect modes of participation: N. Zhao, China, s 3.2 (minimum age requirement of eight years); B. Rešetar and N. Lucić, Croatia, s 3.2.1 (maximum age requirement of 14 years); R. Schuz and T. Morag, Israel, s 2 (minimum age requirement of six years); or regarding litigation rights: N. Dethloff and D. Schröder, Germany, s 3.3.1 (minimum age requirement of 14 years).
130 N. Dethloff and D. Schröder, Germany, s 3.1.

views on matters affecting them.[131] To conclude, there are different options from open norms to strict age limits or, most commonly, a combination of both, and a wide range of ages is used. Questions remain regarding which type of age and maturity requirement is the most appropriate and whether a best practice can be determined in light of empirical legal research or knowledge from social sciences.

In addition to, or at times instead of, age and maturity requirements, a number of other requirements are used for the different modes of participation. A common requirement with the appointment of a representative for the child is the existence of a 'conflict of interests' between the child and their legal representatives, for example their parents. Another requirement – albeit less common – is parental consent to child participation. This can mean children are dependent on the will of their parents regarding participation, but there are some jurisdictions where courts can override this lack of parental consent when necessary.[132]

Finally, there is the universal issue of funding children's participation in family law proceedings, which is not so much a legal concern as a practical one. On the individual level, children are rarely expected to finance their own representation or litigation – instead either their parents must pay or the state bears the cost. When child participation is dependent on parental funding, there must be vigilance about the potential for inequality arising between different groups of children. On the national level, how participation is funded may hamper the practical use of the participation rights afforded to children by the law. In several country chapters, authors noted the negative effects of funding restrictions on the opportunities for children to participate effectively.[133] It is important, therefore, to consider not only the legal regulation of child participation in family law proceedings, but also the practical conditions needed.

6. INFORMATION AND FEEDBACK

For Hannah and Ammar it is pleasing to see that different opportunities for their participation are available. However, if they are not aware of these opportunities, how can they exercise their rights? This section addresses this important and practical right to information. More specifically, the manner in which children are informed of the opportunities to participate and how they are subsequently informed of the decisions made following their participation (so-called feedback) will be compared. This issue was not addressed by all the jurisdictions, so only

131 N. Taylor, New Zealand, s 2.1.

132 A. Nylund, Norway, s 3.1.1.

133 See B. Rešetar and N. Lucić, Croatia, s 4; N. Taylor, New Zealand, s 3.2.2; E.K.M. Tisdall, Scotland, s 4.1.

the expressed methods of informing children will be discussed. In itself, the fact that it was not discussed in a number of chapters may indicate that it is not a topic of priority, or even a topic considered, in those jurisdictions.

Commencing with the information provided to children prior to their participation, how do children find out about the legal proceedings and their rights in those proceedings? In three jurisdictions children are informed of their right to express views by means of a letter sent to their address. In Belgium and the Netherlands children aged 12 years or older are invited to a direct hearing with the judge, while in Scotland children receive a 'Form F9', which they may fill in and return to the courts.[134] In Denmark the child is also directly informed, albeit by means of a contact person offered to them by the administrative authorities.[135] This contact person informs the child about their rights and the various support options available to them, including the option of a support person who is publicly funded and supports the child by, for example, joining the child in meetings.[136] In contrast to these more direct modes of informing the child, in China the judge requests the parents to bring the child for either a direct hearing or another mode of expressing their views.[137] Similarly in Germany and Romania children are summoned through their parents to attend court for a direct hearing by the judge.[138] In both these jurisdictions parents may face sanctions or coercive measures if they refuse to bring the children.[139] In Croatia the parents (or special guardians depending on the circumstances of the case) are obliged to inform the child about the course of the proceedings.[140] In Norway, when the proceedings are at the mediation level, parents have the duty to inform their children of the right to participate, although this duty is not enforced.[141] Subsequently, when proceedings do reach the court, the judge must ensure that children are informed of their right to be heard and the different modes thereof.[142] It is not entirely clear from the country chapter whether the judge will do this themselves, or whether they will ensure that a parent or expert has done so. Finally, in Italy the law contains the obligation to inform children of the nature of the proceedings and the effects of the hearing, but how this is to occur is not regulated and therefore the practice is inconsistent.[143]

Information is not only provided before or after participation, but children are also informed of certain matters at the time of participation. They may be

134 I. Boone, C. Declerck and E. Vertommen, Belgium, s 3.1.2; M. Bruning and W. Schrama, The Netherlands, s 3.2; E.K.M. Tisdall, Scotland, s 3.1 and 4.1.

135 C.G. Jeppesen de Boer and A. Kronborg, Denmark, s 3.1.

136 C.G. Jeppesen de Boer and A. Kronborg, Denmark, s 3.1.

137 N. Zhao, China, s 3.1.

138 N. Dethloff and D. Schröder, Germany, s 3.1; S. Florescu, Romania, s 3.1.3.

139 N. Dethloff and D. Schröder, Germany, s 3.1; S. Florescu, Romania, s 3.1.3.

140 B. Rešetar and N. Lucić, Croatia, s 2, 3.2.1 and 3.2.2.

141 A. Nylund, Norway, s 3.1.1.

142 A. Nylund, Norway, s 3.1.2.

143 E. di Napoli and F. Maoli, Italy, s 3.1.

informed of their right to express views, as well as their right to refrain from speaking, or of the level of confidentiality applied to their expressed views.[144] Children may also be informed about how their views will be weighed in the decision-making process or how the outcome will be communicated to them.[145]

Following their participation, how are children are informed of the agreement made or decision taken and the weight granted to their expressed views? Various options exist in the 17 jurisdictions. One involves directly informing the child, either by the judge verbally or through written communication. For example, in New Zealand and Norway it is possible for the judge to meet with the child and inform them of the outcome, although this is one of several methods in both these jurisdictions and not the most common.[146] In Germany children over the age of 14 years are informed of the decision through a letter or formal notification sent to them directly; however, there is no provision as to how younger children should be informed.[147] Another option is for children to be informed by their representative if one was appointed, such as a special guardian in Croatia or lawyer in New Zealand,[148] or by the party who conducted the indirect hearing of the child, such as the social worker from the welfare unit in Israel or the Cafcass officer in England and Wales.[149] A different indirect option is for the child's parents to inform the child of the outcome of the case.[150] In the Netherlands the law is silent with regard to informing the child as it is presumed that parents will inform their child. However, more recently, some judges have started drafting 'child-friendly' judgments to communicate the decision to the child. In Italy the child must receive information on the effects of their expression of views, but according to the author of the country chapter it is not clear how or by whom and the current practice is inconsistent in this regard.[151] Finally, it is possible that the child is not informed about the decision taken – although this was not mentioned so explicitly in the country chapters. These are the methods by which the child is informed, but it is also relevant to note that in addition to the conclusion of the proceedings, in some jurisdictions the child is also informed of their opportunity to appeal, for example in Croatia and New Zealand.[152]

---

144 See for example M. Freeman and N. Lowe, England and Wales, s 3.2.1.1; N. Dethloff and D. Schröder, Germany; A. Nylund, Norway, s 3.1.2.

145 See for example B. Rešetar and N. Lucić, Croatia, s 3.2.1 and 3.2.2; M. Freeman and N. Lowe, England and Wales, s 3.2.1.1; N. Dethloff and D. Schröder, Germany, s 2.

146 N. Taylor, New Zealand, s 3.2.1; A. Nylund, Norway, s 3.1.2.

147 N. Dethloff and D. Schröder, Germany, s 3.1.

148 B. Rešetar and N. Lucić, Croatia, s 3.2.2; N. Taylor, New Zealand, s 3.1.1.

149 M. Freeman and N. Lowe, England and Wales, 3.1.1; R. Schuz and T. Morag, Israel, s 2.

150 See for example, I. Boone, C. Declerck and E. Vertommen, Belgium, s 3.1.8; B. Rešetar and N. Lucić, Croatia, s 3.2.1; N. Taylor, New Zealand, s 3.2.1; A. Nylund, Norway, s 3.1.2.

151 E. di Napoli and F. Maoli, Italy, s 3.1.

152 B. Rešetar and N. Lucić, Croatia, s 3.2.1; N. Taylor, New Zealand, s 3.1.1.

7. CONCLUSION

It is morning in Germany and Ammar sends a message to Hannah, who has just eaten dinner in Australia. He tells her that he is going to see the judge tomorrow to share his views on the arrangements after his parents' divorce. Hannah is glad to hear this, but wonders how different speaking to a judge is, as she spoke with a family consultant instead. In this chapter, not only have the different modes of participation been compared, as Hannah and Ammar have done, but also the multiple facets of child participation in family law proceedings. What are the key conclusions? There is commonality across all 17 jurisdictions as they each provide children with modes of participation in family law proceedings. This is the minimum. More notable is that a direct mode of participation is available in all these jurisdictions. This comparison has further shown that there is a wide array of possibilities with regard to the modes of participation and the specifics thereof. For example, the requirements attached to modes of participation differ, although age and maturity requirements are very common, as are conflict of interests requirements for representatives.

What conclusions can be drawn regarding the types of proceedings? First, the modes of participation are generally dependent on the types of proceedings and the manner in which the proceedings are conducted. In each jurisdiction, the available modes of participation may depend on the type of family law proceedings; for example, specific modes may only be available in certain proceedings or different requirements may apply to different proceedings. In addition, there is often a difference between contentious and non-contentious proceedings, especially regarding the separation of parents with minor children. There are multiple jurisdictions where the child's views are not sought when parents have reached an agreement themselves.[153] Finally, there are also clear differences between opportunities for child participation in court proceedings or administrative proceedings versus those in alternative dispute resolution settings. In only a few jurisdictions is the right for children to participate in alternative dispute resolution regulated by law. In light of the trend towards more mediation in family law proceedings, this calls for extra attention.

Let us now turn to the different modes of participation. This comparison has shown that in all jurisdictions children have the opportunity to express their views through direct modes of participation. In most jurisdictions there are also different forms of representation and indirect participation available to children. Party status and opportunities for a child to litigate on their own behalf are more limited. More generally, in this chapter the different domestic modes have been compared on the basis of a categorisation into direct modes, representation

153 See for example B. Rešetar and N. Lucić, Croatia, s 3.1; C.G. Jeppesen de Boer and A. Kronborg, Denmark, s 3.2.

modes, indirect modes, and party status and litigation. As previously remarked, it is not always simple to fit the domestic modes into one of these four categories. For example, in the chapter on England and Wales the court welfare report was discussed under the heading of representation, whereas in the present chapter it is categorised as an indirect mode of participation because of the task and method of the reporter. At the comparative, or international, level there is a lack of common language regarding the specific modes of child participation. A common language is needed so that various key questions on the aims and methods of participation can be addressed. When is the communication of a child's views through a representative direct representation and when is it indirect participation? Can indirect participation actually be considered participation when the aim of the reporter is also to report on the child's welfare and not solely the child's views? In addition, can the calling of children as witnesses in family law proceedings be considered participation? To what extent can and does child participation have the collection of evidence as its aim? These are questions for which this chapter has no answer, but which are relevant to consider in the light of children's rights, both at the domestic level and internationally.

Comparative lawyers have historically questioned whether there is a common versus civil law divide. Child participation is a relatively recent development and is therefore less historically intertwined with the development of legal systems. This also makes it difficult to draw robust conclusions on this issue. While it appears to be more common to use indirect modes of participation or to allow party status in common law jurisdictions,[154] these are equally possible in civil law[155] or mixed jurisdictions.[156] More noteworthy are perhaps the Nordic jurisdictions, where mediation and administrative authorities are key in dispute resolution.[157] The implementation of child participation in family law proceedings is a topic with similarities and differences across borders, but also across and within legal families.

It is one thing to know the law, but what about child participation in practice? It is striking that it is not uncommon for participation rights and opportunities to be legally regulated, but for the actual use of them to be limited. Child participation in practice requires more than laws and regulations: it requires, amongst other things, funding, adequate information provided to the child, a shared will by the authorities involved, and the training of judges and others in hearing children. The qualitative research on participation conducted in the jurisdictions surveyed also emphasises these additional conditions needed

154 Understood to be, in this comparison, Australia, Canada, England and Wales, New Zealand and the United States.
155 Understood to be, in this comparison, Belgium, China, Croatia, Denmark, Germany, Italy, the Netherlands, Norway and Romania.
156 Understood to be, in this comparison, Israel, South Africa and Scotland.
157 In this comparison, Denmark and Norway.

for participation in practice. More generally, it is interesting to see the wide assortment of quantitative and qualitative research reported. There is not yet enough research, however, to answer more specific questions. For example, turning back to Ammar, Hannah or a child from one of the other 15 jurisdictions, it may appear that legally different requirements apply to these children, but are these requirements – for example, age and maturity requirements or those regarding a conflict of interests – so different in practice? If we were to draft a test case with the same child in multiple jurisdictions, would their experience really differ in practice? And if so, would it be due to the laws in place, local practice or the discretion of the judge? These are comparative questions which would benefit from further domestic and comparative research.

Finally, this comparative analysis was based on the broad selection of 17 jurisdictions from different geographical regions as well as from different types of legal families. These jurisdictions have revealed a great variety in child participation modes, requirements, etc. The question remains how child participation is regulated in the other 170-plus jurisdictions in the world. More comparative research may provide us with additional innovative modes of child participation, different requirements, and new insights. In any case, the future of child participation is bright, not only because of new research, but especially due to the pilots and experimental models of child participation currently running in several jurisdictions.[158] Comparing the results of these, as well as existing legal practices, can offer new inspiration for jurisdictions worldwide.

158 See for example R. Schuz and T. Morag, Israel, s 4; E. di Napoli and F. Maoli, Italy, s 2; M. Bruning and W. Schrama, The Netherlands, s 3.2.

CONCLUSION

Mariëlle BRUNING, Wendy SCHRAMA,
Marilyn FREEMAN and Nicola TAYLOR

1. INTRODUCTION

This Handbook has provided insights into how children participate in national family law proceedings nowadays and how this relates to relevant developments regarding children's right to participate from the human rights and social science perspectives. Thus, it endeavours to contribute to the growing body of research and literature in the field of children's rights, particularly the child's right to be heard, through both legal and psychological lenses.[1] Bringing together the findings of this Handbook in a concluding chapter has been quite a challenge, since it contains so much information on many relevant dimensions: human rights law, national family law in 17 jurisdictions, private international law and social science research. Collating the various chapters has, however, enabled us to identify several key issues and themes, which we combine with our more general reflections.

To start with a few obvious conclusions: a clear one, as pointed out by many, if not all, of the contributors to this Handbook, is that decisions in family law proceedings can have a substantial impact on children's present and future

1 This growing body of scientific research on the child's right to participate is sometimes very broad in scope (e.g. A. DALY, *Children, Autonomy and the Courts: Beyond the Right to be Heard*, Brill/Nijhoff, Leiden 2018) and sometimes focuses on specific elements of the child's right to be heard, such as the research project *Rewriting Children's Rights Judgments – From Academic Vision to New Practice* of Helen Stalford, Kathryn Hollingsworth and Stephen Gilmore (Hart Publishing, Oxford 2017).

lives and, for that reason, opportunities for children to participate in these proceedings are essential. Hearing the child's views can significantly improve the quality of the decisions made, as well as assist with the child's adjustment to his/her post-separation living and contact arrangements. A trend is also evident in national jurisdictions, private international law and human rights to pay more attention, and attach greater weight, to child participation to ensure that children have a real say in matters that affect them. A third general conclusion is that the rights of children in this domain are often diffuse and the result of processes developed over time, which has led to fragmentation. Even though this Handbook demonstrates clear developments favouring child participation in family law proceedings, much work remains to be done. We therefore identify a roadmap for future work in this field.

2. HUMAN RIGHTS

Clearly, human rights have had a major impact on the law, with six international instruments containing participation rights for children: the UN Convention on the Rights of the Child, the African Charter on the Rights and Welfare of the Child, the European Convention on Human Rights, the European Convention on the Exercise of Children's Rights (1996), the Council of Europe's Guidelines on Child-friendly Justice (2010) and the Guidelines on Children in Contact with the Justice System of the International Association of Youth and Family Judges and Magistrates.[2] Their content depends on the specific instrument. No uniform design for child participation is recognised, but key forms of child participation can be distinguished: (i) the right to be heard directly; (ii) the right to be heard indirectly via a representative such as a parent, lawyer, judge or other professional; or (iii) child litigation. Without doubt, Article 12 of the UNCRC is the cornerstone that has catalysed the development of the other international and regional instruments in this regard. The six instruments each set out various conditions that apply in implementing the child's right to participate – these include, for example, that the child must be capable of forming or communicating his/her own views, and that due weight should be given to the child's views. While the phrasing and presentation of the respective conditions vary across the instruments, one core requirement, regarding the child's maturity, is shared by them all. However, the child's maturity is also variously expressed through reference to other factors such as age, capacity, or sufficient understanding or discernment. None of the six instruments provide

2 Although the latter guidelines are not 'soft law', as the CoE Guidelines are, they do provide relevant best-practices and are a form of international professional standards; see the chapter by M. Bruning and C. Mol in this Handbook.

a blueprint for how children's procedural inclusion is best achieved in practice. The practical implementation of how children can and should participate needs more attention. Ideally, this should be more closely based on the existing body of social science research evidence and legal insights.

A more general reflection to emerge from the insights of the various Handbook chapters concerns how human rights instruments set general norms that then have to operate across diverse cultures, societies and contexts. Therefore, it is to be expected that children's participation rights are quite general, although the ECtHR case law is at times specific. The human rights domain (instruments, bodies, monitoring systems, documents, etc.) could perhaps play a more significant role in this regard by providing, at regular intervals, up-to-date knowledge about children's right to participate in legal proceedings to governments, professionals and academics. Imagine, for instance, that the UNCRC Committee develops a revised General Comment on child participation which is based on the actual, state-of-the-art knowledge in the social and legal sciences and incorporates jurisdictional developments like some of those discussed in the country chapters of this Handbook. This could have the potential to strengthen children's right to be heard, and enable research to be undertaken that could further support implementation of the child's right to be heard, as this is currently not always possible in some jurisdictions.

Another way of strengthening the child's right to participate is by updating children's participation rights in international instruments on the basis of contemporary knowledge and insights. International human rights treaties tend to be less likely to be regularly reviewed and reformed (which is why they adopt their very general approach), but this is not a reason for not reflecting more deeply upon this option despite the challenges it presents for the international community in reaching new agreements and consensus.

3. PEDAGOGICAL INSIGHTS

The social science chapter illuminated historical developments and the shift in child images and status over time. This changed position of children lies at the heart of the participation rights they now enjoy. In a relatively short period of time, from the latter part of the 20th century, immense changes have occurred in the societal position of children and our expectations of their competence and autonomy. Further, the chapter showed that child participation, and how we perceive this, involves a balancing act between the goals of protection versus empowerment of children in the legal arena. This balance has shifted over time in the direction of more child involvement as a result of prioritising child empowerment. Furthermore, social science research seems to indicate that the majority of children who participated in decisions about their post-separation arrangements felt good about being consulted and heard. This implies that child participation impacts children's development and wellbeing but, at the same time, this domain is still somewhat unknown territory. From the national perspectives, it may be deduced that in many countries little research has actually been undertaken regarding how children feel about (non-)participation, reflect on it and benefit from it. It is also unclear how the best interests of the child relate to the views of the child. Children's participation rights would flourish if more research occurred worldwide on how participation affects children and which factors impede, or promote, good outcomes in terms of (i) the person/agency involved and the training needed; (ii) location/venue; and (iii) information and feedback. The legal dimension of child participation requires the legal system and practice to take into account any differences between children. A focus on an autonomy-supportive environment has been demonstrated to benefit children in many ways. The chapter also identified a number of barriers to effective child participation. Providing sufficient, understandable information to children is an indispensable requisite: informing children adequately both before and during the proceedings can increase their level of participation. Moreover, a safe environment from the child's perspective is important, as are the professional skills of the judge, lawyer, social worker or other professional who talks with the child. As can be deduced from the national perspectives reported in this Handbook, there is room for improvement in this respect.

4. PRIVATE INTERNATIONAL LAW

Child participation rights are not often at the core of research on private international law, but Part II of the Handbook provided various relevant insights on this issue. Private international law is a diverse area of law, where the rules and sources tend to depend on the specific type of proceedings, such as divorce, parental authority or child abduction. For each topic specific sets of rules apply, which might involve rules from various sources such as UN treaties, EU regulations and domestic law, stemming from different law-makers (UN, EU, nationally). It is important to note that private international law plays a different role in promoting child participation rights as opposed to substantive family law at a national level. In general, child participation rights in family law proceedings are a matter for national family and procedural law. However, the Handbook authors highlighted a growing trend towards greater attention being given to child participation in private international law in interaction with human rights. While the fragmented area of private international law interacts with human rights instruments on child protection, international child abduction, parental responsibility and maintenance, the way in which this occurs depends on the topic and the relevant body. The older 1980 Hague Convention on the Civil Aspects of International Child Abduction, which predates the UNCRC, pays less attention to child participation rights than more recent instruments, such as the 1996 Hague Child Protection Convention. In the more recent EU Brussels II*bis* and II*ter* Regulations, children's right to have a say and be heard are reinforced in child abduction and parental responsibility cases.

In sum, there seems to be a tendency to include participation rights more frequently in private law instruments, but only those concerned with international families with private international conflicts. These create indirect duties and involve careful nudges by supranational legislators to better respect children's right to participate. In this sense, this might create incentives to cautiously move national procedures in a positive direction to provide more opportunities for child participation. In fact, for some private international law topics, better safeguards are evident for child participation rights in family law disputes for cross-border families than for families whose dispute or issue is tied to 'just one' jurisdiction.

In thinking of ways to promote children's involvement in international cases, the nature of private international law, with its scattered topic-related nature and the diverse law-making bodies, must be taken into account. This makes it more difficult to create and implement a coherent system of child participation rights; on the flipside, it binds more jurisdictions than just one.

5. NATIONAL PERSPECTIVES AND COMPARATIVE ANALYSIS

National jurisdictions have developed children's rights in family law proceedings. However, it has been human rights that have sparked the impetus to take a closer look at the position of children in this field and to strengthen children's participation rights. This could perhaps partially be related to the historical shift of the position of the child described in the chapter on pedagogical insights, which inspired law reform in legislation and practice in many countries.

The comparative analysis shows that the delineation between various types of family law proceedings differs between jurisdictions and also that child participation opportunities are often fragmented between different types of proceedings even within a single jurisdiction. In most jurisdictions, the modes of participation available to the child depend on the type of proceedings. Sometimes these modes are available in most proceedings but, at other times, they may only be available for a very specific type of proceedings. The question is whether this makes sense. Given the colourful palette of options available under domestic laws, the logic is not always easy to identify. This can be explained by different jurisdictions having different child participatory options on offer because this reflects their legislation, history and/or the types of professionals they have available to meet and talk with the child. We think this needs more attention since a child's right to have a say should not depend on the type of family law dispute which affects him/her. In addition, further research is recommended to encourage jurisdictions to improve their child participatory approaches anchored in different contexts and with different backgrounds. Therefore we mark this as an issue for further research.

In all 17 jurisdictions the hearing of a child by a court is possible. In the majority of these jurisdictions this is an oral meeting, but in some countries children can express their views in writing. It is encouraging that a direct mode of participation for children is available nowadays in all 17 jurisdictions from different geographical regions and different legal families (such as common law and civil law), especially since states belonging to the common law tradition often used to favour indirect hearing of children.[3] This indicates, to us, the pleasing global trend towards children being taken more seriously in legal proceedings. In most of these countries, both an age limit as a minimum standard in combination with the possibility of younger children being heard directly on the basis of open criteria such as 'maturity' or 'discernment' are included in domestic legislation and policy practice. Age limits differ between these countries, but it is clear that in several of the 17 countries young children – i.e. children younger than 12 years of age – are being invited to contribute to judicial meetings. There is still much to be learned about hearing children younger than 12 years of age. Future research is much needed and should also focus on child-friendly methods to encourage effective participation for children in the age range of four to 12 years old (elementary school age). The concept of child-friendly justice should also be reconsidered since it is plausible that this concept could be different for various groups of children, for example very young children from four to eight years of age compared to children from 12–18 years of age. We expect that in the near future younger children will increasingly be included in family law proceedings and will be offered more options to be heard.

Furthermore, the national perspectives and comparative analysis illustrate that not only domestic legislation but also national policy and practice are decisive in how children are being heard in family law proceedings and from what age children are being heard. In some countries the minimum age in legal practice for children to be heard is lower than the age limit included in domestic legislation. This indicates that when conducting comparative legal research, both legislation and legal policy and practice should be incorporated.

On the other hand, in relation to representation of the child in family law proceedings, many different modes were identified in the country chapters. These representatives are mostly lawyers, but non-legal representatives were also evident, such as lay persons, relatives, recommended citizens, psychologists

---

3 A. Daly, *Children, Autonomy and the Courts: Beyond the Right to be Heard*, Brill/Nijhoff, Leiden 2018, p. 194.

and pedagogical experts. The purpose of representation also varies between representing the child's views/wishes and/or the child's best interests/welfare. The aims of child representation (views or interests or both) is a topic for further scientific research and debate.

Child participation could be seen as a middle ground between two other options: the child as a litigating party or the parents representing their child in the legal arena. Taking into account the nature of family law proceedings, where – in particular in post-separation and divorce contexts – parents can, and often do, focus on their own interests, which might easily conflict with each other and with the best interests of the child, the right of the child to express his/her views is crucial. In other scenarios outside family law, parents can more easily be presumed to be able to represent the child and act in his/her best interests. Child participation is also a middle ground in the sense that it does not affect the idea that parents can represent the child in the legal arena; it leaves parental responsibilities untouched. One step further lies a new horizon of child litigation. Currently, even though the status and position of children have altered significantly, these changes do not go as far as granting independent party status to children. In general, parents (or those with parental responsibilities) legally represent children in the legal domain, also in family law proceedings, but backed up by child participation rights. The lack of party status for children in family law proceedings was common across the 17 national jurisdictions. When thinking about future developments to further children's right to participate in legal proceedings and improve their access to justice, children having independent party status is worthy of greater consideration as a future step in the evolution of children's rights: from participation to being part of the proceedings.

In comparing direct participation modes, indirect participation modes and child litigation, a difference can be discerned in the criteria used to determine whether a child is allowed to participate. Age and maturity are often used for direct modes of participation and for litigation by the child. It is of less relevance for the indirect modes and representation modes of participation, where only a number of jurisdictions apply such criteria. This is an interesting finding calling for further attention: does it make sense to have different approaches in this respect?

Child participation rights are promising if one looks at statutes and laws, but in practice there is a world to win, as is remarked on by many country chapter authors. It will be a challenge for future research, policy and practice to promote the implementation of the right to participate. This is even more compelling when consideration is given to the incorporation of these rights for children with different backgrounds and younger ages, or with disabilities, and for other children who might need extra attention or support to effectively participate and be heard in family law proceedings.

6. FUTURE DEVELOPMENTS

As well as the ideas identified above, what could future work focus on? Perhaps most important is the development of a coherent framework of child participation. A recurring observation is the rather fragmented nature of child participation rights in law in all the sources studied in this Handbook: human rights, private international law and, most clearly, in substantive family law, with child participation often developing on a step-by-step basis; change taking place through a gradual process instead of via significant major reform. Future work could aim at developing a more coherent framework that includes all the modes of child participation (direct, indirect and child litigation). Social science research findings are essential, as well as empirical legal research, to build such a framework, which should include who, how, why, when and under what conditions children have a right to participate in family law proceedings.

Recent developments regarding child participation in family law proceedings should initiate new thinking about the other trends that may emerge over the next decade. We can speculate that the position of the (older) child will become more independent from the parents and that there will be more focus on the child's position in the legal domain. One of the interesting dilemmas is how to balance children's rights and interests with the rights and interests of parents. The child's right to participate is often appropriately used by parents to influence the legal dispute between them. At times, however, the child's right to participate is used by parents to influence the parents' own personal or legal interests. Case law of the ECtHR illustrates this.[4] A more child-focused approach is advocated based on the Handbook chapters, which hopefully can contribute to less instrumentalisation of children's rights for parents' purposes. This also requires a fresh look at the fact that in many jurisdictions children are mainly represented in the legal domain by their parents. Overall, this general principle is a sound one, except in those cases where conflicts of interests easily exist or can arise, namely in family law disputes and, in particular, in complex divorce- and separation-related issues. There are better ways to disentangle these rights and interests by appointing a separate person or body to advance the child's views and interests, as indeed some jurisdictions already do.

Another interesting dilemma for future research is the balance between the best interests of the child and the views of the child. There seems to be little attention so far to the potential tension between these two perspectives. If a child expresses views as to his/her wishes that contradict his/her best interests, how do – and should – courts weigh the child's views and decide the outcome? Child participation rights have a procedural nature, but they should also have

[4] For instance, ECtHR *Iglesias Casarrubios and Cantalapiedra Iglesias v Spain* (Appl. No. 23298/12), 11 October 2016.

a direct impact on substantive outcomes. The current focus on the procedural right, which still seems predominant, should evolve towards a combined right for children of a procedural and substantive nature for some of the family law issues. We could imagine such a trend for topics that particularly affect the personal status of the child, such as adoption, name and gender. A substantive right in family law would require a child's consent. This would automatically imply the child's right to express a view. In some jurisdictions, for minors of a specific age this is already required in relation to topics like adoption.

Finally, it has been our pleasure to co-edit this Handbook and to work with such a talented and expert group of contributing authors who have shared their perspectives on child participation in family law proceedings in international and domestic contexts. This Handbook promotes a humane and constructive approach to child participation that benefits the child and also improves the quality of the decision-making process for parents, family justice professionals and the courts. The Handbook brings together the latest thinking on human rights, private international law and social science, as well as the approaches to legal policy and practice in 17 jurisdictions with a comparative analysis of the global similarities and differences. Since child participation rights are primarily vested in national legal systems, more work needs to be undertaken internationally to capture this diversity, including in those countries with customary and religious laws. This way countries can learn from each other and look to implement and refine those particular modes of participation that are most effective.

INDEX

European Family Law Series

1. *Legal Recognition of Same-Sex Couples in Europe*, K. Boele-Woelki and A. Fuchs (eds.)
2. *European Family Law in Action Volume I: Grounds for Divorce*, K. Boele-Woelki, B. Braat and I. Sumner (eds.)
3. *European Family Law in Action Volume II: Maintenance Between Former Spouses*, K. Boele-Woelki, B. Braat and I. Sumner (eds.)
4. *Perspectives for the Unification and Harmonisation of Family Law in Europe*, K. Boele-Woelki (ed.)
5. *Family Law Legislation of the Netherlands*, I. Sumner and H. Warendorf
6. *Indépendance et interdépendance patrimoniales des époux dans le régime matrimonial légal des droits néerlandais, français et suisse*, B. Braat
7. *Principles of European Family Law Regarding Divorce and Maintenance Between Former Spouses*, K. Boele-Woelki, F. Ferrand, C. González Beilfuss, M. Jänterä-Jareborg, N. Lowe, D. Martiny and W. Pintens
8. *Inheritance Law Legislation of the Netherlands*, I. Sumner and H. Warendorf
9. *European Family Law in Action Volume III: Parental Responsibilities*, K. Boele-Woelki, B. Braat and I. Curry-Sumner (eds.)
10. *Common Core and Better Law in European Family Law*, K. Boele-Woelki (ed.)
11. *All's well that ends registered?*, I. Curry-Sumner
12. *Model Family Code – From a global perspective*, I. Schwenzer and M. Dimsey
13. *Harmonisation of Family Law in Europe. A Historical Perspective*, M. Antokolskaia
14. *Brussels II bis: Its Impact and Application in the Member States*, K. Boele-Woelki and C. González Beilfuss (eds.)
15. *Tensions between Legal, Biological and Social Conceptions of Parentage*, I. Schwenzer (ed.)
16. *Principles of European Family Law Regarding Parental Responsibilities*, K. Boele-Woelki, F. Ferrand, C. González Beilfuss, M. Jänterä-Jareborg, N. Lowe, D. Martiny and W. Pintens
17. *Juxtaposing Legal Systems and the Principles of European Family Law on Divorce and Maintenance*, E. Örücü and J. Mair (eds.)
18. *Convergence and Divergence of Family Law in Europe*, M. Antokolskaia (ed.)
19. *European Challenges in Contemporary Family Law*, K. Boele-Woelki and T. Sverdrup (eds.)
20. *Children and their parents*, M. Vonk
21. *La capacité de l'enfant dans les droits français, anglais et écossais*, L. Francoz Terminal
22. *Joint Parental Authority*, C.G. Jeppesen de Boer
23. *Debates in Family Law around the Globe at the Dawn of the 21st Century*, K. Boele-Woelki (ed.)
24. *European Family Law in Action Volume IV: Property Relations between Spouses*, K. Boele-Woelki, B. Braat and I. Curry-Sumner (eds.)
25. *Foundational Facts, Relative Truths. A Comparative Law Study on Children's Right to Know Their Genetic Origins*, R. Blauwhoff

26. *Imperative Inheritance Law in a Late-Modern Society. Five Perspectives*, C. Castelein, R. Foqué and A. Verbeke (eds.)
27. *Juxtaposing Legal Systems and the Principles of European Family Law on Parental Responsibilities*, E. Örücü and J. Mair (eds.)
28. *La justice des mineurs en Europe*, Y. Favier and F. Ferrand (eds.)
29. *The Future of Family Property in Europe*, K. Boele-Woelki, J. Miles and J. M. Scherpe (eds.)
30. *The Place of Religion in Family Law: A Comparative Search*, J. Mair and E. Örücü (eds.)
31. *Reconstructing Marriage. The Legal Status of Relationships in a Changing Society*, C. Sörgjerd
32. *Legal Recognition of Same-Sex Relationships in Europe*, K. Boele-Woelki and A. Fuchs (eds.)
33. *Principles of European Family Law Regarding Property Relations Between Spouses*, K. Boele-Woelki, F. Ferrand, C. González Beilfuss, M. Jänterä-Jareborg, N. Lowe, D. Martiny and W. Pintens
34. *Der nacheheliche Unterhalt: Grundlagen und Ausgestaltung im deutschen Unterhaltsrecht und in den Prinzipien der Commission on European Family Law*, P. Beuermann
35. *Family Law and Culture in Europe: Developments, Challenges and Opportunities*, K. Boele-Woelki, N. Dethloff and W. Gephart
36. *Children's Rights in Intercountry Adoption. A European Perspective*, C. Fenton-Glynn
37. *Nordic Cohabitation Law*, J. Asland, M. Brattström, G. Lind, I. Lund-Andersen, A. Singer and T. Sverdrup
38. *European Family Law in Action Volume V: Informal Relationships*, K. Boele-Woelki, C. Mol and E. van Gelder (eds.)
39. *Divided Parents, Shared Children. Legal Aspects of Residential Co-Parenting in England, the Netherlands and Belgium*, N. Nikolina
40. *Family Forms and Parenthood. Theory and Practice of Article 8 ECHR in Europe*, A. Büchler and H. Keller (eds.)
41. *The Child's Interests in Conflict. The Intersections between Society, Family, Faith and Culture*, M. Jänterä-Jareborg (ed.)
42. *Same-Sex Relationships and Beyond. Gender Matters in the EU*, K. Boele-Woelki and A. Fuchs (eds.)
43. *Nacheheliche Verantwortung in Frankreich und Deutschland*, K. Kaesling
44. *The Future of Registered Partnerships: Family Recognition Beyond Marriage?*, J.M. Scherpe and A. Hayward
45. *Plurality and Diversity of Family Relations in Europe*, K. Boele-Woelki and D. Martiny (eds.)
46. *Principles of European Family Law Regarding Property, Maintenance and Succession Rights of Couples in* de facto *Unions*, K. Boele-Woelki, F. Ferrand, C. González Beilfuss, M. Jänterä-Jareborg, N. Lowe, D. Martiny and V. Todorova
47. *Die Familienschiedsgerichtsbarkeit in Recht und Praxis: Eine Rechtsvergleichende Untersuchung des Deutschen und Englischen Rechts*, S.C. Zellerhoff
48. *Elderly Care and Upwards Solidarity: Historical, Sociological and Legal Perspectives*, E. Alofs and W. Schrama (eds.)
49. *Party Autonomy in EU Private International Law: Choice of Court and Choice of Law in Family Matters and Succession*, J. Gray
50. *The Interaction between Family Law, Succession Law and Private International Law: Adapting to Change*, J.M. Scherpe and E. Bargelli (eds.)